RAILROADING
FROM THE REAR END

Books by S. Kip Farrington, Jr.

PACIFIC GAME FISHING

ATLANTIC GAME FISHING

THE DUCKS CAME BACK

RAILROADING FROM THE HEAD END

RAILROADS AT WAR

RAILROADING FROM THE REAR END

GIANTS OF THE RAILS

INTERESTING BIRDS OF OUR COUNTRY

A BOOK OF FISHES

SHIPS OF THE U.S. MERCHANT MARINE

Juvenile

BILL THE BROADBILL SWORDFISH

The Head-End over the Rear-End. S.P. Extra #4228 East with 4-8-8-2 type engine Class AC 10 with 83 cars passes over its own caboose ascending the grade in making the circuit of Tehachapi Look. Photo Courtesy Southern Pacific R.R.

S. KIP FARRINGTON, JR.

COWARD • McCANN inc • NEW YORK

RAILROADING
FROM THE
REAR END

Published simultaneously in the Dominion of Canada by Longmans, Green & Company, Toronto.

Designed by Robert Josephy

MANUFACTURED IN THE UNITED STATES OF AMERICA

Dedicated to the memory of my great friend, sportsman, and fellow townsman, the late William Carter Dickerman, who gave almost a half century of his life to the railroad industry throughout the world and was admired by all who knew him as well as others who shared his many interests.

INTRODUCTION

Great performance engenders great enthusiasm. Nowhere is such a response better reflected than by Kip Farrington in his series of books telling the story of the greatness of our railroads and of their epic war performance. To his *Railroading from the Head End* and *Railroads at War* he now adds his present book on *Railroading from the Rear End* to complete a picture packed with the romance that power, movement, and action always bring.

To me it is deeply gratifying to pay tribute in this introduction to the American Railroads and to express the admiration and deep loyalty my years of association with them in World War II developed.

Closest to my heart is the performance of those railroaders in the Transportation Corps of the Army, some forty-five thousand strong, who ran the military railroads for our overseas forces all over the world. They were formed into units sponsored by various railroads of personnel selected by them to form completely balanced organizations to do the job. And what a job our military railway services did in North Africa, in Italy, in France, Belgium and Germany, in Iran, in India, in Alaska, and in Luzon. Everywhere the bottlenecks disappeared, the traffic moved, our forces were rapidly supported. Our allies were amazed to see the impossible accomplished. Now, the globe over, there is respect for the American railroader.

The performance of our railroads at home, however, was no less magnificent. They fulfilled their transportation mission so well that the full war might of the United States as a nation in arms was brought to bear on our enemies to achieve overwhelming victory. In the first World War they had learned through bitter experience the lessons of transportation in war. Through the intervening years they had preserved those lessons; indeed, had taught them at the Army War College as fundamental maxims of war. As a result, the American Railroads were better prepared for war at the time of Pearl Harbor than were the armed services. From that day forward, although constantly denied federal help in manpower and materials, they took in stride the ever-expanding load clear through unto the end. They overcame their obstacles by strongly united action and by constant improvements in efficiency. Courage, energy, initiative, decision, co-operation, the will to do, were in their fiber. They knew the vital character of time. They, too, had their Pattons.

As a result there is a deeper appreciation by the public than ever before of the essential role the American Railroads play in our national life. It was widely felt before the war that the railroads were being displaced by our motor highways and our inland waterways. But when the war came, what happened? More than 90 per cent of War Department freight moved by rail, scarcely 9 per cent by highway, and the small remainder by inland waterway. No better proof, it would seem, were needed to show that our railroads are essential to our national defense, that they must be maintained in a high state of efficiency. This will be truer in the future than in the past, for with the release of atomic energy wars will be sudden and swift and the principle of movement will take on overwhelming importance. Federal operation is not the answer. One need only compare the inefficiency, and the burdening deficits resulting therefrom, of governmental operation in World War I with the superb performance and present sound financial condition characterizing private operation in World War II, to shun such a solution. Happily, there is real hope that with growing public appreciation of their proper role, of their proven worthiness, of the energy and vision which they are showing in meeting their peacetime mission ahead, the railroads will no longer be a political football, but as a private enterprise under wise regulatory control they will receive the public support so necessary to insure for us all a favorable national destiny.

As the Head End whistles its approach and as the Rear End goes roaring by I salute the American Railroads and the fine men who make them click.

August 20, 1946   C. P. Gross,
                                     Major General Retired,
                                     Formerly Chief of Transportation,
                                     U. S. Army, 1941–45.

CONTENTS

xiii

FOREWORD

The railroads of America are alert and progressive. By constant research, study, and improvement they will continue offering patrons the last word in reliable transportation, a rail service that is safe and dependable and is consistently becoming faster and faster.

"Of the four principal systems of transportation, the railroad is the only one that owns and maintains its fixed plant facilities and pays taxes upon all of them. Other transportation systems have been spared the expense of building and maintaining their fixed plants. The taxpayers have provided them with magnificent highways, elaborate and expensive air terminals and services, and costly inland waterways. All that the other commercial forms of transport need to carry out their operations are the vehicles and equipment and something to keep them in repair.

"To illustrate, if a highway bridge is swept away by flood water, the commercial trucks and busses simply use another highway while some government agency makes the necessary repairs. But if the same flood water destroys a railroad bridge, the railroad must purchase the materials necessary for repairs and make these repairs at its own expense; and at the same time suffer financial loss due to interrupted traffic.

"More than 300 terminal-type airports have been constructed in the United States by various city, state, and federal governments. These airports are almost wholly operated and maintained at public expense.

"A sound, solvent and efficient national railway system is essential to continued economic progress. The progress of American commerce and industry is measured in terms of transportation—rail transportation. The railroads are so vital to the safety of our country in time of war, and to the welfare of the nation in time of peace, that they must continue to operate successfully. Subsidies that give one system of transportation competitive advantages over another are not in keeping with the American system of free enterprise—the system under which America was founded and has grown to greatness.

"All the railroads ask is that the principle of free, competitive enterprise apply to all; that the service each renders the nation be the measure by which its existence is justified. Real progress comes not through the oppression of one industry to promote another, but through equal opportunity for all. The railroads seek only that."

So let us make it our motto "to travel and ship on the railroads of the United States and Canada."

I am particularly indebted to the publishers of the *Railway Age* and *Trains* magazines for their many courtesies in helping me prepare this book. My appreciation is also due the American railroads and their officials for permission to spend so much time on their locomotives, freight trains, and property while securing data. I am only sorry that it is not possible to include all of them in this volume. I am indeed grateful to Olive B. Flannery, Herbert Worthington, and Charles Tyler for their work on the manuscript. My most sincere thanks are again due H. W. Pontin of the Rail Photo Service, Preston George, Richard H. Kindig, and Otto C. Perry, four of the nation's leading railroad photographers, for the use of their many fine pictures.

S. KIP FARRINGTON, JR.

East Hampton, New York
August 22, 1946

RAILROADING
FROM THE REAR END

CHAPTER I

THE LITTLE CABOOSE

Last but Not Least

At the rear end of every one of the thousand freight trains that every hour begin to roll down the steel rails of America is a "little shanty," the caboose.

The big steam or Diesel freight engine on the head end provides the power to start these trains, but it is the conductor who waves the highball, the signal to go. His hand goes up, or there is the bright gleam of his electric lantern doing its little dance in the dark, and fifty, a hundred, a hundred and fifty cars away the locomotive shouts twice. The driving wheels begin to creep, the slack runs out, and the caboose moves forward with a jerk. Another freight train is "getting out of town."

It is not until the flagman of the freight hangs up the markers—the rear-end signals—that a string of cars officially becomes a a train. Somberly blinking red eyes, slipping away around the bend, mark the passing of another caravan of the roaring main line.

Bryant wrote something that might have been an ode to a freight train, "The innumerable caravan, which moves to that mysterious realm . . ."

The freight train with its little caboose travels down the rails with the necessities of life for the farmer and the city dweller— for every man, woman, and child in America. Three-quarters of the transportation burden of the country is handled by the railroads. Gondolas, hoppers, refrigerator cars, tank cars, flatcars, stock cars, and the boxcar—the conductor in the caboose is a mother to every one. His "wheel report" includes the origin, destination, and content of each and every car. Through these

1

reports, any of the country's 1,800,000 freight cars can be immediately located at any time.

The caboose is the field headquarters of the freight train, the command car. It is the outpost, the galley, the office, the bunkhouse at times, and the observation car. It contains lockers for clothing and supplies, an icebox, a water cooler, table, stove, bunks, a fuel bin or tank, and a cupola. The toolbox under the caboose, sometimes referred to as the "possum belly," holds rerailing frogs, chains, blocking jacks, tools, and other equipment.

Caboose crews are immaculate housekeepers, and many among them are famous for their cookery and their recipes. On the stove there is always that American institution, the coffeepot.

Not long ago someone raised the question as to why the caboose still clung to the farmhouse variety of coal-oil lamp when the modern locomotive has electric lights. Of all the various pieces of railroad equipment, the little caboose, it seems, has been the last to come in for up-to-date appliances. But finally it has been included in the modernist trend. It has been given a voice in the form of radio and Inductive Train Communication. The Baltimore & Ohio and other roads are giving it a bay window, and there are electric lights. From the Denver & Rio Grande Western we learn that the "Flying Ute" fast freight, operating regularly between Denver, Colorado, and Salt Lake City, Utah, not only is equipped with two-way short-wave radios, which include a power unit, but electric lights in the little old shanty behind the train. More cabooses on the Denver & Rio Grande Western are being thus modernized at the present writing.

Truly, it is a great day for the caboose. Not only can the conductor "air" his views to the engineer and the operator in the station beside the track, but he can also enjoy the luxury of electric lamps.

The origin of the word "caboose" appears to be a little vague. It has been called the "conductor's car," the "cabin car," the "way car," not to mention such railroadese terms as the "buggy," "hack," "crummy," and others. The name "caboose" appears to have been first employed back around 1859 but was not generally used until the seventies. The name was included in the first *Master Car Builders' Dictionary*, published in 1879, according to

2

D. L. Joslyn of the Southern Pacific. In 1884, in the second edition of the *Car Builders' Dictionary* the following was recorded:

Cabooses are often made with a lookout for displaying train signals to locomotive and following trains, and to give trainmen a view of the train. They are increasing in use, but the majority of cabooses as yet do not have them.

At the time of the joining of the rails at Promontory, Utah, in 1869, neither the Union Pacific nor the Central Pacific had cabooses with cupolas. It is said that the first Central Pacific caboose with a cupola was built in the Sacramento shops in 1875.

There has been much controversy concerning the cupola's origin. Among the claims advanced is the one which asserts that a conductor on the Chicago & North Western first suggested the cupola, and that two cabooses with cupolas were built in the road's Clinton, Iowa, shops in 1863.

The early western cabooses were simply boxcars with windows and a side and end doors. These early-day cabooses were also used as passenger cars, dignified by the term "accommodation cars." Sometimes they served as baggage cars. Their color was a pale red bordering on orange, and they were treated to a coat of varnish, the same as passenger cars.

Until the early twenties, the caboose was the living quarters of the train crew much of the time. Many conductors were assigned regular cabooses, and some of these cars were pretty fancy affairs, with lace curtains and pictures. Often the standard barroom type of chair was replaced by a more comfortable variety. The more fastidious conductors even went in for soft mattresses, white sheets, and bedspreads.

The floors of these cabooses received frequent scrubbings, and there was periodic house cleaning. Woe was the lot of the person who entered these sanctums on a rainy day without first carefully wiping his feet. We are reminded of the story of a rather slovenly boomer who was called as a middle brakeman on a run with one of these housewifely conductors. The boomer so far forgot himself as to expectorate tobacco juice behind the stove. That was the last ever seen of him.

The trainman, as a general rule, no longer has occasion to

3

make the caboose his home. Thus it has lost its once-sociable atmosphere, as well as many a fine culinary artist. But the old caboose will long continue to hold a warm place in the heart of many a railroad veteran.

In 1937 the Southern Pacific built fifty steel cabooses. These were the first of their kind on the road's Pacific lines. Their interiors were tongue-and-groove lined, with half-inch board-type insulation placed between the lining and the steel exterior to keep the cars cooler in summer and warmer in winter. This insulation extended to the cupola. The flooring consisted of a subfloor laid diagonally. A layer of insulating paper was placed between the subfloor and the finished tongue-and-groove flooring.

The cupola extended the full width of the car body, with both side and end windows. There were Pullman-type seats on each side to accommodate four men. These cabooses had cast-steel truck side frames with Barber lateral rollers and elliptic springs. The length was slightly over 35 feet outside and 29 feet, 3 inches inside.

These cars were built at the Los Angeles General Shops, and at that time represented just about the last word in caboose styling. However, as this is being written, the Southern Pacific has under construction a fleet of caboose cars without cupolas. In its place, this new caboose has bay windows on the sides.

The Baltimore & Ohio Railroad came up with the first bay-window caboose in 1930. Thus, close to seventy years after the pain of birth, the caboose cupola found its life hanging in the balance. Whether it will live or die remains to be seen. Possibly, along with the coal-oil lamp, the faithful cupola is treading the path of the vanquished.

But wherever the trend may lead, there will always be a caboose behind the freight train.

Riding the Rear End of the Manifest

A caboose associates with a vast hitchhiking army of freight cars. They are inveterate wanderers. The caboose herds them in their going, as the cowboy trail-herded the cattle that once came streaming out of Texas. The caboose lines them out, gathers up the strays along the way, checks their brands, trails them to their destination, and then slips away to the home corral—the "caboose track"—to await the next drive being assembled in the classification yard.

In wartime a boxcar traveled as far as 15,000 miles in a little over three months, touching more than half of the states in the Union.

To understand better what happens on the rear end when fast freight is on the move, we are going to ride a manifest on its night run between a city at tidewater and an inland gateway.

A fast freight is known variously as a "manifest," a "time freight," a "preference freight," a "red-ball train," a "symbol train," or perhaps just a "hot-shot." Its consist may include perishables, livestock, or general merchandise of the l.c.l. (less than carload) variety; also other bulk consist.

Our train is representative of the hundreds of fast freight trains delivering the goods by day and by night all over the country. Various leading roads have come to employ famous fast-freight fleets—trains like the "97's" of the B.&O., which we will have a look at later, the "92's" of the Chesapeake & Ohio, the Southern Pacific's "Los Angeles Overnight," the "Fruit Trains" and named freight trains of the Santa Fe, and the Burlington's No. 62, the fastest livestock freight in North America—or anywhere else, for that matter.

Freight cars with wheel trucks capable of speeds up to ninety miles an hour are building, and have been built. The fast freight, the manifest, the symbol train—call it what you will—is on the way to writing a new page in American history. The red-ball caravan is rolling.

You are riding west tonight on the rear end of the Seaboard Dispatch, old No. 257. And you hold a particular affection in your heart for this train, for you have watched its going many times.

There is something about a fast freight—something that gives you swelling pride in American railroads. You have turned back the pages tonight as you walk toward the Big Yard. Years ago this 257 held an exciting fascination for you when it came down

5

around the curve and roared through your town. It was a symbol of speed and power.

You remember that in those days it was called the "Cannonball"; you remember, too, the way its lusty being attracted you, and you were not alone. In the late dusk of the summer evenings you found yourself gravitating toward the railroad station, one of the faithful who worshiped at this railroad shrine.

You knew the time when 257 came around the bend; you knew she never disappointed you. Her exhaust was silent when she dropped off the grade. You saw the bright gleam of her headlight before you heard her. Then there was a white plume jetting upward from her dome. Her whistle screamed and the stack erupted, all in the same breath. The board was green, and the long tangent dipped through the sag, the rails extending a gleaming invitation.

The engine was a Pacific, or one of the new Consolidations. It was rocking a little as the exhaust ripped the roof off the world. You moved away from the platform edge and grabbed your hat. There was the breath of the hot oil and steam, a blur of crashing drivers, and the bright gleam of the ashpan; then swirling dust and a mad stampede of brawling wheels. And then, before you could draw more than a couple of jubilant breaths, the caboose was zipping past.

You looked down the track and saw the glow from the firebox painting the trailing smoke banner and the twinkle of the red marker lights, fast fading in the west. You swelled with pride at the tempestuous flight of the 257. In those days the old Cannonball was just about the cream of the crop.

Locomotives grew; the rail was heavier. Freight cars moved faster. Your town watched the slow passing of the old order, almost without realizing what was happening. It seemed that almost everything was fast freight now. The Cannonball became the Seaboard Dispatch, but to you it was still No. 257, picking up its loads in the Big Yard at tidewater and striking inland like a steel tornado. No. 257 had a symbol now—SB1.

You have the proper credentials, and you rather gingerly pick your way through the yards. It is fall, and there is a little bite in the air. Lights are glowing in the windows of the yard offices, and

6

dancing blades reach out across the dark waters of the channel. Great warehouses and grain elevators lift their bulk against the sky. There is the giant framework of the drawbridge, and beyond the husky voice of a tug is shouting. The bridge of the gantry is like a Christmas tree, gleaming with colored lights.

Tracks reach away into the deepening twilight. There are the lurking purple lights of dwarf signals. Everywhere you see the dark shapes of freight cars. A switch engine is puffing a short distance away, and lanterns are winking. You identify the Seaboard Dispatch by the illuminated SB1 in the number brackets high on the jacket of a big 4-8-4 locomotive. Back along the train the probing beams of air-brake inspectors flicker over trucks and air-hose connections.

The conductor is under the cab, comparing his watch with the engineer's. They go over the orders, and you introduce yourself. The engineer nods, and the conductor remarks that they will be getting out of town in a few minutes. You walk toward the caboose with him. He is, you judge, a man in his late fifties, and probably began railroading back around 1908. The thing that impresses you is his look of absolute competence.

A freight conductor is called "Skipper," and sometimes "the Brains," usually the "Old Man." You know that he is a veteran, or he wouldn't be running one side of the Seaboard Dispatch. You learn that he has been a conductor since 1911, which means that he has plenty of "whiskers," which is to say seniority.

"Not too much tonnage tonight," he tells you. "We'll roll." A fast run, you feel, is right down your alley.

There are forty loads, the conductor reveals. You notice that most of them are yellow refrigerator cars; also, there is an express car ahead of the caboose. The others, you learn, are cars with high-speed trucks. The rear brakeman, or flagman, is beside the rear steps of the caboose. The conductor hands him the orders, and he reads them carefully.

There is an overhead bridge up at the narrowing throat of the Big Yard, and you remember when you used to go there to watch 257 start her night run. You remember seeing a coal-oil trainman's lantern doing a little jib back there almost to the

7

main ship channel, which seemed to be the sparkling fuse that started things.

The blade of the semaphore drops, SB1's whistle barks twice. the lazy smoke rolling from the squat stack suddenly shoots straight into the air, and the engine coughs—hard. This is followed by a steady, labored breath from those iron lungs, which grows rapidly into a powerful chant. It is the opening volley of the cannonading Cannonball.

Silhouetted against the dusk, there on the head car, is the shape of the head brakeman, a jaunty figure—a knight of the roaring road, riding the steed that is SB1 in her conquest of time and distance. From your seat in the cupola you can see the glimmer of his lantern and his toylike outline against the smoky glow of the floodlights as he rides the top out of town.

You take a deep breath, feeling that this is your big adventure, and you wonder if that little group of railroad enthusiasts in your town will be there on the platform of the red-brick depot, watching for old No. 257—SB1—to go through.

The wheels of the caboose clatter on the crossover beyond the drawbridge, and the grimy roundhouse on the right slips past. A passenger engine is drinking on the lead; another is under the coal chute. Other steel monsters of the rail are there, holding solemn conclave like cardinals.

You glance down at the conductor, starting his clerical work, the two shaded, wall-bracketed lamps casting a mellow glow over the papers on his desk. There is a calendar on the sheathed wall, pictures. You notice the dial of the air gauge, the conductor's valve, by means of which he can set the brakes and stop the train in an emergency.

The flagman, the rear-end brakeman, climbs into the cupola and flops down on the padded seat opposite you. Like the conductor, he is a veteran, spare-framed, keen-eyed, with that same look of capability. These railroad men, you reflect are, as the late Irvin S. Cobb once expressed it, "by temperament, training and test, the best equipped for their jobs of any like group in America."

"So you're a writing guy," the rear-end man says, eying you curiously.

8

You work at it, you tell him; but when it comes to setting down adequately on paper the story of a train like the Seaboard Dispatch, you have a feeling of frustration.

"Just write that we wheel 'em to beat hell," he says helpfully. He nods at the roof of the special refrigerator express car ahead of the caboose. "Codfish today; chowder tomorrow."

It is something to think about, for the fish in this car has only that afternoon been loaded and iced at a fish pier. Tomorrow a housewife 425 miles away will be purchasing that fish for dinner.

The close press of suburban homes drops behind the markers of the SB1. The distant staccato bark of the exhaust comes back to you. The night is full of it. The whistle wails for frequent highway crossings, blatant, restless. The forward surge eases as we come into an outlying city. There are factory lights ablaze along the river and tall chimneys sticking up like dark fingers.

The SB1 is straining at a grade now, but it has soon whipped it, and you feel the pace quicken. The locomotive shouts at a tower and goes through a junction with a rush. Small towns slip past; you catch the highball wave of operators. The rear-end man returns their salute.

The Seaboard Dispatch pounds through a sizable yard and attacks the hill beyond. "We used to pick up a helper here," the man beside you says, "but the grade is just part of the day's work for these engines we've got now. Right here is where the old man"—indicating the conductor—"used to write up his first 'delay.'"

The "hill" is twelve miles of curves and sharply lifting grade, and you feel the drag of it. The dual-purpose 4-8-4, however, seems unawed by its full-breasted ramparts, and the battering exhaust comes back to you with bold assurance.

You glance down at the conductor and notice that he is studying his watch. "We've got a passenger train behind us," the rear-end brakeman remarks, "the Colonial Limited; and even the Dispatcher don't want to give her a stab, or the Superintendent will yell to high heaven."

The SB1 finally breaks over the hump, and for the first time your stomach tightens up a little when the caboose snaps off a curve. "It's downhill from here in," you are informed, "and the track is fast." It is a comfort to know that the rail and ballast is of a weight and quality to take punishment, for that is what it is getting now. You have a full awareness of why they call it *fast* freight. The exhaust is a continuous roar, and the caboose seems to have taken wing.

You brace yourself by putting your feet on the seat facing you and dig in your elbows, as you begin to have a new respect for the thing called "manifest." Why are the railroads so much concerned with getting a lot of boxcars over the railroad at this speed? And you remember reading that freight traffic produces about 80 per cent of the company's revenues. This is the gravy train and hot as a firecracker. The speed of freight trains has come up as much as 75 per cent in the past decade.

You wonder where it will stop.

The rear-end man beside you keeps a watchful eye on the fast-moving train, maintaining a sharp lookout for possible hot journals on the curves, in particular.

It is getting close to time to head in for the Colonial Limited when SB1 slows to pick up a "19" train order. The rear-end man catches the second hoop from the steps of the caboose. The order gives the Seaboard Dispatch ten minutes on the limited, and there is also a message informing the conductor and engineer that the "middle" at Whitewater and the westbound siding are blocked.

"Looks like we can go in ahead of her," the rear-end man says. He is referring, of course, to the Colonial Limited, coming behind us.

The conductor nods. "We'll make High Bridge Yard if our luck holds." High Bridge, you are told, is the end of the run for the crew on this first leg of SB1's night run. He adds that SB1 usually goes into the "hole," or passing track, at Whitewater for the Limited.

But our luck does not hold. East of River Falls, SB1 slows for a yellow block, a caution signal. It continues under control until it is stopped by a red block. Apparently, an extra westbound freight has been cutting it a little too fine and has failed to clear the rampaging SB1.

Our fast freight crawls ahead, but you can see the smoky flare of a red fusee, and you know SB1 will have to wait until it burns out. The rear-end man, muttering curses, picks up his red and white lanterns, some torpedoes and fusees, and starts back as the SB1 grinds to a stop. However, in a couple of minutes the engineer on the Dispatch "whistles in the flag"—five intensely curt blasts.

The rear-end man comes on the run. The conductor is on top of the caboose, and his lantern swings a "highball" before the flagman has caught the grab irons.

"Good-by High Bridge for the Limited," pants the rear-end man.

The flagman, on the rear platform, yells something at the engine crew of the extra when the caboose slides past, and it is not a greeting. The conductor writes up the delay. It is not much, but sometimes it can mean a lot to a fast freight.

West of River Falls the grade drops away to wind along the river. You hear the close pant of a locomotive on the eastbound, and a parade of freight cars streams past. The hills close in and there is only blackness; then you see scattered lights, and the caboose lurches onto the long curve just east of your town. The engineer's brake application registers on the dial below you.

The wheels are spitting fire, and now, released of the grip of brake shoes, the SB1 falls off the steep curve with a rush. It whips into a reverse curve, and the distant signal there by the bridge is showing green. The whistle on the 4-8-4 wails in delight, then the exhaust breaks out and the caboose lurches forward, running like a scared deer.

As the rear end sweeps around the bend you have a glimpse of the lights of Main Street, sprinkled off there on the right like star dust. You move across to the right side of the cupola, wondering if there are folks in your town who still go to the depot to watch SB1 slam past. You see pale faces in the swirling dust, and you know that today, tomorrow, and always Main Street folks will find a heartening thrill in watching a fast freight go through.

The conductor looks at his watch. He is concerned with the problem, you assume, of where to head in for the Limited. The rear-end man leans over and glances down at him, then touches you on the arm. "Keep an eye on the Skipper; this might be one for the book."

The Skipper's lean face is a study in bronze. You notice the set of his jaw and that little muscle beginning to twitch.

"Whitewater is out," the rear-end man is saying. "Our best bet is Millville, twelve miles beyond, but it's at the bottom of a sag, and we generally wheel through there like a bat out of hell."

You nod, suddenly catch your breath as the SB1 plays snap the whip with the caboose on a curve.

The flagman continues, "There is a long middle and a siding at Millville, but No. 8, the Pilgrim, will be coming east in about twenty minutes, and the chances are that some extra will duck into the middle to clear her. A pickup job, a local freight, is ahead of us, and if they have much work to do—switching—at Millville, their caboose and part of their train will be down at the west end of the siding. If we go in behind them, by the time we back out and get squared away after the Limited goes, our running time will be shot. We'll be late into High Bridge Yard, and the next crew will be stabbed before they start."

You know that there are heavy grades out of High Bridge on the second leg of SB1's run, so readily understand the problem confronting the conductor. That thirty minutes lost might easily grow into an hour or more by the time the Seaboard Dispatch reached the inland gateway.

SB1 roars between the columns of freight cars on the siding and in the middle at Whitewater. A lantern waves, indicating "it's all black," meaning that the watcher beside the rail has seen no hotboxes or sparks which might indicate something dragging, and the rear-end man opens the cupola window and acknowledges with a flip of his lantern.

Your manifest train is doing just about all the law allows, and maybe a little bit more, when it approaches Millville. There is a backward surge then as the brakes take hold. You know that the head-end brakeman is out on the tender, watching for a signal from the rear end. Will SB1 take the siding for the Limited here, or are they going to run for it?

That decision rests with the conductor. He is the boss—the brains. You look down at him. He is studying his watch, tight-lipped, frowning a little. And then he waves his hand at the rear-end man.

"Let's go!"

The man beside you grins, reaches for his electric lantern, flips the long-beam switch. He slides a window open and leans out, and the bright spark of his lantern gives the head end the high sign. Highball!

Forty cars away down those swaying car roofs, a pin point of brightness answers. The 4-8-4's whistle yells twice, exultantly. The exhaust roars—and the race is on.

The SB1 goes into the sag at Millville like a runaway thunderbolt. There *is* an eastbound freight in the middle, and you see the engine of the local working a factory spur. And there are cars and a caboose far down the long westbound passing track.

Your right hand freezes to one of the cupola stanchions, for you have a feeling that they're liable to snatch the caboose right out from under you. You promise yourself that you will never forget that ride from Millville to High Bridge Yard. *Never!*

"If the West End Yard is plugged," the rear-end man calls to the conductor, "and we have to back across the eastbound, your name is mud."

There is the high drone of the steel trestle under the wheels of the caboose; then the brakes go on. The rear-end man squirms out to the running board on top of the caboose. The conductor is on the rear platform, leaning out, peering ahead. The distant signal, operated from the tower, is yellow. You have joined the conductor. He is talking to the angels. "Come on, you square-head, give us the board."

Far ahead, a sternly forbidding dot of red becomes a buoyant green. The exhaust picks it up again, and the Seaboard Dispatch weaves slowly into the High Bridge Yard.

A scant, a very scant, ten minutes later the Colonial Limited whistles for the High Bridge Tower, and the stainless-steel cars come streaming down the ranks of freight cars. Her markers wave a brief hail and farewell and fade around the bend.

Almost as soon as SB1 buckles to a complaining stop, a switch engine snags onto your caboose and takes it away, for here the crews change. The 4-8-4 is cut off for servicing—coal, water, lubrication. Cars are cut out of the Seaboard Dispatch; other loads are picked up.

You board another caboose and are sized up and accepted by this new conductor and rear-end man. The train line—the air-brake connections—is coupled, the brakes are pumped up and tested, and SB1 is once more ready to roll.

It is a battle every foot of the way for the next fifty miles. There are frowning mountains, and the steel climbs steadily. The manifest loses time, but, thanks to the fact that she arrived at High Bridge on time, you are assured that it will be made up "over the hump." The second leg of the manifest run is completed on time. The rush down the final stretch begins. It is level country now, and your "ball of fire" storms west to the great yards of the inland gateway. Here the train will be broken down and the cars made up into other fast freights for various destinations.

Since leaving High Bridge there have been three stops to pick up and drop cars. Including all stops and delays, the Seaboard Dispatch has averaged better than 40 miles an hour. The conductor's book shows an average tonnage of 2,040 tons over the 424 miles the SB1 has covered.

Watching the locomotive blasting through at the head end of the hurrying freight, you have, until tonight, given little heed to the caboose behind the train. You have noticed a man in the cupola; perhaps a couple of figures on the rear platform, but you regarded them in the light of subordinate cogs in the make-up of the clattering string of freight cars. But you know now that the little caboose is the "command car."

CHAPTER II

INDUCTIVE TRAIN
COMMUNICATION

Early Experiments with Train Communication

At last the little caboose behind the train has been given a voice. Until the development of the present train communications systems the caboose was articulate only over a distance determined by the lung power of the often sorely tried conductor. The engineer had his whistle; the telegraph operator had his "Morse" key or telephone; the dispatcher's authoritative orders flashed over the wires; but the conductor of the long freight drag, from his outpost at the rear end, could only express himself by wildly swinging his lantern, "pulling the air," or walking a country mile.

Now, however, the conductor can make a phone call. He can pick up his transmitter and tell the engineer where to head in. He can talk with the operator beside the track, and he can converse with the crews of other trains. He can report conditions as seen from the caboose, instruct his head brakeman, quickly get word to the dispatcher through the medium of the operator, and generally tell the world that he is the captain of his soul.

Denied adequate means of communication, many a freight conductor has been close to apoplexy as he helplessly watched a situation develop that not only spelled delay to his own train but threatened the smooth flow of traffic in general. Perhaps the operator at some station suddenly "swung him down"—signaled him to stop. The engine is out of sight around a curve, and the conductor is left no alternative but to "pull the air"—open the conductor's emergency valve.

The train will stop, no doubt about that; but will it be all in

15

one piece? The emergency application of brakes from the rear end can play havoc with a long freight. Drawbars may be yanked out; cars may even be derailed. Everything will be stopped, while the crew get out and pick up the pieces. But it is different now, for the conductor has a voice.

Back in 1937–38 the Bessemer & Lake Erie Railroad installed on Locomotive No. 609 and Caboose No. 1904 a Union Switch and Signal Company's train communication system. It was called I.T.C. (Inductive Train Communication). This "voice" system was employed on freight trains having an average length of 109 cars and a maximum length of 160 cars. The following are some of the purposes for which this communication system was used:

To convey information for air test; to control switching movements in yards; to report flagman on train after flag stop; to report conductor on train; to request change of train-line pressure to release sticking brakes; to report hotboxes and exchange information between the engineer and conductor regarding train movements during the emergency; to report caboose clear of a siding switch; to stop the train because of a hot bearing on a pusher engine; to couple train under difficult hand-signal conditions; and many more.

With a train communication system it is possible for the engineer to notify the conductor of the cause of a train stop, and in turn the conductor can inform the engineer regarding conditions at the rear end. There is nothing like the utter frustration of the conductor who discovers that his mile-long drag has pulled out of the yard without him. And it has happened.

However, from the early days to the present time the railroads have worked to reduce the hazards and complications constantly arising.

During World War II the ore move on the Bessemer & Lake Erie was vastly expedited because of its adoption of the Union Train Communication System.

The Pennsylvania Railroad since 1940 has been installing Union Switch and Signal Company Inductive Train Communication equipment in its yards and on its trains. All of their

16

streamlined class T-1 locomotives are equipped with I.T.C. when they roll out of the shops of the Baldwin Locomotive Works. Train Communication equipment has further been installed on two of the busiest divisions of the Pennsylvania Railroad between Harrisburg and Pittsburgh.

Modern systems of communications are used so widely that the miracles of telephone, telegraph, and teletype between fixed locations have become commonplace. Because railroading requires a high degree of co-ordination in the activities of thousands of men at widely separated and continually changing locations, railroads fully utilize these systems, and the desire has grown to provide facilities which will also bring the men on the trains within the communication network.

Before examining this thing called I.T.C. in detail, let us go back and consider for a moment the early developments of train communication. The question immediately arises as to why radio was not adapted to railroad use long ago. During the war emergency, because of unfortunate train accidents, radio commentators and newspaper columnists raised the cry that the railroads were delinquent in the adoption of radio as a means of preventing accidents.

As far back as the decade from 1920–30, intensive research and development in the field of train communication was carried on. Trial installations based upon the fundamental principle of radio were made on the Virginian; New York, New Haven & Hartford; Pennsylvania; Chesapeake & Ohio, and other railroads. There were, however, certain inherent deficiencies in all systems based on the radio principle.

In the first place, there was the loss of communication in tunnels; and communications were seriously affected by steel bridges. There was loss of communication when hills came between the front end and the rear end of long trains. To overcome the fading under these circumstances, the power of the radio transmission would have had to be increased to such an extent that serious interference with other radio communications, in some cases as far as hundreds of miles from the train, would have resulted. Other objections were: (1) permission required from Federal Communications Commission; (2) assignment of wave length by the F.C.C.; (3) licensed operator required [1] (4) radio sets along the line could pick up the conversations.

Additional expenses necessary and restrictions imposed by the government tended to detract from those systems based on the use of radio; as a result, companies promoting such communication systems largely gave up this field.

In the report of the committee on Radio and Wire Carrier Systems in the *Proceedings* of the Telephone and Telegraph Section of the Association of American Railroads of 1934, the following statement appears:

As the Federal Radio Commission has discouraged applications from the railroads for wave-length assignments in the spectrum where previous equipment has been developed, manufacturers have done considerable development work with high-frequency or ultra short-wave equipment that would utilize railroad rails and the adjoining plant without following the theory of space radio.

In addressing members of the New York Railroad Club in October, 1944, W. R. Triem, General Superintendent of Telegraph of the Pennsylvania Railroad, said:

The conclusions to be drawn from the facts developing in the hearings before the Federal Communications Commission are that space-radio is not now in use on railroads because no completely satisfactory system has heretofore been available for the frequencies which it appeared would likely be assigned for such use. Space-radio might have been successfully adopted some ten or twelve years ago if the radio frequencies most suitable then for the purpose could have been permanently assigned to the railroads. But there was uncertainty as to the assignment of radio frequencies, which then, as now, were insufficient to meet the demands for their use in the public interest. The Federal Communications Commission had just been established. Its predecessor, the Radio Commission, had refused railroad applications for frequencies, and it was felt by many railroad men that permanent assignment of radio frequencies by the F.C.C. was, at best, uncertain.

[1] The Federal Communications Commission, under an order dated August 21, 1945, provides that railroad personnel using radio transmitters and receivers in the usual course of their business need not be licensed by the Commission but must be examined by the railroad rules examiner at biennial intervals on simple rules relating to radio.

In the early twenties the Union Switch and Signal Company undertook the development of a front-end to rear-end train communication system, employing the train line of the air-brake system on freight trains as a medium through which impulses of pressure could be propagated from one end of the train to the other and translated into a whistle code. The time required for such propagation was too great, however, and the scheme was abandoned.

The General Electric Company in 1927 developed a Carrier Current Inductor Telephone System. This was tried out on the Chesapeake & Ohio during the early part of 1928, and was later tested on the Pennsylvania Railroad, along with their tests of other train communication systems offered by the Union Switch and Signal Company and the Radio Corporation of America.

The communication system offered by the General Electric Company necessitated the installation of a conductor on the pole line throughout the territory within which train communication was to operate. At intervals of approximately a thousand feet connections had to be made from the conductor on the pole line to the tracks on which equipped trains would be operated.

While this system was not presented as incorporating radio principles, it so closely approached these principles that the Federal Radio Commission took the position that its influence upon radio communications would be such as to necessitate the train communication system operating on an assigned wave length. The General Electric Company ceased to promote this particular train communication system because a considerable investment was required in the installation of wayside features, and, further, because of the questionable outcome of the position the Federal Radio Commission might take with regard to the assignment of wave lengths.

During the later twenties, the Union Switch and Signal Company concentrated its research upon the possibility of utilizing carrier, rail, and earth currents as a medium of transmission of front to rear-end communication. This system was based upon an entirely different fundamental principle from that of any other train communication system brought out. It employed a carrier telephone system transmitting usually the upper side band of a 5,700-cycle carrier and ordinarily feeding the signals conductively into the rails and picking them up inductively from the rails.

Now let's stop a minute and get acquainted with *induction*. Induction is the act or process by which an electrical conductor or a magnetizable body becomes itself electrified or magnetized in the presence, but not necessarily with actual contact, of an electrically charged body, a magnet, or in a magnetic field produced by an electric current.

Our mute freight conductor at the rear end of his mile or so of train now is on the way to finding his voice. He is being introduced to I.T.C.—*Inductive* Train Communication.

The ability to utilize the track rails and earth as a medium of transmission of the carrier current is a characteristic which makes this system peculiarly adaptable to train communication, as the sphere of influence of the transmission is restricted to a comparatively short distance from the track. In consequence, communication is restricted only to those who are interested in the information transmitted.

I.T.C. does not encroach on the radio field; it does not come under the control and regulation of the Federal Communications Commission; it does not require licensed operators; it is not influenced by tunnels, bridges, or intervening hills—and conversation is private. Railroad men being what they are, the last-named is not without its advantages. With I.T.C. there is no chance of some lady adjacent to the right of way inadvertently tuning in on a conversation that might cause her to blush.

As a result of early road tests on the Bessemer & Lake Erie, it was found that by placing the communication equipment in a wayside office it was possible to carry on conversation with train crews for distances as far as a hundred miles away. This experiment lead to subsequent special research in the field for providing a system to maintain communication between a fixed wayside point and moving trains.

Additional tests on the Bessemer & Lake Erie revealed that communication could be conducted with the front end of the train disconnected from the rear end and separated by a distance as great as seven or eight miles.

The first I.T.C. communication system for use in classification yards was installed on the Cleveland, Cincinnati, Chicago & St. Louis in the Sharonville Yard in July, 1940. Soon other installations were made on the Louisville & Nashville in the DeCoursey Yard, and on the Pennsylvania in the Columbus Yard. These were known as one-way communication systems, in which the facilities provided means for the yardmaster to issue verbal instructions to the engine crews, but did not provide means for crews to converse with the yardmasters.

In 1942 the Norfolk & Western installed a two-way communication system in its yards at Roanoke, Virginia. This system provided facilities for conversation between yardmaster and engine crews.

Further research by the Union Switch and Signal Company resulted in communication facilities at yard terminals which provided independent communication between yard offices and crews in different yards. In other words, the conversation going on in an eastbound yard in no way interfered with the communication system in operation in the westbound yard.

The importance of two-way main-line communication cannot be under estimated. No sooner has the system been installed than it becomes indispensable. In classification yards it has already found wide application, and more and more roads are applying it to freight trains.

I.T.C. is likewise important to the movement and safeguarding of passenger trains, except that communication between the two ends of the train, while desirable, is not as essential.

Centralized traffic control has given the dispatcher a long arm that can reach out over the division and actually shuffle trains at will; still, even with this modern miracle, time is frequently lost while the conductor makes a telephone call concerning some train movement, or to report conditions.

The voice from the moving train, out there in the darkness, fog, storm, keeps the dispatcher fully advised all during the run as he gets his report from the nearest wayside station equipped with I.T.C.

Conductor Smith, for instance, picks up his handset, moves a lever on the control box, causing the sounding of a distinctive note in the loud-speakers of receivers operating on the same frequency within the operating distance, and says, "Hello, Wayside. This is Conductor Smith, Extra 4673 West. We are at Lost Siding, doping up a hot box." He does not have to walk to the nearest dispatcher's telephone.

The operator immediately notifies the dispatcher, who, informed of the delay to Extra 4673, can plan the train movements in the vicinity accordingly.

But, you will say, this Train Communication System does employ radio waves. Granted. However, they are of low frequency and below the 10 kilocycles where government regulation begins.

We are going to ask S. B. Schenck, Special Engineer, Bessemer & Lake Erie Railroad to explain it.

"The system," says Mr. Schenck, "is based fundamentally on long-wave radio transmission principles utilizing carrier waves of 5,700 cycles per second, and it differs in numerous respects from the usual short-wave broadcasting.

" 'Long-wave' means transmission at relatively low frequency —that is, below 10 kilocycles, where government regulation begins, and far below the frequency used for general broadcasting. For illustration, we have broadcast station KDKA, operating on 985 kilocycles, and its companion short-wave station, W8XK, operating on 15,250 kilocycles, while the train communication system operates on 5.7 kilocycles.

"Furthermore, the low-frequency carrier waves do not go out into space to the same extent as general broadcasting does, but are bound much closer to any near-by metallic circuit, thereby permitting the rails to be used as the main path for signal transmission, assisted by any parallel telephone or telegraph wires.

"The carrier waves of constant frequency are sent out continuously when a message is being transmitted, and the speech rides, as it were, on the top of these waves. The actual mechanism for transmitting and for receiving messages requires vacuum tubes, transformers, and other apparatus similar in some respects to the radio receiver in so many of our homes, but housed differently to withstand exposure to weather and to take the slamming around it gets on a freight train. Suitable power for operating the equipment is provided by a storage battery on the caboose and the headlight generator on the locomotive."

The Inductive Train Communication System in no way interferes with telephone, telegraph, or other communication facilities, strictly minding its own business. Sad to say, it does not pick up hockey games, ball scores, hot music, or radio commentators.

Strangely enough, Inductive Train Communication is not the pert young debutante we had thought. It is really an old maid who married late in life and started stepping out. Sadly enough, she was not courted in her bright and blooming youth, although sixty years ago Old Man Railroad, a gay young blade then, was making eyes at her. In 1885 a man named Phelps experimented with the notion that communication could be established between a station and a moving train. What was more, it worked. But for some unknown reason train telegraphy, as developed by Mr. Phelps, died ingloriously.

The *Scientific American*, issue of February 21, 1885, published an article describing "a new system of train communication by use of electrical induction." A wire, cased in a wooden box, was laid between the rails. Other wires were suspended below a railway car, containing telegraph equipment. Messages sent from this moving car were received on a telegraph sounder in a wayside station. Also, impulses flashed from the station were picked up by the operator in the speeding car.

This all happened on the Harlem River Branch of the New Haven Railroad. In 1885 the *Scientific American* wrote:

Mr. Phelps would seem to belong to that class of men who have made America famous for mechanical ingenuity. These men never accepted anything as a fact in natural law without first demonstrating it to their individual satisfaction. They rarely follow where the crowd leads unless the goal is really in sight.

So the goal was in sight sixty years ago when the forgotten Mr. Phelps foresaw the needs of the roaring main line.

How It Works

The railroads of America today are on the threshold of vast achievement. They smoldered through the years of lethargy, to awaken suddenly to the fact that the truck, the motorcar, and the airplane menaced their very existence. Weeds were starting to grow between the rails. Too long the railroads had been content to jog along at a pace but slightly accelerated over that of Old Dobbin.

They staggered groggily out of World War I, slogged through the depression gumbo, and ran head on into World War II. That jolt awakened them. It also opened the eyes of the country as a whole to the fact that without the railroads the war would have been lost before a man or a ship went over seas.

The Iron Horse, girding up its armor, performed a magnificent feat in the transportation of men and materials of war, but today's hero can be tomorrow's goat unless he continues to live up to his press notices.

More efficient transportation is the order of the day.

For nearly three-quarters of a century the Union Switch and Signal Company has worked with the railroads in the development of signal systems and other devices for safeguarding and expediting train operation.

The sole objective in the development of I.T.C. has been to provide a system of voice communication exclusively for railroad use. The conditions confronting them had no counterpart in any other communication system, private or commercial. These conditions were far more exacting than all other railroad communication services.

Having gained extensive experience through the development and production of continuous coded cab signals involving the use of train-carried electronic devices, the Union Switch and Signal Company was in a position readily to adapt itself to the development of a voice communication system for railroad use.

Dependability of operation was the prime requisite. Also there had to be satisfactory performance under adverse weather conditions and with the movement of trains at high speed. Further, the system required sturdiness and simplicity of operation. Ease and economy of maintenance were important. In designing Union I.T.C. it was imperative that the equipment be capable of servicing at locomotive terminals.

After extensive research and experimentation, the Union Switch and Signal Company came up with a train communication system which began its tryout on the Bessemer & Lake Erie Railroad in April, 1937.

The standard receiver and transmitter used in the Union I.T.C. system looks like an ordinary telephone handset, and is provided with a "press-to-talk" button. This handset is connected to a small control box which may be installed in any convenient location. A loud-speaker is also provided. A red light in the control box shows when the power is turned on and the equipment is in operation.

The first step in sending a message is to move a lever on the control box. This causes the sounding of a distinctive note in the loud-speakers or receivers operating on the same frequency within the operating distance, as we have explained. The person calling then presses the button on the handset. A white light on the control box shows that the carrier current is going out.

The caller speaks into the microphone, or transmitter of the headset, identifying himself and naming the person wanted. A second flashing red light indicates that the voice of the speaker is adequate. He then releases the button and waits for the response.

The person called takes his headset from its hook, presses the button, acknowledges the call, releases the button, and waits for the message. Some installations are so arranged that the loud-speaker is cut out when the handset is off the hook.

Remember, the power for transmission is provided by that storage battery in the caboose and by the headlight generator on the locomotive. Let us follow through and see what happens when the conductor on the rear end starts talking.

The sound waves set up by the conductor's voice are a form of energy. When these waves strike the transmitter in the handset, they produce in the electric current of the microphone circuit variations which are identical in character with the sound waves which produce them.

25

These voice-frequency current variations are of very low power and are not suitable for transmission. In order to transmit them from one station to another, it is necessary to impress their characteristics upon a carrier current of higher frequency and greater power. This is accomplished in the following stages: The power of the voice-frequency carrier current is increased in the *amplifier*. A higher-frequency carrier current of greater volume is supplied by the *oscillator*. These two currents are mixed in the *modulator*, which impresses the voice current, as frequency modulations, on the carrier current supplied by the oscillator.

Going back to our modulated carrier wave, we trace it next to the *driver*, where the relatively weak output from the modulator is made stronger, and sent on to the *power amplifier*. Here the signal is still further amplified and goes from there to the *output transformer*.

All equipment for these steps in the transmitting process is contained in a compact equipment box installed on the vehicle in any desired location.

The function of the output transformer is to change the voltage delivered by the power amplifier to that required by the *transmitting loop*. The modulated carrier current is not beamed or broadcast, but is *fed inductively into the rails* by the transmitting loop. The ground provides the necessary return path for the resultant rail current. The rail current, in turn, *inductively energizes the adjacent line wires*.

Because of leakage to the ground, attenuation (thinning out) of track currents is extremely great, and a system depending on these currents alone would have only a limited range. That is why this system makes use of the line wires which parallel the track—an element that is almost as common on railroads as the rail itself.

Power which is picked up inductively by the line wires is transmitted for greater distances with less attenuation, and at these great distances the line-wire current induces voltage in the track which in turn induces voltage in the receiving coils of the receiving vehicle. The Union I.T.C. system is characterized by this transmission in which the inductive steps are the following: (1) from the transmitting loop to the rails, (2) from the rails to the line wires, (3) from the line wires to the rails, and (4) from the rails to receiving coils.

Neither the wires nor the rails form complete metallic circuits. In the case of the rails, the return circuit is through the ground. The circuit of the line wires is also completed through the ground, by way of the capacity between the line wires and the ground. This may be considered the equivalent of an infinite number of condensers, with the wire as one plate and the ground as the other, and the air as the dielectric. The flow of the current consists, as far as this part of the line-wire circuit is concerned, of the charging and discharging of these condensers in succeeding half-cycles. The result is a continuous flow of the high-frequency alternating current of which the signal is composed.

A circuit established in this way continues to function even if the line wires or rails, or both, are broken in many places between the sending and receiving stations.

This use of rails and line wires as circuits, with ground return and mutual electromagnetic coupling as necessary elements in the transmission and reception of communication, is another distinctive feature of the Union I.T.C. system.

At a receiving point on the train, the carrier energy is picked up from the track by a pair of *receiving coils*. Since the signal is very weak, the first step is to build it up, and that is the function of the *pre-amplifier*.

The pre-amplifier increases the voltage of the incoming modulated carrier wave. Further amplification of this signal can be accomplished more satisfactorily both from the standpoint of gain and from the standpoint of selection by changing it to another frequency. This is done in the *converter*, where a current supplied by an oscillator is modulated by the incoming signal. The oscillator frequency is constant and is mixed with the varying carrier frequency to produce a varying intermediate frequency, which may be higher or lower than the carrier frequency.

Undesired frequencies are filtered out, and the resulting intermediate-frequency signal is amplified in the *intermediate-frequency amplifier* and in the *limiter*. The intermediate-frequency amplifier and the limiter may be combined into two or three stages of amplification which have a definitely limited output.

27

The intermediate frequency carries, as modulations, the voice frequencies which were carried as modulations on the original carrier current sent out by the transmitter.

The next unit in the receiving apparatus is the *discriminator*, which separates the voice frequency from the intermediate-frequency signal.

The voice frequency is then passed on to the *audio-frequency amplifier*, which increases its power to such a point that it can be used to energize a loud-speaker or a telephone receiver.

The equipment at a wayside station is essentially the same as that on a vehicle, except for the method of coupling. Receivers at these points may, in some cases, be inductively coupled to the line wires, but are usually connected directly to the rails or to both the rails and the line wires. In the transmitters one lead of the output transformer is connected to the rail, and the other to one or more existing line wires. The type of connection used depends on the type of communication service handled by the existing line wires.

It will be noted from the foregoing description that Union I.T.C. is definitely set apart from radio and other proposed arrangements for train communication by three outstanding basic principles: (1) The rails, ground, and existing adjacent line wires are utilized for transmission of a carrier current. (2) The carrier current is received on vehicles by induction through receiving coils placed in inductive relation to the rails. (3) In transmission from vehicles the carrier current is fed inductively into the rails.

This somewhat technical examination into the seemingly involved mysteries of train communication may strike the layman as going to extremes over so small a matter as providing the rear end of a freight train with vocal cords, but to the conductor it offers final release from years of almost penal solitude in his distant outpost.

"Let freedom ring!" shouts Conductor Smith. "The little caboose behind the train is on the air!"

CHAPTER III

EMPIRE BUILDER

The Great Northern's Magic Carpet

Great railroad men never die. Six feet of earth can neither claim nor long imprison the spirit of the empire builder. It rides wild and free, its voice triumphant. In storm and in darkness, in sunshine and in shadow, the locomotive shouts the glory of its conquest on the mountain and the prairie.

The whistle of the Empire Builder rises in the foothills of the northern Rockies, and a mountain wall hurls the echo back, loud and clear, and the name it shouts is James J. Hill, the man who spiked a railroad down in the great Northwest.

When you look at those white peaks of the Continental Divide and the shining bands of steel that point the way of the Empire Builder, words seem futile, for you are standing before the throne of the Great Northern.

The Great Northern and the Alps of America. Names are there, burned on a mountain range—Singleshot, False Summit, Rising Wolf, Marias Pass. And off there in the distance the peaks and the glaciers of Glacier National Park, with its eye-filling glory and its bighorns—the Rocky Mountain goat, supreme on its high crag, and the trade-mark of the Great Northern Railway.

The Great Northern crosses the Rockies in Montana through Marias Pass, the lowest pass in any northern state. And here, immortalized in stone, stands the statue of John F. Stevens, the man who discovered the pass. In the Cascade range to the west the rails of the Great Northern drive eight miles straight through a mountain, the longest tunnel in the Western Hemisphere.

For nearly sixty miles the Great Northern tracks skirt the

southern boundary of Glacier National Park, the only national park on a railroad main line. At Rising Wolf, five miles west of Glacier Park station, the snow-blanketed peaks lift close beside the rails in breath-taking beauty, and you feel that this is the glory that reflects America. This is the frontier of the Empire Builder.

But it takes more than scenery to make a railroad. There must be brawn and courage and an iron will. Behind the flashing Pullman train there must be endless caravans of freight cars, for this north country is a land of mines and forests, of agriculture; it is range country, with vast herds of cattle, great flocks of sheep; a land of sawmills and factories and docks and ships. This is the great Northwest, the land of the Great Northern.

During World War II the Great Northern handled an enormous amount of war freight, representing as much as 200 per cent increase in freight traffic over its western lines, the contributing factors being the rapid industrialization of the Pacific Northwest, the feeding of vast quantities of supplies for the Pacific war theater into the port of Seattle, and the transportation of men and materials of war safely and speedily between the Great Lakes and Puget Sound. The Great Northern further hauled from the iron-rich Mesabi, Cuyuna, and Vermilion ranges of northern Minnesota to the ore docks on Lake Superior 29,000,000 long tons of the red dust that is iron ore, or a third of the district's total production, during one season ending December 5, 1942.

When war cracked down, war plants mushroomed up in this Northwest, and the steel and lumber required in their building moved over the steel rail. The three great roads of the Northwest —the Northern Pacific, the Chicago, Milwaukee, St. Paul & Pacific, and the Great Northern—rallied to the support of Uncle Sam. During an earlier era of the building of this vast empire the bugle call was "boots and saddles!" But now the conductor's waving lantern flashed "highball!" and the whistles of the engines shouted the cry of the forward-marching ranks of the legions of the freight car.

Over 100,000 carloads of lumber and shingles; 50,000 carloads of logs, poles, and ties; 472,000 carloads of iron ore; 50,000 carloads of coal; 25,000 carloads of cattle and sheep; 26,000 carloads of potatoes; 77,000 carloads of wheat, barley, and rye, or a total of *all* raw materials and manufactured products for 1942 of 1,267,576 carloads, or 59,469,046 tons!

Included in this grand total was armament, steel, explosives, magnesium, foodstuffs, moving in a thundering parade across the northern Rockies.

It is interesting to glance down the list of commodities coming out of this great empire.

Products of Agriculture
Wheat
Corn
Oats
Barley and rye
Flour and meal
Apples
Other fresh fruits
Potatoes
Vegetables
Flaxseed
Sugar beets

Products of Forests
Logs, posts, poles, cordwood
Pulpwood
Lumber and shingles

Animals and Products
Cattle and calves
Sheep and goats
Hogs
Fresh meats
Poultry
Eggs
Butter

Products of Mines
Anthracite coal
Bituminous coal
Lignite
Coke
Iron ore
Ore concentrates
Gravel and stone
Crude petroleum
Asphalt
Salt

Manufactured Products
Petroleum products
Sugar, syrup, and molasses
Metals—pig, bar, sheet, and pipe
Machinery and boilers
Cement, brick, lime, and plaster
Agricultural implements
Automobiles and trucks
Beverages
Newsprint and other paper
Canned food products
Paper bags and paperboard

31

There is also a host of miscellaneous manufactured articles and products of the soil.

The approximately 8,000 miles of road owned or operated by the Great Northern thread their way into the states of Wisconsin, Minnesota, North and South Dakota, Iowa, Montana, Idaho, Washington, Oregon, California, Manitoba, and British Columbia.

The Great Northern coined the expression, "See America First," and the Rocky Mountain goat that rears its rampant head on Great Northern freight cars has for years been spreading the gospel to all America. Bill of the "Big G" has poked into almost every town and hamlet that boasts a length of rail, and once seen is seldom forgotten. Car initials, names, emblems, and trade-marks, marching in parade when a freight train rolls past, are mostly soon forgotten, but not this proud mountain goat of the Rockies, the legend of the Great Northern.

In one year the car-miles of loaded freight on the Great Northern have reached to over 588,000,000 miles, with the car-miles of empties registering 281,498,000 miles, for a total of over 1,000,-000,000 car-miles. A billion dollars doesn't mean much any more, but a billion car-miles is an imposing figure for a railroad.

Winter railroading on the Great Northern, up there along the Canadian Border, is rugged. The cold is intense and the snowfall heavy, particularly around Marias Pass, where the average is over 200 inches, and a total of 300 inches is not uncommon. But years of experience have taught the Great Northern how to whip this white-bearded old patriarch who comes blustering down from the Arctic. Many concrete snowsheds have been built at places where snowslides are most likely to occur. And when the blizzard strikes, a snow-fighter, called a "snowdozer," springs to arms. These snowdozers were especially designed for the Great Northern, and, since they make almost passenger train speed, the line is rapidly cleared. However, when the fall is very heavy and there are drifts, the big rotary plows of the Great Northern's western lines are employed to keep the track open.

Considering the rugged country traversed by the Great Northern, we are surprised to learn that there are only 55 miles of main line on the entire railway at elevations of 4,000 feet or over, for in this country you have the feeling always of being high under the eaves of the sky.

Between Williston, North Dakota, the eastern terminus of the western lines, and Seattle, Washington, there are seven stretches of double track aggregating 172 miles, the longest extending between Shelby, Montana, and Blackfoot, 51 miles away on the eastern slope of the Rockies. The grades across the water divide were kept at a maximum of 0.8 per cent in general, with a few short stretches of 1 per cent grade and one of 1.8 per cent over 18 miles eastbound from Walton, Montana, to Summit in Marias Pass.

It would take many pages to review the motive power of the Great Northern. There is a vast variety of class and type, but we cannot allow this opportunity to pass without including mention of one outstanding Great Northern locomotive. Let's briefly run through the specifications.

The type is 4-4-0; the cylinder dimensions, 12 inches x 22 inches; the drivers are 63 inches; the boiler pressure, 120 pounds; weight without tender, 55,400 pounds; tractive force, 4,700 pounds.

The class is William Crooks; the builder, Smith and Jackson. And the date—1861. A great engine, the William Crooks, with its long, slender pilot and funnel stack. Pretty as a picture in her day, and pretty still, for she has been maintained in her original condition for display purposes.

And there were later 4-4-0's, numbered from and including the 187 to the 228, some of which were built by Brooks in 1882 and by Rogers in 1887. And the crest on their tenders was old Rocky Mountain Bill.

The Great Northern 4-8-4, S-2 class, was the first to mount 80-inch drivers. Those big drivers and that silver jacket, there on the front of the Empire Builder, made just about as striking a combination of motive power as you would find anywhere. Later, it was the smokebox of the locomotive that was silver, and a sight it is, looking at one of these engines against the background of snow-capped peaks out there on the Continental Divide. And now we have the Diesels, just as inspiring.

The spirit of Jim Hill is still a part of the Great Northern, and it is only fitting that this railroad, in cold figures, should be represented as one of the most efficient roads in the country. An unusually high percentage of the Great Northern's tonnage originates on its own lines—some 84 per cent, as compared with an average of 65 per cent for other leading western roads.

There are a number of factors permanently favorable to the Great Northern, and we find much of the remaining source of lumber in the United States in the Puget Sound country, south-central Oregon, and the Rocky Mountain area in Montana and Idaho, all of which are served by this line. The Great Northern and the government have co-operated in an endeavor to encourage extensive scientific and diversified farming in the territory served by the road. Government irrigation and power projects are constantly opening up new farming areas, thus stimulating the industrial growth of the country.

Another factor entering into the picture was the building of the mighty Grand Coulee Dam, with its source of electric power. This Northwest has long been a land of golden opportunity, and it will continue to be a frontier in much the same sense as the frontier of the Old West. From the days of the Lewis and Clark expedition, away back in 1804–6, and the Louisiana Purchase, the Northwest has truly been the land of the Empire Builder in every sense of the word.

It is a little difficult to imagine, as we explore the dim and dusty archives of those things we learned in school, that part of the territory now served by the Great Northern and those other roads of the Northwest, once belonged to France, and was ceded to the United States in 1803 through the efforts of far-seeing President Jefferson. Thus, boldly and in the face of loudly voiced opposition, this great president paved the way for the present route of the Empire Builder.

In keeping with the tradition of Jim Hill, the Great Northern remains the only western line which has never been in receivership.

The history of the Great Northern goes back to the Minneapolis & Saint Cloud, which was incorporated on March 1, 1856, by the territorial legislature of Minnesota. The first portion of the road was completed in 1882. In the following year the property was sold to the St. Paul, Minneapolis & Manitoba. On September 18, 1889, when it owned no physical property, the name of the Minneapolis & Saint Cloud was changed to the Great Northern. From February 1, 1890, the company operated under lease. The property of these other companies it acquired later.

The Great Northern was built in three major stages. The first covered a considerable period of years marked by land grants and homesteading. One small road after another was built to develop the wheat and lumber resources in Minnesota. Between April 1 and November 18, 1887, a 643-mile line was completed from Minot, North Dakota, to Great Falls and Helena, Montana. The road had no land grant in respect to lines west of Minneapolis and had to get the mileage into operation quickly to warrant the building of the extension. The following year the line was pushed through to Butte, Montana.

This road served the coal mines near Great Falls, Montana, the copper-mining industry at Butte, and the intervening wheat country. Surmounting many difficulties in the way of engineering problems, a route for the third major segment of the road was finally surveyed, and by January, 1893, the line was extended across the Rockies through Marias Pass. It then moved on through the Cascade Range, crossing this mountain bulwark by means of twisting switchbacks until 1900, at which time the original Cascade Tunnel was built. The Great Northern's steel now had reached the shore of Puget Sound at Everett and Seattle.

The Great Northern and the Northern Pacific jointly acquired control of the Chicago, Burlington & Quincy in 1901 and formed the Spokane, Portland & Seattle Railway in 1905. The leased lines of the various wholly owned railroad subsidiaries of the Great Northern were acquired during 1907, the principal properties comprising those of the St. Paul, Minneapolis & Manitoba— about 3,877 miles—and the Eastern Railway Company of Minnesota—about 503 miles.

The line serving southern Oregon and northern California is connected with the rest of the system by long-term trackage rights over the Oregon Trunk Railway, the Southern Pacific, and the Spokane, Portland & Seattle. These lines, with those of the Western Pacific south of Bieber, California, and those of the

Santa Fe south of Stockton, California, form a north-and-south through route on the Pacific Coast, and between the Northwest and California. The Great Northern operates between Seattle and Portland over the lines of the Northern Pacific and the Spokane, Portland & Seattle.

The Spokane, Portland & Seattle Railway and its subsidiaries operate 944 miles of road in Washington and Oregon, including the line from Spokane to Portland, which affords the Great Northern its most direct access from the east to Portland and a river-level route through the Cascade Range.

The Spokane, Portland & Seattle, with its subsidiaries, the Oregon Trunk Railway and the Oregon Electric Railway, is a valuable feeder for the Great Northern, as it originates a large amount of lumber and other forest products, as well as canned fish and a variety of manufactured articles.

In 1928 the Great Northern hewed and hammered and blasted the Cascade crossing down a full 500 feet. It straightened the track and eased the grades and drove a bore straight as a rifle barrel through a mountain range, and 5,250-ton freight trains rolled over the 73-mile stretch of electrified line between Wenatchee and Skykomish, Washington.

In 1942, near Belton, Montana, and Scotia, Washington, trackmen again drove their picks into the ramparts of the Rockies' western slope, whipping the right-of-way into a straighter steel path for the trains that came thundering through, and again schedules were reduced while the tonnage mounted on this the road of the Empire Builder.

The Great Northern owns at this writing 805 steam locomotives, 12 freight Diesels, 15 passenger Diesels, and 15 electric locomotives. Its freight cars number 30,386, and its passenger cars 685. It has shops and facilities for the repair of cars and motive power, including two large Diesel repair shops completed in 1945. Between 1939 and 1945 it built or purchased 7,152 50-ton boxcars and 2,500 75-ton ore cars. More Diesels are on order.

The latter part of 1946 will find four completely new lightweight passenger trains in operation on the route of the Empire Builder. Exclusive of their Diesel locomotives, the estimated cost is $4,800,000. Each of these streamliners will represent the last word in modern de luxe equipment, and will include a baggage-mail car, four coaches, a lunch-counter car with dormitory for the dining-car crew, a diner, four sleeping cars containing room-ettes, bedrooms, drawing rooms, and a limited number of open sections, and a lounge-observation car.

The colors of the scenic Northwest will be featured in the decorations of the interiors of the trains, together with murals reproduced from original paintings of Blackfeet Indians. Other Indian pictures will provide the motif of the panels of the obser-vation-lounge car.

Starting with the 4,000-horsepower Diesel-electric locomotive at the front, the streamlined exterior will have a background of olive green. A broad window band of orange and a narrower band of orange edged in yellow, and a stripe of silver below the entire length of the train will complete the color scheme. The crest on the front of the locomotive will be Old Bill, the Rocky Moun-tain goat, with the name that symbolizes this empire of the Northwest—the Great Northern.

The new trains will operate on a 45-hour schedule, saving one night between Chicago and the Pacific Northwest, and a full business day on coast-to-coast journeys. Other streamliners are building.

The Great Northern and the Northwest offer much to the traveler and the homeseeker, for here is a land of opportunity, of unsurpassed grandeur. The bright, reaching rails of the Great Northern have broken the trail as they thread the land of the cattleman, the wheat-grower, the sheep-raiser, the miner, the lumberjack, the orchardist. They serve the manufacturer and the sportsman, the vacationist and the homesteader. Here, truly, in the world of Jim Hill and the Empire Builder you ride a magic carpet, and F. J. Gavin, the present president of the road, fol-lows in his footsteps, performing even a better job.

CHAPTER IV

CENTRALIZED TRAFFIC CONTROL
ON THE SANTA FE

When a retired operator on the Santa Fe returned not long ago to visit his old office at Fullerton, California, he found some changes. He had heard, of course, about Centralized Traffic Control, but he had never seen it in operation. In his day train movement had been regulated by timetable and train order, while he received "OS" reports from operators on the division, indicating trains passing their respective stations. But it wasn't done that way any more.

Now small colored lights winked on and off. The operator pressed buttons and flipped little switches on the panels of a three-section cabinet. Inked pens mechanically noted down the positions of trains. Occasionally the operator held a brief telephone conversation with someone out on the line. And that seemed to be all there was to it.

Centralized traffic control—C.T.C., as it is known to railroaders—is a mechanical brain. It is an intricate machine which gives the operator complete control of all switches and signals over extended distances of track. It eliminates train orders and time lost by trains "in the hole"—waiting in sidings—and enables a single-track railroad to operate up to 75 per cent of double-track capacity.

With C.T.C. "running meets" are possible. Trains move safely and efficiently, making up valuable time on stretches of track thus equipped.

By means of signals and switches controlled through his C.T.C. board, and by a little "jawbone" over a telephone, the operator's long arm of authority guides and controls traffic over

38

a territory covering a hundred miles and more of track in the mountains and desert of the Santa Fe.

Concise, up-to-the-minute knowledge of train progress is furnished to the operator at the C.T.C. control machine by indications on a "track model" at the top of the panel in front of him. Red, green, and amber lights on this model tell him the exact location of all trains and the conditions of all switches and signals in his territory, and he can change the indications of any signal or the position of any switch merely by turning a small lever and pressing a button on his board.

Because speed, safety, and efficiency—the watchwords of the railroad—are combined in Centralized Traffic Control, this comparatively new wrinkle was a prime factor in the enormous movement of war transport during World War II and afterwards. C.T.C. has been heralded as one of the greatest advances in railroading in this century.

Constantly on the alert for developments to improve the service provided shippers and passengers, the Santa Fe was one of the earliest users of Centralized Traffic Control, and now has this system in operation on more than 520 miles of railroad with a total of more than 660 miles of signaled track.

Installations of C.T.C. on the Atchison, Topeka & Santa Fe are located between Vaughn and Belen, New Mexico; between Holliday and Olathe in eastern Kansas; between Kinsley and Dodge City in western Kansas; between Fullerton and San Diego, California; between Fullerton and Riverside, California; between Melrose and Joffre, New Mexico; and between Algoa and Houston, Texas.

All of these installations, with the exception of the Holliday-Olathe territory, which is double track, are located on stretches of heavily traveled single track, which might have developed into bottlenecks under the strain of the unprecedented flow of war materials and fighting men which began to move over them after Pearl Harbor.

The old-time operator examined the dispatching machine with mingled curiosity and amazement, together with growing admiration. What he saw was a semihexagonal metal cabinet about five feet high and made up of three panels—a center panel, 5 feet wide, flanked by wing panels, each of which was 2½ feet wide. At the top of the panels was a diagram in miniature of the entire track layout in the territory controlled by the board. This indicated the location of all switches and signals between Bandini on the north and El Toro on the south.

On the part of the diagram representing the main line were small lights between all passing sidings, and also *on* the sidings. Presence of a train in that territory, he was told, was indicated by the illumination of these lights in red.

Immediately below the track model, the old-timer saw two rows of levers. The top row, he was told, controlled the switches by means of electrically operated switch machines, located in the field at each controlled switch. The second row of levers, he learned, controlled signals located in the field at each end of passing sidings.

"These switch levers, you notice," said the operator, "have two positions—normal and reverse. The signals are controlled by these three-position levers below. The normal position of a switch is indicated by a green light over the normal position of the miniature switch-control lever. Reverse position is indicated by an amber light over the reverse position of the lever.

"Now if a lever controlling signals at the end of a siding is in center position, all signals show *stop*, which is indicated by a red light over center position of the lever. Moving the lever to the left clears the northbound signal, and movement to the right clears the southbound signal. Clear signals are indicated by green lights over corresponding lever positions."

"What won't they think of next?" said the old-timer.

"You see these toggle switches," continued the operator. "There are 17 of them here just below the signal levers. These toggle switches control electric locks installed at all main-line hand-thrown switches, thus preventing trainmen from throwing the switch unless a release is obtained either automatically with a safety time period or from the C.T.C. machine sending out a control code to effect an electric unlock. Those are the code-starting push buttons there under the toggle switches.

"Under the code-starting buttons, you notice there are more toggle switches. These are for calling the maintainer in case of trouble. By using one of these switches," the operator explained, "I can light an indication light at field locations equipped with telephones, and if a maintainer is around he answers a telephone located there.

"These field locations at ends of passing sidings or other controlled points are small concrete or steel housings beside the track. They contain equipment for electric operation of switches and signals, as well as necessary batteries, relays, and other mechanisms with a network of safety circuits which protect the operation against human failure."

At that moment a telephone at the operator's elbow rang. It was the engine foreman of a switch crew working on a siding off the main line. He was calling from a field location at an electrically locked hand-thrown switch.

"I want to work on the main," he said, as he identified himself.

The operator consulted his track model, checking the location of trains in his territory. He glanced then at the train sheet to determine what trains soon would be entering the territory, and then checked the time by the railroad clock on the wall.

"Okay," he told the engine foreman, "you may have until two-fifteen." He then turned a couple of levers to change indication of signals at the desired location, threw the toggle switch, and pressed the code-starting button to unlock the hand-thrown switch. This done, he marked a small tag with "X," followed by the number of the foreman's engine, and hung the tag on the switch lever to remind him that the switch crew was working on the main line at this point.

At about 2:10 the telephone rang again. "All through," came the voice of the foreman. "All switches have been lined and locked for main track."

The operator removed the tag, threw all levers and switches back to their former positions, and the operation had been concluded. "Just like falling off a log," he told the old-timer.

"That's something!" growled the old-timer. He had been eying the automatic train graph, protected by plate glass, and set into the center section of the horizontal ledge of the C.T.C. machine which served as a desk. "And what's that thing?"

41

"That," the operator pointed out, "is the train graph mechanism. A telechron clocklike device continuously operates this parallel-lined chart, which is printed for a direct reading of time. The space between each pair of lines on the graph represents two minutes. The chart passes under magnetically operated pens and forms a record of track occupancy. An individual pen is provided to make a recording on the graph each time a train passes an "OS" or train report section within the territory. By connecting the dots on the graph with my fountain pen I make a complete chart of the progress of each train in my territory, showing the exact time it passed a particular point and where and when the various meets were made.

"At the end of the day the graph sheet is torn off and filed away as a permanent record of all train movements on that date."

"By golly," said the old-timer, "I would kind of like to play with that thing." He looked at the trim C.T.C. cabinet and shook his head. "I was born thirty years too soon."

The basic principles of C.T.C. operation have been employed in interlocking plants at junctions and terminals for years. At first they were operated by hand levers; later they were electrified. Only in the past few years have these electric controls been developed to a point where entire districts and divisions can be safely handled by enormously expanded interlocking methods.

Under today's C.T.C. system any train may move at maximum speed permitted at that location when the signal governing movements in the desired direction shows green. It may move at restricted speed when the governing signal shows yellow. And it must stop when this governing signal displays red.

Obedience to these three simple rules is the only requirement imposed on the locomotive engineer. The signals grant him full authority for the movement of his train from one end of the district to the other. They authorize him to proceed, and they command him to stop. His only duty is to obey.

Behind the display of these simple signals and underwriting their integrity is a network of interconnected safety circuits in the field controlled by the C.T.C. machine in the office. It is one of the most intricate and exact systems ever designed by electrical and signal engineers.

Technically, the machine which caused the old-timer to blink his eyes in amazement, together with the field equipment, is an interlocking system of electrical circuits, each dependent upon the sequential functioning of the other, guarding and controlling the elaborate system of relays and codes which operates the plant.

No switch can be changed until red signals safeguard it for a safety period and during its movement. No signal can be cleared until the route is safe, with the switches locked and the block clear. All signals give ample warning in advance and provide sufficient braking distance for the fastest trains to be safely controlled to meet all operating conditions.

As the train moves forward a mantle of protection precedes it and follows it, preventing opposing movements and spacing following trains by red signals, with yellow warning signals located more than maximum stopping distance in the rear.

All controls to the entire system are carried to a centralized point where they are placed in the cabinet of the C.T.C. machine and handled by the operator. He constantly exercises finger-tip control over every signal and every siding switch and moves the trains continuously toward their meeting points. He can at any time make last-minute decisions as to where these meeting points will be.

Pecos Division Installation

Perhaps no better example of what C.T.C. means to a busy division can be found than that territory on the Santa Fe between Belen and Vaughn, New Mexico, known as the Pecos Division, Second District. Here Centralized Traffic Control governs operations on a single-track district 109 miles in length. One C.T.C. board controls an entire operating district.

This Pecos Division is rugged, with heavy mountain grades and wild and rough Abo Canyon. All heavy freight trains and some passenger trains require helper service from Belen to Mountainair.

The greater proportion of transcontinental freight tonnage passes over the Pecos Division en route to and from the Pacific coast. Westward tonnage from the eastern lines joins the tonnage from the Gulf lines at Texico, New Mexico, and moves on across the Pecos Division to the entrance to the coast lines' double track at Belen. Eastward, the traffic follows the reverse routing. At times it seems that all of the wandering freight cars in the world converge for a convention on the Pecos Division, and it requires a bit of stouthearted railroading to keep them sorted out and moving.

Western history has blazoned the word "Pecos" in large letters, and the Sante Fe has adhered to tradition as they fought the battle of the Pecos with steel rails and thundering engines.

At the outbreak of World War II, immediate attention was directed to the Pecos Division. With its single track, mountain grades, and limited water sources it threatened to become a bottleneck of startling proportions. Santa Fe officials realized early in the game that the Pecos Division was certain to be called upon to handle the heaviest traffic in all its colorful history. And no threatened stampede of the cattle trails ever held so ominous a menace as the wild rush gathering momentum on the borders of the Pecos immediately following the morning of December 7, 1941.

The Santa Fe men knew full well that the capacity of the line would have to be increased, and quickly. It was going to be a case of forcing open the jaws of frowning Abo Canyon, or dipping into their bag of tricks and coming up with a piece of magic sufficient unto the needs.

The Santa Fe was hewn out of the wilderness by men of courage and resource in the long ago. Happily, those who came after were no less pioneering and determined souls, and they were not at all disheartened by the threat of the approaching storm. Black clouds hung low over those glowering mountains, with their trailing veils waving like battle flags, but Santa Fe men were not easily intimidated.

Having made their decision, they rolled up their sleeves and went to work. Already they had settled on Centralized Traffic Control as a means of relieving the growing congestion, but it remained to prepare the Pecos Division for the C.T.C. installation. Tawny men with picks and shovels and machines were thrown into the battle.

Sidings were lengthened, in some cases two or three miles. Long turnouts were placed in running tracks and sidings, making for high-speed train movements. Curves were reduced, water stations were rearranged, new sources of water were developed, heavy rail was laid on both main line and siding, and the Pecos Division was on its way to becoming a fighting division.

The entire construction and reconstruction district was integrated with the newly installed C.T.C. system to produce the greatest possible capacity on a single-track line. The result was that the Pecos Division handled more than double the traffic with C.T.C. than it had previously handled, and in less time, terminal to terminal.

Break-in-two problems and delays were reduced by eliminating the many starts and stops for heavy freight trains. Water stops were reduced by providing continuous movement. The productivity of motive power was greatly enlarged by the increase in train speed on the division.

The C.T.C. installation lifted serious burdens of congestion from the terminals by affording free movement whenever trains were made up and ready to go. It also furnished opportunity for proper spacing of trains into the terminals, thus avoiding congestion.

Benefits were spread far beyond the Pecos Division itself. There was a freer movement of trains and a wider use of power over the entire Southern District. The problem of Abo Canyon was solved. A mountain bottleneck had been smashed, and the Santa Fe had demonstrated that a champion is hard to whip.

The high point of the Pecos Division at Mountainair, New Mexico, is 6,492 feet. The elevation at Belen, to the west, is 4,806 feet and at Vaughn, to the east, 5,958 feet. It's pretty rugged country, out there west of the Pecos. There is the Manzano Range and the great Chupadera Mesa—and Abo Canyon.

And there is the shining single-track steel of the Santa Fe, winding, twisting, dropping, climbing. There are mighty engines and long dragonlike trains, clawing for a foothold on mountain iron—and there is Centralized Traffic Control.

45

Eastward from Belen Yards, the line lifts constantly on a grade ranging from 0.5 to 0.6 per cent for the first 13 miles to Becker. From there the grade ascends at rates ranging up to 1.25 per cent for the remaining 26 miles to Mountainair. On this grade between Belen and Mountainair the railroad is in the canyon of the Abo River for about 13 miles between Sais and Abo, and in this section there are seven 4-degree curves and six 2-degree curves. The locomotives assigned to through freight service are rated at 4,500 tons, and each eastbound train has a helper which is cut in at Belen and cut out at Mountainair.

From the summit west of the station at Mountainair, the grade descends eastward for 68 miles to Vaughn at varying rates between 0.3 and 0.6 per cent, except for 16 miles between Silio and Dunmoor and 4 miles between Encino and Carnero, where the grade ascends eastward at 0.1 to 0.6 per cent. Throughout the Mountainair-Vaughn territory, the railroad is in more or less open country, the curvature being very light, with no curves of more than 1 degree.

In the operating arrangement previously in effect, train movements were authorized by timetable and train orders, with single-track automatic block signaling protection controlled on the

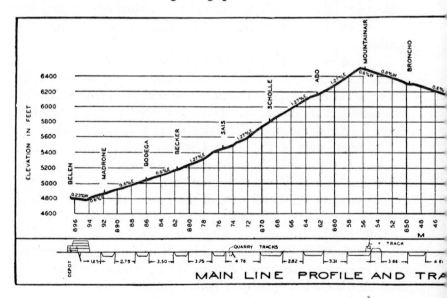

overlap basis. Spring switches were in service at both ends of 14 sidings, and interlockings at both ends of 3 sidings. One siding had a capacity of 90 cars, 5 sidings a capacity of 110 cars, and 12 sidings a capacity of 130 cars.

The schedule included 2 through passenger trains each way. A local freight was operated each way daily except Sunday. Prior to World War II, the remainder of the freight traffic was handled in 2 to 3 through freight trains each way daily. Thus the total traffic in the years 1930 to 1937 averaged from 12 to 16 trains daily, not including 2 to 3 light engine helper moves westward between Mountainair and Belen.

With the coming of the war, the number of passenger trains daily increased to an average of 3.2 eastbound and 5.7 westbound, and the freight traffic increased to a daily average of 762 cars eastbound and 812 cars westbound, totaling about 30 trains daily, in addition to about 10 light engine moves when helpers returned from Mountainair to Belen. This increased volume of traffic caused serious train delays, especially on the grade between Belen and Mountainair. As a result, in this section the average speed of passenger trains was reduced to 31 miles per hour westbound and 29.9 per hour eastbound, and freight trains

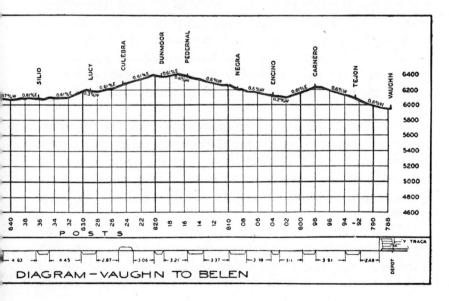

DIAGRAM — VAUGHN TO BELEN

to 14.8 m.p.h. westbound and 7.2 m.p.h. eastbound. Helper engines encountered serious delays in getting back down the hill to Belen, so that the number of engines assigned to this service had to be increased to an average of 6.9 daily.

Faced with the necessity not only of expediting train movements but also of handling an ever-increasing wartime traffic, a decision was made to lengthen the sidings and install Centralized Traffic Control, including power switches and signals for authorizing train movements, thus obviating the train stops and delays which were inherent in the timetable and train-order method.

An outstanding feature of C.T.C. on the Pecos is the use of very long sidings, and we mean long. At 13 stations the sidings were extended to 2 miles or more in length, and at 6 other stations the sidings range from 1.2 to 1.8 miles in length. In addition to a siding 3.4 miles long at Mountainair, there are also two other sidings, one with a capacity of 62 cars, and the other 111 cars. The car capacities of sidings, based on 55 feet to the car, include Broncho, 218 cars; Abo, 237 cars; Scholle, 270 cars; Pedernal, 200 cars; Negra, 209 cars; and Tejon, 186 cars. And there are many more, ranging between 105 cars and 162 cars.

The purpose of lengthening the sidings was not to "hold" more trains, but rather to provide track length for a train to keep moving while making a meet with an opposing train. On these sidings, the track is constructed and maintained to standards which permit trains to be operated safely at speeds up to 40 miles per hour. At 17 sidings new No. 20 turnouts were installed to permit trains to enter and depart at speeds up to 40 miles per hour.

All of the 21 sidings are equipped with track circuits which serve two purposes: (1) to control indication lamps on the track diagram on the C.T.C. machine so that the operator may be reminded of the presence of trains on sidings, and (2) these track circuits enter into the control of signals for directing trains to enter.

When a switch has been reversed and a signal cleared for an approaching train to enter a siding, the signals inform the engineman that the siding is unoccupied and therefore he can pull his train through the turnout and into the clear with promptness, rather than dragging along prepared to stop short of a train. Thus the train can use the turnout at the speed for which it was designed.

Having gotten his train into the clear on a siding, an engineman can reduce speed but keep moving. In the meantime, the operator at his C.T.C. board can return the entering switch to normal and clear the signal for the opposing train to be met. Generally the opposing train clears the far switch in time for it to be reversed and for the leave-siding signal to be cleared so that the train in the siding need not stop, but can be accelerated and pull out promptly.

Another item of importance is that the leave-siding signals are the three-aspect type which display yellow if only one automatic block ahead is unoccupied, or green if two or more automatic blocks ahead are unoccupied. When yellow is the best aspect on a leave-siding signal, an engineman cannot accelerate to maximum permissible speed until he reaches the first intermediate signal. But with the green aspect he can pull his train through the turnout at the speed for which it was designed, and then promptly bring his train to main-line speed.

As stated previously, the sidings were lengthened for the purpose of aiding in making nonstop meets, rather than to "hold" trains. On the other hand, in rare instances it is handy to double a train in on a siding behind a train of the same direction which is already occupying the far end.

As applying to any of the 13 long sidings on the Second District of the Pecos Division between Belen and Vaughn, which are equipped with intermediate block signals, if the rear of the first train is beyond the intermediate automatic signal on the siding, the head-in signal can be cleared by C.T.C. control so that the engineman of the second train will know that the siding is unoccupied as far as the intermediate signal, and therefore this second train can be pulled in to stop short of the intermediate signal. If the intermediate signal were not provided, as is true on the 8 shorter sidings, a second train would be stopped at the entering signal, and then would enter the siding under flag protection.

The possibility of making nonstop meets between opposing

trains depends not only on long sidings, but also on short time-spacing between sidings, so that frequently a train can be directed to move on over to the next siding and enter on short time, rather than being held back at the previous siding.

Train speed and distance are the factors which determine the time-spacing between sidings.

The maximum permissible speeds in this district are 90 miles per hour for passenger trains and 50 miles per hour for freight. Restrictions below these maximums are, of course, necessary on the grades as well as on some of the curves.

Between Belen and Mountainair the distances between sidings are comparatively short, ranging from 2.7 to 3.5 miles. The outstanding exception is the 4.7 miles between Sais and Scholle. Here the grade is 1.2 per cent, ascending eastward. The speed is slow for eastbound trains, increasing the train time. The situation cannot be easily remedied because the track is in a canyon, with no available space for another siding. Thus, with few exceptions, the time-spacing between sidings is short, not only because of short distances but also because of the long turnouts and the signals which permit trains to enter and leave sidings promptly after C.T.C. was installed.

Although the number of freight cars handled daily increased from 762 to 891 eastbound and from 812 to 991 westbound, the average speed of freight trains increased from 14.8 to 24.5 miles per hour westbound, and from 7.2 to 14.6 miles per hour eastbound. On account of delays when returning from Mountainair to Belen, a helper locomotive and crew could be used for only one trip each day. Now the delays have been reduced to a point where a helper engine can help two, and sometimes three, trains daily up the hill and return to Belen.

When changing over to C.T.C., the old semaphore mechanisms, spectacles and blades were scrapped. The masts were shortened and reused to mount the new searchlight-type signal heads. These signals are equipped with 250-ohm operating coils for operation at 8 volts d.c. The signal lamps are double-filament type rated at 8 volts.

So that the aspects may be seen as far as practicable, all signals on sidings as well as on the main track are high signals. All sig-

New York Central #68, with Engine #6010, new class S-1B, running around BN-2, new Pacemaker fast freight, with Engine #3100, Class L-4, at Garrison, N. Y., on the Hudson Division. Courtesy New York Central Railroad.

S. P. Engine 4159 Class AC5 4-8-8-2 type pushing Rotary Snow Plow on the Sacramento Div. at Snowshed 47. Photo "Courtesy" Southern Pacific R.R.

Steel gang stands aside as three-engine 83-car S. P. eastward freight train passes them out of Bakersfield, Calif., on San Joaquin Div. Photo Courtesy Southern Pacific R.R.

Great Northern #449 westward fast freight with Engine #2049, class R-2, 2-8-8-2 type, crossing Gassman Coulee with 98 loads on the Third Subdivision of the Minot Division 5 miles west of Minot, N. D. Photo by H. W. Pontin. Courtesy Rail Photo Service.

B.&O. St. Louis-94 fast quick-dispatch freight train with 5,400-h.p. 4-unit freight Diesel overtaking eastward coal drag with Engine #7606, 2-8-8-4 type, class EM-1, entering Keyser Yard, Cumberland Division. Photo by H. W. Pontin. Courtesy Rail Photo Service.

The great N.&W. class-A engine, 2-6-6-4 type, with a westbound time freight at Narrows, Va., on the Radford Division. Courtesy Norfolk & Western Railroad.

The rear end and the head end about to meet. Caboose of N.&W. time freight #99, and Engine #2165, 2-8-8-2 type, class Y-6A, with white flags and a coal drag near Elliston, Va., on the Radford Division. Courtesy Norfolk & Western Railroad.

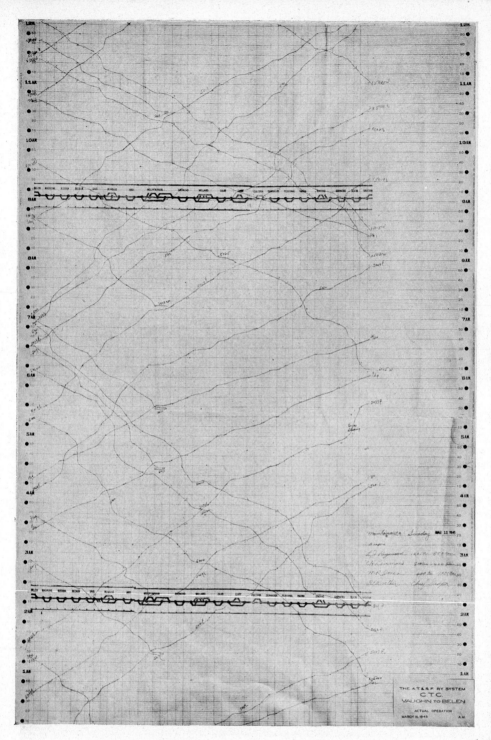

Graph off the C.T.C. machine at Mountainair, N. M.

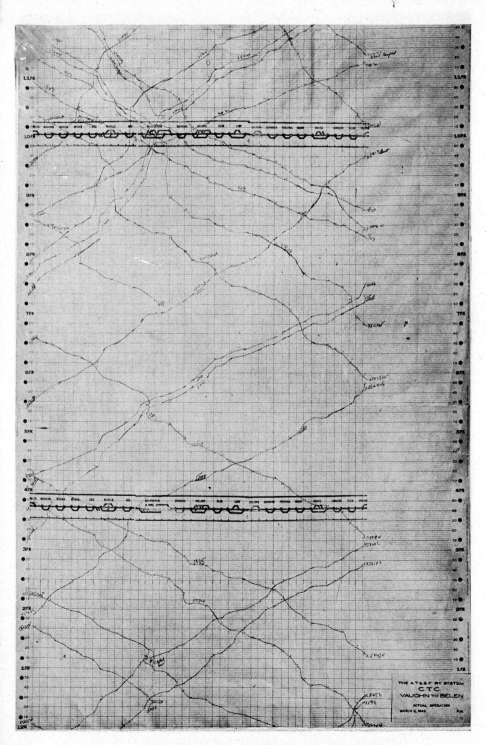

Graph off the C.T.C. machine at Mountainair, N. M.

The C.T.C. machine at Mountainair, N. M., showing the track diagram, graph, switch and signal levers, and code and starting buttons, with the operator clearing a signal at Willard on the Santa Fe's Pecos Division. Courtesy Santa Fe Railroad.

Santa Fe Extra #5022, east with GFX at west end of Mountainair siding west of Mountainair, N. M., on C.T.C. territory, Pecos Division. Note the searchlight signals and high masts. Courtesy Union Switch & Signal Co.

nals are at the right of the track which they govern. Where possible, the sidings were moved over to 18-foot track centers to allow clearance for a high signal on a mast. When space was not available, the signals were placed overhead on bridges or cantilevers.

With certain exceptions, each signal displays three aspects—red, yellow, and green. Where signals are equipped with an additional light unit so that they can display yellow over yellow, this aspect requires medium speed and indicates that the train may approach the next signal at reduced speed. A point of importance is that if either light is burned out when the signal is supposed to show yellow-over-yellow, there will be no hazard because a single yellow is more restrictive than two yellows.

The power switch machines are d.c., low-voltage, rated to operate in 14 seconds with 24 volts at the motor. In the No. 20 turnouts, the switch points are 30 feet long, and to prevent flexing of the points a second operating connection is attached to a tie rod approximately 14 feet from the main connection.

The C.T.C. control machine for the territory is located at Mountainair, and, like the one at Fullerton, California, has a 5-foot panel and two wing panels.

The illuminated track diagram includes a lamp to repeat the occupancy of: (1) each "OS" switch detector section; (2) each passing siding; (3) each section of main line opposite a siding; and (4) each section of single-track main line between two sidings. The switch and signal levers are equipped with indication lamps above these levers, as previously described.

Electric time locking is provided in connection with the signals at switches. If a proceed signal aspect is taken away by the lever control, electric time locking by time-element relays at the field location becomes effective in preventing operation of the power switch, as well as the clearing of an opposing signal until a certain predetermined time has elapsed. So that the operator will know when the time-element relay is operating, the red "stop" indication light over the signal lever remains dark. Any attempt by the operator to move the switch while the timing device is in operation will be ineffective.

Below the levers there are two rows of toggle switches, one row of which controls the electric locks on the hand-throw main line switches and the other the maintainer's call lamps at each field location.

Above each portion of the diagram representing a section of main track between sidings there is a double-headed arrow with two lamps. When the machine controls are established to permit the clearing of a signal for a westward train movement, the lamp to the left, which is green, is lighted. Or, when eastward, the right-hand lamp, which is yellow, is lighted.

The C.T.C. system is a form of time code for multiple line application, using biased polar line and starting relays. The transmission of control codes and return indication codes are handled on two line wires.

The territory between Vaughn and Belen is divided into three separate sections of code line. The code line west from Mountainair handles the 40.8 miles to Belen. Then there is a code line from Mountainair to Culebra, to the east, and a code line from this point to Vaughn. However, controls can be sent to or indications received from the three sections simultaneously.

Part of the work in this territory included the construction of a pole line over the entire district. A.c. power is supplied from commercial sources. The two power-distribution line wires are bare copper. The two C.T.C. line wires are weatherproof covered. Storage batteries trickle-charged from the a.c. power system through rectifiers, are used for feeding the line code equipment, the power switch machines, and the line circuits. Signal lamps are fed normally from a.c. with storage battery stand-by.

The signaling between sidings is so arranged that opposing train movements are positively blocked while following movements are permitted. Only one of the two opposing station-leaving signals can be cleared at one time, and all of the signals, including the intermediate automatic signals, are provided with electric circuits so interconnected that no signal can clear unless the mechanism of the opposing signals are in the stop position. The direction of traffic is set up by the dispatcher clearing one of the C.T.C.-controlled signals for train to enter a block. The signal lamps remain unlighted until a train approaches. This latter feature is called "approach lighting."

Train movements through signaled sidings are handled in the same manner as train movements from siding to siding, in that opposing movements are positively blocked while following movements are permitted.

This Pecos Division installation also includes motorcar indicators by means of which the men on motorcars are informed of the approach of trains on those sections where curves and high banks reduce the sighting distances. These indicators are mounted either on the signal cases or on short poles beside the track and with the lens so directed that it can easily be observed by the trackman on his motorcar or speeder.

Other Installations

Adjoining the Vaughn-Belen installation on the Pecos Division, Centralized Traffic Control has been put in operation between Melrose and Joffre, New Mexico. Here we find 97 miles of single-track road with 16 sidings, for a total of 132 miles of signaled track. The board is located at Clovis, New Mexico.

Another C.T.C. installation on the Santa Fe system is located on the Gulf lines between Algoa and Houston, Texas. It was here that another bottleneck threatened, and nothing can so thoroughly jam a railroad as a lot of freight cars with no place to go. There were only 22 miles of single track and 5 miles of double track involved, but those fleets of long, perishable freights slogging onto the Santa Fe line at Algoa over the Missouri Pacific with their Rio Grande Valley harvest were a little more than the Santa Fe could comfortably swallow, and so once more the Train Dispatcher's "Mechanical Brain"—the C.T.C. control board—was employed to sort out the tangle.

A siding controlled by the board at Alvin was constructed at Algoa. It provided accommodations for two 100-car trains, and here the slower hauls awaited their turn on the main line while the faster trains ran around them. The congestion was promptly eased, and a lot of headaches were relieved. Finding a way to overcome difficulties is an old story on the Santa Fe.

The first Centralized Traffic Control installation on the Santa Fe went into operation between Kinsley and Wright in the wheat-growing belt of western Kansas on December 23, 1930, and it was extended from Wright to Dodge City, being completed January 29, 1931.

December 30, 1930, also saw another section in operation on 13 miles of double track between Holliday and Olathe, Kansas. Grades on this territory had caused serious congestion when wheat was on the move. C.T.C. promptly eased the operating problem by enabling the Santa Fe to run trains over either track in either direction. The control board was located at Holliday.

Holliday is a big name on the Santa Fe, for it was Cyrus K. Holliday who started the construction of the Santa Fe something like 62 years before Centralized Traffic Control went into operation at a place called Holliday, Kansas, a small matter of about 50 miles from where the first shovel of dirt was turned on the present great Santa Fe System.

Examples of What C.T.C. Can Do

TRANSCRIPT OF RUN—BELEN TO VAUGHN—PECOS DIV. SANTA FE R.R.
SECOND DISTRICT

Drag Extra East—Engine 5026

90 Loads   8 Empties   4,984 Tons December 19, 1944

Eastward grade feet per mile shown between stations

Weather clear and calm
Temp. 26 at Belen

Meets	Station	Arrived	Dept.	Dist.	Running Time	Average Speed	Capacity of Sidings
	Belen		11.15a.m.				
	31.7						
	Madrone		11.30a.m.	4.4	15″	17.6	170 cars
	31.7						
	Bodega		11.38a.m.	6.0	8″	45.0	170
	31.7						
	Becker		11.46a.m.	4.5	8″	33.7	171
	66.0						
	Sais		11.55a.m.	6.1	9″	40.6	153
	66.0						
X5017	Scholle		12.12p.m.	6.6	17″	23.1	276
	66.0						
1-1 3761	Abo	12.35p.m.	12.45p.m.	6.7	23″	17.4	246
	66.0						
X5004	Mountainair	1.05p.m.	1.10p.m.	6.5	20″	19.5	W 310 E 116
	o.						
2-1 Main 3722	Broncho	1.18p.m.	1.21p.m.	6.4	8″	48.0	226
	o.						
X 5021	Willard		1.38p.m.	7.2	17″	25.4	121
	31.7						
	Silio		1.46p.m.	6.3	8″	47.2	148
	31.7						
X 5002	Lucy		1.56p.m.	7.0	10″	42.0	178
	31.7						
Work Ex 1815	Culebra		2.10p.m.	5.4	14″	23.1	130
	31.7						
	Dunmoor		2.24p.m.	3.9	14″	16.7	170
	31.7						
X 5009	Pedernal		2.38p.m.	4.0	14″	17.1	208
	31.7						
X 3820	Negra		2.52p.m.	6.7	14″	28.7	218
	31.7						
X3855 Main	Encino		3.00p.m.	5.0	8″	37.5	101
	31.7						
	Carnero		3.08p.m.	5.8	8″	43.5	165
	o.						
	Tejon	3.20p.m.	3.25p.m.	5.7	12″	28.5	194
	o.						
	Vaughn	3.40p.m.		4.8	15″	19.2	

Sais to Scholle on 1.25 grade
Seven 4° curves
Scholle to Abo six 2° curves
Mountainair to Vaughn no curves over 1°
Compiled by S.K.F. Jr. who was riding engine. Engineman P. W. Eckley

109 mi. 4 hr.25″ 23 min. detention
10″ Meet #1 at Abo
5″ Cut off helper eng. Mountainair
3″ Flagged by Ex-Gang Broncho
5″ Leak in air hose & brake sticking Tejon

TRANSCRIPT OF RUN—VAUGHN TO CLOVIS—PECOS DIVISION
FIRST DISTRICT

Drag Extra East—Engine 5026

Double track Vaughn   90 Loads   8 Empties   4,984 Tons
to Joffe—Melrose
to Clovis   C.T.C. Joffre to Melrose

December 19, 1944
Weather clear—light wind
Temp. 28 at Vaughn

Eastward grade feet per mile shown between stations

Meets	Station	Arrived	Dept.	Dist.	Running Time	Average Speed	Capacity of Sidings
	Vaughn	3.40p.m.	3.55p.m.				
	0.						
X 3866	Iden		4.05p.m.	4.9	10"	29.4	
	0.						
End of dbl. track	Joffre		4.18p.m.	6.9	13"	22.6	107
	10.2						
X 5005							
2-43	Duoro	4.30p.m.	4.40p.m.	6.7	12"	33.5	211
	31.7						
	Cardenas		4.50p.m.	7.2	10"	43.2	200
	0.						
	Buchanan		5.00p.m.	5.7	10"	34.2	200
	0.						
X 3817	Largo		5.07p.m.	5.9	7"	50.5	200
	0.						
X 3707 Main	Yeso		5.13p.m.	6.3	6"	63.0	200
	0.						
	Evanola		5.20p.m.	6.9	7"	59.1	200
	0.						
	Ricardo		5.27p.m.	6.7	7"	57.4	200
	15.8						
X 5011	Agudo		5.36p.m.	5.9	9"	39.3	212
	0.						
X 5000	Ft. Sumner		5.47p.m.	7.6	9"	50.6	101
	31.7						
	La Lande		5.55p.m.	6.7	8"	50.2	186
	31.7						
X 5024	Taiban		6.14p.m.	7.3	19"	23.0	240
	31.7						
	Tolar		6.20p.m.	4.3	6"	43.0	150
	31.7						
	Krider		6.30p.m.	5.4	10"	32.4	200
	31.7						
	Cantara		6.38p.m.	5.9	8"	44.2	200
	26.4						
Beg. of dbl. track	Melrose		6.48p.m.	6.4	10"	38.4	W 102 E 100
	11.1						
1-23 5025 and 3753 cpl.	St. Vrain		6.58p.m.	7.9	10"	47.4	
	13.7						
	Grier		7.05p.m.	5.5	7"	47.1	W 103 E 112
	11.1						
2-23 3767	Gallaher		7.12p.m.	5.2	7"	44.5	
	12.7						
	Clovis	7.20p.m.		5.5	8"	41.2	

Total time 1st and 2nd Districts 239.8 miles 8 hr. 5 min. with 48 min. delay—7 hr. 17 min. running time Compiled by S.K.F. Jr. who was riding engine. Engineman A. O. Wells, Fireman Robert E. Lee

130.8 mi. 3 hr. 25 min. 15 min. detention at Vaughn—service engine—water NO STOPS 10 min. detention Ex 5005 west Duoro going through siding

Typical Transcripts of Runs over C.T.C.-equipped Pecos Division

January 26, 1946

Diesel 169—2/GFX-W-OT, 75 loads, 25 empties, 100 cars

4,805 tons, including 9 perishable

2nd District—

Conductor R. K. Gentry
Engineer F. R. McNeill
Fireman P. V. Steele
Brakeman C. D. Pugh
Brakeman E. V. Elliott

Helper engine 5024 Belen to Mountainair

Engineer P. W. King
Fireman B. Y. Steele

Weather partly cloudy, calm to strong west wind, 26—40

Left Belen 9:06 a.m.—Arrived Vaughn 12:50 p.m.—3'44"

Delayed Mountainair 10" cut off helper and inspect train.

Met 39-Z, Forwarder 43-W, and TDF-X without delay.

1st District—

Conductor C. C. Hastings
Engineer L. A. McQueen
Fireman C. W. Crews
Brakeman L. H. Rosson
Brakeman W. A. Katzberg

Dispatchers—J. C. Collins—8 a.m. to 4 p.m.
         D. D. Boler—4 p.m. to 12:01 a.m.

Weather partly cloudy, calm to light west wind, 30—38

Left Vaughn 1:35 p.m.—Arrived Clovis 5:50 p.m.—4'15"

Delayed Ricardo 25" Forwarder 33-W which train was stopped by extra gang at Agudo.

Met 1/23-Y and 2/F-33-V on double track between Melrose and Clovis.

January 30, 1946

Diesel 163—PGX-BI, 93 loads, 7 empties, 100 cars

5,100 tons, including 63 perishable

2nd District—

Conductor C. W. Ross
Engineer M. L. Nichols
Fireman L. T. Brown
Brakeman J. H. Hawkes
Brakeman R. H. Ely

Helper engine 5019 Belen to Mountainair

Engineer P. W. King
Fireman B. Y. Steele

Weather clear, calm to light west wind, 27—36

Left Belen 11:55 a.m.—Arrived Vaughn 3:35 p.m.—3′40″

Delayed Mountainair 04″ cut off helper.

Met 2/F-33-Z and TDF-A without delay.

1st District—

Dispatcher D. D. Boler

Conductor C. C. Hastings
Engineer P. W. Curry
Fireman J. E. Clark
Brakeman S. M. May
Brakeman L. H. Rosson

Weather clear, brisk to strong west wind, 29—44

Left Vaughn 4:05 p.m.—Arrived Clovis 9:20 p.m.—5′15″

Delayed Agudo 05″ meet 1/23-BI. Fort Sumner 1′00″ meet Main 2870 West, Work Extra 1129, Local No. 37-CJ, 2/23-BI and DHQ PS 1659.

Also met 9/43-BG and F-43-BH without delay.

February 3, 1946

Diesel 162—Forwarder 43-A, 95 loads, 3 empties, 98 cars

4,223 tons, including 11 cars livestock

1st District—

Conductor H. C. Price
Engineer C. E. Rehorn
Fireman A. L. Hughes
Brakeman C. W. Franse
Brakeman C. H. Reno

Weather clear, calm, 42—50

Left Clovis 7:15 p.m.—Arrived Vaughn 12:20 a.m.—5′05″

Delayed Taiban 12″, inspect train. Evanola 10″ meet Main 3639 east Duoro 08″ meet 14/GFX-A (Diesel 169).

2nd District—

Conductor J. W. Achen
Engineer W. A. Riggs
Fireman D. B. Stephenson
Brakeman M. E. Bussey
Brakeman W. W. Gardner

Weather clear, medium west wind, 34—42

Left Vaughn 1:05 a.m.—Arrived Belen 5:00 a.m.—3′55″

Delayed Scholle 20″ meet 1/GFX-A, 05″ 1/24-B, 10″ 2/24-B. Bodega 05″ meet 13/GFX-B and WMB 70289 (Navy train east).

March 2, 1946

2nd District—

1-44-BG, engine 5023, 41 loads, 61 empties, 102 cars, 4,416 tons

Conductor J. L. Lewis
Engineer E. R. McManus
Fireman M. L. Nicols

Brakeman B. C. Rogers
Brakeman E. A. Weinhart

Helper engine 3902—Belen to Mountainair

Conductor pilot J. W. Doolen
Engineer P. W. King
Fireman B. L. Wilson

Weather clear, calm to light west wind—temperature 52—68

Left Belen 7:55 a.m.—Arrived Vaughn 12:30 p.m.—4'35"

Delays: Bodega 20" 14-43-BG, Becker 15" No. 1-BH, Mountainair 04" cut off helper, Willard 10" water and inspection

1st District—

Had 40 loads, 66 empties, 106 cars, 4,531 tons

Conductor J. T. Murrell
Engineer L. A. McQueen
Fireman C. W. Crews
Brakeman H. E. Nunn
Brakeman R. D. Todhunter

Weather clear to part cloudy, calm to light west wind—Temperature 68—74

Left Vaughn 1:10 p.m.—Arrived Clovis 5:10 p.m.—4'00"

Delays: Duoro 10" FWD 33-BG, MP 736 05" Extra gang, MP 716 thru shoo fly. West end Clovis yard 20" get in yard.

March 6, 1946

2nd District—

1-GFX C-7, engine 5028, 61 loads, 33 empties, 94 cars, 4705 tons

Conductor R. P. Armstrong
Engineer W. D. Houston
Fireman W. E. Haragon
Brakeman G. R. Bost
Brakeman J. Cassano

Helper engine 5030—Belen to Mountainair

Conductor pilot C. H. Craig
Engineer M. E. Johnson
Fireman W. G. Cherry

Weather clear, calm—temperature 26—30

Left Belen 2:35 a.m.—Arrived Vaughn 6:55 a.m.—4'20"

Delays: Sais 12" DHQ CS 41—Scholle 16" 1-24-D, 11" 2-24-D 10"
WMB 73978—Mountainair 5" helper, Willard 10" water

1st District—

Conductor R. L. Johnston
Engineer J. P. Thompson
Fireman R. K. Williams
Brakeman J. B. Massey
Brakeman J. L. Kim

Weather clear, calm to light west wind—temperature 44—50

Left Vaughn 9:10 a.m.—Arrived Clovis 1:05 p.m.—3'55"

Delays: None

CHAPTER V

THE MILWAUKEE

A Railroad Hauls the Atom

Contrary to popular belief, an American community and not Hiroshima, Japan, first became a victim of the atomic bomb. Six hundred square miles were abandoned; and more than 1,800 families evacuated. And it all happened almost with the suddenness of a striking tidal wave.

The town was Hanford, Washington. The area evacuated included the Priest Rapids and Richland areas of the Columbia River Valley. Men, women, and children, their goods and their chattels were displaced as completely as if a plague had visited the land.

The Hanford Branch of the Chicago, Milwaukee, St. Paul & Pacific strikes off in a southerly direction from the road's main line at Beverly on the Columbia River. Hanford stands at the end of the line, 46 miles away. Before the opening of World War II, Hanford boasted a rail service represented by one train a day each way. Except for the brief flurry attendant on the arrival of the afternoon train, nothing much happened to disturb the tranquillity of sleepy Hanford. Folks went to the station to see the train come in; they waited at the post office for the mail to be put up and lingered a little to talk of the war; then went about their affairs.

Life in Hanford was pleasant; folks were neighborly. Nothing ever happened in Hanford. The mighty Columbia flowed down from the Priest Rapids on its way to Columbia Bar and the broad Pacific. It was a good country; the folks, the solid sort of Americans you find in small towns everywhere.

They worked and played and closely followed the war news.

But the war seemed distant, unreal. True, it claimed Hanford boys. They went away to training camps, to the far-off war theaters, leaving a bit of heartache and loneliness in some home. But so far as the actual deep wounds of war were concerned—the misery and the devastation—Hanford felt secure in this pleasant inland world of south-central Washington State.

The radio and the papers cried of bloodshed and terror, of casualties, of the graveyard of the Murmansk run, of the submarine menace and American ships and men lost. And folks read of millions of miserable people uprooted from their homes and forced to try to put down roots again in new and strange places.

Hanford folks found greater appreciation of their own simple way of life, of their security. Nothing so starkly tragic, they were confident, could ever touch them.

Possibly the sleepiest spot in Hanford was the depot during the hours before the arrival of No. 415 at 2:30 in the afternoon. Even the telegraph sounder and the whispering relays seemed subdued and drowsy. Now and then the tongue of the sounder sputtered, while the agent listened to the gossiping voice of the telegraph wire.

Perhaps it lazily rattled off a message for someone in town; perhaps some operator up the line merely wanted to relieve the tedium with a bit of conversation concerning the weather or John Smith or Sam Jones.

And then, this February day in 1943, the sounder at Hanford depot rapped out a curt call. Gone was the easy flow of dots and dashes; gone was the peaceful atmosphere. Suddenly the air seemed charged with a tense something. It brought the operator to the key with a vague sense of uneasiness, a grave premonition of impending disaster. Could it be possible that far up the Columbia at the great Grand Coulee Dam something terrible had happened? Could saboteurs have penetrated this closely guarded area and planted dynamite charges that had released the waters of this vast man-made lake? Was a wall of water at this moment sweeping downstream?

Folks had talked of the possibility of the destruction by enemy agents of the two mightiest water barriers created by man, Boulder Dam and the Grand Coulee Dam.

63

The Hanford agent flicked the key open and clicked a quick "I-I," signing the station's call letters. The telegraph sounder broke into a rapid chatter, a lightning flood of Morse characters. The agent copied the message, his somber face reflecting a growing incredulity. When he had finished he sat back in stunned amazement. He read and reread the words before him, unable immediately to adjust his thinking to the full realization of their import.

He remembered now the strangers that had appeared in Hanford during the past weeks, grave, keen-eyed men whose business there had remained a close-kept secret—until now.

Hanford town was done—the old, sleepy Hanford, with its one train a day, had been inexorably caught in the grim jaws of war, just as surely as though it had suddenly found itself in the path of an invading army.

The message the agent at Hanford had copied ordered the full and complete evacuation of the town—at once. This flash from the wires was only the beginning.

The United States Government quickly followed it up with orders which resulted in the abandonment not only of the town of Hanford but of a total of 600 square miles of the near-by countryside.

Now it can be told. Hanford, Washington, was to become the site and the scene of a project of earth-jarring proportion, and the home of one of the three atomic bomb plants in the United States. The town of Hanford, instead of a sleepy hamlet, was to become the "Hanford Project," its purpose the manufacture of a weapon of war that might well have been spawned by men from Mars.

No time was lost, for war does not wait. The Milwaukee Railroad's Agricultural Development Department and other agencies speedily arranged for the relocation of the dispossessed families —600 in Hanford; 1,800 in all—thus clearing the way for the making of the atomic bomb.

Instead of one passenger train, together with the small dribble of going and coming freight cars, that had moved through Beverly Junction, there now began a tide of cars carrying scientific and industrial materials and equipment that grew to the equivalent of a freight train 350 miles long.

As many as 100 cars a day rolled behind the wall of secrecy that surrounded the Hanford Project—43,633 carloads of freight went into the building of the atomic bomb between April 1, 1943, and July 31, 1945.

From the beginning, the production of this new weapon, the impact of which was to smash all existing concepts of war, was a closely guarded secret. The men of the Milwaukee Road who knew of the development and its magnitude, the crews who operated the heavy trains and other employees, down to the last man, remained tight-lipped through the entire operation.

We still do not know the secrets of the atomic bomb, and possibly never will. We know only that as many as 100 loaded freight cars moved to the Hanford Project in one day—and that nothing but empty cars came out.

That's the story of Hanford that now can be told.

Only America's railroads had the capacity and the flexibility which enabled the government, science, and industry to marshal the nation's resources anywhere, in any quantity, for any undertaking, no matter how gigantic.

Whether it is moving "X" materials for a weapon to end all weapons, the transportation of big guns from coast to coast at high speed, the hauling of PT boats and landing barges and tanks direct from factory to the docks, the speeding of millions of fighting men to training camp and to waiting convoy, the carrying of tons of servicemen's mail, or any other of a vast variety of transportation jobs—only the railroads of the United States are capable of performing the task of bulk transport necessary to the movement of men and materials of war, as well as adequately serving the needs of the nation in peacetime.

Like the Milwaukee, the Southern Railway played an important part in the creation of the bomb that rocked the world, for it was at Oak Ridge, Tennessee, that the Southern delivered the atom in the raw.

And out in New Mexico, at Los Alamos, where the atom bomb was also worked on, the Santa Fe each year handled millions of dollars worth of materials and equipment employed in

65

the bomb experiments over the 18-mile Santa Fe branch from Lamy to the state capital where it was received from the New Mexico Division.

It is entirely possible that without the railroads the terrifying atom might have remained a prisoner of the test tube.

The Fast Mail

On March 13, 1946, the Milwaukee Road completed 62 years as a mail carrier for Uncle Sam between Chicago and the Twin Cities. Trains No. 56 and 57 are the Milwaukee's splendid carriers of the mail sack. The road's Fast Mails make connections with the Great Northern's famous 27 and 28, which serve the Northwest and Alaska.

It was back in 1884, we are informed by Carl F. Rank, Manager of Mail Traffic, Chicago, that the Postmaster General proposed to the Milwaukee that it operate a fast train from Chicago to St. Paul-Minneapolis.

It did not take the Milwaukee long to make up their minds. And, having arrived at a decision, they went into action with a bang. At two o'clock on the morning following the proposal the Milwaukee mail train began operation, which we feel free to venture established some kind of a record.

The Milwaukee, literally and figuratively, "carried the mail" for eight years, bound by iron-clad contract. Winter and summer the Fast Mail roared through, with many a battle with the elements. And then, in 1892, the Post Office Department decided to discontinue the exercising of written contracts, and it was verbally agreed that the Milwaukee should continue to handle the mail so long as the service continued to be satisfactory.

There isn't much to add to that, except that the Milwaukee is still carrying the mail.

The distance from Chicago to Minneapolis is 420.8 miles. No. 57 covers this distance in 9 hours and 15 minutes, which requires some very fancy running. The Fast Mail comes booming out of Chicago at nine in the evening. It makes stops at Milwaukee, Portage, New Lisbon, Camp Douglas, Sparta, La Crosse,

Winona, Red Wing, and St. Paul, arriving in Minneapolis at 6:15 a.m. The Great Northern's No. 27 picks up the mail in the Twin Cities and starts the long haul to Seattle.

No. 56 receives mail from the Great Northern's No. 28 and starts its night run for Chicago, leaving Minneapolis at 8:40 p.m. and arrives at the Chicago Union Station at 6:30 a.m. The Milwaukee "Postman" is a veteran now, but time has not dimmed the glory of the Fast Mail.

The New Caboose

On the Milwaukee Road the caboose has at last yielded to progressive redesigning, which includes the removal of the cupola, a subject which we have already touched upon. The little old caboose, on some roads, loses its cupola only to see it reappear on passenger coaches in the form of a glorified glass-domed observation point. In the meantime, the freight-train brakeman moves downstairs into a bay window.

In its shops in Milwaukee, Wisconsin, the Chicago, Milwaukee, St. Paul & Pacific, in 1945–46, began the task of rebuilding 900 cabooses, removing the cupolas and in their place installing side bays.

As viewed on the Milwaukee, the removal of the cupola has permitted the elimination of partitions inside of the car, making for a roomier, airier, and more easily heated caboose. These Milwaukee cabooses are equipped with the latest type of stove, both for heating and cooking. This stove has various safety features which include doors that cannot be thrown open accidentally.

Side seats 6 feet in length are built in. These are upholstered in leather and can easily be converted into beds, for use when the crew is away from his home terminal. A better and more efficient type of oil lamp has been installed.

The caboose has 3 clothes lockers, a washstand with water supply, a built-in refrigerator, and a tool locker, also a toilet.

The ceilings of the Milwaukee cabooses are finished with plywood, which makes for greater warmth in winter and insulates against heat in summer. Aluminum paint brightens the interior,

67

giving it a cheerful and sanitary appearance. Thus the freight crew's accommodations assume the proportions of parlor, bedroom, and bath.

No longer will the little red caboose adorn the rear end on the Milwaukee, for the remodeling of the caboose includes the rather startling innovation of a silver color scheme edged with black. The exterior is finished with aluminum paint. The running gear, platforms, grab irons, and ladders are done in black. Thus we witness on one road a modernistic trend that seems to threaten a long-established custom. But, as we have previously stated, railroad fashions at last have reached down the long line of the freight train to the lowly caboose.

The contrast of black against aluminum at the rear end, the Milwaukee points out, provides an added safety feature, since it tends to set off the caboose against the headlight rays of an oncoming engine.

CHAPTER VI

RAILROADING ON THE BOSTON & MAINE

"It's a Hell of a Way to Run a Railroad!"

The Boston & Maine is the Main Street of northern New England, and probably more of the folks along this street have a voice in its affairs than on any other railway system—from Aunt Mathilda on brocaded Beacon Hill to the champion checker player in Center Ossipee, New Hampshire.

And don't think for a minute that the criticisms and the suggestions of the Boston & Maine's neighbors are not carefully considered and weighed. President Edward S. French, when he took charge back in 1931, promptly adopted the policy that the customer is always right. "We are selling transportation," he told his associates. "Find out what the folks want—and give it to them."

There you have in a nutshell the policy of the Boston & Maine. President French was talking horse sense. And horse sense is a staple commodity in New England.

At a time when better than one-fourth of the railroads in the country were in the hands of receivers, the Boston & Maine was far from traveling a primrose path. But it was along about this time that Edward Sanborn French and staff hitched Old Dobbin to the wagon and went to town. A lot of the way it was uphill, but it takes more than a hill to stop a New Englander. His forefathers had long ago tackled the job of wrestling a living from those hillside farms. Half of every crop he harvested was stones, but he laid up fences with the stones—and kept right on plowing.

Because the Boston & Maine would not recognize defeat, it is today providing northern New England with the last word in modern transportation—whether it is hauling fish or plutocrats. It brought out, to quote from *Life* magazine, the first and only appealing timetable in the United States. It put on a radio program that broadcast weather reports, temperatures, tides, and hot music; also introduced Boston & Maine employees to the Main Street neighbors.

Where else would you find a railroad taking time out to stage a banquet for veteran commuters, each of whom received a 50-year-commuter pin? Galen A. Parker, at 93, was the "life of the party." "Mr. Parker," John O'Connor, of the *Boston Herald*, wrote, "proudly pointed out that Abraham Lincoln was still in the White House in 1865 when he hopped aboard the Boston-bound local at Reading station to begin the first of his 75 years as a steady Boston & Maine passenger."

Each commuter group had its own table. There were those who rode the Flying Yankee, the Minute Man, the Pine Tree Limited. Names breathing of the essence of New England, of its traditions and immortal history. Fifty-seven were at the party; ten for various reasons were unable to be present.

As homespun as the yarn from the old spinning wheel, this northern New England railroad. Friendly, gracious, neighborly. And efficient.

What is the Boston & Maine?

The Boston & Maine is 16,000 men and women working and living in northern New England and providing transportation for rural communities, for farms, for industries in Maine, New Hampshire, Vermont, Massachusetts, and a portion of New York. It is 1,789 miles of road; 3,430 miles of track; it is 530 locomotives, close to 8,000 freight cars, and 1,158 passenger cars, representing an investment of $269,570,102.

The Boston & Maine in 1944 carried 4,014,285 interline-ticket passengers, 11,513,766 commutation-ticket passengers, and 15,-403,202 single-fare passengers.

That's all for statistics.

Statistics don't tell of the conductor who helps an old lady with her luggage, or of the trainman who goes out of his way to deliver a forgotten parcel to a commuter, or of the ticket seller

70

who says, "Thank you, sir." Little things—yes. But they are the kind of little things that create good will.

A lady, changing trains at Greenfield, Massachusetts, discovered that she had left her purse on the Minute Man, and so found herself without money, ticket, or eyeglasses. She took her troubles to the ticket agent. Immediately this gentleman went into action. He telephoned the station at the Minute Man's next stop; he called the local police sergeant on duty, arranging for a special messenger to return the purse; he invited the lady to be his luncheon guest; and he arranged for a cab, should she wish to relieve the tedium of waiting by visiting the local points of interest.

That is selling transportation. Think how different the picture might have been if this agent had been a "sour-puss." Instead of the lady going home to sing the praises of the Boston & Maine to her friends and neighbors and writing a heart-warming letter to Vice-President and General Manager J. W. Smith, she not only would have been provoked because of her forgetfulness but keenly resentful of the curtness and indifference of the grouchy agent.

There is bound to be a sour-puss now and then, just as sometimes there is a flat wheel on a freight train. But for the most part the Boston & Maine family is made up of neighborly folks, the kind you find in every New England community.

On a railroad every employee who comes in contact with the public is a salesman, and on the Boston & Maine they hold to the opinion that the only place in which a crab becomes an asset is in a salad in the dining car.

When a railroad patron finds the service he has bought and paid for unsatisfactory, the B.&M. *Employees Magazine* points out, he'll give his future business to some other form of transportation. Once stung, a customer becomes mistrustful of bees, regardless of the fact that they produce honey.

Your New Englander is traditionally a sharp trader, but he is inherently honest. It was said of a country storekeeper we knew that he would break a cracker in half rather than give an ounce over; yet he was just as meticulous in making certain that he was

71

not giving short weight. He died a rich man, honored and respected by every person in that village.

For over a hundred years the Boston & Maine has served northern New England faithfully and well, come hell or high water, and there has been plenty of both. Another trait of the Down East Yank is his outspoken frankness, his direct approach to the matter at hand. He doesn't beat about the bush. The Boston & Maine has adopted this Yankee trait in its advertising, and the folks on Main Street like it.

In a country that employs a lot of ballyhoo in its sales campaigns, some of the Boston & Maine's advertisements are as refreshing as a salty breath of that east wind off the north Atlantic. After scanning the average railroad advertising page, you gather that an overnight trip on the X.Y.&Z.'s Pussy Willow will provide the most soul-satisfying experience this side of Paradise.

Imagine then—if you can—a Boston commuter boarding the morning local and opening his favorite paper to read a Boston & Maine advertisement, with the black-face type fairly screaming, "IT'S A HELL OF A WAY TO RUN A RAILROAD!"

And yet that is exactly what happened. Puritan New England, this was, where once they'd put you in stocks and spit on you if you even said "heck."

Now we're getting back to the voice of the people. It so happened that during a New England "thaw" (a New England thaw is two feet of snow and quite a blow) a suburban train arrived finally at North Station more than somewhat late. A group of disgruntled commuters disembarked, and growlingly one was overheard to remark, "That's a hell of a way to run a railroad!"

The Boston & Maine snatched the words right out of the gentleman's mouth. It is not difficult to envisage the mingled emotions with which the commuter, not long thereafter, discovered that he had unwittingly provided the Boston & Maine's able publicity department with copy when he aired his views that stormy morning.

There it was, spread all across the page. "It's a hell of a way to run a railroad!" Reading on, the commuter learned why the train was late. The advertisement explained the difficulties that confronted a railroad during a blizzard, and how the operating department fought to overcome them. It took the commuter behind the scenes, and for the first time the folks on the 8:15 came to understand a little of the intricate business of licking Old Man Winter.

Again, after a disastrous fire swept the Mystic River drawbridge in Somerville, Massachusetts, an advertisement appeared in the Boston papers. "IT'S A HELL OF A JOB TO BURN UP A RAILROAD" (especially the Boston & Maine).

The advertisement went on to explain that this key drawbridge over the Mystic River carried the four main-line tracks of the Portland Division, and that over these rails rode the thousands of commuters to and from Malden, Melrose, Wakefield, Reading, Lawrence, and other points, as other thousands passed over this important bridge in traveling to New Hampshire, Maine, the Maritime Provinces, and all points east.

And yet, the advertisement revealed, 35 hours and 13 minutes after the fire swept the structure the railroad was giving service as usual.

It was two hours after the fire was discovered before engineers could begin to check on the damage. They found that not one track was safe. The timbers and ties were gone, rails bent and twisted, drawbridge machinery and signal apparatus destroyed.

The weather was as hot as the fire. Railroad men had scattered to the beaches, lakes, and mountains for the week end, and yet in a matter of a few hours workers were rushing to join the fight—laborers, trackmen, carpenters, electricians, signalmen; craftsmen of every sort. Scores of officials and employees—men and women—rushed to general offices and key points to organize emergency substitute service.

The advertisement thanked the B.&M. patrons for their forbearance during the emergency—gave them a little pat on the back—and concluded, "Oh—well. Probably that's a hell of a way to run a railroad.— *But* the railroad always runs."

Compared with many railroad giants, the Boston & Maine is not large, but it is one of the biggest little packages in these United States. An article in the *Reader's Digest* bore the heading, "Country's Liveliest Railroad."

73

When trucks started siphoning freight from rails to highways, the Boston & Maine, in 1932, bought a fleet of trucks of its own, giving its patrons a door-to-door service. When passenger busses started cutting hunks out of the passenger revenue, President Edward French started the first bus line hooked up with a railroad. He also organized the first railroad-owned air line, providing daily service between Boston and points in Maine, New Hampshire, and Vermont.

A long time ago we engaged in a little family brawl with our British cousins, and Ethan Allen proclaimed, in effect, that "you can't beat a Yankee."

This fact has been borne out in various conflicts since, including two earth-jarring world wars. When the Kaisers and the Hitlers started swinging punches our way, they failed to take into consideration certain qualities that include not only intestinal fortitude, but Yankee ingenuity. The sort of ingenuity employed by the Boston & Maine when a 10,000-ton freighter rammed the Boston Elevated's bridge structure between Boston and Charlestown.

The mishap presented Boston with its most critical transportation tie-up in years, coming, as it did, at the very peak of the Christmas shopping rush. This bridge was the sole main artery between the Boston and Charlestown-Everett area, and the accident isolated in their Everett terminal cars sorely needed at the Boston end of the elevated system. The situation assumed further alarming proportions due to a critical steel shortage and the threat of an impending steel strike.

And yet, as a result of the spirit of co-operation existing between the Boston & Maine and the Boston Elevated, a temporary bridge was in place and elevated traffic had been resumed within 73 hours.

It simply goes to show what neighbors can do when they all pull together. It also provides an example of your New Englander's ability to extemporize, to improvise. Down East they call it "tinkering." They tinker everything, from decrepit hay rakes to railroad bridges.

When "El" officials were tearing their hair, certain gentlemen, from their windows in the Boston & Maine's General Office

74

Building, looked over and appraised the situation. Of course, they immediately offered their assistance, and Chief Engineer T. G. Sughrue, of the B.&.M., at once cast about for some means of tinkering up this bridge until such time as permanent repairs could be made.

There was, he remembered, an 85-foot turntable at Mechanicville—a spare one that was just kicking around. No steel girders long enough to span the gap were available, but a turntable, Mr. Sughrue reflected, should make a very good substitute in a pinch. This one he had in mind was of sufficient length, but it was some 200 miles away—just a "whoop and a holler," under the circumstances.

Promptly the departments of Engineering, Operating, and Mechanical put their heads together. A wrecker loaded the 40-ton turntable on three flat cars at Mechanicville, and the cars were run in with Diesel-powered RB-2's regular train. RB-2 is a fast freight. The run from "Mickeyville" (Mechanicville) to Boston was made in 5 hours and 38 minutes, including a stop for a hotbox.

RB-2 arrived in Boston at 6 p.m. the day following the mishap. A switcher immediately cut the cars, moved them to Yard 13, and a wrecking crane lifted the turntable aboard trailer trucks. Two hours and 50 minutes later the turntable structure was on its way to the damaged double-deck highway and railway bridge.

The turntable was inverted across the gap and blocked into place. The sagging "El" structure was jacked up, posts were installed, and emergency repairs completed. Of course, Old Man Winter took a hand about this time, powdering the landscape with a foot of snow, but come 10 o'clock Monday morning elevated trains were again rumbling overhead.

However, in the meantime, the Saturday thousands who normally ride the Charlestown "El" had combined with the other thousands of regular Boston & Maine commuters and Christmas shoppers to create an unprecedented jam in North Station, B.&M. terminal. A howling blizzard had developed, with everybody wanting nothing so much as to get home and away from it all.

Making for greater confusion was the fact that certain commuter trains had been shifted from their regular berths because these tracks were occupied by special cars loading with Christmas mail and express matter. Because of the press of the crowd, freedom of movement was restricted, making it impossible for these hundreds of people to locate their trains. Folks jostled and shoved; tempers were brittle.

Threatened with a serious situation, Station Superintendent Arthur J. Rodgers, from his little glass cubicle overlooking the concourse, began directing this solid mass of humanity, his voice calm, cool, reassuring.

Out of chaos order came; the tension lessened. Strained faces relaxed; folks began to grin. Someone said, "It's a hell of a way to run a railroad!" The man going to Waltham said, "Must be that tie-up on the El." "I guess so," said the man going to Everett; "I never saw it this bad. Well, Merry Christmas if I don't see you again."

Drifting snow in the yards slowed train movements, and the long lines of coaches crawling out past Tower A were jammed to the doors, but they were going home, and everybody was mighty happy about it.

Shortly after five o'clock the station began emptying and by six o'clock traffic was close to normal.

Many of these commuters leaving North Station this December 19 remembered another night—a night they would never forget. . . . The city was emptying. The concourse was crowded. Outside of North Station sounded the high cries of the news hawks, the rumble of elevated trains, and in the background the city's ceaseless murmur. Over it all the air seemed charged with a voiceless something, pressing hard against the earth.

Came a gush of wind, followed by a breathless calm. A second gust exploded. People stopped, shocked by the savagery of it. There was a terrifying roar, and the world came crashing down. The hurricane had struck.

This was at the height of the commuter rush on the late afternoon of September 21, 1938. The Boston & Maine already was faced with serious flood conditions. The six-o'clock weather report on the morning of September 18 showed rain at some points. Subsequent reports up to the morning of September 22 indicated an almost steady downpour. By the twentieth the wires were hot with messages reading: "River rising . . . Slides over track . . . Bridge out . . . Water over track . . ."

The Connecticut River was on the rampage; the Millers River was 3.5 feet above the 1936 flood stage; the Chicopee was 5.5 feet above; the Deerfield, 5 feet 9 inches above; the Ashuelot, 2 feet above; the Merrimack, rising; the Contoocook, close to the 1936 stage. Other rivers and their tributaries were raging torrents, adding to the growing menace.

The interruption of train operation began on the night of September 20. A locomotive and three cars were off the track in a washout west of Naukeag on the Cheshire Branch; train No. 5500 was marooned at Bellows Falls; No. 325, the Alouette, and No. 63 were marooned. On the morning of the twenty-first, 13 other trains were stranded at various points. Conditions during the day grew worse. Trains were being maneuvered around washouts and washed-out bridges. Everywhere men were fighting desperately to maintain some semblance of service, but waging a losing battle.

And then the hurricane.

Trees and telegraph poles went down. Lightly constructed buildings were wrenched from their foundations, and their wreckage was flung about like jackstraws. Tracks still open to traffic were blocked. A factory roof crashed onto the main-line tracks of the Fitchburg Division. Communications failed; power lines quit.

Staggering, groggy under the deluge of flood waters, New England now received the coup de grâce at the hands of the tempest gods. At seven o'clock the order went out on the Boston & Maine, "Stop all train operations."

There were still hundreds in the North Station waiting to get home. And yet it was an orderly, good-natured collection of folks. They seemed to know that the railroad would take care of them—get them home somehow.

At 9:33 p.m. a Haverhill work train pulled out with a passenger train behind it. The Lexington Branch trains were released at 9:20. A train left for Lowell at 10:27. The Gull pulled out at

77

11:18, followed by a fleet of Eastern Route trains over the Portland Division.

Not a single accident marred the movement of the heavy suburban fleet that night, and more remarkable still was the fact that on the morning of September 22 these commuters found all trains arriving at the scheduled hours to take them into Boston.

It was after the floods of 1927 that people said, "It can't happen again." But it did—in 1936. And again in 1938, with a hurricane to top it off—a hurricane the wind velocity of which in some places reached 100 or more miles per hour.

For 20 days and 20 nights, from September 20 to October 9, inclusive, the Operating Department of the Boston & Maine, from office boy to the high office, was on a 24-hour basis. During that period the Boston & Maine wrote a page in railroad history that will live forever.

When the floods had receded a check revealed that there was major flood damage at over 300 locations, with 27 bridges and culverts damaged or destroyed, 206 major washouts on main and branch lines, 22 landslides, and 45 submerged locations.

The Cheshire Branch of the Fitchburg Division was washed out and flooded out for practically its entire length. The city of Keene, New Hampshire, was entirely isolated.

At Millers Falls, on the main line of the Fitchburg Division, the Millers River changed its course, completely washing out the roadbed for a distance of 1,600 feet and to a depth of 20 feet. Immediately east, there was another washout 550 feet in length.

Also, in this district east of Greenfield, Massachusetts, 4 big double-track main-line bridges were either completely washed out or their approaches, abutments, piers, and superstructure so badly mauled that they were close to a total loss. So it went all up and down the Boston & Maine system, with the exception of the Portland and Terminal Divisions, which escaped serious disruption and were out of service but a few hours.

On September 22 a total of 977 miles of road, including 593 miles of main line and 384 miles of branch line, were out of commission. Of this staggering total, 279 miles were restored to service in 2 days. In 4 days 535 miles were in operation; in 10 days, 760 miles; in 12 days, 795 miles. At the end of the 15th day 97 per cent of the Boston & Maine's flood-torn right of way was in shape to handle traffic. A railroad on its knees had come back fighting.

That was public service. It was the spirit of Bunker Hill—the spirit that has made America great. The spirit of free men and free enterprise, cradled in New England, to the lasting glory of those stalwarts who founded our nation.

What is the Boston & Maine?

The Boston & Maine is D. H. Connell, Portland Division trainman, heating a nursing bottle over a lantern for a baby of travel-weary parents. It is John Sweeney and Jimmy McGrath, of Salem, Massachusetts, for five years attentive and kindly in their treatment of draftees at the Salem station. It is Charley Campbell, attendant in the North Station men's room, finding and turning in a sailor's wallet containing papers and $121 in cash. It is R. W. Dockendorff, conductor on the Minute Man, commended by a passenger for "marked courtesy and service."

The Boston & Maine is Tower A and its train directors, moving, without delay, without mishap, the 320-odd passenger trains that daily converge upon North Station, Boston, from north, east, and west. It is the roaring main line between Boston and Mechanicville, the western gateway. It is a 5,400-horsepower Diesel locomotive tramping down the rail with a mile of freight cars. It is "Casey Jones," steam locomotive number 4115.

The Boston & Maine is the Santa Claus who at Christmas time passes through the trains arriving at Concord, New Hampshire, with cheery greetings and candy for every boy and girl aboard. It is an eleven-year-old boy, proud in the knowledge that the mighty locomotive No. 4111 carries the name "Trojan," which he suggested. It is the nursery in North Station for traveling mothers and their babies. It is the Credit Union for B.&M. employees. It is the "Garden," run by Walter Brown, the first sports arena in a railroad station, and New England's largest assembly place for all indoor attractions. The home of the Boston Bruins Hockey Club, where great ice names have made history, Dit Clapper, Frank Brimsek, Jack Crawford, Bill Cowley Shore, and the Kraut Line, not to mention Art Ross, Sr., who managed them all, Coney Weiland, Tiny Thompson, Hitchman, and the rest.

The Boston & Maine is an iron artery, pulsing through northern New England, binding its communities together. It is a neighbor and a friend.

When the whistle of a Boston & Maine engine is heard in Brattleboro, Vermont, the wheels of press and justice stop. At least, that is the way the *Brattleboro Reformer* reports it. Their caption reads, "Many Dignified Adults Retain a Small-Boy Love for the Choo-Choos."

The *Reformer* then goes on to say:

The editorial room of the *Reformer* has one person whose hobby is railroads or anything pertaining to them and who jumps to the window the moment a whistle is heard, explaining, "That is one of the 4100-Class." Wednesday morning the wheels of justice were completely stopped in Municipal Court as Judge E. J. Shea said, "Pardon me a moment, I want to see that new Diesel engine," and hurried to the window to watch No. 703 go through, proving that many dignified adults retain a small-boy love for the Choo-Choos.

Small-town stuff? Don't you believe it. We know city folks—bankers, lawyers, executives—who like to drive to a favorite spot beside the tracks of an evening just to watch the trains go by. Or perhaps Dad will say, "Mother, I'm going to take the kids down to the station to see that new streamliner." And Mother knows darn well that it is *Dad* who wants to see the train—probably more than the kids.

The Boston & Maine is forward-looking and progressive. It has kept pace with the times in signaling, in streamlining, in motive power and train dispatching. It has pioneered; it has expanded its facilities. It has been a rock standing firm when economic disaster threatened; it has come through fire, flood, hurricane, and war with head unbowed, as it prepares to face the world of tomorrow.

It is "folks" that make a railroad—the men and women who run it, and those it serves. Main Street folks. The farmer in Putney, Vermont, the clerk in Boston, the millionaire down

Rockport way. They're not so far apart. Their eyes get misty when there is sadness, and they laugh at the same old jokes.

There was a time when the Boston & Maine was referred to as the "Broken and Maimed," but that day has long since passed, thanks to old-fashioned Yankee thrift and dogged perseverance. Under the heading "Boston & Maine Trail Blazer" an editorial in the *Boston News Bureau* read:

The Boston & Maine Railroad has for years been a trail blazer. The men responsible for its management, public relations and advertising, have been quick to catch new ideas and to use imagination and boldness.

It was so with the establishment of the Boston Garden. . . . It was so with the starting of the "Snow Trains," which gave the first major lift to winter sports in New England. This was an idea widely copied subsequently by other roads and applied not only to winter sports but also to other diversions. . . .

More about the Snow Trains in another chapter.

In connection with the sports angle, we are reminded that shortly after the turn of the century the Boston & Maine owned and operated a professional baseball team at Concord, New Hampshire, in the old New England League. It was successful in every way, except financially. That was the year the Boston & Maine won a pennant. They have won a lot of pennants since— but not in baseball. Concord, the home of St. Paul's School, a typical American institution, with all its New England beauty and background, the cradle of American amateur hockey, where Hobey Baker, Archer Harmon, Stewart Iglehart and other "greats" learned to play the game.

Trainman H. R. Woodhead, a few years ago, was enthusiastically describing to a group of passengers on the Flying Yankee the modern trend in trains, as exemplified by the luxurious, brightly colored East Wind. Later, someone remarked on his apparent attempt to "sell" the new train.

Trainman Woodhead's reply was a classic. "At times it requires very little effort to help feed the goose that lays the golden eggs."

The "goose"—the folks who travel and ship by Boston &

Maine lines—lays the "golden eggs" which go into the pay envelope of Boston & Maine employees. The trouble with most of us is that we forget that even a goose has to be fed now and then.

In 1944 the Boston & Maine gave tangible evidence that it was planning for new and better things when it set up a chair-measuring device in its North Station terminal. Thousands of people passing through saw other folks being measured in natural sitting positions in an effort to determine the type of car seats most suitable for the comfort and relaxation of train passengers.

The record cards filled out for these persons volunteering for the test were so arranged that the cards could be coded and tabulated. They contained such data as elbow height, hip breadth, back height, stature, and weight—all essential to the purpose of finding a standardized dimension for the most comfortable passenger coach seat obtainable.

Perhaps you think the folks didn't get a lot of fun trying to think up names for those 3700 and 4100-class engines, from young to old. A boy suggested the "Swallow," because, he wrote, he thought they would want a name meaning speed and power. And Swallow it was for the 4112, with the name on the plate telling the world who suggested it.

The 3716 is the "Rogers' Rangers," the 3718 is "Ye Salem Witch," the 4106 is "Little John," the 4108 is "Lily Pons," to name but a few.

When a new train or a new engine goes into service, the Boston & Maine holds open house, and the folks are invited in to inspect the latest in equipment and motive power. Sonny and Dad sit in the engineer's seat; Mother and Sis examine coach appointments. That's showmanship, and salesmanship.

There are study tables and typewriters in North Station for students waiting for trains. And you never know whether you will find a menagerie or a cowboy band around. Whatever it is, it will help to pass the time away—and pleasantly.

The Boston & Maine runs "Whoopee Trains" and "Hike Trains" and "Barn Dance Trains," and those "Snow Trains" we're going to tell you about.

These Yankee railroaders—what they don't think about!

Located high above the Central Square bridge in Lynn, Massachusetts, there are two illuminated clocks, giving a 24-hour correct-time service; and for 16 hours a day the "light-writing" neon signs below show what time the next train leaves for Boston.

The Boston & Maine maintains a labor-management suggestion system, paying out thousands of dollars to employees who suggest new and better ways of doing things.

And there is that nursery in North Station, with its cribs and high chairs and automatic electric bottle-warmers and regulation table to aid in changing those "three-cornered pants." And the walls and flooring are decorated with bunnies and bears and storks, just to give it all the right atmosphere.

Well, maybe that is a hell of a way to run a railroad, but it just goes to show you how they do things on the Boston & Maine.

"We thank you!"

CHAPTER VII

THE NEW YORK CENTRAL'S
S-1-CLASS NIAGARA

Fittings and Equipment

Niagara! Eye-filling, earth-jarring Niagara. Once you have looked at mighty Niagara and know the thunder of it in your ears, you never forget it. Here is power, beauty, majesty beyond compare. Is it possible, you ask, for a man to fashion with his hands anything to compare with Niagara? The answer is yes. Not perhaps in immensity and grandeur, but in general characteristics.

Out of iron and steel the American Locomotive Company wrought it. The New York Central developed and named it "Niagara"—471,000 pounds, 6,000-horsepower, class S-1B 4-8-4 type.

Locomotive No. 6000, delivered by the American Locomotive Company to the New York Central early in the spring of 1945, represents another forward step in the progress of the New York Central's Equipment Engineering Department in the development of the steam locomotive.

In my book, *Railroading from the Head End*, I outlined the development of the class J-1 and J-3 4-6-4 Hudson-type locomotives. The class J-1 type was introduced in 1927. This was followed by the class J-3 ten years later. The high-stepping Hudson proved itself to be an engine of distinction and found ready acceptance by various roads in many parts of the country. It was a 4-6-4 Hudson-type Santa Fe locomotive that waltzed through from Los Angeles to Chicago on a record run in December, 1937.

The New York Central developed and refined its class L

work-horse 4-8-2 freight locomotives, adapting them finally to high-speed passenger service. These were the famous Mohawks, the first of which made their bow in 1942. The class L-4.

The Mohawk, with its big six-foot drivers, was a lot of engine, capable of hauling heavy freight on the Water Level Route or zipping through on the Twentieth Century Limited.

And on the Boston & Albany, a division of the New York Central System, there were the mighty Berkshires, with a 2-8-4 wheel arrangement, designed to whip the heavy grades of the famed Berkshire Hills in western Massachusetts.

But today it is the Niagara toward which we turn our eye. You are impressed by the power and the glory of the Niagara roaring down the rail, exactly as you view with awe the mighty falls for which it was named. This Niagara is just about as sleek a piece of motive power as ever rolled down the main line. Smooth and clean as the waterfall starting its downward rush.

The development of the class S-1A locomotive, known as the Niagara, began with the intention of bringing out a new class of the L-type locomotive with some expansion of boiler capacity. As the developments progressed, however, it became evident that to attain the full possibilities of increased boiler capacity, a 4-8-4 type of wheel arrangement was required.

The maximum indicated horsepower of the class J-3 4-6-4 locomotive was close to 4,800, and the class L-4 4-8-2 type was 5,400. In comparison, the class S 4-8-4 develops an indicated 6,000 horsepower.

The boiler has been increased both in diameter and length from that of the class L-4 locomotive. Built without a dome, it has 100 square feet of grate and 6,600 square feet of combined heating surface. The outside diameter of the third course is practically at the clearance limit.

The grate area has been increased 24.7 square feet over that of the L-4, and the depth of the combustion chamber 29½ inches. The length of the tubes has been reduced from 20 feet, 6 inches to 19 feet. The boiler has been designed for a maximum working pressure of 290 pounds, which is required with the 79-inch drivers. The L-4 carried 250 pounds of pressure and had 72-inch driving wheels.

In lieu of a dome, from which to collect steam, the steam dry pipe, closed at the rear end, has a series of twenty-eight 1-inch transverse slots across the top, each with a clear chord length of 5 inches. The dry pipe, 11 inches in inside diameter, has an internal cross-sectional area of 95 square inches. The steam gathering area through the slots is 140 square inches.

GENERAL DIMENSIONS, WEIGHTS, AND PROPORTIONS OF THE
NEW YORK CENTRAL 4-8-4, CLASS S-1A LOCOMOTIVE

Road class	S-1A
Road number	6000
Date built	March, 1945
Steam pressure, lb. per sq. in.	275 [1]
Drivers, diameter, in.	75 [1]
Cylinders, number, diameter and stroke, in.	2—25 x 32
Rated tractive force engine, lb.	62,330
Valve gear, type	Baker
Valves, pistons, diameter, in.	14
Maximum travel, in.	8½
Steam lap, in.	1 9/16
Exhaust clearance, in.	3/16
Lead, in.	5/16
Cut-off in full gear, per cent	83
Dimensions:	
Height, rail to top of stack, ft. in.	15—1¾
Height, rail to center of boiler, ft. in.	10—7½
Width overall, ft. in.	10—7½
Cylinder centers, in.	92
Wheel bases, ft. in.:	
Driving	20—6
Rigid	13—8
Engine, total	48—9
Engine and tender, total	97—2½

[1] These dimensions apply to the locomotive as delivered by the builder with 75-inch driving wheels. When these wheels are replaced with the 79-inch set, the working boiler pressure will be increased to 290 lb. per sq. in., and the rated tractive force will be 62,400 lb.

Weights, lb.:

Front truck	91,000
Drivers	275,000
Trailing truck:	
Front	48,000
Rear	57,000
Engine, total	471,000
Tender (⅔ loaded)	337,400
Weight on drivers, per cent weight of engine	58.39
Weight on drivers ÷ tractive force	4.41
Tender:	
Type	Bed
Water capacity, gal.	18,000
Coal capacity, tons	46
Wheel arrangement	4-10-0

Baffle plates, which extend out below these openings on each side of the steam pipe, have proved effective in preventing moisture carry-over. These are 50 inches in length and are welded at the ends to vertical end plates which fit over the steam pipe and extend up close to the inside of the boiler shell at the top.

The shell courses of the boiler are carbon-silicon steel. This material is estimated to have permitted a reduction in weight of about 7,000 pounds as compared with carbon steel. Other construction details closely follow those of the boiler of the L-4.

The circumstantial wrapper and outside throat-sheet seams and the butt joints of shell courses at ends of longitudinal seams are seal welded.

The American arch is carried on five 4-inch arch tubes. Coal is fired by a Standard HT stoker, with the engine on the tender. The grates are Firebar. The feed-water equipment consists of the Worthington No. 7SA feed-water heater and a Nathan No. 4000 injector on the right side.

A Barco low-water alarm is applied.

One of the bottlenecks in the maintenance of uninterrupted road service of coal-burning steam locomotives in modern fast, long-distance train movement is limited ashpan capacity. The ashpan on the S-1A locomotive has a volume of 86 cubic feet, with 4 hoppers. The ashpan on the L-4A was limited to 50 cubic feet. The ashpan volume, in cubic feet per square foot of grate area, is 0.86 on the S-1A, 0.66 on the L-4A and 0.76 on the J-3A locomotives. The body of the pan is of welded construction, and the hoppers are cast steel.

The foundation of the Niagara is a cast-steel engine bed, which includes the locomotive cylinders with integral back cylinder heads, the air-pump brackets, and the main reservoirs. The boiler is supported by sliding shoes at the second course and at the front and rear ends of the firebox.

The driving wheels are mounted on hollow-bored axles, and the roller-bearing assemblies are of the Timken split-housing type with two-roll bearings. Alco lateral-motion devices are applied on the front and intermediate pairs of drivers. They permit a controlled lateral of ⅝ and ⁵⁄₁₆ inches per side, respectively.

The engine truck has a roller centering device for the bolster and a combination coil and elliptic spring suspension. The truck wheels of this class S locomotive, number 6000, are 36 inches in diameter; the inside journals are fitted with Timken roller bearings. The front wheels of the 4-wheel trailing truck are 36 inches and the rear 44 inches in diameter. These axles are fitted with outside Timken roller-bearing boxes.

The Niagara is driven by a complete set of Timken roller-bearing rods. These include bearings on the crosshead wrist pin and the 4 crank pins. The roller bearings are mounted on the crank pins, and the rods, with spun-brass liners, are slipped over the outside bearing races. A single rod on each side leads from

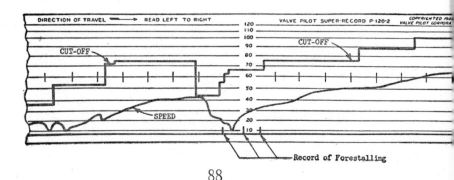

the main to the front drivers; in order, outside of this on the main pin, are a main-to-intermediate side rod, the main rod back end, and another main-to-intermediate side rod. Between the ends of the two main-to-intermediate rods on the intermediate pin is the front end of the back side rod.

The one-piece pistons are of electric cast steel, designed for the Central's lip-type packing rings. The hollow piston rod is Timken alloy steel, with the Timken type crosshead connection. The crosshead shoe is of aluminum. The guides are not attached to the rear cylinder heads.

In counterbalancing the locomotive, only the main drivers are cross-balanced. The total revolving weights on each side of the engine amount to 3,064 pounds, and the reciprocating weights to 1,547 pounds, of which 25 per cent is balanced. This requires an average overbalance per wheel of about 97 pounds and leaves a reciprocating unbalance per ton of total engine weight of 4.94 pounds.

The reciprocating parts and crank pins, with the exception of the front, are chrome-nickel-molybdenum steel. The main and side rods are manganese-vanadium, and the locomotive axles carbon-vanadium steel. The crank pins in the front drivers are of carbon steel.

Loop-type hangers are used in the driving and trailer spring rigging. Coil springs are inserted in the hangers at the engine-bed connections in from the No. 1 driving wheels and at the connection to the trailer frame back of the rear trailing-truck axle.

The 14-inch distribution valves are driven by the Baker valve gear, with needle bearings. This gear provides a maximum travel

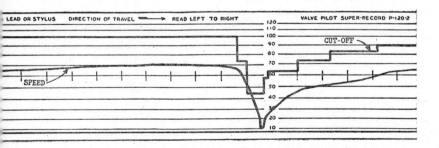

of 8½ inches. The valve motion is controlled by the Franklin Precision reverse gear, which is attached to a bracket on the engine bed and not to the boiler.

The larger boiler diameter permits better superheater proportions. Particular attention was given throughout the steam passages from the boiler to the exhaust to bring the pressure drop to the minimum.

The minimum area through the superheater tubes is 86.6 square inches. This compares with 70.5 square inches on the L-4 Mohawk.

Lubrication of the Niagara is supplied by a Nathan DV-8 42-pint lubricator. From this lubricator are 2 feeds to the steam pipes, 2 feeds to the cylinders, 1 feed, with a 4-way distributor, to the guides, and 1 feed to the stoker engine.

The chassis lubrication is by Alemite and Rex oil fittings. Alemite soft-grease fittings are used on the valve gear, including the Valve Pilot fittings, on the radial buffer, on the valve-stem crossheads, on the water-scoop piston rod, and on the lateral-motion-device spring seats. Alemite fittings using valve oil are applied on the driving-box pedestal faces. Rex oil fittings are installed for engine-truck-box, trailer-truck-box, and tender-truck-box pedestals, and on the crank pins and roller-bearing wrist pins. The power reverse-gear cylinder is lubricated by a Norgren No. 401-4 lubricator, with Alemite soft-grease fittings on the reverse-shaft bearings and the reach-rod connections.

Alemite hard-grease fittings are applied on the back ends of the eccentric rods, and also on the spring-rigging pin and loop connections.

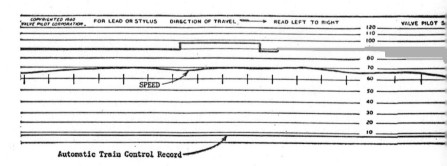

Engine oil is used to lubricate the firebox expansion shoe castings, engine-truck and tender-truck center plates, as well as miscellaneous points.

The Niagara's cab is built of aluminum and is supported on the boiler by cantilever beams. The running boards, front platform, and air-pump shield, the smoke-lifting shields at the front, casings, gauge-boards, and other installations are also of aluminum.

Two saturated-steam turrets are mounted on the boiler just ahead of the cab, one on the right and the other on the left side. The right-hand turret provides connections for the cab radiator, the smoke consumer, the coal pusher, the headlight generator, and the injector. From the left turret steam is taken for the steam-heat reducing valve, the stoker, the feed-water pump, and the coal sprinkler. Superheated steam is furnished for the blower and the whistle. The whistle is mounted *beside the stack on the smoke box.*

The headlight generator is back of the rear driver on the right side, and the exhaust is piped to the ashpan. The aluminum sand box, of limited capacity, on top of the boiler has two rectangular tubes which lead down under the jacket to right and left steel boxes under the running boards. The New York Air Brake sand traps at the lower ends of these sand boxes distribute sand in front of the front and main drivers.

The air brakes are the New York Schedule 8ET with relay valve. The two 8½-inch cross-compound air compressors are supported directly on the bed casting under the smoke box. A fin-tube aftercooler is placed in the air line between the two main

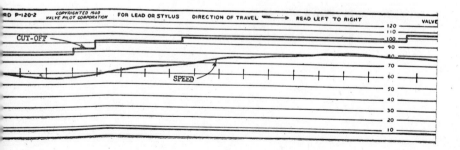

reservoirs. Removable portions of the front deck permit access to the air filters. The air compressors are built with integral lubricators.

All wheels on the Niagara's locomotive and tender are braked. The engine-truck brakes are operated by a single cylinder; the driver brakes by two cylinders, one on each side.

The Tender

When the characteristics of the S-1 class locomotive were first receiving consideration in 1942 by the Equipment Engineering Department of the New York Central, authority was secured to build 5 tenders of the bed type, carried on one 4-wheel leading truck and 5 pairs of wheels mounted in pedestals on the tender-bed casting. The objective of this design was to provide approximately the same coal and water capacity as that of the large tenders of the conventional type carried on two 6-wheel trucks which were received with the class L-3 and L-4 4-8-2 type locomotives, but to have a wheel base about 6 feet shorter. This would permit the 4-8-4 type locomotive, with its longer engine base, to be handled on the 100-foot turntables generally available on the main line between New York and Chicago. Built by the General Steel Castings Company, this is the finest coal-carrying tender in service today, and they ride like a business car.

These tenders, with their capacity of 46 tons of coal and 18,000-gallon tanks, have incorporated in them a venting system

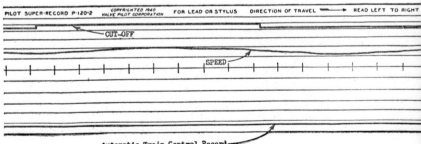

for scooping water without reducing speed, similar to that built into the large tenders of the L-4 Mohawks.

The tender wheels, equipped with Timken journal bearings, are 41 inches in diameter.

The Niagara Goes into Service

For the purpose of investigating the effect of driving-wheel diameter on locomotive performance, No. 6000 was delivered to the New York Central with 75-inch drivers, but a set of 79-inch driving wheels was provided for later use.

Originally it was intended to conduct performance and capacity tests of the Niagara while equipped with the 75-inch drivers; then to replace them with the 79-inch driving wheels and increase the boiler pressure to maintain the same tractive force. However, these plans were changed, and the locomotive went directly into road service with the 75-inch drivers.

After several weeks' service between Harmon and Chicago, the 79-inch drivers were installed, and the Niagara was assigned to one side of the Commodore Vanderbilt. This is a heavy train, making a number of stops, and will prove the mettle of any engine. No. 6000 piled up a mileage of about 27,000 miles a month, and by the middle of August, 1945, had accumulated a total of better than 60,000 miles.

In October, 1945, the 6000 was withdrawn from service for complete boiler-performance and capacity tests at Selkirk. These were followed by road tests.

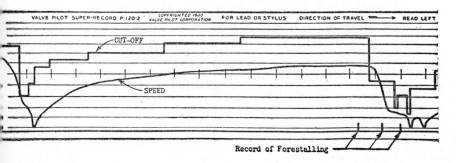

Many of the Central engines were war-weary, and before the 6000 was completed an order had been placed for 25 additional S-1 locomotives. Because of the inability to test the 6000 before the new engines were ordered, the length of the combustion chamber in the boilers of these locomotives was reduced from 92½ inches to 81¼ inches, and the tubes and flues correspondingly lengthened.

The new engines, the S-1B class, had 79-inch drivers, and the cylinder diameter was increased from 25 to 25½ inches to accommodate a working pressure of 275 pounds.

A further change was made in the trailer, which was given two pairs of 41-inch wheels, replacing 36-inch wheels in the front and 44-inch wheels in the rear, thus allowing a further increase in ashpan volume to 98 cubic inches. It also permitted a better shape in the design of the pan slopes.

A twenty-seventh locomotive was built to the same proportions of the 25 S-1B class. It, however, differs from these engines in that the Franklin poppet-valve system of steam distribution is installed. This locomotive, designated class S-2A, is to be subjected to comprehensive acceleration, capacity, and performance tests for direct comparison with the S-1 class, which has large piston valves and the Baker valve gear.

At this writing the Niagara is handling 18 cars at high speed on several districts, and doing a sweet job in passenger service. In freight service, the 6000 has hauled a new overnight freight train between New York and Buffalo, some 435 miles, in 10 hours and 45 minutes, for an average of 39 miles per hour, and this includes stops at Albany, Utica, Syracuse, and Rochester.

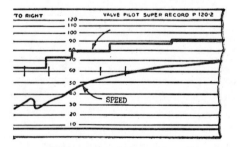

Valve Pilot tape off New York Central class S-1B engine 6016 hauling Train No. 68, 16 cars, Chicago-Elkhart, Western Division

I rode the 6020 between Syracuse and Utica, 51 miles, with 3 stops, in 52 minutes, with 17 cars and have had countless other fine demonstrations around the system.

The Niagara gives every indication of becoming as great and as famous a locomotive in its class as the two champions of earlier design and class, the Hudson and the Mohawk. Hats off to the American Locomotive Company.

Dynamometer Car

The Dynamometer Test Car looks like a misplaced caboose that got coupled into the train behind the engine on the head end by mistake, but it is the most important behind-the-scenes piece of equipment on the railroad.

The Dynamometer Car is the doctor. It takes the temperature, the pulse, and the blood pressure of the locomotive. It X-rays this boisterous giant, applies a stethoscope to its heart and thumps its chest, and charts its every reflex and reaction.

Let us assume that you are a strapping six-footer, with the pink flush of health on your cheeks. You walk into the office of the insurance doctor. Does he just take a look at you, smile, rub his hands, and exclaim, "What a perfect hunk of manhood!" He does not. On the contrary, he regards you with a slightly jaundiced eye and tells you to strip.

Then he starts to work. He probes and taps and explores. He puts you in a test tube and takes you into the laboratory. He listens to you tick and takes down your family history.

And this, in effect, is what happens when a new type of locomotive like the New York Central's 6000-class Niagara is applying for a job on the railroad. They put it in a test tube, and a corps of experts sit down at their instruments and go to work. The Dynamometer Car is coupled in behind the engine, and when this railroad doctor is through, the locomotive has no secrets. What the "doc" doesn't find out you could cover with a thin dime. They staff the Dynamometer Car with test engineers and a chef, and turn them loose on the main line.

Testing a locomotive often takes weeks; so the staff lives

aboard the Dynamometer Car. Mile after mile they ride; day after day. They watch flickering instruments and chart their readings. They take the pulse of the cylinders, sample the smokebox gases, weigh every pound of coal, and record the pull of the drawbar. For every yard the car travels, automatic recording pens write their findings on paper rolls.

The development of the steam locomotive has been reduced to the finest balance between maximum efficiency, speed, and tractive power. An athlete is trained and conditioned long before he takes part in big-league competition. It is the same with an engine. That thundering giant pulling the Twentieth Century Limited had to prove itself before it was coupled onto the "flagship" of the New York Central's steel fleet.

In 1923 the New York Central built in its West Albany shops one of the first completely equipped Dynamometer Cars of its kind. This car and installed apparatus cost approximately $70,000 at that time.

Weighing 62 tons, the car was sturdily built to stand the roughest kind of treatment in freight service that it might conduct its tests under actual conditions. It is 52 feet long and 8 feet, 8 inches wide, and affords complete accommodations for its crew.

A space of 15 feet, 9 inches is reserved at the forward end of the car as the dynamometer compartment. A ⅝-inch steel plate extends under the entire compartment floor to add strength and to take the high stresses incident to the measuring of the drawbar pull and buffing.

The dynamometer weighing head is extremely simple and rugged in construction. It operates on a hydraulic principle with a diaphragm. The pull or buff from the drawbar is imposed without loss through the diaphragm to the liquid mixture in the weighing head. The large cylinder or buff takes shocks up to 1,250,000 pounds, while the smaller cylinder takes a drawbar pull or load up to 500,000 pounds.

Directly behind this compartment is located the dynamometer recording table, where the dynamometer record is made and where the dynamometer operator is stationed during a test.

The chronograph table is provided with indicating gauges and recording pens whereby records are made of such features of train and locomotive performance as: location, drawbar pull, speed, time, distance, train-line air pressure, brake-cylinder air pressure, boiler-steam pressure, buffing shocks, integration of drawbar pull curve, curvature of track, coal fired, steam indicator cards, right and left sides, position of reverse lever and throttle.

As a test is in progress the dynamometer operator is able to communicate by telephone or buzzer with the cab of the locomotive being tested, or with the helper if one is used.

The crew operating the Dynamometer Car during a test consists of the dynamometer engineer, his assistant, a dynamometer operator, 11 apprentices, a mile-post recorder, an engineer, a fireman, 2 coal passers, and a chef from the Dining Car Service.

Six of the 11 apprentices are special apprentices—men who have a degree from a technical school—and 5 are regular machinist apprentices, selected from the shop and enginehouse forces of the Motive Power Department.

The engineer and fireman are selected from regular service for their known ability. The coal passers are also firemen, shoveling coal onto a scale for weighing before it passes into the firebox.

During the running tests, the crew members are stationed in positions ranging from the pilot of the locomotive to the interior of the Dynamometer Car, and even so far removed as in the Dynamometer Office Car, which waits at the end of the division on which the test car is working.

Protected by a windbreak on the pilot, the two indicator men work there and on the running board of the locomotive; also protected by windbreaks are the apprentices recording drafts and pressures, and collecting flue gases for analysis. Two more apprentices are located in the cab, and a third in the tender, weighing the coal shoveled by the coal passers.

In the Dynamometer Car are seated the dynamometer operator at the chronograph table, an apprentice recording temperatures, and a mile-post observer who has unobstructed vision through a windowed cupola.

The dynamometer engineer and his assistant might be found wherever their presence is necessary at any of the apprentice stations. Usually, however, they are located either in the locomotive cab or the Dynamometer Car.

In the Dynamometer Office Car are the calculator and his

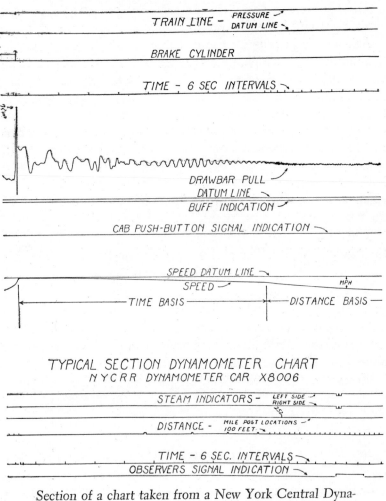

TRAIN LINE - PRESSURE
DATUM LINE

BRAKE CYLINDER

TIME - 6 SEC INTERVALS

DRAWBAR PULL
DATUM LINE
BUFF INDICATION

CAB PUSH-BUTTON SIGNAL INDICATION

SPEED DATUM LINE
SPEED
MPH
TIME BASIS
DISTANCE BASIS

TYPICAL SECTION DYNAMOMETER CHART
N Y C R R DYNAMOMETER CAR X8006

STEAM INDICATORS - LEFT SIDE
RIGHT SIDE

DISTANCE - MILE POST LOCATIONS
100 FEET

TIME - 6 SEC. INTERVALS
OBSERVERS SIGNAL INDICATION

Section of a chart taken from a New York Central Dynamometer Car. Courtesy New York Central Railroad.

assistant. At the end of a particular test all data, charts, and indicator cards are handed over to the calculator for preliminary calculations and compilations of the daily report. The calculator

THE MILWAUKEE ROAD

01803

JULY 27-1939

New B.&W. 5,400-h.p. 4-unit freight Diesel with MB-2 crack Mechanicsville-Boston fast freight. Courtesy Boston & Maine Railroad.

With Glacier National Park and the snow-capped Montana Rockies just ahead, first #1, the old Empire Builder, climbs the 1% grade into Triple Divide, Mont., on the Second Subdivision of the Kalispell Division. Photo by Wm. J. Pontin. Courtesy Rail Photo Service.

Great Northern #27, the Fast Mail, leaving Whitefish, Mont., on the Third Subdivision of the Kalispell Division hauled by a 2-unit 4,000-h.p. passenger Diesel. Photo by H. W. Pontin. Courtesy Rail Photo Service.

Cab of new New York Central coal-burning 4-8-4 type, Class S-1B. Courtesy New York Central Railroad.

Wheels and valve gear of the new New York Central S-1B, showing Timken roller-bearing rods and valve pilot cam box over #2 driver. Courtesy New York Central Railroad.

New York Central Dynamometer Car and Engine #3016, 4-8-2 type class L-3, equipped for the test and train ready to leave Utica, N. Y., on the Mohawk Division. Courtesy New York Central Railroad

Here's where they tell what the locomotive is doing. A New York Central Dynamometer table and chart with operator during an actual test. Courtesy New York Central Railroad.

New York Central Dynamometer Car office, showing chart table. Courtesy New York Central Railroad.

Close-up view of a New York Central Dynamometer Car showing cupola. Courtesy New York Central Railroad.

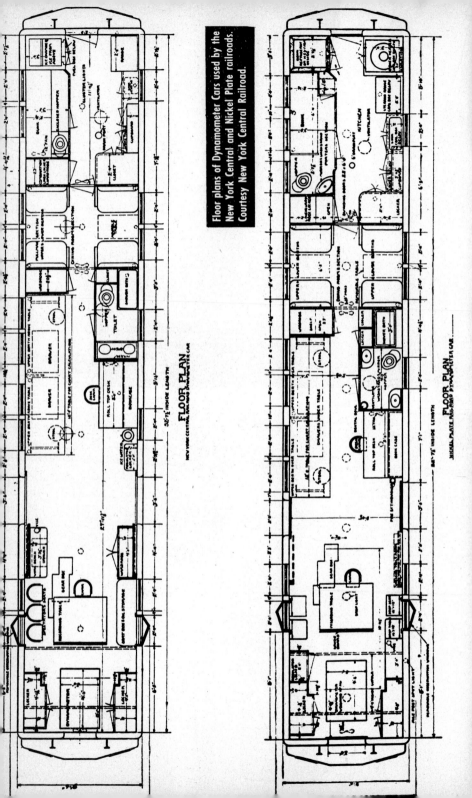

Floor plans of Dynamometer Cars used by the New York Central and Nickel Plate railroads. Courtesy New York Central Railroad.

FLOOR PLAN
NEW YORK CENTRAL RAILROAD DYNAMOMETER CAR

FLOOR PLAN
NICKEL PLATE RAILROAD DYNAMOMETER CAR

#19 Santa Fe Chief, Engine #3785, 4-8-4 type, and two 3800-class 2-10-2 type helpers with 15 cars passing Wootton, Colo., with Raton Tunnel just ahead. The grade is 3.5% and the battle with the country's heaviest main-line grade is nearly over. Courtesy Santa Fe Railroad.

New York Central hotbox alarm cartridge being inserted for use with roller bearing. Courtesy New York Central Railroad.

New York Central smoke alarm for hotbox with friction bearing. Courtesy New York Central Railroad.

New York Central roller-bearing hotbox alarm being tested. Courtesy New York Central Railroad.

also assists the dynamometer engineer in making up the final reports on the results of all running tests.

Many different kinds of tests, all with the purpose of seeking improvement over established performance, are undertaken on each new class of locomotive entering service.

Thus we have Dynamometer Car X8006, which looks like a glorified caboose, coupled in behind a Mohawk L-3 locomotive, making exhaustive tests which will pave the way for the design of the L-4. And the tests conducted behind the L-4 become the germinating seeds that lead finally to the development of the class S, the Niagara. The staff of the Dynamometer Car then put this class S 6000 into the test tube, again pointing toward the higher breeding of the locomotives of the Central.

Boiler Tests

Locomotives are fast approaching their maximum size. The problem of the engineers now is to combine tractive force with higher speeds in the same engine and to develop more steam power in the gigantic locomotive boilers. Engineers are seeking at the same time to cut fuel costs, thus creating still greater economy. The average coal-burning locomotive in freight service today uses 1 ton of coal every 8.9 miles it hauls a train, and any economy that can be effected in the operation is worthy of consideration.

It was back in 1939–40 that boiler tests were conducted at Selkirk, New York, under the direction of W. F. Collins, Engineer of Tests of the New York Central System. W. F. Collins and his staff at that time used for a guinea pig a J-3 steam locomotive, the 5408, a 4-6-4 Hudson type. For over a year this engine stood in a corner of the Selkirk shops, undergoing various standing tests.

These standing tests offer a method for study of the effect of changes in the design of smokebox arrangements where uniformity of conditions can be maintained. Here these changes can be closely observed and the subsequent road performance predicted without incurring either the uncertainties or difficulties of procedure attending road tests.

"It may be pointed out," Mr. Collins explains, "that the standing tests are suitable not only for the study of smokebox problems but for other tests in which the performance of the boiler is involved, such as the performance of the feed-water heaters, fuel, stokers, and so forth.

"The method for controlling the temperature of the exhaust steam during the standing test," Mr. Collins has told us, "is through the medium of the spray of water mist in the cylinder which is subsequently removed in its entirety. The locomotive standing test with the exhaust temperature thus controlled produces a more accurate and economical method for study."

As a result of these standing tests, certain changes were made in the front end. These involved the stack, exhaust nozzle, and spark arrester screen. The stack was enlarged and made longer to allow for a stronger draft of greater volume; there were adjustments of the exhaust nozzle; and the netting box was enlarged to contribute a free passage of exhaust gases. The final result was an 8 per cent increase in boiler efficiency.

During these tests the first motion pictures of a locomotive firebox in operation were taken. The pictures were taken in color and showed fire conditions up to rates as high as 13,000 pounds of coal consumed per hour. These pictures gave evidence that at higher rates of firing, when the temperature in the firebox is at 2,400 degrees Fahrenheit and the speed of the gases, or draft, reaches 200 miles an hour, the unburned coal loss is approximately 25 per cent. And this remains the problem which engineers are still attempting to solve.

The Hotbox Alarm

Since 1933 "smoke-and-odor" type hotbox detectors have been under continuous trial and evolution in the laboratory of the New York Central System, with the result that a practical hotbox alarm has been perfected, and is being installed on all passenger rolling stock and locomotives.

A word first about this New York Central Test Laboratory. The laboratory was established in 1892 and consisted of two rooms in Building No. 1, adjacent to the Car and Locomotive Shops at West Albany, New York. At that time only chemical work was done, but the laboratory has grown steadily since that time, both in size and importance.

The activities of the West Albany Laboratory have been extended to the Bacteriological Laboratory at Selkirk, where all drinking water for stations, dining cars, and passenger cars is tested, to sister laboratories at Collinwood and Beech Grove.

The Central laboratories test metals, paints, oils, greases, coal —in fact, everything connected with the railroad system, including certain sleuthing for the Claims Department.

A hot journal on a fast passenger train can quickly develop into a serious threat to the safety of the train. With a view to further safeguarding the trains of the Central, the laboratory staff persistently attacked the problem of developing a satisfactory hotbox alarm. As far back as 1934, 500 alarm-equipped bearings were applied to the tenders of J-1 4-6-4 locomotive tenders, and these applications were followed by running tests. By 1936, 16 actual cases of hotboxes had been detected through the functioning of the alarm device.

The alarm system employs two indications—smoke for observation outside of the train, and a distinctive and unpleasant odor which conveys the message to the interior of the train. The alarm was designed primarily for application to frictional bearings, but has been adapted to roller-bearing journal boxes.

In its present form this alarm consists essentially of two containers, or "cartridges," which are placed in cavities provided in the bearing for that purpose. Each cartridge is filled with a different liquid and has a small orifice sealed with a fusible metal, which melts at a predetermined temperature, releasing the liquid. At this temperature the liquid vaporizes and escapes through the orifice. The liquid from one cartridge produces a penetrating odor which will reach into the cars, including those which are air-conditioned; and the liquid from the other produces a dense white smoke. The discharge continues until both cartridges are empty, or a period of from 8 to 10 minutes.

The gases from both of these liquids are noncorrosive and when diffused in the atmosphere can be inhaled without harmful effect. The melting temperatures of the fusible elements are 220 degrees Fahrenheit for roller bearings and 320 degrees for grease-lubricated friction bearings.

The journal bearing is drilled longitudinally to provide cavities to receive the cartridge. The cartridges for roller bearings are inserted in pockets in the face of the roller-bearing housing.

The Snow-Melting Machine

Two giant snow-removal machines especially designed to scoop up deep snow from the railroad track and melt it in a large steam-charged tank have been acquired by the New York Central for attacking heavy snowfalls.

A single complete machine consists of two units, a snow loader and a snow melter, each mounted on a heavy flatcar and having a combined weight of 66 tons. When in operation the machine is pushed by a powerful locomotive at speeds from 2 to 6 miles per hour, depending on the depth and density of the snow. Snow is first scooped up by the loader, which has a capacity of 30 cubic yards per minute. It is then carried upward on two continuous belt conveyors, to be dumped into a hopper on top of the snow melter.

The snow-melting unit is a large double tank. One tank, of 4,500-gallon capacity, contains water which is brought to boiling temperature by steam at boiler pressure from the locomotive. In the other and larger tank, of 16,000-gallon capacity, the snow is dumped and melted.

At the beginning of the cycle of operation, boiling water is admitted from the smaller tank into the larger to a depth of about a foot. As the snow is then dumped in, steam jets are opened to melt the snow. Fourteen steam jets can be used to control the speed of melting. When both tanks are full, the locomotive is backed to a convenient catch basin or drain, where the larger tank is dumped. Water is retained in the smaller tank and again brought to boiling temperature before a repetition of the operation is begun.

Two men operate the machine. One, seated in a cab on the loader, controls the scoop and conveyors, which are driven by a 52-horsepower gasoline engine; the other controls the steam jets from the top of the melting tank.

The snow-melting machines were designed and constructed by the Barber-Greene Company of Aurora, Illinois, in co-operation with the New York Central's Equipment Engineering and Maintenance of Way departments.

CHAPTER VIII

ON THE CHESAPEAKE & OHIO

The Trackman

The wheels are clicking off the rail lengths. Twin ribbons of steel are slipping away behind the train as you look back from the observation car. There is the blurred pattern of ties, the clean-tailored roadbed, reaching away to the horizon. You notice overall-clad figures moving out of the right of way ditch to resume their labors, and your thoughts turn to the rails you ride and the men who maintain them.

You have read somewhere that a standard rail is 39 feet long and that its weight is 131 pounds to the yard on most heavily traveled main lines. Your thoughts revolve around these figures, and you take out a pencil and do a little figuring on the time-table in your hand. You are not too good at mathematics, and you frown and check the figures, half-doubting their correctness. A steel rail, you have discovered, weighs about 1,700 pounds. There are 271 steel rails to the mile. The weight of these rails, then, is close to 462,000 pounds, or 231 tons. You estimate your speed at about 60 miles an hour. Thus, every minute your train is passing over 231 tons of rail. Every minute! You are amazed. It seems impossible, and yet the steel rail is only one part of the track. When you have finished your trip, you hunt up a track-man and discover that supporting this rail over every mile there are 3,250 ties, 6,500 tie-plates, 2,700 rail anchors, 13,000 spikes, and 1,084 bolts, besides the ballast and culverts and bridges, together with all of those signals and switches and frogs.

It is something to think about when you are watching the track fast disappearing behind you.

The romance and adventure of track laying passed when the

104

frontier railroads built through to the Pacific. The steel rail then was challenging a raw new world. It took men of brawn and courage and a handy trigger finger to whip the wilderness. "Hell on wheels" paced the railway builders, and writers dipped their pens in blood and gun smoke in recording the deeds of the trackman in that brawling era.

And then, suddenly, track work became an unsung and humdrum occupation, with no more appeal than washing dishes after a party. The locomotive and the speeding train caught the fancy of the article writer and the fictioneer, and the man at the throttle came in for the glamour and the glory. The trainman and the telegraph operator had their share of fictional window dressing. Even the track walker got into the picture now and then.

But the nearest the lowly trackman came to fame was when someone tacked the name "Gandy Dancer" on him. The track laborer wielded tamping bars, claw-bars, picks, and shovels manufactured by the old Gandy Manufacturing Company of Chicago, hence the name. The track foreman was dubbed "King Snipe," for what reason historians are vague.

Until recent years the trackman seemed destined to leave little for posterity. He was, it seemed, neither mouse nor man, appearing to occupy a place somewhere in between. His individuality was lost in a group or a gang, and his part in the general railroad scheme, so far as it was apparent to the traveling public, was to stand idly in the right-of-way ditch and watch the trains go by.

The passenger is dimly conscious that the train's pace is fast and smooth. He is confident that he will arrive safely at his destination; but seldom, except perhaps in the vaguest sort of way, does he associate his general comfort and well-being aboard the speeding train with the blurred faces of the overall-clad figures beside the track.

And yet the trackman is one of the most important cogs in the vast and intricate railroad machine. He is the pillar of the road, the slogging foot soldier of the mighty army of that department known as the Maintenance of Way. The trackman is eternally on guard up and down the endless miles of the rails we ride.

The locomotive has grown in size and power; the train has grown in length and weight; speed has increased. And the fiber of the track has been strengthened to meet the demands thrust upon it. The trackman has grown from a lowly laborer, swinging a pick and spike maul, to a man skilled in the use of a constantly increasing assortment of labor-saving machines.

Primitive man one day discovered that by joining two round slabs cut from a log, with a pole for an axle, he could move loads he had previously been unable to lift or drag. With his crude cart he was released from dependence on the river or lake for transport. Unseen worlds were opened to him, and the inevitable result was the growth of trade and the spread of civilization.

Having created a wheeled conveyance, the primitive inventor discovered that a road was required, and the smoother the road, the larger the load he could transport. All down the centuries man has continued to improve both the conveyance and the highway.

Dirt roads sufficed during the day of the ox- and horse-drawn vehicle. The automobile traveled over dirt and gravel roads when conditions were favorable, but it traveled faster and farther and with heavier loads when there were roads of brick and macadam and concrete.

The early locomotive joggled along over strap-iron rails weighing 12 pounds to the yard. Came a better locomotive and a better rail. The early T-rails weighed 50 pounds per yard; then 75 pounds, approaching the turn of the century. Again it was the old story—the limitation of the load was governed by the motive power and the track.

The rail grew to 131, to 152 pounds per yard on some lines, and giant locomotives went storming down it. Keeping pace with the growth of locomotive and rail went the constant improvements in roadbed structure and increasing efficiency in its maintenance.

And right here we are going to examine some of the many track problems resulting from the increase in the volume of railroad traffic. We will take, for example, the Chesapeake & Ohio.

The C.&O. has the distinction of having the greatest traffic density, principally bulk freight, of any railroad in the world. There are certain territories on this road in which the traffic density has exceeded 52,000,000 gross ton-miles per mile of track per year.

Except to the statistician and the adding machine, figures don't mean much. The inclusion of too many figures in a railroad book might justifiably cause the reader to draw the conclusion that the author merely thought of a lot of big numbers. Of late years the common man has been fed so many staggering figures that his brain has become slightly numbed. So we are going to steer clear of big numbers as much as possible while we break all these gross ton-miles down into factual items that are easy to digest.

Just bear in mind that behind it all there stands the lowly figure of the trackman.

What the Track Takes

Better to pave the way for an understanding of the beating the track takes, we will start with a brief word concerning the locomotives that roar through on the main lines of the C.&O.

Some of these great freight haulers, including tender, weigh pretty close to 600 tons. Train loads of 15,000 tons are not uncommon. These loads the track must safely carry with the locomotive and train moving over it at high speed. Enormous forces are built up—forces forever attacking the rail and roadbed structure.

The movement of the tonnage figure we have given you includes coal trains, manifest trains, and high-speed passenger trains, covering every possible sort of terrain from mountains to lowlands.

Heaviest of the C.&O. locomotives are the class H-8, 2-6-6-6 Articulateds, or the Allegheny type. These engines are capable of handling the heaviest tonnage at speeds that would have made the old-time trackman gray before his time.

Then there are the L-2's, or 4-6-4 type passenger engine, with their 78-inch drivers, designed to handle heavy passenger trains at the high sustained speeds necessary to maintain schedules; the forty 2-10-4 class T-1 which haul 13,500-ton trains many trips each day; and their great 4-8-4 type class J-3 used in passenger service on heavy grades.

The class K-4, 2-8-4 type locomotive, which we will cover in another chapter, was designed for use in fast freight service. And there are many more of these motive-power giants. It can be readily appreciated that track and roadbed must be of the highest standard to withstand the day in and day out punishment to which the track is subjected.

Use of Heavy Rail: The contact between load and track is established through the medium of the rail, which on the Chesapeake & Ohio main lines are in general 131-pound-per-yard American Railway Engineering Association Standard Section. In some instances in territory where the traffic is lighter 112-pound rail is used. Because the loads carried by track are rolling loads, it is evident that correct line and surface must be maintained if passenger and freight is to be transported comfortably and safely.

Reduction of Joint Wear: A feature of travel on the Chesapeake & Ohio is the comparative lack of joint click. Annoying as this may become to the passenger, it is a still greater source of worry to the trackman. For to him it means that the continued pounding of the joints will batter the rail ends and result in rough-riding track. This must be corrected by "tamping up" low joints and rebuilding these rail ends by welding on new metal. On the C.&O. it is the practice to retard this damaging effect by heat-treating, or hardening the rail ends to a greater degree than the original rolled hardness of the steel.

Reduction of Curve Wear: Another annoying feature of rail travel is the screeching of car wheels in rounding curves. This noise is caused by the grinding of the wheel flanges against the rails. It is extremely detrimental to both the wheel and the rail. The resulting wear of metals requires premature renewal of rail and retooling of flange. This trouble is alleviated to a large extent by a distribution of automatic flange- and rail-greasing machines on the main lines.

Tie Renewals: The Chesapeake & Ohio is fortunate in that it traverses a section of the country that is heavily timbered, hence track ties of suitable dimensions and of selected hardwood are available. Formerly the renewal of ties constituted one of the largest labor items in the yearly program of the trackman. A replacement of over 300 ties per mile is not unusual.

However, modern scientific methods in the application of chemical preservatives have materially cut down the number of ties removed because of decay. This, together with the installation of large steel plates between rail and tie, which largely eliminates the wearing of the wood, has reduced annual renewals in some years to less than 100 per mile.

Ballast Renewal: The transmission and distribution of rolling loads to the subgrade or roadbed is accomplished by means of ballast of a minimum depth of 12 inches.

Ballast being the only unit of the three major components that make up the track, by means of which line and surface adjustments can be made, it is essential that the gravel or stone used should be of the finest quality available, and it further should be well drained. To accomplish this it is necessary to clean out the dirt that accumulates; also to remove all recurrent weed growth. The removal of this weed growth is largely a hand operation, but the application of weed-killing chemicals by means of tank cars is also used. The burning of weeds beside the track in the late fall aids in deterring the spread of seeds.

The sources of the dirt accumulation in the ballast include the cinders and ashes from passing trains, earth washed in from the right-of-way ditch, dirt from subgrade working upward, and particles from the ballast itself. The greater part of the stone ballast is cleaned by off-track machines or other equipment designed for the purpose.

Curve and Grade Reduction: During the period of rapid railroad development in the nineteenth century, many railroads were hastily built under the urge of reaching an objective ahead of the other fellow. Many roads were poorly financed, and in no case did the builders anticipate the tremendous increase in the speed of trains and the weight of loads lurking just around the bend. The result was the imposition of a heavy maintenance burden on the roads in later years. Thus the reduction of grades, elimination and easement of curves, widening of embankments, and other work had to be carried out at a later day and while the trains were rolling.

Regardless of the high quality of materials which compose the railroad track, it will not long retain its best riding qualities unless supported by a stable roadbed, the essential elements of which are good drainage and adequate slopes.

Modern Ditching Train: One of the most difficult problems encountered along the right of way is that of widening cuts and raising embankments, for on main track the work is subject to interruptions from traffic. Unless there is room for an additional track, it would not be economical to work a power shovel on the ground.

It was some forty years ago that the idea of mounting the shovel on the work train itself was conceived. The original method was to use a small steam shovel which was pulled from car to car. But it was a cumbersome method and was finally replaced by a more modern system of operation.

The new method consisted of mounting the shovel on a flat-car, which was placed between two side-dump cars. However, the capacity of these cars was limited to the dumping radius, or reach of the ditcher bucket, and only 16 to 20 cubic yards could be loaded in each car. Further, the loading was confined to two cars at a time, and when these cars were loaded, either a run to the dump was necessary, or a switch of cars had to be made. Too, the limited loading radius of the car-mounted shovel prevented the general use of the longer dump cars employed on construction. These cars are usually of 30-cubic-yard capacity and are mechanically dumped.

A study of the subject by C.&O. engineers resulted in the development of equipment that removed the restriction on loading capacity. It also eliminated much of the time lost in running to dumps. This was accomplished by providing the 30-yard dump cars with drop ends of sufficient strength to support a tractor-mounted shovel. This shovel travels from car to car, loading each in turn. Cars sufficient to accommodate the entire day's loading can be utilized, thus reducing the runs to the dump to a minimum. With such equipment it is also possible to operate two or more shovels on the same train, further speeding the work.

Power Machinery: Paddy and his pick wrote history in America. They built the first railroads in the land and maintained them down the years. But, like the steel rail and the Iron Horse, they grew up. Still a soldier in the Maintenance of Way corps on the Iron Road, the trackman finally was provided with new tools to work with, just as your modern doughfoot's equipment has supplanted that of the infantryman who carried a musket.

On the railroad a constant battle is being waged—a battle against periods of labor shortage, against days of financial stringency, against the thundering surge of traffic. Unless the railroad advances with the times, it is whipped. Once out of step with the trend of the day, it is difficult to again get into stride with the onward march.

The Chesapeake & Ohio, along with the other great railroads of the nation, has not only kept faith with the passenger and the shipper, but has lived up to the tradition of the American railroad, which is without equal on this earth.

The C.&O. has kept rank with other great carriers through the acquirement of the latest and best in track machines, co-operating always with the manufacturers of power equipment.

The cry has been raised that laborsaving machines are a menace to the worker and his job. The answer to that is—*no!* We will grant that the machine lessens the need for pick-and-shovel men, *but* it increases the need for skilled labor—labor to operate these machines, labor to manufacture them. In another chapter we will show how the railroads offer a bright field to men of skill, and provide the pick-and-shovel man with greater opportunity for betterment.

On the Chesapeake & Ohio, machines for maintenance of track include self-propelled cranes for rail laying, bolt tighteners, spike pullers, mechanical adzers, spike drivers, rail drills, and wood borers. There are electric and pneumatic tie-tamping tools, air compressors for operating rock drills, paint sprayers, and other equipment. Repairs to rails, frogs, and switch points are accomplished by the latest welding methods, together with electric arc generators and power grinders.

The trackman, always on guard along the right of way, has at his command today every modern appliance better to maintain the rail and roadbed.

Portable Industrial Plant: The past few years have witnessed radical changes in the handling of maintenance operations. The introduction of gas- and electric-powered machinery has simplified many major problems, but paradoxically this has greatly complicated the job of the supervisory officer. As an illustration, planning the work and scheduling the moves of a track gang of more than a hundred men in such a manner that lost time will be minimized and interference with traffic will be avoided becomes a delicate and involved proposition.

The equipment of a fully mechanized gang of this size represents an investment of $40,000 to $50,000, and represents a production plant of no small proportions. In a factory, the raw material is brought in and processed along a definite production line. But on the railroad the rail-laying plant must move to the scene of operation, deliver its own raw material, and come up with a finished product there in the field.

Standardization of Work: In most lines of manufacture, competition is keen, and if the owner desires to remain in business he must devise methods that are both economical and efficient. The routine of manufacture must move at an even pace and without interruption. The layout of machines, the number and the contribution of each must contribute its share to the set schedule. This is exactly the result demanded of a track gang.

Fortunately, the introduction of machines in the performance of track work has been gradual, and it has been possible to readjust the organization of the work to meet and mesh with the new production schedule. That, however, is but one phase of the problem. It is further necessary to reconcile the varying individual ideas of handling the work. The best ideas developed in the various track gangs are gradually consolidated into a standard pattern.

In applying this principle, the motion picture has been of inestimable value. An old Chinese proverb tells us that one picture is better than a thousand words, and the Chesapeake & Ohio quickly discovered that a camera could do more to convey the general idea of certain accepted practices in 5 minutes than any long-winded discourse on the subject. A lot of folks go to sleep during a lecture but remain alert and attentive during the showing of a moving pictire.

There are, too, the advantages of a permanent record of the track work. Also, defects in the progress of the work may be detected and corrected. Time studies may be made, and these results in turn co-ordinated, exactly as a football coach looks at the pictures of a gridiron battle and discovers weakness in the line or errors in the backfield.

In the practical application of the motion-picture formula it is a simple matter to study and analyze the individual operations of the various track gangs, selecting then the most promising methods for standardization. When this has been done, complete pictures are taken. These pictures, with suitable captions, are shown to those in charge of other gangs for information and study.

Repairs and Reclamation: At Barboursville, West Virginia, the Chesapeake & Ohio maintains a well-equipped machine shop for the overhauling and repair of the track machines. Work-weary equipment is quickly rebuilt and returned to service.

In addition to this work, the shop forces rebuild frogs and switch points, crop and rebore rail ends, re-form angle bars, and repair equipment for the water-supply and signal departments.

It is all a vital part of the maintenance of track and the rest of the railroad plant, with the trackman eternally on guard down the endless miles of shining steel.

The Work Train

Scant acclaim and little attention is the lot of the all but forgotten work train, and yet it is as important to the railroad system as the manifest and the passenger train. The work train, the drudge of the road.

A big K-4 Berkshire locomotive roars through at the head of C.&O. Manifest No. 92, and you watch it with a little thrill. Or perhaps it is the popular George Washington, the F.F.V. or the Sportsman streaking past, and your eyes grow bright and your pulse quickens at the sight of it.

But let a work train come plodding around the bend, and you regard it almost with distaste. There is an old frump of an engine and a waddling string of untidy flatcars loaded with dirt. You are half-inclined to wonder why the railroad let the thing out onto the main line.

That is life. The star of the show gets the applause, and the son of toil who sets the stage is forgotten. And yet without the work train the prima donna of the rails would be left at the switch.

The work train hauls stone, gravel, cinders, steel rails, rail-laying machines, ties, bridge timbers, drain pipes, frogs, switches, and what have you. It puts them down where and when they are needed and then goes scuttling for its burrow to get out of the way of the manifest and the passenger train.

There is no rest for the work train. Before it has completed its labor of the current season, next year's stint is being planned. Worn ties are spotted for removal, the new tie program is lined up, ballast- and rail-renewal schedules are laid out. And there are proposed bridge and building repairs and renewals, requisitions for materials, and endless other tasks, largely of a menial nature as viewed by glamour-hunting folks on the side lines. But you can't run a railroad on glamour alone, any more than you can operate a store simply by dressing up the show window.

The Northern Subdivision of the Cincinnati Division is representative of a heavy-tonnage line. It requires large quantities of maintenance material and a corresponding amount of work-train service. It begins at NJ Cabin, Kentucky, on the south, and ends at Parsons, Ohio, near Columbus, on the north. A heavy movement of coal from the West Virginia coal fields, flowing constantly to the industries of the great manufacturing centers, passes over this 94 miles of double track. The handling of work trains is an important part of the track supervisor's duties on this heavily traveled subdivision.

Let us take a typical work-train movement and follow it through. This is a July afternoon, and the track supervisor has been informed that 30 cars of ballast will be delivered the following day. He immediately calls the dispatcher on the telephone, saying that he wants a work train out of Russell Yard, Kentucky, at 6 o'clock in the morning for the rest of the week.

"Right," replies the dispatcher. "What are the working limits?"

"Between Greggs and Wheeler. Tie the work train up at Robbins."

The track supervisor then calls the operator at VA Junction, Ohio. "We've got a work train coming out of Russell at six in the morning. Take a message."

The message instructs the work train to pick up ballast at Greggs, Ohio, and unload on Blakeman Fill, Apex, and on mile 16, both tracks. A message also goes to the foremen at Robbins and Fallen Timber, saying that they are to work together unloading the ballast, and to have their ballast chains with them.

At the roundhouse in Russell early the next morning we find a hostler coaling and watering the engine assigned to the work train. The crew caller has rounded up the work-train crew, and they arrive about 5:30. The conductor picks up his orders and clearance and at 6 o'clock the work train pulls out.

It passes MS Cabin and approaches Riverton and is given a highball, or go-ahead signal. The engineer whistles an acknowledgment, and the train proceeds westward to NJ, where it receives instructions for the day's work. It moves on past Wheeler and Robbins to the Greggs Yard. Here the ballast is picked up.

When the work train is ready, the conductor calls the operator at Robbins, asking permission to cross over to the eastbound main so that he can return to the point of unloading. The orders are issued, the crossover is lined, and the work train gets under way.

(There are times when a work extra may be given orders over certain trains, but it must protect itself against such trains, as set forth in the rules. Again, it may be given exclusive right between designated points between times designated by the dispatcher. Work extras must give way to all trains as promptly as possible.)

Our work extra pulls out of Greggs with 30 cars of gravel. It stops at Robbins for coal and water and delivers orders regarding a line-up of trains. The section foreman and his gang board the train, which continues then to Blakeman Fill. Here the section foreman from Fallen Timber is waiting with the gang.

The foreman from Robbins instructs the conductor as to the exact place the ballast is to be unloaded, requesting that the work train operate at no more than 6 miles per hour. The conductor orders his flagman back to protect the work train, and the section men apply the ballast chains to the hopper doors. These chains provide a means of regulating the flow of ballast. In this case the chains are adjusted to allow only enough ballast to escape from the hoppers to fill in the track, to the end that it may be surfaced and restored to top condition.

When the work train arrives at the point designated, the foreman calls, "Knock the first two loose." The hoppers are opened to the limit of the chains, and the ballast is spread along the track as the train moves slowly forward until those cars with chains have been emptied.

Perhaps a train whistles on the westbound main now, and there is the cry, "Everybody clear!" After it has passed, more hoppers are chained—usually 6 or more at a time. So the work continues until it is time to move to another location.

The track where the ballast is dumped, we discover, has been "cribbed out." The work continues at this location until it is time to "clear a train," at which time the work extra heads for the nearest siding.

They are slow miles—stopping, crawling forward, pouring ballast to carry these heavy main-line rails. At last the entire 30 cars have been unloaded, and the work train returns to Robbins for more ballast.

At noon the empty cars are set off at Marshall, say, and the work extra goes huffing back to Robbins for dinner. Men pile off and make a rush for the camp cars and the long tables of grub.

Come night, the work train is tied up at Robbins, and the conductor notifies the operator that the day's operations are finished. A hostler has been ordered to report at Robbins, and he takes charge of the locomotive—cleaning the fire, dumping the ashpan, taking on coal and water, and watching the engine until the regular crew take over in the morning.

At times there may be as many as three work trains operating in a certain territory, unloading new materials and loading and hauling away old materials. The track gangs "spread down" road-bed, scarify ballast, deepen ditches, remove slides, and perform may other operations that have to do with the maintenance of track.

The track supervisor keeps a close watch over the work, checking with the dispatcher, arranging for the movement of the work extra in such a manner that it will interfere as little as possible with the traffic flow, as it concerns extras. Above all, the track must be kept open for the manifest train and the haughty star of the show—the lady with the varnished train.

So the work of the trackman goes on. And on the main line a man beside a telegraph pole speaks into the transmitter of his field telephone. His voice reaches out to the train dispatcher. "The track is clear. . . . Let the trains roll."

CHAPTER IX

THE SOUTHERN PACIFIC

The Los Angeles Overnight

The Southern Pacific is symbolic of the West. Born of a rough-and-ready parent, the Central Pacific, the S.P. has grown from a two-fisted frontiersman into a polished gentleman of the old school. The rails of the S.P. spin their silver threads across the highest mountains, the great valleys and down that eternal highway of kings—El Camino Real—in California.

Today these rails of the Southern Pacific reach out half across the nation; they are thrust into the Northwest, the Southwest, and deep into Old Mexico. But California, the land of the Dons and the Padres, the Gold Coast, is the home to which their speeding trains always return.

The Southern Pacific [Erle Heath writes] is a monument to the enterprise and the vision of Leland Stanford, Colis P. Huntington, Charles Crocker and Mark Hopkins, the Sacramento merchants, famed in later years as the "Big Four."

They were to the Southern Pacific what Jim Hill was to the Great Northern, what Cyrus K. Holliday was to the Santa Fe. They were the empire builders. And their spirits ride today in gleaming splendor on the Daylights and the Larks and the City of San Francisco, and all the others.

But it is not with the flashing passenger trains that we are concerned now, but fast freight—the Los Angeles Overnight. However, before we board the rear end of the Overnight, which soon will be storming south from the Bayshore Yard in San Francisco, we will first set the stage with a little background scenery that you may better appreciate the obstacles these roaring carriers must surmount in their flight.

California abounds in scenery of a variety and startling contrast not to be found in a like radius anywhere. Scenery—and climate. And in both it reaches violent extremes. An Eskimo or a Zulu could find in California the climate exactly adapted to him —from 40 below zero to 135 above. In winter in the Sierra Nevadas the mercury lurks frigidly at the bottom of the thermometer, and in summer in the Sacramento and San Joaquin valleys and the southern deserts the mercury boils over the top.

This in a land where they have roses in December and snow in July. Mt. Whitney, the highest spot in the United States, and Death Valley, the lowest point, are actually within sight of each other. For every mile of flat country in California, there is a mile standing on end.

No Southern Pacific train can get in or out of California without crossing a mountain or a desert, or both. No passenger or ton of freight can take a journey of any consequence without discovering, as the Forty-Niners did, that this country is rugged. There are the Sierra Nevadas—"the Hill" to S.P. men—the Cascades, the Siskiyous, the Tehachapis, the Santa Lucias, the Santa Susanas, the San Bernardinos, the San Gabriels, and Beaumont Hill.

It is a perpetual scramble to climb a mountain or to get down from one. Motive power consists of about one-third road engines and two-thirds helpers. Locomotive stacks get hot going up, and the wheels get hot coming down. It is a ceaseless battle to lift trains almost straight into the sky and safely drop them down again. But these S.P. railroaders do it, and with amazing speed and absolute safety.

The Southern Pacific's fleet of Overnights is a legend in the West. Rushing down the rail, the Overnights provide speedy overnight freight service between San Francisco and Los Angeles; Oakland and Reno, Nevada; Los Angeles and Tucson, Arizona; Oakland and Dunsmuir, California, with connections at the latter point for Portland, Oregon; this service soon to be run through.

The run from San Francisco to Los Angeles involves climbing

the Santa Margarita grade and negotiating the grade and tunnels of the Santa Susanas. The S.P.'s speedy passenger train, the Lark, makes the run in 12 hours. The Overnight wheels its fast freight through close to the passenger's running time.

This writer rode the rear end of the Overnight, 374, out of the Bayshore terminal in San Francisco, leaving an hour and thirty minutes ahead of No. 76, the Lark, which was still forty minutes behind us at Burbank.

This provides a good example of the manner in which the railroads are highballing freight. Later we will have something to say about the last word in freight trains, further indicating the kind of postwar speed merchants that will serve the shipper.

The Los Angeles Overnight, flagship of the Southern Pacific's fast freight fleet, leaves the San Francisco Bayshore Yards every evening, except Saturday and Sunday, at 7:40. The train is limited to 60 high-speed freight cars, and it is hauled by a GS (General Service) 4-8-4 type locomotive. The drivers of this engine are 80-inch, and that is a big driving wheel for a freight train on any railroad.

The Overnight picks up Oakland cars at San Jose and usually one or two at Watsonville Junction. It stops at King City for inspection, Santa Margarita for a helper, and San Luis Obispo and Santa Barbara to change crews. These are the only stops, ordinarily, in the run of close to 480 miles.

The cars used as cabooses on the Los Angeles Overnight trains are unique in that they are rebuilt passenger coaches with bay windows on the sides instead of the usual cupola on top. They were among the early cabooses of this type to make their appearance on American railroads.

The caboose on 374 runs through from Bayshore to Los Angeles, instead of being changed at points where crews change, as is customary. It is my impression that the Overnight cabooses were the first to be operated over more than one division in ordinary freight service. These caboose cars, of course, were used because of their ability to stand the blistering pace set by the Overnight. They are fitted with the usual caboose equipment which we have described in the opening chapter.

At 6:30 p.m. the Bayshore freight house is a veritable beehive of activity, for this is the peak rush hour. The freight handlers we find hurriedly loading the last of the l.c.l. consist billed to Los Angeles. There are about 25 cars on the house tracks on either side of the freight house. Here are piled the boxes, crates, and barrels that have been trucked in by the San Francisco shippers late in the afternoon. And there are, of course, those last rushes that must be billed and loaded before the 7:15 deadline.

The little tractors and their trucks dodge and squirm and dash everywhere. They clatter across the steel aprons into freight cars, and expert handlers stow the assortment of lading, using care in spite of the rush to load the cars in such a manner that breakage will be reduced to the minimum. Hand trucks dart in and out like busy ants, yet in spite of the seeming confusion the work is accomplished speedily and with an amazing precision.

At 7:15 on the dot, the car doors are banged shut, almost as though they were actuated by a master switch. Already a switch engine is bumping the coupler at one end of a 25-car cut and only awaits the signal that all doors have been secured and seals attached. Then it growls away with this part of the Overnight's make-up.

A second switch engine puts the caboose on, air hoses are hooked up, and air-brake inspectors begin their task of checking the train.

The venerable J. J. ("Jimmie") Jordan, Superintendent of the Coast Division, is there. We find him talking to the conductor beside the caboose. Jimmie never goes home until the Los Angeles Overnight highballs out of Bayshore. J. J. Jordan is typical of your railroad man. He has been through the mill and was "made" on the Sacramento Division, the crucible from which many an S.P. man has come to take his place in the high ranks of West Coast railroaders.

Often you also find J. W. Corbett, Southern Pacific Coast Line's General Manager, and R. E. Hallawell, Assistant General Manager, down there in the Bayshore Yards keeping an eye on things when the pressure is on. During the war days, when the railroads were straining to keep traffic moving, the untiring efforts of these men untangled or forestalled many a snarl. Too much credit cannot be given men of their breed. These two are tops as all-around railroaders, also having grand dispositions and personality.

Tonight we pull out onto the main line at Visitacion Tower, 1.7 miles east of Bayshore Yard, at 7:55 p.m., running ahead of No. 154, a local passenger, and roll down the rails toward San Jose. The engine is the 4427, and we have 42 loads. The average running time to San Jose is 37 miles an hour. Here we pick up 9 cars from Oakland and highball at 9:35.

The 53 miles to Watsonville Junction are covered in 1 hour and 11 minutes, for a 42-mile-an-hour average. We pick up two cars and leave at 11:02, 23 minutes ahead of the Lark.

We roll into King City at 12:15 a.m., and after the inspection are moving again at 12:27. It is remarkable how the same type of engine that pulls the Lark and the Daylights can knuckle down and do a job on a freight like this 374. The exhaust is sweet to listen to as we rush toward Santa Margarita.

The Southern Pacific is the only road in the country that still computes tonnage by the "M" method; thus our tonnage of 5850 M's is 2925 tons. The General Service engines with 80-inch drivers are only rated for 1800 M's between Santa Margarita and Cuesta, where there is about 2½ miles of 2.2 per cent grade. The 374 is therefore given a helper at Santa Margarita. To save time the helper goes on through to San Luis Obispo.

The 16.6 miles from Santa Margarita to San Luis is one of the hottest and most important stretches of track anywhere. The grade is 1 per cent on each side of Serrano, the summit, and on the east slope this becomes 2.2 per cent for a distance of 9 miles.

This is C.T.C. territory, and it provides one of the best examples of the advantages of Centralized Traffic Control to be found in the United States.

We have been rushing through the fertile Salinus Valley toward the dim outline of the Santa Lucia Mountains, thundering past towns the Spaniards named—Gonzales, Soledad, Paso Robles. We passed the old Mission at San Miguel. Now we're on the famous Santa Margarita grade on single track. And it is on this piece of single track that all trains that leave San Francisco and Los Angeles at the same time meet, including both the morning and noon Daylights, the Larks and the Overnights.

Here the dispatcher at his C.T.C. board maneuvers these east- and westbound trains through their meeting points with magic speed and safety. You are rushing along on a single track. Lights signal the engineer into a passing track. There is the hot beam of a headlight, the rapid bark of an exhaust, and the westbound Overnight crashes past our caboose. We have also met the Coaster, No. 69.

A word here concerning our reference to *east*- and *westbound* trains between Los Angeles and San Francisco. The latter city, of course, is north of Los Angeles, but the trend from this southern city is westerly. Even many residents of California, until they look at their map, do not realize that Santa Barbara, "up" the Coast, is pretty nearly due west of Los Angeles, and that all S.P. trains heading toward San Francisco are westbound and odd-numbered.

The Southern Pacific's ocean line consists of two divisions—the Coast Division and the Los Angeles Division—and both are tough. The rails of the former climb out of the Salinas Valley, cross the Santa Lucias, and drop down to the Pacific. The rails of the Los Angeles Division strike inland from Ventura, threading through the Simi Valley to the Santa Susanas and the 7,369-foot tunnel which opens into the San Fernando Valley. Between Santa Margarita and Goldtree there are 6 tunnels.

It is when dropping down the beautiful Santa Lucias that passengers on the eastbound Daylights get their first view of the Pacific Ocean, the blue of it like the blue of the lupine fields when California is putting on its spring flower show.

The Los Angeles Overnight pulls out of San Luis Obispo ahead of the eastbound Lark, leading this fast-stepping train into the great Taylor Yard in Los Angeles, and the shipments loaded there at Bayshore, San Francisco, the night before are in Los Angeles for morning delivery by the vast fleet of P.M.T.— Pacific Motor Lines—trucks.

The Southern Pacific Coast Division is a heavily traveled railroad artery, handling an enormous amount of traffic, as revealed by the following table of train movements. The movements

TRAIN MOVEMENTS—SEPTEMBER, 1945—COAST DIVISION

	SF Bayshore		BAYSHORE Red. Jct		SJ W. Jct		W. JCT Salinas		SALINAS S. Marg.		S. MARG. SLO		SLO S.B.		Total All Points Per Day		
	E	W	E	W	E	W	E	W	E	W	E	W	E	W	E	W	Total
1	60	59	44	44	23	17	25	19	14	12	16	21	15	11	197	183	384
2	47	48	26	26	18	17	17	18	12	11	12	11	9	12	141	143	284
3	47	45	35	33	16	14	18	15	14	11	15	11	13	12	158	141	299
4	59	61	43	43	18	17	20	20	12	12	16	20	13	13	181	186	367
5	65	68	47	44	20	19	18	20	12	14	16	17	12	13	192	195	387
6	64	64	44	44	20	18	18	18	12	14	13	14	12	12	183	184	367
7	60	63	46	45	21	18	18	19	12	13	14	13	9	14	183	185	368
8	65	66	43	45	25	18	18	26	10	15	17	17	10	12	187	199	386
9	41	44	29	32	18	19	17	19	11	13	16	18	10	10	142	155	297
10	68	65	44	47	20	17	20	18	12	12	14	18	12	13	190	190	380
11	67	65	47	42	22	20	22	23	16	15	17	18	15	16	206	199	405
12	63	64	44	48	18	18	22	19	14	15	21	19	12	11	194	194	388
13	65	66	49	47	21	21	19	24	11	16	16	19	11	14	192	207	399
14	59	62	44	47	22	20	22	24	15	16	16	20	11	12	189	201	390
15	65	60	43	44	21	19	22	21	15	13	17	17	14	13	194	187	381
16	42	40	33	32	16	14	15	16	11	11	15	13	14	12	146	138	284
17	54	55	46	49	23	20	18	19	13	14	17	17	13	11	189	185	374
18	67	66	46	48	20	21	18	18	15	13	15	17	11	13	192	196	388
19	64	64	46	46	16	18	18	22	11	13	15	14	12	15	182	192	374
20	64	66	46	45	25	22	21	22	12	14	16	15	11	16	195	200	395
21	65	65	46	49	23	24	21	26	11	16	14	13	11	14	191	207	398
22	61	63	45	48	22	21	23	22	13	12	17	20	10	10	191	196	387
23	43	43	32	33	26	17	19	20	11	12	15	14	12	12	158	151	309
24	59	55	45	45	23	24	25	26	13	14	13	17	12	13	190	194	384
25	69	70	45	48	24	22	25	25	11	12	17	15	14	14	205	206	411
26	66	67	47	47	24	23	27	25	14	13	16	18	12	11	206	201	407
27	63	63	50	50	20	19	23	19	14	12	17	18	12	14	190	195	394
28	69	69	48	44	23	18	24	24	14	16	17	17	14	14	209	203	412
29	59	65	45	49	21	23	22	21	14	14	17	17	10	13	188	202	390
30	46	44	32	32	20	20	18	24	10	16	16	15	12	15	154	166	320
	1786	1705	1280	1206	620	578	620	622	370	404	461	491	357	285	5524	5581	11105

listed covered the month of September, 1945. During October and November coast division traffic was even heavier.

The Hill

The Mountain Subdivision of the Southern Pacific's Sacramento Division extends from Roseville, California, to Sparks, Nevada. Railroaders on the S.P. call it "the Hill," and you will go far to find another stretch of track as tough. Here the double track of the Overland Route lifts to 7,000 feet in crossing the mighty Sierra Nevadas. The distance is 138.2 miles over the eastward track and 138.7 miles over the westward track.

The snowfall between December and April in this portion of the Sierra Nevadas is the heaviest of any place in the United States. The fall is the greatest between Gold Run, at an elevation of 3,228 feet on the west slope, and Sparks, on the east slope. This is also one of the coldest spots in the country, and I have seen the thermometer at Verdi when it registered a blood-chilling subzero 42. The wind seems to sweep down off the North Pole as it piles the snow into towering drifts, at times close to 70 feet.

The elevation at Roseville, on the edge of the Sacramento Valley, is only 162 feet. At Norden, 80 miles to the east, the rail lifts over a mile. The grade here varies from 79 feet to 131 feet to the mile. However, the right of way was engineered to eliminate sharp curves, there being only about a mile of 10-degree curvature. Both tracks are completely rock-ballasted, and the entire division is laid with 130- and 131-pound rail.

The elevation at Sparks, on the Nevada side, is 4,225 feet, climbing to 6,965 at Summit, with a high point of 7,017 feet a little to the east.

All track on the Hill in slide areas is protected with slide-detector fences. Against the 40 miles of snowsheds employed in days gone by there are now some 17 miles of sheds. There are 18 tunnels on the eastward track in the 31 miles between Rocklin and Colfax, and 1 tunnel between Colfax and Norden. Be-

'tween Truckee and Summit on the westbound there are 13 bores, with 4 on the eastbound.

Normally there are 5 regularly scheduled eastbound passenger trains moving over the Hill each day, with an additional train on the days the City of San Francisco operates. The westbound count is 5, except in the case of the days the latter train is going through. An almost endless parade of extra trains is constantly hammering at the ramparts of this mighty mountain range.

The Sierra Nevadas are really the stamping ground of the cab-ahead articulateds, for it was here that these locomotives were first used. The reason for this arrangement was that by placing the cab in front, the engine crew escaped the suffocating smoke and gas from the stack that had previously made operation in tunnels and snowsheds very tough.

The AC-6 to AC-12 class locomotives are rated at 2,400 tons from Roseville to Colfax and 1,450 tons, Colfax to Norden, where the going gets tough. This, of course, is eastbound. Westbound, Sparks to Truckee, the rating is 3,650 tons. From Truckee to Summit it is 1,850 tons. There are no AC-9 class in service on this division.

The average tonnage on the Hill is from 2,800 to 3,500 tons. As we have indicated, the Southern Pacific employs the M system in figuring tonnage, each M being 1,000 pounds. However, here we are dealing in actual tons. The usual procedure is to cut one AC helper in 10 cars ahead of the caboose for the climb from Roseville to Colfax. At this helper terminal another AC is cut in 4 cars ahead of the caboose, or two 2-8-0 type engines. The heaviest grade is encountered between Colfax and Emigrant Gap. Here the second helper is usually dropped, but the Roseville helper goes through to Norden.

Westward, the road engine hauls the train from Sparks to Truckee unassisted. At Truckee two AC helpers are cut in. These helpers are placed in the train 4 and 10 cars ahead of the caboose, as at Colfax, with an eye to avoiding as much as possible smoking and gassing both train and engine crews. All engines are equipped with respirators.

Braking on the Hill requires experienced railroaders in every department, and the conductor and swing brakeman are extremely proficient in the tricky work of cutting the helpers in and out of the drag.

Railroading on the Hill has come a long ways since this writer first rode the head and rear end of freight trains over the Sacramento's Mountain Subdivision. I was 9 years old, and they were using the old staff system then. The crews, I remember, coming out of Roseville changed at Blue Canyon, 60 miles to the east, and at a point 80 miles from Sparks. These heavy drags now cover the entire run across the Sierras as quickly as they used to take to run the trip to those early division points.

The best cabooses on the Southern Pacific are in service on the Hill, and they have lanterns with reflectors mounted just behind the wheels of the rear trucks. These lights provide track illumination and enable the crews to maintain a constant vigil as they watch for any telltale indications of dragging equipment. When the ties and roadbed indicate that something is down, the train can immediately be brought to a stop. These track lights have been the means of averting possibly serious trouble.

Another feature of the Mountain Subdivision is the electric-lighted train-order signals, placed upwards of a mile in advance of the train-order office at points where the visibility is poor because of curves and snowsheds.

I have a particular affection for the Hill and for its railroaders, and when I am on the coast and the opportunity presents itself I never fail to head for Roseville and this Mountain Subdivision. And I don't know of any place where you can better view this land of the Sierra Nevadas and more intimately come to know the men who play a vital part in the movement of these trains toiling in the mountains than in the caboose behind the train.

Let us ride the rear end of one of these Southern Pacific freight trains over the Hill. Here the magic carpet of the rail provides unexcelled grandeur and a sense of leaving the trials and tribulations of the world behind. You are going to ride straight into the sky—a mile up from the great valley of the Sacramento—where the air is clear and crisp, and the clouds are so close you can almost touch them.

The crew dispatcher has called us at the Riverside Hotel in

Roseville at 5:30 in the morning, and we are informed that engine 4177 class AC-8 has been assigned to train 482 called for 6 o'clock. We dress and eat breakfast and hurry to the yards, where we locate the caboose and climb aboard.

It is September. The fruit rush is on, and there are long lines of cars readying for the long journey east. Our train, however, contains no reefers. The conductor gets aboard with his waybills, which list 99 cars—30 loads and 60 empties, totaling 6120 M's, or 3,060 tons. Our helper has been cut into the train. It is 4277, an AC-12, the last of this great class to be received by the S.P.

Leave Roseville	6:55 a.m.

Standing inspection of train pulling out. Conductor and brakeman inspecting each side.

Pass Newcastle	7:40 a.m.
Arrive Colfax	8:15 a.m.

Road engine and helper take water. Cut in helpers 2811 and 2822, 4 cars from rear end.

Leave Colfax	8:35 a.m.
Arrive Towle	9:15 a.m.

Flagged by work train. 30-minute detention.

Leave Towle	9:45 a.m.
Arrive Emigrant Gap	10:55 a.m.

Cut out rear helpers. Take water. 20 minutes for crew to eat.

Leave Emigrant Gap	11:40 a.m.
Arrive Crystal Lake	12:00 m.

Inspection.

Leave Crystal Lake	12:08 p.m.

Arrive Norden	12:45 p.m.

Take water. Cut out helper. Turn up retainers.

Leave Norden	1:10 p.m.
Arrive Sanford	1:38 p.m.

Inspection of train.

Leave Sanford	1:45 p.m.
Arrive Truckee	2:05 p.m.

Pick up 10 cars. Put retainers down.

Leave Truckee	2:20 p.m.
Arrive Sparks	3:40 p.m.

Total time, 8 hours, 45 minutes. 55 minutes delay beside dead time.
Weather calm and clear. Temperature Roseville 59; Norden 41; Sparks 52. September 27, 1944.
Met 6 westbound freight trains and 7 main trains.

The train is braked so perfectly the slack action is negligible on the rear end. The conductor has completed his wheel report and other clerical work upon our arrival at Colfax, after which he assists the other crew members in watching the train and track. During the entire run the train is under the close observation of these men in the caboose. They inspect westbound trains, which we meet en route, and constantly scan the track and right of way for signs of trouble.

Little escapes the vigilant eye of railroad men on the Hill. They have no fear of this mountain road, but they respect it, for high steel holds a potential threat always.

Supply Train

One thing that impresses you when you are riding the rear end is the enormous quantities of supplies required in the operation and maintenance of the railroad—spikes, bolts, nuts, rails, tools, lanterns, paint, lumber, gasoline, motor and switch-lamp oil, and switch assemblies, to mention a few of the 3,000 items listed by General Stores.

In an earlier chapter we referred to the material required for one mile of single track—3,250 ties, 6,500 tie plates, 13,000 spikes, over a thousand bolts. Multiply these figures by 2 for double track, and again multiply the result by the 138 miles of a division such as we have seen on the Hill. The amount you finally arrive at will be staggering.

We have written in another chapter of the track work constantly in progress. Aside from the maintenance of the line, the job of supplying the materials constitutes an enormous task. These supplies come from the railroad's General Stores. Here we find them loaded onto supply trains and peddled at various locations, thus satisfying the never-ceasing flood of requisitions that descend on the Stores Department.

The supply train provides pickup and delivery service, for it must gather scrap and rail and surplus and released materials as it goes along. Roadmasters, signal supervisors, agents, and others make their requests for a three months' supply of required items, which are delivered on the ground.

The Sacramento supply train works from Fresno, California, north to Portland, Oregon, and east to Ogden, Utah. The Los Angeles train works from San Jose and Fresno south and east to El Paso, Texas, and Tucumcari, New Mexico. These supply trains consist of 28 to 33 cars, 12 to 16 of which are specially equipped for supply-train service. The balance will be flats, gondolas, and boxcars. On the eastern run, the Los Angeles train takes about 36 days to make the trip. Each morning before leaving terminals the supply-car storekeeper makes a list of all regular stops for the day. This list is distributed to the superintendent of the division, trainmasters, and the chief dispatcher so as to avoid interruption to regular traffic.

The supply train is manned by a storekeeper, 4 assistants, and a crane operator. Though the supply train looks like an ill-assorted freight train, it is actually put together in an orderly and careful manner. Everything is arranged to expedite the unloading of materials at the various stops. Included in the make-up of the train is a coach car equipped to serve as an office and living quarters.

The gasoline-operated crane has a lifting capacity of 7½ tons, and its 40-foot boom permits of a sizable reach on either side of the track. The crane is completely revolving, and it also moves back and forth on rails the length of the 52-foot flatcar which carries it. The loading of scrap is facilitated by the use of a powerful magnet which snatches up all metal objects with which it comes in contact.

Good housekeeping is the order of the day aboard a supply train. Car interiors are brightly painted, and all bins and racks are planned for neatness and efficiency. There's a place for everything, and everything is in its place. Gasoline is pumped from tank cars to underground storage tanks; also signal oil. Motor oil is carried in large tanks in a boxcar and in drums.

As a supply train nears a stop, all supplies are arranged near the doors to aid in speeding delivery. The crew of a supply train spend 75 per cent of their time on the line.

The two supply trains which serve the S.P.'s Pacific lines operate out of the Sacramento General Stores and the Los Angeles General Stores.

Storekeeping on a railroad is something that most of us fail to appreciate in the order of its importance, but no railroad could long maintain its track or efficiently operate the trains that go roaring through without the quiet, efficient, but unsung railroad man from General Stores.

Detector Car

Riding the rear end, we look back at small twin glassed-in cars moving out onto the singing steel of the main line behind us.

The lettering on the side reads: DETECTOR CAR SP-0-1000. This is the Southern Pacific's railroad "detective"—the detective that searches out the villain in the form of the lurking flaw in the rail, the invisible fracture in the steel structure, which under the constant hammering of the trains might one day become a broken rail, a deadly menace.

The Detector Car itself is pulled by a gasoline-engined power unit. These units are in operation continuously as they cruise over the system, painstakingly searching for defective rails.

All main-line rail on the S.P. is tested twice a year by these Detector Cars. They move at a speed of about 5 miles an hour, and the Detector Car's magic instruments continuously record their findings on tapes. When the sensitive pen indicates a possible flaw, the car is stopped and the rail double-checked. If it indicates a hidden fracture, it is marked for immediate removal. Most of these flaws are invisible to the human eye.

Most rail defects are caused by separation of molecules in the metal. These tiny separations in time grow to a size that might weaken the rail. The job of the Detector Car is to locate such faults before the rail is dangerously weakened.

This is another contribution to your railroad's constant search for ways and means of providing both speed and safety down the magic carpet of the rails you ride.

S.P. Shorthand

Every S.P. locomotive has a little story stenciled in shorthand on its cab. Many people wonder what these strange hieroglyphics are all about. When you have translated these figures and numerals, you know all about this big S.P. engine—its class, its weight, the size of the cylinders, and if it is equipped with a superheater and feed-water heater.

The translation of this S.P. shorthand is found in the road's book of locomotive classification and assignment. Let's take this big 4427 that hauled the Los Angeles Overnight. We find the following on the cab under the number:

$$\text{GS-80} \ \frac{26 \quad 267}{32 \quad \text{B-109}} \ \text{SF}$$

The "GS" means that this is a General Service 4-8-4 locomotive. The "80" represents the diameter of the drivers. The numerator of the fraction following, $\frac{26}{32}$, is the diameter of the cylinders; the denominator is the stroke. The figure "267" indicates the weight on drivers in nearest even thousand pounds. "B" means that the engine has a booster, and the "109" following is the weight on trailing truck in nearest even thousand pounds. The letter "S" informs you that the locomotive has a superheater, and the "F" indicates feed-water heater.

Likewise, the designation of an AC Mallet would read:

$$\text{AC-63} \ \frac{24\text{-}24}{32} \ \text{475-SF}$$

This would apply to the 4-8-8-2 type of the 4100 class. "AC" is Articulated Consolidation. The cylinders are 24 x 32. The weight on drivers is 475,000 pounds, and it has a superheater and feed-water heater.

The letter or letters at the beginning of the classification are always the type designation, as "DES" for Diesel-electric switcher, "T" for ten-wheeler, "P" for Pacific, "C" for Consolidation, "Mt" for mountain type, and so on.

Thus, once you become acquainted with it, S.P. shorthand is both simple and informative.

CHAPTER X

THE BURLINGTON'S PANORAMIC COACH

The Vista-Dome Car

Those who once envied the brakeman his countryside view from the cupola of the caboose can now, for the price of a railroad ticket, enjoy the same view from a passenger coach penthouse.

In the early part of 1945 the Chicago, Burlington & Quincy Railroad built at its Aurora, Illinois, carshops what is believed to be the first American railway passenger car with a steel-framed, glass-enclosed observation compartment extending upward through the roof of a day coach. The first silver Zephyr streaking down the rails had the folks all agog, and this penthouse on a passenger car created no less a sensation.

The idea proved as catching as a new style in ladies' hats, and soon several railroads were placing orders for these cars for their postwar trains.

The Burlington's Vista-Dome car made its initial test run on July 23, 1945, and it almost jumped the neighboring populace out of its boots. However, upon discovering that it was neither a circus car nor a new kind of a caboose, John Q. Public sidled up for a closer view. What he saw pleased and amazed him, but the big thrill was that first ride.

Seated in a deep-cushioned comfortable chair, you lean back and look at the cloud effects, the far horizons, and you rather get the feeling that you have never been outdoors before. And when, out of the distant haze, there appears the thin white line that is the snow-capped Rockies—well, there are just no words to describe the panorama spread before you. Suddenly the world is at your feet—plains, a sea of golden wheat, a harvester at work, a cluster of cottonwoods, thunderheads billowing under the eaves of the sky. And the Rockies rushing to meet you.

Americans are the greatest travelers on earth. They want to see the country, as more and more they appreciate the fact that the United States offers a variety of scenery without compare. With that fact in mind, the Burlington people set to work to throw open the doors, to provide the passenger with a new kind of observation point, a place aboard the speeding train where he could look all around the horizon, and the answer was the Vista-Dome.

One of these sky-line observation cars is a sight-seeing bus, a mountain lookout, and an airplane ride, all in one. You see everything there is to be seen and still keep one foot on the ground.

Regardless of what the weather is like outside, you are in perfect climate in a Vista-Dome. The dome compartment is thoroughly insulated. The top glass is double-laminated safety glass, separated by a ¼-inch air space, the outer pane having heat- and sunray-resisting properties. Side windows have one pane of ¼-inch heat-absorbing glass, a ¼-inch air space, and a ⅜-inch pane of safety glass on the inside.

Positive air conditioning of the car and dome is assured. And in spite of the increased air-conditioning load resulting from the glass dome, temperatures of the dome compartment during tests were kept down to 78 degrees Fahrenheit with a maximum outside temperature of 103 degrees.

Car heating is arranged to provide amply for the additional dome space in the coldest weather. Attractive and effective electric-light fixtures are installed in the observation section, which contains 24 de luxe seats.

In connection with the famous Burlington Zephyrs, which carry these Vista-Dome cars, it is interesting to note that these silver cars of the Burlington "speedway" are equipped with Timken roller bearings. It was back in 1935 that the first Zephyr was placed in service—the Mark Twain, running to St. Louis. Since that time 13 other Zephyrs have made their entrance on the scene, and these trains have rolled up the amazing total of over 25,000,000 miles.

Probably the most important preservice demonstration ever made was with the dawn-to-dusk nonstop train that streaked down the rails from Denver, by the Rockies, to Chicago, by the Lakes, on May 26, 1934. The distance of 1,015.4 miles was covered in 13 hours and 5 minutes, for an average of 77.6 miles an hour.

This demonstration of sustained high-speed running was the preview of an overnight service between the Colorado capital and Chicago which was to bring them hours closer. The previous shortest running time was 25 hours and 15 minutes. The silver Zephyrs, with their roller-bearing-equipped motive power and cars, reduced this to an amazing 15 hours and 38 minutes.

The dome-type construction was originally suggested by General Motors' proposed "Astra Liner," for car designers were already experimenting with this revolutionary observation-dome idea.

The work of constructing the Burlington's Vista-Dome car was unusually difficult due to the necessity of building this dome into an existing car, using only such materials as were readily available and without drawing on critical war materials. Where the General Motors designs called for a depressed center section, the Burlington car was rebuilt without changing the underframe and main floor. Seats in both the dome compartment and the main car body under the dome were arranged in such a manner as to take advantage of the decreased headroom required when sitting as compared with standing.

The car from which the Vista-Dome was built was a 79-foot, 8-inch streamlined stainless-steel chair car, constructed in 1940 by the Edward Budd Company. It provided 52 seats for passengers, not including seats in the women's lounge and the men's smoking room. As redesigned, the seating capacity was for 58.

The height of the original car from the top of the rail to the roof was 13 feet, 6 inches. The height with the dome added became 16 feet, 2 inches. Clearances, it had been determined, were ample for the Vista-Dome to be operated anywhere on the Burlington system. The glass dome compartment is approximately 22 feet, 6 inches long, 10 feet wide, and extends 2 feet, 8 inches above the former roof. This places the passenger's head and shoulders well above the roof line, providing a good view in every direction, including forward and back over the top of the train. The seats are reversible to suit the direction of car movement.

The distance from the floor to the ceiling of the dome compartment is 6 feet, 2 inches. The weight of the car is 130,000 pounds, compared with 110,000 before the dome was added. However, the Burlington builders have pointed out that if the car had been built new it would not have weighed much more than the original 110,000 pounds.

The trucks used under the rebuilt car were the original trucks, which were equipped with Timken roller bearings, lateral and vertical snubbers, and stabilizers to resist car sway. While the car was easy riding in the extreme, other tests with improved trucks have since been tried out in an effort to determine the type most effective in cushioning road shocks.

Owing to the unavailability of curved glass or suitable transparent plastics in wartime, the windows and roof of the dome were built of flat double-plate glass. This air space acts both as an insulator and a preventive against fogging or frosting.

Coincident with the installation of the dome compartment, the main floor of the car was remodeled and refinished. The main passenger compartment contains 18 reclining chair seats in conventional arrangement. Beneath the dome space are 16 seats, four of which may be used to form a card-playing section, with 12 placed back-to-back along the center of the car, facing outward toward the windows. These two rows are separated by a glass partition. A short stairway leads up to the dome compartment. A modern and attractive women's lounge and a spacious men's room are located at opposite ends of the car.

Any woman would delight in the many well-lighted mirrors in the lounge. The finishings are in turquoise green for the built-in settee and salmon for the chair and dressing table. This color also is incorporated in the drapes. The floor covering is a light-brown linoleum. Walls are beige cream; also the ceilings. The white vitreous enamel lavatory and dental fountain are enclosed in stainless steel. This boxed-in construction both conceals the pipes and provides covered space for used towels.

The men's lounge is done in antique tan leather for the settees, and the floor is a blue-green linoleum. The upper walls are beige and the lower a cinnamon brown. The same boxed-in construction of lavatory fittings is used as in the women's lounge. Light fixtures built into the box construction at the upper side walls utilize the rounded translucent plastic shield to give an attractive modernistic effect. All trim in this room and throughout the car is stainless steel. Suitable prints, mounted in stainless-steel frames, are used for decorative purposes in both lounges.

In rebuilding and reconditioning this car at the Aurora shops, both design and construction details, as we have pointed out, were dictated in many instances by the fact that the car was not a new design. For example, the limited headroom available with a straight instead of a depressed-center construction placed definite limitations on the amount of space available under the dome compartment. In view of the urgent need at the time for employing only such materials as were, for the most part, readily available, many substitute materials and fabricating methods were of a necessity employed.

Stainless-steel sheets and pressings, joined by the Budd Shot-weld process, were used when available in the desired thickness, but it was necessary to use arc-welded carbon-steel structural shapes for the dome frame and aluminum sheets for some of the wainscoting and ceiling below the dome. Exterior roof and side sheathing is entirely stainless steel.

Longitudinal forces in the rebuilt car were carried through the dome section by means of reinforcing plates and shapes inserted in the car sides just above the windows. This reinforcement was extended well ahead and back of the dome itself in order to assure a strong, rigid, and permanently straight construction. The floor of the dome performs many of the functions of the roof, such as tying the upper portions of the sides together, and resisting torsion and latitudinal bending.

Structural partitions transmit such forces from the roof to the dome floor. Longitudinal beams in the dome floor are supported by structural partitions at the ends and middle of the dome region. Even the staircase, which gives entrance to the dome, is designed so that some of the step treads and risers, as well as the staircase sides, perform structural functions.

All glass in the dome is sealed in steel frames. This frame is lined on the inside with a thin layer of wood, both for insulation and for looks. Except for the center ceiling duct, wood is utilized for all trim in the dome. The center ceiling duct in the original car was cut out at the dome section and replaced by an air duct passing vertically upward through glass walls in the center window at the front, thence into the center ceiling duct, which is equipped with circular outlets for the cool air. Side ducts and outlets below the window level also distribute cool air in the dome compartment. The return air duct in the front wall just above the floor simply transmits air to the lower car floor, whence it circulates back through the car into the overhead return duct.

Positive circulation of cool air to all parts of the car is assured by an electric-driven blower. The car heating equipment utilizes the ducts and outlets which we have described. Fin-type radiation units located along the floor on each side of the dome are controlled by thermostatically operated valves.

Attractive and effective electric-light fixtures were installed throughout the rebuilt car, including aisle lamps and an individual light on each side of the steps leading to the dome section. Individual magnifying-lens reading lamps were installed over the longitudinal seats beneath the dome compartment; also over cross seats in the card-table section. Center ceiling and baggage-rack lights in the main passenger compartment were unchanged.

In the redesigned coach the seats and carpets are peach color, and the window drapes in the main passenger section are blue. The lower walls under the dome compartment are a red tile, and the upper walls pale-yellow paint on metal inside finish. The glass panels above the center seats serve the double purpose of providing privacy and permitting a desirable decorative effect. The dome compartment is finished in gray and green with a maroon carpet. The stairway below the handrail is stainless steel; the upper walls are finished in surf green.

A recessed luggage space is provided at the sides of the stairway. Here your bags are easy of access and yet are out of the way.

At the present writing Vista-Dome cars are being included in new coach, parlor, and lounge car equipment on order by the Burlington, Rio Grande & Western Pacific, for service between

Chicago and Minneapolis, and between Chicago and Oakland.

That there will be many changes and refinements in these Vista-Dome cars there is no doubt, for this type of cupola coach offers a new and fertile field for the car designer. From the reception it has received it is evident that folks have been sold on the idea. The passenger finds a new thrill in every passing mile. From the Vista-Dome you get a first view and a last view of constantly unfolding grandeur, for it is an *observation* car in every sense of the word, and you also get a better look at the railroad you are riding over, and it would be a good thing if more of our citizens knew about them.

In keeping with its policy of constantly striving to provide the traveler with every luxury on his journey, the Chicago, Burlington & Quincy has once more added to its laurels by providing a "panoramic" passenger car from which to view better the wonders of America. It is the Burlington's contribution to further breath-taking adventures on the railroad's magic carpet.

CHAPTER XI

THE NORFOLK & WESTERN

The Railroad That Coal Built

The seed of the present great Norfolk & Western Railway system was planted in the earth millions of years ago. It grew in the form of luxuriant vegetation, which was absorbed finally by the forces of upheaval that marked the slow process of a world in the making. Out of this vast and turbulent crucible of the gods, mountains and valleys and rivers were molded, while deep beneath the earth's surface the once lush vegetation was subjected to heat and pressure. Gradually this vegetable matter took the form of sedimentary rock, consisting mainly of complex carbon compounds. And so, in labor, coal was born. The coal that built a railroad.

Coal generates 55 per cent of all the nation's electricity. It is the base for 85 per cent of all plastics. It is essential in making 100 per cent of the country's steel. It heats 4 out of 7 American homes. The annual value of coal mined in the United States is greater than that of all metals combined—5½ times the value of all gold; 22 times the value of all silver; 7 times the value of all copper; and 7 times the value of all iron.

Coal and the Norfolk & Western have had a vital part in the building of industrial America.

In 1946 the Norfolk & Western had been in operation 108 years, and today is one of the world's greatest coal carriers. The road has seen wars and depressions, hard times and good, and has continued to grow and thrive, its strong heartbeat the economic rock there in central Virginia. The principal contributing factors to the Norfolk & Western's strong position today are efficient operation, a huge volume of coal traffic, the finest type of rolling stock and roadbed, financial security, and, last but not least, its able and loyal family of employees, who number approximately 22,000.

The Norfolk & Western system, serving the vast bituminous coal fields in southwestern Virginia, southern West Virginia, and eastern Kentucky, comprises some 4,690 miles of track. In addition to lines in these states, the road operates in Ohio, Maryland, and North Carolina.

It was in 1881 that Vice-President Frederick J. Kimball discovered rich coal deposits in the town of Hutton, now called Pocahontas. This is the site of the famous Pocahontas coal seam. Immediately a new era of railroad building got under way, with the Norfolk & Western blazing a trail of steel through the mountains and gorges into the coal fields.

A railroad man is of a tenacious breed, refusing to be easily turned from his purpose or belief. We have as an example Fred J. Kimball's persistent search for coal in the Virginia mountains, in spite of certain adverse reports by geologists. Had he not read the notes of the great Thomas Jefferson—notes which referred to coal and other mineral wealth in Virginia? He pressed his search, and one day, accompanied by his wife and one or two others, went exploring in Abb's Valley in Tazewell County. The first actual mining operations in the history of coal were in the Midlothian mines about 1750, and it was in this year that Thomas Walker discovered coal in several places, including an outcrop of the Pocahontas seam.

But it was not until Fred Kimball dug into a hillside with his penknife in Abb's Valley, uncovering the thing called "black diamonds," that the development of the coal fields served by the Norfolk & Western began in earnest. Kimball and his associates immediately began the projection of a line into the area, and on March 12, 1883, the first carload of coal rolled from Pocahontas Vein No. 3. This was used for fuel by the railroad.

On March 17, Saint Patrick's Day, the first carload of coal from the Pocahontas vein was delivered to the mayor of Norfolk as a gift to the city.

During that year of 1883 some 100,000 tons of good Pocahontas coal were hauled by the Norfolk & Western. Four years later the tonnage had climbed to nearly a million tons. Today the figure has reached more than fifty million.

Between 1881 and 1892 the Norfolk & Western built three lines into the coal fields of Virginia and West Virginia and also extended their trackage into Ohio. The New River line, from New River Depot (now New River) to Pocahontas, Virginia, was opened in 1883. The Clinch Valley road, from Bluefield (Graham then) to Norton, Virginia, a distance of about 104 miles, was opened in 1891. Construction of the Ohio Extension from Elkhorn, West Virginia, to Ironton, Ohio, 195 miles, was completed in 1892. In July, 1890, the Norfolk & Western acquired the Scioto Valley & New England Railroad, extending from Coal Grove to Columbus, Ohio, a distance of 128.6 miles. In December of the same year it purchased the Shenandoah Valley Railway, operating 255 miles of main line and branches between Roanoke, Virginia, and Hagerstown, Maryland.

It was on September 24, 1896, that the Norfolk & Western Railroad was reorganized as the Norfolk & Western Railway Company. Later in the same year it purchased two lines running from Virginia into North Carolina: the Lynchburg & Durham Railroad, operating between Lynchburg and Durham, North Carolina, a distance of 115 miles, and the Roanoke & Southern Railway, 123 miles, running between Roanoke, Virginia, and Winston-Salem, North Carolina. Both of these roads had been operated by lease for a number of years. The Cincinnati, Portsmouth & Virginia Railroad, which operated between Sciotoville, Ohio, and Cincinnati, was conveyed to the Norfolk & Western in October, 1901.

This brief review of the Norfolk & Western tells nothing of the road's struggles and hardships, of the unflinching courage and determination of those men who guided its destiny—men like William Mahone, who bossed the heartbreaking, backbreaking job of laying track through Virginia's great Dismal Swamp, and all those others of steel will and iron heart, right on down to William J. Jenks, of the present-day Norfolk & Western system, who rose from telegrapher to the president's chair.

The most impressive single fact about the Norfolk & Western is the coal that it hauls. In 1943, the biggest coal year, 54,400,000 tons moved out to the various gateways. This represented 76 per cent of the total revenue freight handled, or 71,456,000 tons. Fifty-nine per cent of the system's freight revenue is derived from this coal traffic. Besides coal, the Norfolk & Western hauls lumber, wheat, tobacco, cotton, milling products, fruits, vegetables, livestock, refined petroleum, sheet and structural iron, fertilizer, cement, brick, and lime.

But it is coal with which we are mainly concerned—coal by the trainload, flowing in an endless black flood to the ends of the earth. Coal from the great Kenova district, from the Tug River fields, from Pocahontas No. 3. Coal for Minnesota, South Dakota, Kansas; coal for the Midwest, the ports on the Great Lakes, the South; coal for New York and New England; coal for the Irish Free State, the Scandinavian ports, for Holland, the Mediterranean; coal for the Far East, for Cuba, for South America. More than 61,000 tons of coal have been dumped at the Norfolk & Western tidewater terminal at Lambert Point, Virginia, in one day.

Forty-nine thousand coal cars and 310 locomotives are required to move this enormous volume of bituminous coal, and this equipment must be maintained in top shape always. The motive power of the Norfolk & Western includes great compound Mallets, single-expansion articulated combination freight and passenger locomotives and 16 big electric locomotives for work on the heavy mountain grades, 76 miles of which are electrified.

Approximately 180,000 tons of coal come out of the mining districts during an average 24-hour period. This represents the output of 143 mining operations and requires some 3,000 cars, or the equivalent of a solid train 20 miles long. The handling of this tremendous tonnage involves loading, tagging, branch-line haul, and a movement of 25 to 190 miles to classification points at Bluefield and Portsmouth.

Corresponding to and skillfully interwoven with the outgoing movement is the flow of empty cars to the mine tipples. Men and trains move with machinelike precision. Roaring exhausts shout constantly at the hills, and thousands of wheels tramp the rail in solemn black-hooded caravan.

The coal fields served by the Norfolk & Western are divided into 8 districts. Northernmost is the Kenova district, extending from Williamson, West Virginia, to Kenova, near the Ohio-Kentucky-West Virginia border. The Thacker district extends from Williamson to Iager, West Virginia, extending a short distance into Kentucky, Virginia, and West Virginia. The Upper Buchanan and Clinch Valley Nos. 1 and 2 districts are in southwest Virginia. The Tug River district reaches from Welsh to Iager and from Iager nearly to Berwind, West Virginia, bordering the rich and famous Pocahontas district in the extreme southern corner of West Virginia. The Radford district, separated from the before-named group, is divided into 6 smaller groups running between Christianburg and Wytheville, Virginia.

The coal seams in the Pocahontas, Tag River, and Upper Buchanan districts range in thickness from 3 feet to 12 feet. This is low volatile coal—smokeless and high in fixed carbon—of the highest quality. Because of their purity and high heat content these coals have many uses and a wide distribution.

High volatile coal, described as an "all-purpose" fuel, is mined chiefly in the Williamson field in Mingo and Wayne counties, West Virginia; Buchanan County, Virginia; Pike and Martin counties, Kentucky; and in the Clinch Valley field in Tazewell, Russell, and Wise counties, Virginia.

One of the chief assets of coal mined along the Norfolk & Western is its preparation before shipping. In other words, its cleanliness and freedom from foreign matter, and its correct sizing and careful handling, which assures a minimum of breakage.

Electric motors haul the mine cars from the mine, and these cars are unloaded by two methods—a rotary dumper in some cases, and again by tilting the car. The coal is discharged into small hoppers beneath the unloading machinery. Then it is moved to the tipple by conveyors, being fed then onto a series of shaking screens which separate it into the various sizes required for domestic and industrial use. The motion of the tilted shaking screens keeps the coal moving forward. The first screen has very small perforations through which slack coal passes directly to waiting railroad cars below. The next screen has slightly larger holes. These trap the pea-size coal. The remaining coal passes over other screens, sifting out the nut, stove, and egg sizes, leaving finally only the lump coal at the end of the shaking screens.

The next point in preparation of coal is the cleaning. In many tipples, the small sizes are washed, a process based on the difference in the specific gravity of the coal and the usual foreign materials that may have passed through the screens. The foreign matter sinks to the bottom of the washing tank and is drawn off, leaving only clean coal for delivery to the loading booms.

In other tipples the smaller sizes of coal are dry-cleaned, by using air and agitation for separation instead of water.

Larger sizes of coal, after screening, move on to picking tables where alert workmen remove the foreign matter by hand as the coal slowly passes past them. When the screening and cleaning processes are completed, the coal is conveyed to the railroad cars. This is accomplished by means of loading booms which carefully lower the coal into the cars so as to avoid breakage. These booms are simply endless conveyor belts.

The coal tipples in the Norfolk & Western territory were among the first to be equipped with dustless installations. This treatment is accomplished by means of sprays located at the end of the loading booms, which give the coal passing into the cars a thorough coating of oil, calcium chloride, or some similar compound. The result is a product that is not only clean, but dustless as well. This makes for a strong selling point when the dealer offers his wares. It is one of the reasons why this coal mined in these famed fields has been given the name of "Fuel Satisfaction."

Fuel Satisfaction grew out of a meeting between the railroad heads and the mineowners back in 1928. Arthur C. Needles, then president of the Norfolk & Western, said in effect: "Gentlemen, your business is mining coal; our business is hauling it. By putting our heads together we should find a way to make an even greater market for the coal we handle."

As a result of that meeting Norfolk & Western "Coal Bureaus" were established at strategic points throughout the country. These bureaus were manned by fuel and combustion experts,

Southern Pacific #98, the Los Angeles Daylight, running along the Pacific Ocean on the Coast Division. Note the oil derricks in the ocean. Courtesy Southern Pacific Railroad.

C.&O. work train in action near Robbins, Ohio, on the Northern Subdivision of the Cincinnati Division. Courtesy Chesapeake & Ohio Railroad.

C.&O. steel gang laying new rail near Aldson, W. Va., on the Allegheny Subdivision the Clifton Forge Division. Courtesy Chepeake & Ohio Railroad.

urlington, Colorado Southern streamlined
exas Zephyr running over the Rio Grande
uth of Denver where the C.&S. and the
nta Fe have joint trackage rights over that
ad's Pueblo Division. Photo by Preston
orge.

Meeting an eastward freight train from a new
Vista-Dome coach east of Aurora, Ill., on the
Burlington's Denver Zephyr. Courtesy Chicago,
Burlington & Quincy Railroad

The conductor of a Southern Pacific eastward freight train gives a highball to a flagman on #51, the San Joaquin Daylight as they meet on double track near Bena, Calif., on the San Joaquin Division. Coθrtesy Southern, Pacific Railroad.

S.P. rotary snowplow being pushed by Engine #4004, 2-8-8-2 type, Class AC-1, first of the cab-ahead engines at Summit, Calif., on the Sacramento Division. Courtesy Southern Pacific Railroad.

N.&W. first #3 coach section of the Pocahontas, with Engine #600, 4-8-4 type, class J, built at the Roanoke Shops and equipped with roller-bearing rods, descending the west slope of the Blue Ridge Mts. at Bonsack, Va., on the Norfolk Division. The grade is 1.2%. Courtesy Norfolk & Western Railroad.

The great eastbound N.&W. classification yard at Roanoke, Va., showing: (lower left) hump signal, retarders, master scales and scalehouse, retarder control towers, floodlight towers; (far left) ice dock; (outside right) eastward running track, thence cab tracks. Courtesy Norfolk & Western Railroad.

N.&W. freight conductor of Time Freight #99 writing up his conductor's book from the wheel report between Roanoke and Elliston on the Radford Division. Courtesy Norfolk & Western Railroad.

B.&O. #4, the eastbound Diplomat, at Rawlings, Md., on the Cumberland Division hauled by 2-unit 4,000-h.p. passenger Diesel. Photo by H. W. Pontin. Courtesy Rail Photo Service.

and their duty was to provide advice and assistance to distributors and users of coal. An advertising campaign was initiated, illustrated literature was distributed, and the black gold buried deep in the Appalachian Mountains was lifted to the eminence deserved by the most important economic mineral known to man.

The advertisements and pamphlets told the story of coal from its beginning millions of years ago to the glowing fire in the furnace of the home. They told the story of Pocahontas No. 3, a seam 12 feet thick at the point of discovery; the story of mining and of transportation to the steel mill, to the boiler of the electric-light plant, to the kitchen stove. The story of "Fuel Satisfaction."

Industrial history has not produced a greater story of the manner in which the railroads serve the nation.

The Norfolk & Western, hand-in-hand with the coal industry, has developed its facilities and services better to satisfy the fuel markets of the world.

One of the first railroad men on the job when the day's work begins in the coal fields is the car distributor. He is charged with arranging for and providing the right number and types of cars to be delivered to the coal mines each day.

Empty trains start out from Bluefield and Williamson in the morning, working their way into the coal fields—Bluefield, West Virginia, at the eastern border of the coal district, and Williamson, West Virginia, at the western edge. For example, 500 empties will be set off at Eckman to take care of the loading requirements of the 20 mines served from this assembly point. Mine run crews then move the empties to the various tipples of the branch line.

When the loads are picked up, the mine orders the number of empties needed for the next day's loading. The mine run crews gather up these loaded cars at the tipples and bring them out to the assembly point. Here they are made into trains which start the run to classification points.

Eastbound coal is weighed and billed at the Roanoke Yards; westbound loads are weighed and billed at Portsmouth, unless they are destined for points east of Portsmouth, Ohio, in which case they are billed at Williamson, West Virginia. Cars for points between the mines and Roanoke are weighed and billed at Bluefield, West Virginia.

The greatest number of mines served is between Bluefield and Williamson, and the dispatcher at Bluefield will handle an average of 125 trains during a normal day's operation.

When loaded cars are ready to leave the tipple tracks, each car is tagged. Cars move on "mine tags" as far as weighing points, and by waybill from there to their destination. A white tag is attached to eastbound cars to be weighed at Roanoke, while green tags are for westbound loads to be classified at Portsmouth. A mixed blue-and-white tag is put on cars to be moved from the mines to Williamson or points between Williamson and Portsmouth. Orange tags are attached to cars destined for points between the mines and Roanoke. These are classified at Bluefield.

Modern scales maintained at Portsmouth, Bluefield, Roanoke, and Lambert Point are accurate to the nth degree. The weights are typed on the original mine tag by an automatic recorder as the car passes slowly over the scales, thus insuring absolute accuracy.

Coal classified at Portsmouth then moves on to western terminals at Columbus and Cincinnati, some for delivery there, but mostly for shipment to the West, the Midwest, and the Great Lakes region. Coal classified at Roanoke moves to the road's ocean terminal at Norfolk (Lambert Point). Here the coal is dumped into the holds of ships loading for New England and foreign ports. Other coal cars classified at Roanoke move south through North Carolina, while a small percentage of the coal traffic travels up the Shenandoah Valley route to northern points.

The Rear End of a Coal Train

We can better follow the movement of a coal train by riding one, so let's board the caboose of a drag about to pull out of Williamson, West Virginia, bound for the great western terminal at Columbus, Ohio. Over this route moves the greatest portion of westbound tonnage (68 per cent of all coal handled by the Norfolk & Western moves to western gateways).

Our tonnage out of Williamson is 10,000 net tons—enough coal to heat 1,200 homes for an entire winter. The tonnage rating from Williamson to Portsmouth is 13,000 gross tons.

Before we highball we are first going to follow the movement of our conductor, a 24-year veteran of the road. This is pretty much the usual routine with freight conductors anywhere.

The conductor reports for duty at the Williamson yard office perhaps half an hour or so before his train is scheduled to leave. He is informed as to the location of his train; then he compares his watch with the standard clock in the office and notes the accuracy of his watch in a book provided for that purpose. He checks the bulletin board for orders and notices posted since his last trip; he also checks the train register to familiarize himself with movements in and out of the terminal.

You remember, the coal cars in these westbound trains carry their mine tags until they are weighed and billed at Portsmouth.

Our coal-train conductor gets his clearance and his orders. Before the train pulls out, in company with the brakeman, he will inspect the train, looking over brake rigging, draft gear, grab irons, ladders, steps, and so forth. He finally compares watches with the engineer and other members of the crew, and we are ready to go.

In the cabin car the rear brakeman has a fire going in the pot-bellied stove, and the conductor settles down to check over his orders and do his paper work. Our consist has been wired ahead to Portsmouth Yard, and this will later aid in the prompt classification of our coal cars upon arrival. The conductor is busy on his switch list, which will prove a further aid to the yard crews. He also copies the car numbers into his conductor's train book for his own records.

We are moving over a well-tailored double track, winding through the mountains along the bank of the Tug Fork of the Big Sandy. Always there are alert eyes in the cupola watching for hotboxes, sticking brakes, rigging dragging, or anything which might cause trouble. When we meet other trains, the crews shout across the car to each other, "On the railroad," and the flagman goes out on the rear end to inspect the other train. They never fail to observe this important duty on all roads on single, double, or more tracks.

There is a train inspection when we stop at Prichard, West Virginia, for coal and water. The cabin car's coffeepot offers fragrant invitation, and as we leave Prichard behind we sample the rear brakeman's coffee-making ability.

The steady beat of the exhaust comes back to us above the tramp of wheels. The big Mallet is working hard. We pass Kenova and cross the Ohio River. Coal Grove, Ironton, Hanging Rock slip past. Franklin Furnace. Sciotoville. We are thundering toward Portsmouth Yard now—a big, sprawling 10,300-car yard. The whistle shouts, and the barking stack ahead lessens, seeming relieved that the grueling run up from Williamson is done.

The conductor notes the time of our arrival at the yard board and pull-in track on his time slip and switch list. He has made out his register slip, showing the names of his crew, the time they reported for duty, and the time we left Williamson Yard. On the back of this slip there is a delay report form with spaces to indicate any possible delays en route.

A yard crew takes over in Portsmouth Yard. The conductor completes his time slip, showing the time the crew went off duty, checks in at the yard office, registers off, and his job is done.

Our coal train is broken down, the green tags are removed, and the cars are weighed and humped in the classification yard. Within a few hours the waybills are ready, and we prepare to pull out. This, we'll say, is Extra 2115 West, the engine a 2-8-8-2 Mallet. Our tonnage is a little less than we had out of Williamson, for the Portsmouth-Columbus rating is 11,000 tons.

Our new conductor gets his stack of waybills and his C.R. 10, or "wheel report," from the yard office. This wheel report is in triplicate, and it supplies data on the train from headlight to markers.

The wheel report is a large ruled sheet with columns and spaces for the record of each car in the train, its number, contents, net and gross weight. On this report is the entire consist of the train and report of its trip under this conductor, including the number of the engine and the name of the engineer.

It shows the actual leaving time and arriving time, the division, direction, total number of cars, tonnage out of the initial point, and tonnage at the end of the run. There is a space on the back for switching data; also a space in which the conductor makes his weather report. And finally there is the conductor's signature.

These wheel reports are bound in sets and are made in triplicate by the use of carbon sheets. Agents or yardmasters at initial points make out and deliver this report to the conductor before departure of the train. At the end of the run the conductor hands this report to the agent or yardmaster, who must receipt for it in the conductor's train book.

Sheet 3 of the wheel report is retained by the terminal yard and used as a record of cars received. Sheets 1 and 2 are immediately forwarded to the Superintendent of Car Service.

All rolling stock on the road is listed on the back of this C.R. 10 form, including the types of freight cars, their series numbers, capacity in tons, and weight in pounds. There is a list of the non-revenue equipment, such as inspection cars, instruction cars, scale test cars, dynamometer cars, camp cars, and caboose cars. There is a list of locomotive cranes, with their ton capacity and weight in pounds; a list of engine tenders, with their weight loaded and empty and their capacity in gallons. Another space indicates all locomotives and tenders and the numbers, class, and weight in pounds. Passenger equipment is listed, including business cars, baggage and mail cars, dining cars, coaches, and sleepers. And there is a list of the road's steam wrecking cranes, with their series numbers, capacity, and weight.

The total weight of all cars in the train, including caboose, must be shown in thousands of pounds out of initial point and at the end of the run for each district.

As we leave Portsmouth behind a big 2-6-6-4 engine, the conductor begins checking over his waybills and comparing them against his wheel report. The rear brakeman is in the cupola watching the train. The roadbed slips away behind us like a neatly patterned stair carpet. We stop at Renick for water, and there is another inspection of the train. Leaving Renick, we cross the Scioto River. Our train finally pulls into Columbus.

Here the train is broken down in the classification yard again, as cars are sorted out for distribution to other rail lines, the majority of the coal now moving over the tracks of the Chesapeake & Ohio, the New York Central, and the Pennsylvania roads.

Eastbound Movement: A coal train assembled at Williamson Yard for eastbound movement travels first to Eckman, West Virginia, behind steam motive power, but here there is an operational problem requiring the use of electric power. The steep mountain grades demand greater power and efficiency for the movement of tonnage trains. To meet these requirements, a shuttle service employing powerful electric engines is maintained over the 24-mile route from Eckman to Bluefield.

Electric locomotives were found to be more efficient for this job, for their use eliminated the double-heading required when steam motive power was used. An electric engine and crew make several trips in an ordinary day.

At Bluefield steam crews tackle the job again, moving the coal trains on to Roanoke, stopping only at Dry Branch, Blake, and Elliston, Virginia, for water and inspection. Approaching the top of the mountain near Christianburg, where our helper is cut off, the conductor checks the air pressure registered on the cabin car gauge, and we drop down the hill.

The train is broken up for classification at Roanoke, and coal cars soon begin their journeys north, south, and east. Our drag finally rolls on toward seaboard. We cross the beautiful Blue Ridge Mountains and move on across the low country of eastern Virginia to Crewe, with stops at Lowry for water and inspection and at Phoebe for water and coal. Crewe is a small but important division point. Crews change here and trains are combined, since the tonnage rating from this point to tidewater is 12,500 gross tons. En route to the great coal terminal at Lambert Point, one stop is made at Disputanta for water.

At Lambert Point all loads are reclassified and prepared to move onto the piers for unloading. Cars are "motion-weighed" as they move from the classification yard to the docks. Normally about 7,000,000 tons of coal move over this route every year.

Of the total commercial coal tonnage produced on the lines of the Norfolk & Western in normal years, about 32 per cent moves east and 68 per cent west from the coal fields. Approximately 19 per cent of the road's coal haul is delivered to tidewater at Lambert Point, Norfolk, where it rides away down the highway of ships.

NORFOLK AND WESTERN RAILWAY CO.

CHAPTER XII

THE VOICE OF THE SANTA FE

A Great Railway's Communication System

In Baltimore, Maryland, in 1844, tense faces watched the bar of a crude instrument called a "telegraph sounder" fluttering up and down. Slowly it formed a series of dots and dashes—*dot two dashes, four dots, dot dash, dash.* . . . In the United States Supreme Court in Washington, forty miles away, Professor Samuel F. B. Morse spelled out words by opening and closing an instrument called a "telegraph key." When the message clicking over the wire had at last been copied, it read, "What hath God wrought!"

That day the telegraph was born, and the foundation laid for the modern network of world communications.

On September 22, 1851, Charles Minot, Superintendent of the Erie Railway, first used the telegraph in train dispatching. In 1853 Gintl, a Viennese, produced *duplex* telegraphy, whereby two messages could be sent over a single wire at the same time— one in each direction. Thomas A. Edison, in 1874, made possible *quadruplex* telegraphy, which flashed *two* messages each way over one wire simultaneously.

At the Centennial Exhibition in Philadelphia in 1876, the *telephone* was revealed to America, its inventor Alexander Graham Bell of Massachusetts. In 1895 Marconi flashed the first *wireless* message. A great wireless station was erected at Wellfleet on Cape Cod, and in 1903 President Theodore Roosevelt sent to King Edward of England the first wireless message to cross the Atlantic.

In 1946 the Santa Fe Railroad's communication facilities were handling the greatest volume of telegraph and telephone messages of any transportation system in the world.

Transportation and communications are today so closely allied that the need of the one for the other is tightly interwoven in the fabric of the railroad system. The steel rail and the copper wire have been spun into the pattern of the magic carpet that today links the far horizons.

The most remote outpost of the railroad is but a whisper from the heart of its rail empire. The Super Chief, speeding across the great Mojave, is under the finger of the train dispatcher constantly. The fast freight on the Pecos Division becomes a red dot winking across the board of the C.T.C. machine at Clovis, New Mexico. The conductor of the "Spud Special," out of Bakersfield, California, talks with the engineer out of sight around the curve simply by picking up the transmitter of his intertrain communication set. The teletype transmits wheel reports and advance switch lists almost in a twinkling. The stationmaster at the Los Angeles Union station makes announcements to the hundreds of travelers in the waiting rooms and patios over the public address system.

Not only has the Santa Fe pioneered in many phases of railway communications, but it has anticipated developments and paved the way for their introduction. Santa Fe engineers years ago foresaw the application of high-frequency multi-channel operation to its services and began transposing and preparing their communication lines for the things they knew were coming. Pole lines were worked over, iron wire was replaced by copper, telephone circuits were modernized, improving the quality of voice transmission over both the physical and phantom circuits. In other words, the Santa Fe was putting its house in order, as the architect of the modern day included in his blueprints wiring and outlets for the telephone and the radio.

Progress in rail communications has advanced rapidly since the days when trains moved warily over a single track by time card and "smoke orders." The complexity of the present system of communications demands a high degree of skill both in operation and maintenance of an enormous network of pole lines, channels, circuits, switchboards, switching centers, and relay offices, for it involves the harnessing and directing of vast electro-motive forces and impulses. The training and instruction of many specialists is necessary.

A staff of some 2,700 men and women is required to operate the Santa Fe communication system, which is the largest and most modern privately owned communication system on earth. The Santa Fe installations include the following:

		Wire miles
13,123	miles of pole line	
13,310	circuit miles dispatching telephone	26,620
10,734	circuit miles conversational telephone	21,468
3,403	circuit miles phantom telephone	6,806
18,229	circuit miles carrier telephone	37,458
45,676	total telephone circuit miles	92,352
1,539	miles Morse dispatching	1,529
20,403	miles Simplex circuit used in printing telegraph service	40,806
15,149	miles Morse circuits in railroad way service	15,149
15,695	miles Morse circuits in joint commercial way service	15,695
18,146	miles carrier channels in multiplex printing telegraph service	108,876
93,094	total telegraph circuit miles	226,397
139,770	grand total	318,749

The Communications Department of the Santa Fe, under the able supervision of J. A. Parkinson, is charged with the construction, maintenance, and operation of all Santa Fe telegraph and telephone communications, electronics and allied research, the administration of duties incident to the Santa Fe's contract with Western Union, the operating agreements with the Bell and other telephone companies, and construction specifications of foreign line wire crossings and parallelisms on Santa Fe rights of way.

Efficiency of operation and the quick restoration of service is absolutely essential at all times, and upon the following officers rests the responsibility of seeing that Santa Fe communications are kept in order:

E. K. Metzdorf, assistant superintendent
    of communications, Topeka   System Lines
C. O. Overbey, assistant superintendent
    of communications, Los Angeles   Coast Lines
W. C. Hankison, communications manager,
    Amarillo   Western Lines
J. L. Lee, communications manager, Galveston   Gulf Lines

These officers are charged with the maintenance and supervision of relay telegraph offices, telephone and telegraph facilities both inside and outside of plants, and the flow of telephone and telegraph traffic within the designated territories. Each is assisted by a communications construction engineer. Division linemen are stationed on each local operating division. Five line construction crews constantly move about the Santa Fe System lines, handling construction and repair work. This force is augmented as the need arises.

The staff of the Superintendent of Communications consists of an electronics engineer who is in charge of engineering, plan layout, tests, electronics exploration, and development and supervision of installations; a telegraph engineer who supervises installations and maintains telegraph facilities; a telegraph traffic supervisor who supervises telegraph traffic; a communications engineer, supervising maintenance and manufacturing or fabrication work in the Topeka telegraph shop; a construction engineer, supervising on-line construction and pole-line and line-crew work; a telephone engineer, supervising installation and maintenance of telephone equipment; a telegraph and telephone supervisor, directing installation and maintenance of equipment under the electronics, telegraph, and telephone engineers.

Well within the memory of many a man on the Santa Fe is the day when a telegraph engineer required little more than a knowledge of the fundamentals of a crow's-foot battery and resistance coils, a knowledge shared by any Morse operator or lineman. A break in the line was located by a Wheatstone bridge, and a trouble shooter went out and repaired it. That was about all there was to it. The "quads," which made possible the sending and receiving of two messages each way over the same wire, were a bit complicated, but nothing like the intricate mechanisms employed in today's communications.

Each Santa Fe grand operating division has a number of relay telegraph offices. These are staffed by a manager or a wire chief, a night wire chief, a late night wire chief, telegraphers, telegrapher-printer clerks, printer clerks, messengers, and apprentices, who handle some 62,000,000 telegrams transmitted each year over the Santa Fe telegraph facilities. The Santa Fe private branch telephone exchanges (P.B.X.) handle local commercial Santa Fe calls at terminal or population centers, and the 9,500,000 long-distance calls.

A chart prepared by the Communications Department governs the routing of Santa Fe telegraphic traffic directed to other railways. Commercial facilities, with some exceptions, are used for Santa Fe telegrams and telephone calls directed to Santa Fe patrons or Santa Fe offices beyond the Santa Fe premises or territories.

Printing-telegraph service is established with the Santa Fe's traffic offices in Boston, Philadelphia, Pittsburgh, Buffalo, and Washington through a re-perforator switching center located in the Santa Fe's New York offices. The cities of Minneapolis, Milwaukee, Detroit, Cleveland, Cincinnati, Atlanta, St. Louis, and Des Moines are handled through a similar switching center in Chicago. There is, in addition, a two-way printing-telegraph service between the New York offices and the Pullman reservation and information bureaus at Chicago and Los Angeles. Santa Fe Pullman and information bureaus at Chicago, Kansas City, and Los Angeles are provided with especially designed communication installations to meet the service demands at these centers.

Fred G. Gurley, able president of the Santa Fe, has often stated that a railway is no better than its communications. Modern train operation, with its multiplicity of details, fast schedules, and improved services, depends upon the extent and quality of the road's system of communication.

Each step in the progress of the Santa Fe has been marked by enlarged and modernized communication facilities, and in late years this modernization often has preceded other Santa Fe inaugurations and improvements. Almost all Santa Fe offices are serviced by either a train dispatcher's or a network telephone. Convenient intercommunication closely links all the Santa Fe people, enabling them to provide prompt and efficient service to the patrons of the line.

Since its earliest operations, the Santa Fe has made use of the telegraph, train-order signals, and other features made possible by the introduction of the Morse telegraph.

At one time all Santa Fe messages were transmitted by the Morse code, and it still remains an important cog in the communication system of the road. However, the telephone was employed for train dispatching on the Santa Fe between Emporia and Newton, Kansas, beginning in December, 1908. By 1911 the entire main line was thus equipped.

The day-to-day routine of transmitting local Western Union telegrams and Santa Fe company messages at small stations, or those not equipped with printer-telegraph, is by Morse operation. But at terminals and at all points where relay telegraph offices are located, at population centers and sizable traveling and shipping points, modern printer-telegraph and carrier-current systems, using superimposed modulated frequencies (wire radio), provide capacity and necessarily prompt service.

With multi-channel carrier equipment—the newest improvement in telegraphy—the Santa Fe has added onto 2 properly transposed copper wires, up to 3 trunk lines, or, where desired, 2 through telephone circuits and up to 14 duplex printing-telegraph circuits. For example, 2 copper wires used for telephone train dispatching, properly transposed, may be used to carry simultaneously as many as 3 other conversations, or 2 other conversations and as many as 28—14 each way—printing-telegraph messages without interfering with the normal use of the wires for train dispatching.

Multi-channel carrier equipment—30 kc. (type C)—as installed on the Santa Fe, extends from Chicago to the Pacific Coast and to Galveston. Separate units connect Chicago with Topeka, Kansas, Topeka with Fort Worth, Texas, and Fort Worth with Galveston. Another branch connects Topeka with Amarillo, in the Texas Panhandle; still another links Amarillo with La Junta, Colorado. The latter is connected with Topeka,

Kansas, and Albuquerque, New Mexico, over the northern route of the Santa Fe. Amarillo, in turn, is hooked up with Los Angeles, and Los Angeles with San Francisco.

This equipment is the first to combine both wide- and narrow-band circuits in the same speech-frequency channel. For example, between Topeka and Chicago there are 7 narrow-band channels for single teleprinter working, spaced at 150 cycles with intervals beginning at 525 cycles; and 3 wide channels for multiplex working at 1950, 2250, and 2550 cycles. In other sections on the Santa Fe system there are various combinations of wide and narrow channels. At predetermined intervals on each circuit, repeating amplifiers raise the level (voice) of all channels to a high quantity of uniformity. On a Chicago to Los Angeles call this amplification takes place at Corwith and Streator in Illinois, Shopton, Iowa, and Marceline, Missouri, and at similar intervals across the country.

The printing-telegraph machine, commonly called the teletype, or teleprinter, has a standard typewriter keyboard. Its maximum printing capacity is about 60 words per minute. These machines are located in 96 printer offices throughout the Santa Fe system, and they transmit such important items as wheel reports, as we have mentioned, advance switch lists, and data concerning Red Ball freight. Frequently Topeka, Chicago, or other terminals toward which the fast freight is moving receive information well in advance of its arrival concerning its consist, the location of the cars in the train, whether certain cars will need re-icing, possible switching movements, and the like. Often this information is received before the train has left its originating terminal.

Being thus informed, yardmasters may plan switching movements far in advance, and when switching is so expedited the yard capacity is increased. Anything reducing terminal detention is a matter of first importance.

The handling of diversions to carload freight is also an important service dependent on this sort of quick communication. Delivery of freight to consignee and to connecting lines is speeded up.

At Los Angeles and San Francisco, California, Chicago, Illinois, Winslow, Arizona, and Fort Worth, Texas, manual relaying of Santa Fe telegraph traffic has been virtually eliminated by the use of carrier-current telegraph channels and the installation of switching centers. All teletype circuits within the area served by a switching center terminate in a switchboard. Switchboards serving the various centers are linked by trunk lines. A Santa Fe printer office can be connected with as many as 6 offices, transmitting simultaneously a multiple addressed message to all 6 points; also at the same time receive a message from any one of the offices to which transmission is being made.

At Santa Fe switching centers, teletype connections are effected in a manner similar to telephone calls passing through a private branch exchange. An office signals the switching-center attendant, who determines the other office desired and sets up the connection. At the conclusion of the transmission, the sending office gives a "disconnect" signal, and the circuit is restored to normal. If the switching attendant desires, a receiving printer may be cut in and so obtain a copy of the message.

It is never necessary for an originating office to wait for a particular circuit because it happens to be busy. When a desired circuit is reported busy, the calling office is given a re-perforator, which perforates the message on a tape. The message can then be transmitted at such time as the circuit is available. Teletype switchboard circuits are designed for full duplex operation, or the simultaneous transmission of a message each way at the same time.

The Santa Fe has the distinction of having operated the first transcontinental train using radio end-to-end communication. This end-to-end communication took place on the potato train we have mentioned and was highly successful. In the field of electronics, which made possible the establishment of the Santa Fe's telephone network, constant study and observance is under way. Some intricate and highly efficient circuit designs have been developed in the company's laboratories, including the application of vacuum tubes in place of electrically operated mechanical relays.

The practicability of utilizing the facsimile in railway service has been investigated, but research has not developed sufficiently to forecast to what extent or how it may be used.

On the Santa Fe, telegraph line crews handle the important task of conditioning the wires for the high-frequency or carrier-current system. The work consists of transposing on point brackets the telephone circuits used for these carrier systems. This is essential, for carrier circuits will not operate successfully without such transposing. It is a rather complicated process and demands the highest skill on the part of the linemen.

Pole lines are of a suspension type and are subjected to the most adverse weather conditions. Ice loading, wind, and water are the three major causes of pole-line and wire prostration. Failures caused by storms seem to occur in cycles and in about the same areas. Certain sections of the Santa Fe's lines are regularly subjected to attack by the elements, and it means work for the trouble shooter. When flash trouble reports are received, the engineers of the Communications Department know from experience what to look for in the locality of the disturbance, and crews and the proper materials are on the way in a hurry.

The task of transposing the telephone circuits was an enormous one, for it embraced all main-line routes, Chicago to Newton, Kansas; Newton to Belen, New Mexico, via the northern and southern districts of the Santa Fe's western lines; Belen to San Diego, California; Newton to Galveston, and various side routes.

Since the wires are transposed every 260 to 520 feet, every pole on the line had to be worked. However, it was a contributing factor in making the Santa Fe outstanding in the private communications field.

So broad are these communication facilities that the failure of one through route has little effect on the prompt movement of messages, for in almost all cases the route can be by-passed by "patching," or routing messages over an alternate route.

The telephone and telegraph, because they make possible the quick exchange of intelligence, set in motion forces which otherwise would be static for long periods. The telegraph has not only opened the way to a greater transportation world, but also has created broader horizons, scientifically, educationally, and socially.

Electronics enable us to detect odorless gases, to see through fog and storm and darkness, to speed communications. The possibilities in this field appear limitless as we stand on the threshold of even greater miracles. The tiny electrical particles revolving

Santa Fe

Form 933 Standard

TRAIN ORDER NO. 316   OCT 9   19 45

To

C AND E NO 17

C AND E NO 21

C AND E WESTWARD EXTRAS LEAVING FROM MAIN TRACK

At	SHOPTON	X	Opr.	M.

ON NO 2 OR WESTWARD TRACK BETWEEN KENWOOD AND

HURDLAND FROM M P 297 TO M P 298 SPEED LIMIT

80 MILES PER HOUR

MMK

THIS MARGIN NOT TO BE WRITTEN UPON

THIS MARGIN NOT TO BE WRITTEN UPON

Made *Com*   time *8 27* PM.   *Bird*   Opr.

An unusual slow order, the only order of its kind the author has ever seen.

around each atom are being harnessed and controlled, and no man has the vision fully to estimate the wonders of the world of tomorrow.

The expansion of the Santa Fe from a small Kansas enterprise into a mighty transcontinental transportation system has brought about many changes in its operations, including the growth of its first Morse circuit to the present vast modern communication network—the voice of the Santa Fe.

CHAPTER XIII

THE AMERICAN LOCOMOTIVE COMPANY

The Story of Alco at Home and at War

Rommel, storming the gates of Alexandria, was beaten at Sche-nectady, New York, in 1848!

The great German army lost the battle of Stalingrad 100 years ago!

Historians may find it difficult to reconcile these statements with certain recorded facts concerning these great battles, and yet in the last analysis they must stand unchallenged.

The legions of the Desert Fox were drawn up before El Ala-mein. Montgomery was making his last stand before Alexandria. This was to be the crucial battle, with possibly the entire trend of World War II in the balance. This was November, 1942. History was in the making in the crucible of war.

Only a few hundred kilometers—a very few—separated Rom-mel's steel from the British jugular—Suez and the Red Sea. Breathlessly the world waited for news of the battle. And then the vast silence of the great Qattara Depression was rolled back by the ear-shattering thunder of massed belching guns, among them a top-secret weapon—a mobile 105-mm. gun called the M-7.

One thousand of these M-7's, built at Schenectady, New York, by the American Locomotive Company, hurled their shells at the surprised Rommel in such an artillery barrage as the world had never seen. Crushed, stunned, beaten, the Nazis fell back. It was the beginning of the German retreat across North Africa to Cape Bon, to the Italian boot, and beyond.

The Schenectady Locomotive Engine Manufactury, founded in Schenectady in 1848, later became the Schenectady plant of the American Locomotive Company. And American Locomotive, from rough pencil sketch to "mock-up" to hurried final production, created the weapon that played a major part in turning the tide of the battle that sent the Desert Fox and his shattered forces reeling back.

The men and women of Alco (American Locomotive Company) developed and built the mighty M-7 almost from scratch. And they kept their secret. The people of Schenectady watched the M-7's trundling through the streets on the beginning of this mystery weapon's journey to the Aberdeen Proving Grounds—and they kept the secret. . . .

The German hordes were before Stalingrad. Russia was fighting with her back to the wall. Russia desperately needed supplies —guns, ammunition, tanks. Russia was engaged in a life-and-death struggle for her very existence. Russia, for all of her vast storehouse of raw materials and her manpower, was lacking in one thing—the ability to produce in quantity those machines of war that spell the difference between victory and destruction.

The Mediterranean was closed, the Dardanelles were closed, the northern Murmansk route was a graveyard of ships and heroic men. There was but one route, one sure route, into Russia, and that was Iran—Persia. Between the Persian Gulf and the Caspian Sea runs a railroad 650 miles in length—the toughest piece of railroad track in the world.

A thin life line of steel, which now was carrying a small trickle of vital supplies—the quaint, poorly equipped Trans-Iranian Railway, built by a former shah. Over half of the tonnage hauled by the steam locomotives of the Trans-Iranian Railway was coal and water to supply the appalling appetite of its wheezing engines on the journey across the mountains and deserts.

Freighters were piling up supplies on the shores of the Persian Gulf for transshipment to the Caspian Sea and Russia. But that 650 miles of a funny little railroad was the bottleneck that choked them off. "How," cried the generals, "can we break it? How?"

The United States Government turned to the men of the American Locomotive Company and asked, "Can it be done?" And Alco said, "Yes!" All during World War II American manufacturers and American railroads were answering, "Yes!" no matter how difficult the assignment. Never did they answer, "No." Not once—when the chips were down.

American Locomotive technicians moved in on Iran, confident of their ability to whip the toughest railroading job on earth. And it had to be done in a hurry, for war does not wait. The precision-trained armies of the "Master Race," superbly equipped, were counting the battle of Stalingrad already won.

Before we follow through with the tight-lipped men of Alco, let's take a brief look at this Trans-Iranian Railway and the country it traverses. Included in its twisting right of way are 150 miles of desert with temperatures ranging to 170 degrees Fahrenheit; there are 7,000-foot mountain ranges where the thermometer tumbles to 40 degrees below zero. The track threads through 225 tunnels and squirms around dizzy 25-degree curves. It throws its steel rail across deep chasms and canyons and gorges and lesser depressions at 450 places. It is a railroad man's nightmare and an engineer's lunatic asylum.

And yet U.S. Engineers, American Locomotive, and the General Electric Company forged it into a mighty main line, mounted Diesel-electric locomotives on its track, and started a solid stream of supplies over it. It meant the rebuilding of 1,200 miles of twisting track, the construction of a terminal on the Persian Gulf, a 2,000-foot pier on the shore of the Caspian Sea, and the building of special Diesel locomotives capable of muscling heavy trains over the craziest railroad anywhere.

The 762nd Diesel-Electric Railway Shop Battalion, Persian Gulf Command, was organized—sponsored by and with an officer personnel recommended by the American Locomotive Company. More than 50 per cent of the personnel came from Alco and the General Electric Company, its associate in the Diesel-electric locomotive field. Lieutenant Colonel W. C. Rogers, an Alco man, was placed in charge.

The first train under American operation rode into Teheran on March 29, 1943, and by May the Russian daily requirements were exceeded by 18 per cent. Stalingrad held. And another vital phase of the war was history.

On September 3, 1942, officials of the State Department,

army officers, and men of the American Locomotive Company were called into conference. The result was an agreement that found 13 Diesels, already in use on American railroads, being ordered in for immediate conversion to use on the Trans-Iranian Railway. These locomotives were requisitioned by the government and rushed to Schenectady. They were partly dismantled, supplied with 6-wheel trucks instead of the standard 4-wheel type because the Trans-Iranian Railway would not support the weight of a standard Diesel, and started on their long journey to the Persian Gulf. Thirteen of these converted locomotives were delivered within 45 days of their arrival at the Schenectady shops; 44 locomotives of the same type were shipped at the rate of 4 each week, beginning 45 to 60 days after the receipt of the order. By August, 1943, the entire 57 engines were growling their way over the rails of the devil's own track in Iran.

And again a locomotive-building company, born in Schenectady in 1848, had played a valiant part in stemming the mighty German tide. Also, if the vast quantities of American supplies had not continued to move across Persia into Russia, the subsequent Russian offensive would have been impossible.

The Schenectady Locomotive Engine Manufactury, with a capital stock of $40,000, grew into the present great American Locomotive Company, which company in 1948 will celebrate 100 years of locomotive building. The first engine that went huffing out of the original plant was called the Lightning. Followed a period of financial difficulties, during which time the plant was sold. However, the new purchasers were Schenectady citizens whose money had made the original company possible. A new company was formed and incorporated in 1851, and operations began on the site of the present property, bounded by Jay Street, Erie Boulevard, Nott Street, and the Troy Branch of the New York Central Railroad.

The first locomotive built was called the Great Western. It was completed in November, 1851, and was sold to the Buffalo, Corning & New York Railroad Company. Its gauge was 6 feet. The diameter of the boiler was 46 inches, with a length of 12 feet. The firebox, 58 inches deep, measured 53½ by 49 inches.

There were 148 two-inch flues. The cylinders were 16 by 22 inches. The drivers measured 5½ feet.

In 1900 land was purchased east of the New York Central Troy Branch, and a new powerhouse was built. Here between Huron Street and Park Place began the company's use of electric-driven equipment.

The early pay rolls are interesting. Rates of pay ran from 4 cents to 16¼ cents per hour. There were, of course, few men, and the company experienced many ups and downs. It was not until 1887 that over 200 locomotives were built in any one year. Because of the panic of 1857, the following year saw but 2 locomotives built. Came the panic of 1873; 110 locomotives were built that year, but only 9 the year following. Having weathered the panic of 1893-1894, the company continued to move forward.

The locomotive plant in Schenectady was born, grew to maturity, and prospered through 50 years in the hands of a father and 4 sons. The father was John Ellis, a canny Scotchman, who came to this country in 1831. John Ellis was president of the company from 1851 to 1864. John C., the first son, occupied the position from 1864 to 1878. The second son, Charles G., moved into the president's chair in 1878 and remained until 1891. Edward, the third son, carried on the work until 1897. And the fourth son, William D. Ellis, was at the helm until 1901, at which time control of the plant passed to the American Locomotive Company.

John Ellis and his sons built well, and Schenectady is indebted to them for the establishment of its first big industry, which has continued successfully to the present time. John Ellis, who had had no previous experience in locomotive building, proved his ability by surrounding himself with able assistants. The name of one stands out—Walter McQueen, who joined the old firm in 1852 and later became mechanical engineer and vice-president. He gained a reputation as a designer and builder, and for many years the product of the Schenectady Works was known throughout the country as the "McQueen Engine."

The beginning of the second era of the American Locomotive Company found S. R. Calloway as its first president. The incorporation of this company was the result of a merger of 8 locomotive plants. These were located at Schenectady and Dunkirk, New York; Allegheny and Scranton, Pennsylvania; Providence, Rhode Island; Richmond, Virginia; Manchester, New Hampshire; and Paterson, New Jersey. The plant at Schenectady continued to be the only one of the units devoted almost entirely to the building of locomotives.

During the Civil War, the American Locomotive Company built 73 engines for the government for war use. Hundreds of locomotives were built for the Allied Nations during World War I. Something like 2,000 locomotives have been supplied to the War Department in World War II. Most of these were shipped to the various theaters of war—Britain, France, Italy, North Africa, Iran, Russia, India, Burma, Australia, the Philippines, and numerous Pacific Islands, as well as Newfoundland and Alaska.

In addition to locomotives built during the war period, American Locomotive manufactured some 6,000 tanks, 150 marine boilers for Liberty ships, and 850 ship sets of large marine forgings for use in ship construction. And there were those famous M-7's.

American Locomotive built, in addition, M-3 medium tanks, the M-4's, hard-hitting General Shermans, and M-36 tank killers, or "Sluggers," as the Army called them. In 1942–43 Alco produced 75 per cent of the mechanical springs that went into the Gruman Wildcat, Avenger, and Hellcat planes; also the Fairchild Trainer and Sikorsky Corsair.

Half of the king posts, masts, and topmasts for the great Liberty-ship armada came from the Dunkirk, New York, plant of American Locomotive. Prior to 1940 this company had never manufactured a king post or a topmast, but it went into production and turned them out, supplying all requirements of three of the foremost shipyards in the country.

Again and again American Locomotive was asked by the government to undertake strange and difficult wartime jobs. "Experts" raised their hands and cried out that many of these jobs could not be done. But Alco has never employed the word "can't." It was the old story: "The miraculous we do immediately; the impossible takes a little longer."

Forgings for big guns were such an assignment. Between World War I and II, no big guns were manufactured in the United States by any private company. That was a government job, and a mighty fussy one—not to be trusted to outsiders. The result was that when the need arose no large company of experience and know-how was familiar with the process of forging big guns.

In 1942 American Locomotive was asked whether it would undertake so difficult an assignment. Could Alco do it? Alco could! There were tube forgings for 155-mm. howitzers, 75-mm. pack howitzers, 90-mm. guns, and 76-mm. guns.

The experts stood back and waited, tongues in their cheeks. What did a locomotive company know about big guns? After all.

Down at Latrobe, Pennsylvania, Alco turned out hundreds of ingots. These were forged, machined, rough-bored, and heat-treated at Schenectady. And the company had so low a percentage of losses and rejects that representatives of some of the country's foremost steel companies were sent to Latrobe to study the methods employed.

Then there was the case of generator shafts. Early in 1942 some of the foremost turbine manufacturers in the country were lamenting that they could not meet navy requirements because they could not get satisfactory forgings. The Navy turned to Alco. Once more Alco was asked to undertake a job that every expert worthy of the name was shouting could not be done with existing facilities at American Locomotive. But they still didn't know Alco, failing to realize that after close to 100 years of engineering responsibility and the frequent solution of complex and difficult railroad engineering problems, this locomotive company had the ability to do anything asked of it.

The generator shafts were tricky, and out of the first 6, 4 were rejected. Alco made some changes in steel melting and forging practices, then went ahead and turned out 200 of the big shafts with only 2 replacements. It forged 178 motor shafts without a single rejection. Subsequently Alco delivered a great many more shafts, with the result that the critical steam-turbine program was not delayed a single day for lack of American Locomotive forgings or because of the slightest defect in them.

And there were those big marine boilers. Those marine boilers made history. Whoever heard of anything that size coming off a production line? The British were startled almost out of their boots. They were so amazed at the methods employed that newsreels of the process were shown to the folks at home.

It seems that in January, 1941, a fleet of 10,000-ton cargo vessels was being rushed to completion in one of the big State of Maine shipyards for the British, and 90 marine boilers were urgently needed. Now, a marine boiler is big. It stands 15 feet high and weighs 60 tons. Marine boilers are not so simple, and they are not mass produced. At least, that was the understanding in those far-off days of 1941. Since then we have put 10,000-ton freighters and transports on the production line.

The question again was—could Alco build and deliver 3 marine boilers by May 15, 1941, and the balance at the rate of 9 a month? Alco said yes, and signed on the dotted line. In the first place, using mass-production methods, American Locomotive delivered the first 3 boilers 5 days ahead of schedule, and the last of the 90 *nine months* ahead of schedule!

But that wasn't all! They trot out a magic carpet at Alco everytime the occasion arises to do something that has never been done before. In this case the achievement was termed "one of the most ingenious and successfully planned and executed moves in the history of American transportation."

It had originally been planned to transport these marine boilers building at Schenectady to Maine by boat, shipping them to Albany, New York, and loading them onto freighters there. But there were certain risks to a sea voyage, for submarines were on the prowl. So someone at Alco said, "Why not move them all the way by rail?" Again the wiseacres started screaming that it could not be done; it was the craziest thing they had ever heard of.

But American Locomotive officials had an idea that it could, and they called in certain officials of several railroads. Of course, there first must be special gondolas of a sort that have special low-slung frames between the trucks. There were only 100 such cars in the United States, but Alco finally came up with 9. When one of those 15-foot marine boilers was loaded on the special gondola, the top of the boiler was 17 feet, 6 inches above the rail, which was entirely too much for a lot of tight-clearance spots.

The next job then was to scout routes which provided adequate clearance. To begin with, 300 feet of track had to be specially laid in the Schenectady area. Then the track over one New York state bridge had to be raised. In Vermont and Maine, two bridges had to be raised. In various places station canopies had to be altered, and at one spot in the White Mountains 80 feet of track had to be moved and a rock cut widened for several hundred feet. But all of these things are child's play to locomotive builders and railroad men.

The Scotch marine boilers went through. They traveled 380 miles instead of a normal 280, but the thing that counted was that they got there—safely and ahead of time.

The manufacture of synthetic rubber is a rather involved process, and it requires mountains of equipment. Here again American Locomotive put its shoulder to the wheel. Over one-half of the butadiene-producing capacity of the country (butadiene being a key base product of synthetic rubber) was supplied with vital heat-transfer equipment by Alco Products Division of the Company.

American Locomotive forged and machined torpedo caps; manufactured battleship turret rollers, which require unbelievable precision in manufacture; developed and built Diesel engines and generating sets for the Navy; made fragmentation bombs; and performed other vital and intricate jobs necessary to the mighty war program. At Schenectady, at Latrobe, at Richmond—always somewhere there was an American Locomotive plant ready and capable of performing the "impossible."

From that day in 1848 when the old Schenectady Locomotive Works turned out the fussy little Lightning, weighing 15 tons with steam up, through the building of the Union Pacific's "Big Boy," weighing 604 tons ready for the road, to April of 1945, the American Locomotive Company has built 25,041 locomotives.

The Lightning was rated to haul 9 cars at a speed of 15 miles per hour. The Big Boy, the largest engine ever built, is capable of hauling, and does haul, a mile of loaded freight cars at a speed of a mile a minute.

Of the 25,041 locomotives built as of April, 1945, 1,500 were

Diesels. Included in the many famous engines built by Alco is the first streamlined steam engine, built for the Milwaukee Road for its famous Hiawatha. Other notable examples of the locomotive builder's art are the New York Central's 4-8-2, carrying the company name Mohawk, and the new 6000-class 4-8-4, which the Central has called the Niagara, and the UP 4-6-6-4 type, and about all the others that have been built.

The story of American Locomotive would not be complete without some small tribute to the men of the 762nd Diesel Railway Shop Battalion and Lieutenant Colonel William C. Rogers. The job they performed on the Trans-Iranian Railway was one of vital importance. They worked in rain, heat, mud, and dust to keep the trains rolling. They suffered from the various insidious diseases of the East. To quote Captain George F. MacGowan, the men of the 762nd "did a hard, dirty, monotonous, and inglorious job under the worst possible weather conditions."

There were constant sandstorms and unbearable heat. Often they had to "beg, borrow, or improvise" the tools and equipment necessary to the servicing and maintenance of the motive power units. They played a big part in a Persian hell toward turning the tide at Stalingrad.

The New Diesel-Electric Locomotives

The American Locomotive Company and their neighbor in Schenectady, the General Electric Company, recently made a joint announcement of two new Diesel-electric road locomotives. They are what we might expect from two great manufacturers of railroad motive power.

In the first place, they will be produced on an assembly-line basis. You remember, the American Locomotive turned out those marine boilers on a production line, and now we find introduced in the locomotive industry full-scale production of standardized units, a striking contrast to the made-to-order methods followed in the construction of steam locomotives over a long period.

The facilities of the American Locomotive Company plant, covering some 112 acres, are particularly adapted to this method of turning out locomotives, and those who have watched an automobile move down an assembly line can fully appreciate its advantages. The first cost of your Diesel has from the first been considerably higher than that of the steam locomotive, but now the American Locomotive proposes substantial economies in this initial cost, which, coupled with greatly improved design, are expected to give the new locomotives a clear advantage over steam locomotives in a majority of applications.

The first of these locomotives consists of a 115-ton 1,500-horsepower unit, which may be operated in multiples of 1,500 horsepower—namely, 3,000, 4,500, and 6,000 horsepower. The second locomotive is a 150-ton, 2,000-horsepower unit which may be operated in multiples of 2,000 horsepower or 4,000 and 6,000 horsepower.

The new locomotives are part of a complete line of Diesel-electric road and switching locomotives, and these will include (1) a 115-ton, 1,500-horsepower combination road and switching locomotive; (2) a 115-ton, 1,000-horsepower switching locomotive; (3) a 100-ton, 660-horsepower switching locomotive.

The 1,500-horsepower road locomotive is designed primarily for freight service. The 2,000-horsepower locomotive is for passenger service. However, the latter may be adapted to either road work or switching.

Some of the outstanding features of these new locomotives are listed as follows:

1. Capacity to haul more ton and passenger miles at higher speeds over longer distances.

2. Smallest displacement Diesel engine per unit of output in locomotive service. (Two to four times the horsepower output per cubic inch displacement of other heavy-duty Diesels, or 1 horsepower per 18 pounds of engine weight.

3. Low fuel consumption.

4. Locomotives designed to operate one million miles, or three years, without overhaul.

5. New features of design, including unique accessibility of parts.

6. Almost all wearing parts are interchangeable.

7. Gears changed without change in other equipment. Locomotives may be geared to operate in ranges from 65 to 120 miles per hour.

There seems little doubt that these new Diesels in a majority of cases will have an advantage over steam locomotives. We feel by no means that steam is through, for the steam locomotive will continue to have a high place in the scheme of things on the railroad for a long time to come, but there is no evading the fact that the Diesel-electric is rapidly moving to the front.

In switching service, the Diesel has replaced steam almost without exception.

The first Diesel-electric locomotive put in service in the United States was built in 1925 by the American Locomotive Company, General Electric, and Ingersoll-Rand. This was a 300-horsepower switcher, and the remarkable part of it is that it still is in service on the Central Railroad of New Jersey. This switcher was built with two box-type operator's cabs, one at each end. But subsequently American Locomotive developed the hood-type switcher with one cab, and this has become the standard design for the switching locomotive.

War postponed the development of the Diesel-electric locomotive to a considerable extent, but with the coming of peace, progressive improvements of this type of locomotive have been the order of the day. In the attainment of all future goals, the three major elements of the Diesel-electric locomotive are important—the Diesel engine itself, the electric equipment, and the chassis. However, the heart of the problem remains the Diesel motor. Mainly, the problem is to attain the desired horsepower within weight and space limitations, which means that a higher horsepower output must be obtained per unit of engine volume (volume as measured by cylinder bore and stroke). Engine ratings are based upon the power to the generator for traction. An engine actually delivers considerably more than its rated horsepower, the difference being used to provide auxiliary power for the air-brake compressor, lighting, and other items.

In the search for greater horsepower, Alco engineers in collaboration with General Electric engineers found the answer in the application of a wartime development. This was the turbo-supercharger which General Electric had designed and produced for aviation engines. Through the use of "constant-pressure supercharging" and by various design modifications, the horsepower of the Diesel has been stepped up.

Constant-pressure supercharging is a method of utilizing the hot exhaust gases efficiently to drive a gas turbine, which in turn operates a compressor which forces air into the cylinders at high pressure. Getting more air into the cylinders not only thoroughly cleanses the cylinders of exhaust gases but permits more fuel to be burned, thus resulting in a higher power output from the engine.

The application of the Diesel engine to railroad service poses a great many special problems, but years of experience in building both steam and Diesel locomotives has enabled American Locomotive engineers to take these problems fully into account in the development of engines specifically for railroad use.

In addition to engineering problems in connection with the Diesel-electric locomotive, there was another item of major importance, and that was "eye appeal." The new queen who ambitiously aspires to the throne of the rail must have class and style. From the beginning the locomotive has been referred to as "she," possibly because there was once a race of female warriors called Amazons, or viragoes. A virago was a woman of great stature, strength, and courage. But a woman is a woman, and, Amazon or scullery maid, she has an eye for adornment.

Locomotive designers made a stylish lady out of a frump in the steam-engine field, but Diesel designers, starting from scratch, created a new vogue that quickly became all the rage in motive-power circles.

Many of these trim Diesels you see racing past are the work of stylists. Dress and hat fashions for ladies may come from Paris, Hollywood, or Broadway, but the Alco Diesel's latest creation is from the Appearance Design Division of the General Electric Company. G.E. designers found a challenge in turning from the problems of styling household appliances to the new, complex task of designing eye appeal into a giant locomotive, but they really have turned out a lovely dress for Her Majesty, the challenging queen of the railroad.

Three of the Alco-G.E. 1,500-horsepower units were road-tested for a 46-day period between Oneonta and Mechanicville, New York, on the Delaware & Hudson Railroad, covering a total of 13,400 miles. A total of 559,500 tons of freight was hauled, amounting to 49,172,000 gross ton-miles, exclusive of the locomotive itself. Fuel consumption in gallons of fuel per 1,000 G.T.M. was 1.642. The average tonnage southbound, with a ruling grade of 1.36 per cent, was 2,590 tons. The average tonnage northbound, with a ruling grade of 0.8 per cent, was 4,736 tons. The first of the new 6,000-horsepower 3-unit passenger Diesels was the 75,000th engine Alco has built, and was the initial one of a group that are now in service on the Santa Fe's Super Chief.

CHAPTER XIV

THE RIO GRANDE

Laboratory and Research

Judge R. V. Fletcher, Vice-President of the Association of American Railroads, recently said of the Rio Grande: "No railroad in the country surpasses the Rio Grande in its zeal for intelligent research."

Unfortunately, in a book of this kind it is impossible to do more than scratch the surface of modern science as applied to the railroad, its motive power, its communication system, and its equipment. The laboratory and the test tube play a vital role in the ballroom smoothness of the track, the power and speed of the locomotive, the hotel-like appointments of the train, the almost instantaneous control of traffic with "push-buttons," and the communications that are vital to train movement.

Someone has remarked not so long ago that the railroads belong to the horse-and-buggy days. A statement of this kind might be likened to that of the hillbilly who visited the circus for the first time, and upon seeing the giraffe said, "I don't believe it!"

The hillbilly's world did not include giraffes, hence his first sight of one proved more than his mind could assimilate in one fell swoop. The railroad critic, however, has lived close beside the railroad all his life, and still he knows as little about it as the hillbilly knew about the giraffe.

If the horse-and-buggy critic could suddenly be confronted with a composite picture of a modern transportation system in all of its intricate entirety he wouldn't believe it.

I like railroads, and I like railroad men. Perhaps it is because I still retain a small-boy love of engines and trains, and because of that love I have not only ridden locomotives thousands of miles but have poked into shops and roundhouses and dispatchers' offices—and laboratories. And the things I learned amazed me. Retaining all of my old love for the locomotive, I suddenly knew a greater admiration for the men who created and perfected it, and in these pages I have attempted to reveal certain behind-the-scenes facts—something of the private life of the locomotive, from test tube to the roaring main line.

I visited the Denver laboratory of the Denver & Rio Grande Western Railroad and came away with a fuller knowledge of the vital part such a laboratory has in the railroad scheme of things.

The keynote of the laboratory and research program on the Rio Grande, I was told, is "fundamental" rather than "applied" research. In the Rio Grande laboratory, these railroad professors have open minds, and they question certain present techniques and practices, attempting instead to take advantage of our rapidly expanding scientific knowledge to improve equipment and operations.

In the past, railroad research as a general thing has been concerned largely with "applied" research. That is to say, the primary concern has been solely with research suited to the needs and facilities of the railroads themselves. The contention being that the railroads are a service industry, and consequently should leave all problems of basic or fundamental research to the manufacturer.

However, the Rio Grande and a few other railroads are changing that concept, for they are increasingly aware of the aid which new scientific discoveries bring to other agencies of transport, such as the airplane, the bus, and the privately owned automobile. They are beginning to realize that the railroads have as their prime function the manufacturing of ton-miles and passenger-miles at a price which no other manufacturer can meet in the handling of mass transportation.

We have, for example, the Milwaukee's bulk movement of material "X" to the atom-bomb plant at Hanford, Washington. We don't know where material "X" came from, but we imagine it was a long haul, and yet the Milwaukee delivered 100 cars a day to the plant at Hanford. Only the railroad could have delivered in the quantity demanded the material necessary to the building of the atom bomb.

During the amazing expansion of scientific knowledge in the years of World War II, over and above the development of the atom bomb, there have been many developments in the field of electronics, metallurgy, chemistry, and allied endeavors, and the industry which does not take full advantage of this enormous store of scientific knowledge can quickly be crowded out of the picture by others more alert.

It is true that an important part of a railroad laboratory's function is still to test all materials and equipment to be used on the road, and to study the causes for any failures of this material or equipment in an effort to prevent recurrence. But now, superimposed on this program of "applied" research, is the intriguing and important program of "fundamental" research.

Thus the Denver laboratory of the Rio Grande some time ago set out to find new and better ways to make the things that make the railroad run. They have co-operated extensively with the manufacturers of railroad equipment in this program, instead of placing the entire burden for such research strictly on the manufacturer. Previously the railroad was guided, as well as limited, by what the manufacturer was able or saw fit to develop unassisted.

There are many projects which have greatly improved the high art of railroading in recent years which are the direct result of "inductive" rather than "deductive" thinking in the Rio Grande laboratory.

I am going to give you an example, several, in fact, but first let's start with keen-eyed Walter Leaf of the Denver laboratory—the railroad professor.

Somehow we have always associated professors with long-haired, slightly eccentric gentlemen, largely concerned with bugs and butterflies. It was hard to imagine a professor as interested in so noisy and blustering a thing as a railroad locomotive, let alone being vitally involved in its development. But Professor Leaf was just that.

It happened at a photoelastic conference at the Massachusetts Institute of Technology. While working in the laboratory,

Walter Leaf noticed that a beaker of colloidal bentonite—a clay having such small particles there is no tendency to settle out of suspension of water and so light they move exactly where the fluid takes them—formed patterns of light when seen through these polarizing plates.

All of the way back to Denver, Walter Leaf was turning the thing over in his mind. At the laboratory he made a model of a locomotive firebox, using a transparent plastic, including the brick arch design which has been in use for the past 50 years.

With the colloidal bentonite and polarizing plates, he studied the behavior of gases in the firebox. For years the rivets at the top of the firebox have been cut by the high velocity of the gases carrying cinders. Too, the lower fire tubes have been plugged with cinders due to the eddying of the gases around the lower portion of the brick arch. A reduction of power and efficiency, expensive repairs and maintenance, and locomotive failures were the natural result.

By his "fluid flow" study, Leaf was able to redesign the brick arch so that today locomotives utilizing the new design have greatly reduced cinder cutting and flue-plugging.

This was the first application ever made of this technique. Promptly officers of Republic Steel Company saw the possibilities in Walter Leaf's discovery and applied it to the design of their open-hearth furnaces. Engineers of the Bureau of Reclamation gave it their attention and subsequently found it of great value in designing dams, for it completely changed their concept of fluid flow through siphons. The development was studied by aeronautical engineers and employed by airplane builders.

So it was that a laboratory curiosity—a piece of clay suspended in water—captured the imagination of our railroad professor, who, as a result not only made possible greater locomotive efficiency, but also contributed to the general store of scientific knowledge.

This same Walter Leaf who developed the fluid-flow technique, one day sat watching test tubes of heated water, idly observing the bubbles rising to the surface, little dreaming that he was on the verge of making another revolutionary discovery.

Leaf noticed that when large bubbles were formed on the heating surface, no foaming developed. When small bubbles were formed, on the contrary, foaming was encountered.

Foaming of boiler water has always proved a bugbear to railroads, for when foaming takes place water is carried over into the cylinders, cutting out packing and greatly decreasing the efficiency of the locomotive. Castor oil or a product of similar base was the only preventive known.

Those test-tube bubbles floating upward started a new trend of thought in Leaf's brain. Fnally he made a plate with cone-shaped openings. He put this plate halfway down into the water and watched. When large bubbles encountered these openings in the plate, they burst. And when the small bubbles came through the openings, they formed into large bubbles and burst when they reached the surface of the water.

The railroad professor smiled, for he knew that from this moment forward the thinking about the cure for foaming in locomotives would be revolutionized. As this is written, Rio Grande Mallets are being equipped with this mechanical means of breaking bubbles. Out of the test tube has come another long step in the development of railroad engineering. The costly problem of foaming in locomotive boilers is on the way to being licked.

What effect this discovery may have in other lines is still problematical, but it may prove far-reaching. As the Mexican railroad worker would say, "Quien sabe?"—who knows?

The T-rail is almost as old as the steam locomotive itself. It followed on the heels of "strap" rails and "edge" rails. The first T-rails were manufactured in England. A man named Robert L. Stevens whittled the design of the first T-rail out of a block of wood. That was in 1830. Through the years the design of the T-rail has not changed much, but it has increased in size.

The Rio Grande and the railroad professor were the first, and probably the only ones, to install and utilize photoelastic methods for design studies, and this program, among other things, has resulted in an entirely new conception of rail design. It is being applied to rails rolled since the end of World War II, and has resulted in a more efficient use of the rail steel; also has reduced the possibility of rail failure.

The railroad professor in making these studies employed bakelite models and polarized plates, which showed the lines of stress in the model. This model was loaded to simulate actual conditions in the field. And now comes the surprising part of it.

Contrary to the beliefs on which all past rail designs have been based, the studies revealed that there were greater stresses near the top of the web than near the bottom, where most metal has been applied in all steel rails for many years. Strain gauges were used in the field to supplement the laboratory tests. After finding how closely both studies checked, the new rail design was conceived.

Because of the sulphurous acid caused by stack gases, the Rio Grande had a substantial problem of rail corrosion in the 6-mile Moffat Tunnel. And here again we find the railroad professor at work. After a lot of study and thought, it was decided to weld the rail solidly through the tunnel, leaving only 8 joints to take care of the insulation for the signal system.

In co-operation with the Metal and Thermit Company, the laboratory helped develop an entirely new type of weld, using for the first time in railroad practice the "gamma ray" for determining the soundness of these welds. And again the test tube and the professor had added a new page to railroad achievement.

The Denver laboratories of the Rio Grande have produced many "firsts," not the least of which has been the use of the "Magnaflux," or magnetic, method of inspection throughout all shops and roundhouses. The Magnaflux inspection is made by passing electric current of high amperage through a coil placed around the part to be inspected. If there is a crack or a flaw in the part, a magnetic flux creates magnetic poles at that point. Iron powder sprinkled over the surface, when removed, leaves magnetized portions intact, showing the location of the flaw.

The Rio Grande has begun studies with one of the large oil companies for improvements in Diesel fuel and the use of "additives." This study may prove of vast benefit to both the automobile and the railroad industry.

The use of X-ray diffraction units and damping capacity studies of firebox and boiler materials is resulting in recommendations for new materials and for improving fabricating practices for the elimination of residual and fabrication stresses. The Rio Grande has pioneered in the use of short-wave radio, and was one of the first railroads to put trains into regularly scheduled operation while utilizing this method of communication. Much could be written on "fundamental" research as applied on the Rio Grande. Trustees Henry Swan and Wilson McCarthy have been behind it all the way.

Very nearly every physical condition known to railroading can be experienced on the Rio Grande, for here we find elevations up to 10,000 feet on its standard and narrow-gauge lines. There are deserts and high, fertile valleys and the eternally snow- and cloud-capped peaks of the Colorado Rockies. The steel rails lift over the frowning back wall, to drive on through the Moffat bore into a world of rugged grandeur on the roof of the American Continent.

Temperatures vary from 110 degrees above zero to 58 below. By its very nature, the land of the Rio Grande offers a challenge to the railroad man. The road has adopted an aggressive, open-minded laboratory and research program, with the result that train operation is safe and efficient as it moves a volume of traffic which ten years ago was deemed impossible.

The Rio Grande stands high in the rank of American railroads. Untiring effort has brought higher speeds, better equipment, more efficient motive power, better track structures, C.T.C., improved communications, and decreased costs. A salute to the Rio Grande's Denver laboratory and its staff—and to the railroad professor and his test tube!

CHAPTER XV

THE BALTIMORE & OHIO

The "97's"

Out of the east they come—from Maybrook Junction, from the Jersey shore, from Locust Point, from Curtis Bay, from Potomac Yard—a mighty fleet of Q.D. trains. They are Quick Dispatch—the 97's of the B.&O.

Up from the valleys and the lowlands, up from tidewater to ride mountain steel come these fast-traveling caravans of freight. Trains loaded with sugar and spices and fabrics and metals, with the products of the farm and the factory and the mine. A headlight silvers the rail, wheels clatter past, marker lights gleam and fade in the gloom. The night flight of the 97's has begun.

Locomotive voices shout, "Clear the rail! We are trains of importance and speed is our watchword! We are safe and sure and reliable. We answer the challenge of the signal lights. We hail the operator who guards our going. We answer the roll call of the rail—in starlight, in rain storm and driving snow: I am 'CSD-97, the old Central States Dispatch.' I am 'First Chicago-97.' And I, 'Cleveland-97.' And I, 'St. Louis-97.' And I, 'Cincinnati-97.' And I, 'Columbus-97.' And I, 'Springfield-97.'"

There are others: "Philadelphia-97," "Parkersburg-97," "Highcar-97," "Second Chicago-97."

Fast freight is king. The 97's are his courtiers. Their coat of arms is B.&O.

This fleet of time freights originates at all of the principal eastern seaboard terminals, and so the 97's begin their westward movement. They are switched and reshuffled at certain larger classification yards, then again are speeded on their way.

Let us start with the CSD-97. This train makes up in Cedar

Hill Yard, New Haven, Connecticut, far up in New England, where it takes under its wing cars from Boston. It begins its journey over the rails of the New York, New Haven & Hartford. It crosses the Hudson River at Poughkeepsie and rolls into Maybrook Junction. Here the Lehigh & Hudson River road takes over. In turn then the train moves over the tracks of the Central of New Jersey, the Reading, and the Western Maryland, finally being delivered to the Baltimore & Ohio at Cherry Run, Maryland, in the Potomac Valley.

From Cherry Run CSD-97 rushes on to Cumberland, Maryland, arriving at 2:25 p.m. on its daily schedule. Here it is broken up; the cars are reclassified and switched into other westbound 97's, building for various destinations beyond the mountains.

Six 97's from various eastern points, in the meantime, have converged on Brunswick, Maryland. The Brunswick Yard is between Point of Rocks and Harpers Ferry, on the banks of the Potomac River. It is the largest yard on the B.&O., and here nearly all east- and westbound trains are run over the hump and rebuilt into solid through trains.

Now we will take these 97's at their various points of origin and ride them into Brunswick.

New York-97 leaves Jersey City at 9:45 p.m. daily, arriving at Brunswick at 9:20 a.m. Philadelphia-97 leaves at 1:30 a.m.; Bay View-97 (Maryland) at 1:45 a.m.; Locust Point-97 (Baltimore) at 1 a.m.; Curtis Bay-97 (Maryland) at 1:30 a.m.; Potomac Yard-97 at 3 a.m. The last 5 arrive at Brunswick at 9:15, 7:30, 6:30, 7, and 8 a.m., respectively.

These 97's move through the maze of tracks in the great Brunswick Yard, and a few minutes after 12 noon they start rolling west. They have been humped, classified, and made up. Train lines have been coupled, the brakes pumped up, big road engines stand pulsing at the front, and on the rear-end the caboose, the cabin car, has set its markers.

The conductor waves a highball, and First Chicago-97 starts out of town behind the big freight Diesel which at 9:15 this morning brought in Philadelphia-97. Just as sure as death and income tax, First Chicago-97 will take its departure from Brunswick Yard at 12:05 p.m. It consists of a solid train for Chicago and will arrive at Pine Junction, Chicago, at 11 p.m. the following day.

Second Chicago-97 pulls out of the yard at Cumberland, Maryland, west of Brunswick, at 5 p.m., arriving at Pine Junction at 11:55 p.m. the next night. This train has in its consist cars from CSD-97 from New England.

Cleveland-97 leaves Brunswick at 12:10 p.m., arriving at Cleveland at 8:10 the next morning. Pittsburgh-97 leaves Brunswick at 3 p.m., arriving at Pittsburgh at 6:30 a.m.

There are other 97's—the St. Louis, the Cincinnati, the Columbus. It is like taking rabbits out of a hat. St. Louis-97 pulls out of Brunswick at 1:30 p.m., reaching East St. Louis at 4:15 a.m. the second day. A big freight Diesel usually hauls this train between Cumberland, Maryland, and Washington, Indiana. Cincinnati-97 picks up its train and goes storming out of Brunswick at 2:30 p.m. and is in Cincinnati at 8 p.m. the following evening.

Columbus-97 roars out of Cumberland at 5:55 p.m., arriving at Columbus, Ohio, at 7 the next evening.

The rail lifts from the green valley of the Potomac, and the manifest trains hurl themselves at the mountain iron. The Iron Horse is chanting in the hills. Big Diesels are growling upward, whipping famous grades—Seventeen-Mile, Sand Patch, Cheat River. The 97's are rolling.

Out of Cumberland comes Parkersburg-97. It is pulling cars for that place, and other cities on the Ohio line. It leaves Cumberland at 7 in the evening and brings its train into Parkersburg at 8:30 in the morning.

Cars cut out of both the St. Louis and Cincinnati 97's move out of Parkersburg in the Springfield-97. It departs daily at 8:30 a.m., arriving at Indianapolis at 3:30 a.m. and Springfield at 3:15 p.m. the next day.

And there is a train called High-car-97. Because of close clearances on the line between Grafton and Parkersburg, West Virginia, particularly the tunnels, high cars cannot be operated over this line. Consequently all such cars must be switched out of through trains and routed from Grafton by way of Fairmont and Benwood Junction, West Virginia, and Newark, Ohio; thence to Cincinnati. High-car-97 starts from Brunswick, leaving there

188

at 4 p.m. and arriving in Cincinnati at 6:30 a.m. the next day.

On account of the heavy grades through the mountains, the consists of the 97's are changed at important junction points, without materially slowing the schedule. Let us examine the records of New York-97, for instance, on October 31, 1945. This train left Jersey City with 58 loads. At Philadelphia, a 5,400-horsepower Diesel was coupled on, and cars were added for a total of 97.

On the same day St. Louis-97 left Brunswick with 57 loads, pulled by a Santa Fe locomotive of the S-1 class. At Cumberland a 5,400-horsepower Diesel was attached, and she left with 66 loads. Out of Grafton, after crossing the mountains, she had 75 loads; out of Parkersburg, 86 loads and 10 empties; and out of Cincinnati she was hauling 70 loads and 9 empties.

Also on October 31 Pittsburgh-97 had 47 loads out of Brunswick; Cleveland-97, 17 loads and 50 empties; while Chicago-97 had 105 loads with a Diesel freight engine on the head end.

Leaving Cumberland on this date, Pittsburgh-97 had 50 loads; Cleveland-97 consisted of 24 loads and 50 empties; Chicago-97 had 72 loads behind a Diesel. Second Chicago-97 had 25 loads and 38 empties. Columbus-97 carried 40 loads, as did Cincinnati-97. St. Louis-97, with a Diesel, had 66 loads.

Between Philadelphia and Brunswick the motive power is usually the Q-4 Mikado. On the CSD-97 out of Brunswick and Hagerstown the big S-1 Santa Fe's handle the train to Cumberland and Keyser. From Cumberland to New Castle, in the southwestern corner of Pennsylvania, the 97's go through with workhorse Santa Fe's, or 2-10-2's.

Out of Cumberland on the Cincinnati and St. Louis main line the 97's move behind the daddy of steam on the B.&O., the powerful 2-8-8-4 Articulateds. Their job is to drag reluctant freight cars over the mountains. Measuring 125 feet, 9⅝ inches from knuckle to knuckle, these brute-big 7,600-class locomotives take particular delight in whipping Seventeen-Mile Grade, between Piedmont, West Virginia, and Altamont, there just west of Cumberland. The westbound rail climbs at a maximum of 2.2 per cent. The mountains—the Alleghenies—fill with the thunder of them when they go to work wheeling the 97's through.

It is interesting to note that the first Mallet articulated locomotive built in the United States was delivered to the Baltimore & Ohio and exhibited at the Louisiana Purchase Exposition at St. Louis in 1904. This first Mallet and the ones that followed played an important part in whittling the brawling Alleghenies down to size. The Mallets helped pave the way for a mighty fleet of manifest trains—the 97's of the B.&O.

From New Castle, Pennsylvania, on the Chicago line, the motive power consists of Mikados or the new T-3 Mountain Type high-speed locomotives. From Grafton, West Virginia, on the St. Louis line, it is mostly Mikados, the Q-3's.

Three of the six 5,400-horsepower freight Diesels handle the 97's between Philadelphia, Pennsylvania, and Willard, Ohio, and three work between Cumberland, Maryland, and Washington, Indiana.

The companion eastbound trains of the 97's are the fleet of 94's, running on equally fast schedules.

The vast network of steel of the Baltimore & Ohio reaches far, stretching from the Jersey shore to the Father of Waters, to the Great Lakes. It bands the Appalachians; it taps vast industrialized territories and rich farm territory. It serves mighty metropolitan areas. It is an important link in the greatest system on earth—the American Railroad.

And yet, without absolute co-operation on the part of every last employee, it could not operate. From the switchman in East St. Louis to the high offices in the Baltimore & Ohio Building in Baltimore, Maryland, there is a tight bond of unity, an eternal brotherhood that can not only move mountains but move them fast.

Far from least in this rail corps are the men in the caboose. We have taken a quick glance at the fast-rolling fleet of 97's, roaring up from the lowlands to beat at the portals of a mountain chain, ignoring in the tempestuous rush the caboose behind the train. Too often when guns are booming at the front we forget that the command post is behind the lines.

The skipper of the train rides in the caboose. His is the final word. His is the lantern, there in the blackness of the Jersey City Yard that signals New York-97 to begin its westward flight.

Banana Special

The lowly banana rides on a special train on the Baltimore & Ohio, and it travels fast.

During World War II the great United Fruit Company's white banana fleet donned navy gray and sailed away to fight. The banana trains turned from peaceful pursuits to bringing up the ammunition. The banana disappeared from the market. Now it is back, and the banana trains are rolling again.

The handling of bananas through the port of Baltimore is a highly specialized business. Banana ships are scheduled to arrive in Baltimore harbor on Monday and Thursday of each week. In anticipation of the arrival of the vessel, about 40 refrigerator cars are cleaned, conditioned, and inspected. These cars are then placed on car floats, which are moved to shipside. The green bananas are loaded directly into these cars.

When the loading is completed, the floats are towed to Locust Point. Here the special train is made up. Now we will follow one of these trains down the main line.

At 8 in the evening the Banana Special pulls out of the Locust Point Yards and begins its flight westward. It arrives at Cumberland, Maryland, at 1:15 a.m. The distance is 182 miles. Here this early Tuesday morning the first cars are dropped. The schedule provides 25 minutes for this purpose. Cars for Cumberland are set out; also cars for Grafton, Fairmont, and Clarksburg, West Virginia, which are switched into the first outbound manifests leaving for these cities.

Once more the Banana Special gets under way, moving up the Sand Patch grade and on over the Pittsburgh line. It travels fast down the valley of the Youghiogheny River to Connellsville, Pennsylvania. Here the Connellsville cars are set out; also cars for Wheeling and Morgantown, West Virginia, Uniontown and Pittsburgh, Pennsylvania, and Columbus, Ohio.

The Banana Special operates through Pittsburgh over the

tracks of the Pittsburgh & Lake Erie without stopping. The cars dropped at Connellsville are forwarded by fast freight service to their respective destinations, reaching Wheeling at 5 p.m., Morgantown at 12:15 p.m., and Columbus at 11:45 p.m. on Tuesday.

The next regular stop of the flying Special is at Akron Junction, Ohio, where it arrives at 9:40 Tuesday forenoon. It has traveled 450 miles, and the elapsed time of the run, including stops to set off cars and service the train, is 13 hours and 40 minutes. Under 14 hours from tidewater to Akron Junction requires some pretty fancy wheeling. Those marker lights have been riding fast.

Cars for Akron and Cleveland are set off at Akron Junction, and once more there is the highball from the rear end. The Banana Special rushes on across Ohio to Willard, 76 miles away. The train shows at 11:20 a.m. And now the marker lights are taken down, for this is the end of the run.

The remaining cars of the banana train are switched into time freights for various points, including Detroit and Flint, Michigan, Toledo, Ohio, and Chicago. Banana cars absorbed by No. 397 arrive in Toledo at 8:30 p.m.; cars for Detroit arrive at 2 a.m. Wednesday. Chicago cars leave Willard on No. 89 and reach the Barr Yard at Chicago at 3:45 a.m. Wednesday. From the Locust Point Yards in Baltimore they have traveled 795 miles.

Up from the lowlands and the valleys to ride the mountain steel has come the lowly banana, king for a day. On across Ohio into the Mississippi Basin, the Middle West, far from the ship lanes of the banana fleet. The time of those last cars into Chicago has been 32 hours and 45 minutes.

The banana cars are iced or heated as the season requires, and every precaution is taken against delay lest these green bananas ripen before reaching their far-flung destinations. In the banana service, as in all of its multitude of train movements, the Baltimore & Ohio renders fast and dependable service.

Behind the speeding Banana Special rides the caboose, the keen eyes of the man in the cupola watching down the long line of swaying "reefers," or refrigerator cars. He is always there, always on guard, there at the end of the train.

Color Position Light Signals

Guarding the flight of the 97's of the Baltimore & Ohio, the rush of the Banana Special as well as other of the road's vast train fleet, we find in growing numbers the Color Position Light Signal. At the time of this writing, Color Position Light type signals are in service on 1,205 miles of the Baltimore & Ohio System, representing about 50.3 per cent of all automatic block signals.

The Color Position Light Signal was developed by the late F. P. Patenall, signal engineer, for the B.&O. This signal combines the principal features of the color-light and semaphore signals, in that it gives both color and position indications.

The first Color Light Signals were installed in the Howard Street Tunnel, Baltimore, between Camden and Mt. Royal Stations in April, 1921. From that time forward, whenever semaphore signals required replacing, the Color Position Light Signal has been substituted. In some instances entire divisions have been equipped with the C.P.L. signals. Eventually the entire system will be equipped with this type of signal.

Although we find C.P.L. signals in service at many points on each operating division, the following represent the most extensive installations:

1. New York Terminal Territory (Staten Island Lines).
2. Waverly to Carroll, Baltimore, Maryland.
3. Bailey to Riverside, Baltimore, Maryland.
4. Laughlin Junction to Pittsburgh, Pennsylvania.
5. New Castle Junction to Warwick, Ohio.
6. Sterling to Greenwich, Ohio.
7. Attica to Hamler, Ohio.
8. Defiance, Ohio, to Milford Junction, Indiana.
9. Cumberland, Maryland, to Loveland, Ohio.
10. Cincinnati, Ohio, to Dearborn, Indiana.
11. Cochran, Indiana, to Milan.
12. North Vernon, Indiana, to East St. Louis, Illinois.
13. Glenwood Junction, Pennsylvania, to Wheeling, West Virginia.
14. Maynard to Fairport, Ohio.

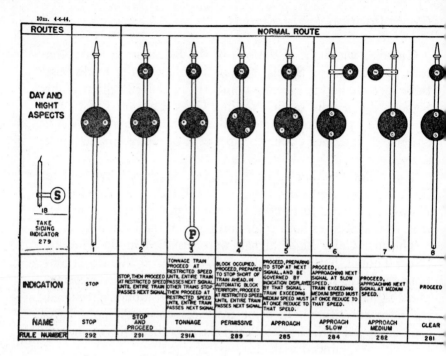

15. Lima to Toledo, Ohio.
16. Alexandria Junction, Maryland, to Potomac River Bridge.

Bay-Window Caboose

The old red caboose, it seems, is on the way to coming in for a few architectural alterations. Whether or not they will be generally adopted is still a moot question among railroad men. However, the Baltimore & Ohio has come out flat-footed in favor of a certain innovation known as the bay-window caboose.

It was back around 1929 that J. J. Tatum, then General Superintendent of the Car Department on the B.&O. (now Assistant Chief of Motive Power and Equipment), began toying with the notion that a caboose with a bay window should have many advantages over the long-established cupola type. It is just possible that Mr. Tatum had wearied of reading about locomotive development, advancements in signaling, and new fashions for the

B.&O. #29 fast mail and express hauled by Engine #7620, new 2-8-8-4 type, class EM-1, running over the west end of the Cumberland Division east of Keyser, W. Va. Photo by H. W. Pontin. Courtesy Rail Photo Service.

Two rear ends and four pushers. Hind end of B.&O. #96 overtaking coal drags pushers on the 2.16% grade coming around the horse-shoe curve west of Terra Alta, W. Va. All four engines are class EL-1A, 2-8-8-0 type. Photo by H. W. Pontin. Courtesy Rail Photo Service.

Rear end of Great Northern #402 fast freight with a mixed consist of lumber and apples approaching Minot, N. D., on a fall evening. Photo by Wm. J. Pontin. Courtesy Rail Photo Service.

Denver & Rio Grande Western #3613, 2-8-2 type, class L-132, with fast freight #61 in the canyon of the Arkansas River west of Princeton, Col., on the Grand Junction Division. The grade is 1.42% ascending. Photo by R. H. Kindig.

Denver & Salt Lake work train at Pine Cliff, Col., on the Moffat Tunnel Route with outfit cars in the background. Photo by Otto C. Perry.

The Santa Fe's famous economy train, The Scout, first #2 coming down the hill past Belva, Okla., with Engine #2928, 4-8-4 type, with 16 cars. Extra #2910 west "in the hole." First District of the Plains Division. Photo by Preston George.

Rear end of Santa Fe #31 New Mexico-Colorado-Kansas fast freight about to enter the east portal of Raton Tunnel. Two more 2-10-2 type engines are on the head end. Courtesy Santa Fe Railroad.

Rotary snowplow working hard on the S.P. Mountain Subdivision of the Sacramento Division near Stanford, Calif. Courtesy Southern Pacific Railroad.

Rear end of the Southern Pacific streamlined all-Pullman Lark near Chatsworth, Calif., on the Los Angeles Division in the early morning. Courtesy Southern Pacific Railroad.

First picture of the new 5,400-h.p. Diesel passenger locomotive with the Sante Fe Chief climbing the 3.5% grade up Raton Pass with 15 cars and no helper. These Diesels run through from Chicago to Los Angeles. Note the heat from the motors. Photo by Preston George.

Denver & Rio Grande Western #116, the San Juan, America's finest narrow-gauge railroad train, whistling for Cumbres after topping the 4% grade up the pass of that name. Elevation is 10,015 feet. The engine is 2-8-2 type, class K-28. Photo by Otto C. Perry.

Denver & Rio Grande Western #482 narrow-gauge 2-8-2 type, class K-36, helping #487 with 21 cars up the 4% grade on Cumbres Pass west of Coxo, Col., on the Alamosa Division. Photo by Otto C. Perry.

Pair of B.&O. 2-8-8-0 types, class EL-3A, pushing #96 eastbound fast freight around the 7-degree curve at Amblersburg, W. Va., while climbing the Cranberry grade between M.&K. Junction and Terra Alta, W. Va. Note the bay-window caboose. Photo by H. W. Pontin. Courtesy Rail Photo Service.

Interior of a B.&O. bay-window caboose showing safety grab iron overhead, bunks, conductor's desk, lockers, stove, water cooler, and lamps. Bay window on left over the seat. Courtesy Baltimore & Ohio Railroad.

MEDIUM ROUTE						SLOW ROUTE		
9	10	11	12	13	14	15	16	17
STOP, THEN PROCEED AT RESTRICTED SPEED UNTIL ENTIRE TRAIN PASSES NEXT SIGNAL	BLOCK OCCUPIED PROCEED, PREPARED TO STOP SHORT OF TRAIN AHEAD. IN AUTOMATIC BLOCK TERRITORY PROCEED AT RESTRICTED SPEED UNTIL ENTIRE TRAIN PASSES NEXT SIGNAL	PROCEED AT MEDIUM SPEED, PREPARING TO STOP AT NEXT SIGNAL AND BE GOVERNED BY INDICATION DISPLAYED BY THAT SIGNAL	PROCEED AT MEDIUM SPEED APPROACHING NEXT SIGNAL AT SLOW SPEED.	PROCEED AT MEDIUM SPEED APPROACHING NEXT SIGNAL AT MEDIUM SPEED.	PROCEED; MEDIUM SPEED WITHIN INTERLOCKING LIMITS, OR THROUGH NON-INTERLOCKED SWITCHES IMMEDIATELY BEYOND THE SIGNAL BLOCK CLEAR.	PROCEED AT RESTRICTED SPEED UNTIL ENTIRE TRAIN PASSES NEXT SIGNAL	PROCEED AT SLOW SPEED, PREPARING TO STOP AT NEXT SIGNAL AND BE GOVERNED BY INDICATION DISPLAYED BY THAT SIGNAL	PROCEED AT SLOW SPEED UNTIL ENTIRE TRAIN PASSES THROUGH SWITCHES APPROACHING NEXT SIGNAL AT SLOW SPEED, AND BE GOVERNED BY INDICATION DISPLAYED BY THAT SIGNAL.
STOP AND PROCEED	MEDIUM PERMISSIVE	MEDIUM APPROACH	MEDIUM APPROACH SLOW	MEDIUM APPROACH MEDIUM	MEDIUM CLEAR	RESTRICTING	SLOW APPROACH	SLOW CLEAR
291	289A	286	283B	283A	283	290	288	287

trains of tomorrow, feeling perhaps that it was about time for someone to begin paying a little attention to improving the forgotten caboose. Being a person of initiative, he decided to do something about it.

The origin of the lookout, or cupola, has been the subject of considerable controversy. However, some time ago a Mrs. E. C. Lane, of El Paso, Texas, wrote a letter to *Railroad Magazine* enclosing a clipping dated at Cedar Rapids, Iowa, December 9, 1898. From this clipping it appears that a Mr. T. B. Watson, formerly a conductor on the Chicago & North Western, originated the cupola idea. Conductor Watson, it was stated, while making a run between Cedar Rapids and Clinton, Iowa, in the late summer of 1863, received orders to turn his caboose over to the conductor of a work train and to take an empty boxcar to Clinton, using this car en route in lieu of a caboose.

The boxcar happened to have a hole about 2 feet square in the roof, and Mr. Watson became intrigued with the idea of sticking his head through this hole, which would not only offer a bird's-eye view of his train but also of the landscape in general. Like all freight conductors, he was a resourceful individual and soon had contrived a seat by stacking the lamp and tool boxes under the opening to a height that allowed him to sit with his head and shoulders above the roof.

Apparently Mr. Watson found the experience both exhilarating and possessed of potentialities in that with a very little labor and material, he no doubt reasoned, a freight conductor could be provided with a kind of pilothouse from which to watch over his train.

We gather that Conductor Watson felt that such an arrangement would be cozy as well as practical, and whatever rancor had been engendered through being deprived of his caboose must have soon been dissipated as he indulged rosy dreams of a permanent cupola affixed to what at that time was termed the "conductor's car." The only fly in the ointment was the dark possibility that the master mechanic might hoot the idea into oblivion.

Upon arriving at Clinton, Mr. Watson sought out the master mechanic and unveiled his brain child. Two cabooses were in the process of construction at the time in the shops, and when they were finished—they had cupolas on them.

From that time forward there has been no radical change in caboose design—not until Mr. J. J. Tatum, of the B.&O., brought out the bay-window caboose.

The caboose was red, and it had a front and rear platform— and a cupola on top. And it seemed destined to remain the old maid of the train, uncourted by progress, to the end of time.

And then suddenly the old red caboose stepped out into society. The occasion was the World's Fair in New York in 1939. For show purposes the caboose on exhibition was painted gray instead of the usual "Devil's red," with zebra stripes, front and back. And the cupola was missing. In its place was a pair of not unbecoming bay windows on the sides.

Besides just about stopping the show, the new caboose started a controversy that is still raging. We can imagine that tongues immediately began to wag in caboose circles, from Maine to California, and that scandalized eyes were raised on many a "hack track." A hack track is the place where cabooses are switched at the end of the run. Until now the gloomy, somber-eyed sisters on the caboose track had only their repair operations and their neighbors to talk about. In the livening buzz of conversation following the announcement of the coming-out party at the World's Fair, it is conceivable that the words "hussy" and "bustles" were employed.

The gray dress of the Baltimore & Ohio caboose, with which the lady had been adorned for her debut, did not remain, but the bay windows did.

The first bay-window caboose was put in service on the B.&O. in 1930. It was of all-steel construction, with the conventional-type roof. Coming, as it did, during the depression years, it remained the only one of its kind for a long time. The B.&O. had no occasion to build more cabooses, there being then a surplus. In fact, there were about 1,000 in service on the system.

But the die was cast; the B.&O. was definitely committed to this new wrinkle in caboose construction. It is claimed for the bay-window caboose that it provides the lookout brakeman on the rear end with a better view of the train, from track to roof, whereas with the cupola type he can only observe the sides of the freight cars ahead of him when the drag is on a curve. There is more floor space because of the elimination of the lockers and cupola seats, and the trainman can move quickly from one side to the other.

As a temporary measure, the B.&O. equipped the old-style cabooses with a glass box over one window on each side. This served as a kind of improvised bay window, enabling the trainman to see the side of the train and still remain within the necessary clearances.

The trucks of the new cabooses are equipped with elliptic springs which add materially to the riding qualities of the car. Ajax brakes and modern air-brake equipment further provide for the safety and comfort of the crew.

The high cushion on the back of the seats in the bay-window section can be adjusted to a position between the seats to form a berth, as in a Pullman sleeper. Also, collapsible tables can be set up in this space when desired.

There are two cushioned longitudinal seats at one end of the caboose, as in the old-type caboose. At the other end is the stove, porcelain washstand with overhead water supply, and steel lockers for the crew's clothing. A safety rod extends below the ceiling from one end of the caboose to the other, providing a safe handhold for members of the crew.

Another safety feature is the small round windows in the ends of the caboose, which replace those of earlier design, as there have been occasions when trainmen have been hurled through these end windows when there has been an emergency application of brakes.

The first bay-window caboose on the B.&O., C-2500, built in 1931, was not of the wagon-top design, as were those built later. Two of wagon-top design were built in 1936, and they were numbered C-2501 and C-2502. Numbers C-2503 to C-2507 were built in 1939–40.

In 1940–41, 100 wagon-top bay-window cabooses were built. These were designated as class I-12 and numbered C-2400 to C-2499 inclusive. On account of wartime shortages of steel, 36 stock and 74 boxcars were converted to caboose cars. The ends were cut back for platforms and steel bay windows were set in the doorways. The stock cars were converted to class I-13 and numbered C-1800 to C-1835. The boxcars were designated as class I-16 and numbered C-2300 to C-2374. In 1943, 99 more

SUMMARY OF BAY-WINDOW CABOOSES

Class	No. Cabooses	Numbers	Year Built	Kind
I-7	1	C-2500	1931	All steel
I-5a	1	C-2501	1936	" "
I-5ba	1	C-2502	1936	" "
I-5b	3	C-2503—C-2505	1939-40	" "
I-5ba	2	C-2506—C-2507	1940	" "
I-12	100	C-2400—C-2499	1941-42	" "
I-12	25	C-2800—C-2824	1945	" "
	133			
I-13	36	C-1800—C-1835	1941	Wood, Steel Underframes
I-16	74	C-2300—C-2373	1942	" " "
I-16	99	C-2700—C-2799	1943	" " "
	209			

boxcars were converted to class I-16 cabooses and numbered C-2700 to C-2799.

In 1945, 25 additional class I-12 bay-window cabooses were added to the fleet. These were numbered C-2800 to C-2824.

The interiors of the new cabooses are painted gray, giving them a bright, clean appearance. The trainmen are provided with practically all of the comforts of home, including home cooking. From personal experience I can testify to the excellence of caboose cookery.

In concluding this chapter I can only say that "something new has been added," but whether or not the bay-window caboose will eventually dethrone the cupola on American railroads remains problematical. At least the Baltimore & Ohio has paved the way for new fashions at the rear end of a freight train. And these "bustles" have given the little old red caboose more publicity than it has had in three-quarters of a century.

Passenger Service

The B.&O. was one of the first railroads to put Diesel motive power on their passenger trains, and the fine on-time performance of them all—including the solid-Pullman Capital Limited between Baltimore, Washington, and Chicago all through the war years is not only a compliment to these locomotives, but a very high one to the Operating Department of a great railroad. Other crack trains to Chicago are the de luxe all-coach Columbian, the Shenandoah, and the Blue Ridge Limited. The National Limited and the Diplomat to St. Louis are beautiful trains, as is the Ambassador to Detroit and the Cleveland Night Express. When you ride these trains from Baltimore and Washington to these points, you will ride the best, eating fine food, seeing great scenery, and enjoying a comfortable trip over a system that links 13 states within the nation.

CHAPTER XVI

THE GREAT NORTHERN'S ORE MOVE

The World's Heaviest Trains

The Great Northern Railroad operates the heaviest and the longest trains in the world—16,740 tons of iron ore! These mightiest of trains, 180 loads, haul ore from Kelly Lake, 5 miles southwest of Hibbing, Minnesota, to the ore docks at Allouez on Lake Superior.

The great Mahoning open-pit mine is the largest in the iron country, and here at Kelly Lake we find a yard with a track capacity of about 2,000 cars. The Great Northern receives its ore from feeder lines which spin their web through the range. During the seasons of 1944–45 one of these mammoth trains was crawling out of Kelly Lake every two hours or better behind a G.N. Articulated.

If you are wondering how one of these 2-8-8-0 engines does it alone, the answer is that the engineer who handles the throttle years ago was aided by the engineers who laid out the line, for the maximum grade is only 0.4 per cent and favors the loaded ore train all the way to Allouez.

The empty trains return from the ore docks 180 strong, moving to Kelly Lake over another line, which leaves the Third Subdivision at Boylston. The majority of the loaded trains operate over the Eighth Subdivision, Kelly Lake to Brookston, a distance of 50 miles, while others are handled over the Eleventh Subdivision, Kelly Lake to Gunn, Minnesota, a distance of 31 miles. It is 51 miles from Brookston to Allouez, and 110 miles from Gunn to Allouez.

The red ore is loaded into Lake boats according to its grade, which is established by metallurgists before its arrival at the docks. The Great Northern docks are the finest and the most up-to-date to be found anywhere.

The track in the ore district is maintained at the highest standard. The rail is 110-pound, and the track has the advantage of excellent drainage. I have covered all of the Mesabi Division in a rail car, and it is like traveling over a steel-banded red carpet, as so much ore has fallen off along the right of way.

It is a thrill to ride the caboose behind 180 ore cars, everyone alike as you realize that 16,700-odd tons of ore are between the rear and head ends. Let's go along with this ore train and see what it is like. In the first place, we learn that every car is equipped with the new Westinghouse AB brake, which represents the last word in air-brake equipment.

Unlike the Duluth, Mesabi & Iron Range, where all of the cars have the train-line hose above the drawheads, these G.N. ore cars can be handled on foreign roads outside of the district. The Mesabi also handles 180-car trains but does not haul as great a tonnage because many of their cars are of only 40-ton capacity. The Duluth, Mesabi & Iron Range is also confronted with heavier grades.

This is Sunday morning, November 12, 1944, and the ore train we are riding is about the last of these trains for the season. When the lakes freeze up, that is all for the ore move until spring. A train of empties has arrived at Kelly Lake, pulling in at 9:15, in charge of Conductor Barilani. Engineer Fosig and Fireman LeBlanc are on the head end. The locomotive is the 2014, and these N3-class locomotives are veterans. They were originally built by Baldwin in 1912 and rebuilt in the Great Northern shops in 1925-1927, and rebuilt again in 1940 for the specialized job of hauling ore. Their weight with tender is 863,700 pounds. The tender has a capacity of 21,500 gallons of water and 24 tons of coal. The drivers are 63-inch; the tractive effort, 106,000 pounds. The 10 coal burners still have their original duplex stokers; the other 15 burn oil.

It is a source of amazement how an engine of this age and type can handle the world's heaviest trains, but they do, and much of the credit belongs to President F. J. Gavin and Vice-President of Operations C. L. Jenks—a great pair of railroaders.

The train crew grab a bite to eat, and by 10:15 the 2014 has taken on coal, water, and sand and is coupled onto the train. Now let's check the movement of this 180-car ore train, the running time of which was 4 hours and 55 minutes, including the 15-minute delay.

Coupled to train	10:15	
Brake test	10:26	Two stickers
Leave Kelly Lake	10:37	
Pass Riley	10:58	
Pass Casco	11:31	
Pass Baden	12:13	
Pass Arlberg	12:28	
Arrive Brookston	12:42	

The fog and early-morning mist which prevail in northern Minnesota at this season, have lifted, and it is possible to get a look at the train stretching away ahead of the caboose. When the weather closes in, ore trains have to stop for inspection halfway between Kelly Lake and Brookston.

From the cupola the engine seems like a toy, there at the head end of those interminable cars of red ore.

The train is inspected at Brookston, and coal and water taken aboard again. One journal is running hot and is rebrassed, which delays us 15 minutes. The conductor waves his hand, and the signal is relayed to the engineer. You instinctively brace yourself when you hear the slack running out, for the sound of it comes back with a growing roar of a big sea; the caboose lunges ahead. Again we check the stations.

Leave Brookston	1:19
Cloquet	2:07
Scanlon	2:13
Carlton	2:20
Bridge 6	2:35
State Line Tower	2:45
Dewey	2:54
Boylston	3:07
Saunders	3:16

| Bridge A-8 | 3:19 |
| Arrive Allouez | 3:32 |

We watch the swaying cars and are amazed at the smooth manner in which Engineer Fosig handles the train. Now and then we glance down at Conductor Barilani, working at his wheel reports, and all of the time we have been thinking that 180 cars is a whale of a lot of cars—16,740 tons. But to the crew it is all in the day's work.

Like the Chesapeake & Ohio's and the Norfolk & Western's 15,000-ton coal trains, the Great Northern ore moves are closely watched and inspected, both from the head and the rear end. The speed limit from Kelly Lake to Allouez is 30 miles an hour, and it is rigidly obeyed. They keep the retainers up on the first 40 cars of each train, all the way down.

The ore move on the Great Northern, in my opinion, is one of the most amazing railroad operations in the United States, and it is another example of the American way of making big jobs seem easy.

From thaw-out to freeze-up, iron ore flows down to Allouez over another of the Great Northern's magic carpets—a carpet of steel on a right of way dyed by the red earth of the Iron Range.

Fast Mail

Nos. 27 and 28—the Fast Mail—daily come booming out of St. Paul, Minnesota, and out of Seattle, on Puget Sound, to start their flights over the rails of the Great Northern. The name "Fast Mail" breathes of speed and high adventure. From the days of the Pony Express, the carrying of the United States Mail has created a colorful page in American history, with the railroads playing a stellar role in the headlong rush of the mail sack.

The distance between St. Paul and Seattle is 1,765 miles, and the westbound schedule calls for a running time of 46 hours and 15 minutes, including 40 minutes "dead time" at Spokane, Washington. Eastbound, the schedule is 54 hours and 45 minutes, with 2 hours out at Spokane. The make-up of 27 and 28 consists of all mail and express cars, with the exception of one passenger coach.

Except for local work between Havre, Montana, and Spokane, No. 27 makes a limited number of stops. Eastbound No. 28's time is slowed somewhat for the reason that it makes more regular stops than the westbound mail train. This land of the Great Northern is a world of vast open spaces, of far horizons, dotted here and there with small communities which must be served. The local trains we know in the more populated sections would lose themselves in the empire of the Great Northern; thus it falls to the lot of the Fast Mail to pause briefly here and there in its surging flight for the accommodation of these fine communities and people of the Northwest.

The remarkable part of it is that these mail trains of the Great Northern can graciously perform a certain amount of neighborly service and still hold to the stiff schedule that it maintains. This road is the only northern route which operates through mail and express trains between the Twin Cities and Seattle.

Westbound mail is much heavier than eastbound, and includes a large amount of letter mail. Heavy eastbound letter mail is handled by No. 2, the Empire Builder. No. 28 hauls non-letter mail, for the most part, which is in not too much of a hurry, and its equipment to a considerable extent consists of deadhead movement.

No. 1, the westbound Empire Builder, carries letter mail only over part of the route. This movement is from Fargo to Minot, North Dakota, and from Shelby, Montana, to Spokane, Washington.

No. 27 picks up mail coming through from the East, including full cars brought into St. Paul for transfer to the Great Northern; it also makes collections along the line to Seattle. No. 28, in addition to the slower mail from the west coast, picks up letter and other mail throughout North Dakota and western Minnesota which funnels in from branches and other rail systems.

Nos. 27 and 28, the thundering mailmen of the Great Northern, serve the wheat-grower and the cattleman, the lumberman and the sheep-raiser, the apple-raiser, the country schoolteacher, and the proprietor of the general store, the St. Paul merchant and the Seattle manufacturer—faithful always to the tradition of the United States Mail.

Throughout her 1,765-mile run, No. 27 carries a 60-foot postal distributing car, together with mail storage cars in whatever numbers are necessary. The mail distributing car maintains a force of about 7 clerks from St. Paul to Fargo; 5 from Fargo to Williston, North Dakota; 3 from Williston to Shelby, Montana; 6 or 7 from Shelby to Spokane; and 9 from Spokane to Seattle.

Between Spokane and Seattle these clerks work up Seattle and Tacoma mail for city delivery, with the result that it is ready for firms or outlying stations upon arrival. Mail bound for Tacoma, 40 miles down the sound from Seattle, is loaded onto a truck which leaves Seattle just 5 minutes after the arrival there of No. 27 at 5 a.m. One hour and 5 minutes later it is at the post office in Tacoma.

The 60-foot distributing cars move east on the Empire Builder, Seattle to Fargo; then are switched into No. 28 for the remainder of the journey to Minneapolis and St. Paul. Seven clerks work up the Twin Cities mail for carriers and outlying stations. They also work other mail.

Nineteen forty-three was the biggest year for No. 27. It handled the equivalent of 1,515 of those 60-foot storage cars, ranging from 102 in August to 207 in December. In 1942 there were 1,259 of these storage cars racing through, with 1,347 in 1944 and 1,308 in 1945.

Down the trail of the Empire Builder rides the mail paced by Old Bill on the shield of the Great Northern Railway.

The Grain Movement

The Great Northern is the principal grain-hauling railway in the Northwest. The harvest that springs from the black soil of North Dakota alone is in an amount that beggars description. A golden sea inundates the rolling prairies. You travel down it for endless miles—100, 200, 300 miles and more. The beauty of it remains with you always. The great North Dakota wheat bin.

Your speeding train seems lost in this world where the yellow horizons never cease, and yet these twin bands of silver shape the destiny of the flood of wheat that comes like a tidal wave from this land of plenty.

The wheat tonnage originating east of the Montana boundary is about twice that which comes from the territory to the west, for North Dakota ranks first as a source of grain among the on-line states.

Minneapolis with its huge flour mills is the leading point of destination for this wheat. In second place comes the movement to the head of the Lakes at Duluth and Superior. The Great Northern serves a large number of the terminal storage elevators here.

Grain originating west of Minot, North Dakota, moves over the Surrey line. It is sampled by Federal inspectors at Willmar, Minnesota, or at St. Cloud, Minnesota. The movement from the North Dakota branch lines and the Grand Forks, North Dakota, main line is usually sampled at Grand Forks.

The vast bulk of the samples goes to Minneapolis or Duluth, and the grain is bought or sold on the basis of this sampling, after which instructions are placed with the Great Northern as to the point to which it will be shipped. Some grain is purchased by interior mills and is diverted to their bins. As diversions are received at hold points such as Willmar, Grand Forks, and St. Cloud, cars are switched in order of destination and trains are made up for movement to the markets indicated.

When the grain rush is on the Great Northern moves the wheat in solid trains. Empties are moved into the grain territory in great numbers in advance of the movement, while long trains of empties are rushed to replace the emptying grain-elevator sidings. These movements are made at high speed, particularly during periods when the boxcar supply is limited, as it was during and following World War II.

From Havre, Montana, west, virtually all grain moves south or toward the coast. It is in the territory west of Havre that high-protein wheat is grown. This may move east or west, but the bulk of it goes to mills in Montana or on the Pacific coast.

The barley and oats harvest starts in southwestern Minnesota in mid-July in normal seasons and flows north and west. While this movement is far less than wheat, 30,000 carloads of barley, oats, and rye of these on-line crops, plus those received from other roads, represent a heavy tonnage—something like 300 or so 100-car trains, just for example.

We still have not included corn, flaxseed, sugar beets, and other agricultural products.

Other Products

Potatoes: Out of the Red River Valley of northwestern Minnesota and eastern North Dakota roll some 20,000 to 25,000 carloads of the humble spud every year, for the Red River Valley is a heavy producer of certified seed potatoes, in addition to those which find their way to the table.

Normally the table stock begins moving in mid-September and will continue until April or May. The seed potatoes are stored after harvesting, starting their move into the Southeast and Southwest sometime between mid-December and the early part of February. In the years between 1936 and 1946, storage facilities were built by growers and growers' organizations in increasing numbers in the Red River Valley. Thus it became possible to spread out the potato movement. It also enabled growers to keep an eye on price trends and market their potatoes accordingly.

At harvesttime the potatoes, so far as possible, are placed in the trackside storage warehouses, as this enables movements to be made at any time. When heavy shipments are in progress the potato finds itself provided with a special train as it starts its journey both to the Southeast and the Southwest.

Apples: Out of Wenatchee, Washington, and the surrounding country come the apples that move over the rails of the Great Northern to the tune of 16,000 to 18,000 carloads yearly. The apple, like wheat and the potato, moves for the most part by the trainload.

The apple travels in a reefer, or refrigerator car. These cars are moved in before the crop is ready, and the cars are serviced at the Great Northern Appleyard terminal. And then when the harvest is under way the cars roll to warehouse sidings from Wenatchee northward to Oroville, 140 miles away. This apple belt also includes a 25-mile-wide belt east and west of Wenatchee.

After the apples are loaded, the cars are assembled at Appleyard for icing or heating, as the season dictates; then are made into trains. The apples moving west are largely for export. However, the bulk movement is eastward and southward. The shipments are watched over with an eye to their further needs en route, with the result that they eventually appear in the market lovely to look at and delicious to the last bite.

Forest Products: The great state of Washington is the leading source of forest products in Great Northern territory, with Oregon just an eyelash behind. The great sawmills and the husky lumberjack provide the lumber harvest, and the falling monarch comes crashing down to the high cry of, "Timber!"

And timber it is that rides the trains of the Great Northern in the amount of around 100,000 carloads. Connecting lines chip in with another 40,000 to 50,000 carloads. Logs, ties, lumber, pulpwood, and associated products make up the movement. Forest products in less quantity from Minnesota and the Rockies are included in the total carloads mentioned.

The shipments are predominantly eastbound, though a considerable amount of lumber finds its way south. A current trend involves the use of wood waste for alcohol and other products, including the manufacture of fireplace logs from sawdust.

More and more the products hauled by the Great Northern are moving in aluminum boxcars, floated on Timken roller bearings. Many of these cars are built in the St. Cloud, Minnesota, shops of the G.N. These new light-weight boxcars represent a saving of 4,057 pounds as compared with standard steel construction—a dead load that becomes a pay load.

Used in connection with roller bearings, these cars are creating new standards in the movement of freight. There are no speed restrictions for roller bearings, which means that the freight train of tomorrow will be riding on frictionless wings.

The roller-bearing equipped cars of the G.N. have come

through their baptism of fire with flying colors, having operated at temperatures up to 120 degrees Fahrenheit and to 35 degrees below zero over thousands of miles of main line.

In the limited space at our command, we have but briefly reviewed the Great Northern and the land that it serves—the land of the Empire Builder. Its rails have blazed a path for commerce and industry in the Northwest—a long trail awinding straight through God's Country.

CHAPTER XVII

TAILORING THE TRACKS ON THE NEW YORK CENTRAL

Maintenance

The heroic achievements of train operation in the United States during and immediately following World War II were in no less a measure matched by the performance of the Maintenance of Way department of the railroads. Few paeans are sung for the track repair and maintenance men. And yet, though receiving less acclaim in a role not as spectacular, the Maintenance of Way has reached high peaks of achievement.

"What are the functions of the Maintenance of Way Department?" you ask. We will let S. E. Armstrong, Maintenance Engineer on the New York Central, answer that. Mr. Armstrong tells us:

Primarily it is the job of the Maintenance of Way Department to keep the tracks in safe operating condition at all times. The rails and track structure must be periodically lined and surfaced; ties must be tamped; close attention must be paid to the alignment and smoothness of curves, maintaining them to the mathematical super-elevation and degree of curvature. New rail in sizable tonnages has to be laid, involving the distribution of the rail and other materials, as well as the removal of released material.

And there is much more, including a vast amount of incidental work. The basic concept in many minds is that mainly the Maintenance of Way Department keeps "two streaks of steel" together and in line so the wheels can roll over them. While this is the ultimate aim and one of the principal functions, there are many and lesser known factors involved.

He goes on to point out that the two component parts of the Maintenance of Way Department, as in other departments, mainly involve *men* and *materials,* to which might be added *machines.* "Men come first," says Mr. Armstrong, "for it is through their combined efforts that materials and machines are effectively used."

Manpower: On manpower hinges the success of any undertaking. Unlike the old question of whether the hen or the egg came first, we know in this machine age that man came first, and on man depends not only the creation of the machine, but its operation and maintenance.

We have explained in another chapter that track work has become mechanized to a great extent. The problems ahead have to do, we are reminded by the Maintenance of Way Department on the New York Central, with maintaining a force of trained men capable not only of performing the necessary track work, but of supervising it.

The time will come when the older and experienced trackmen will be stepping aside, and younger men must take their places. Where they will come from might easily become a major problem. There is a certain appeal in railroading, particularly in the Operating Department, but there is real opportunity in the Maintenance of Way Department.

The wrinkled face of Mother Earth and the elements have challenged the Maintenance of Way forces since the first train went huffing down the railroad. Weeds and brush foul the right of way, retarding drainage; there is the heaving of track from frost action and the pumping of the ties in the ballast when rains creates soft spots. Intense cold solidifies the roadbed, virtually eliminating the wave motion of rail and track, thus intensifying the counterbalance action of the locomotive and the pound of flat wheels. Variations in temperature produce inevitable expansion and contraction of the rails, setting up internal stresses. Low temperatures reduce the impact value of the steel, increasing susceptibility to failure.

The second major item in track maintenance is *materials.* Let us consider the rail. Outwardly, this T-rail remains the same in appearance as it did a great many years ago. However, there is a vast difference in design and in the structure of the rail itself. Through constant improvement from the days of the wrought-iron rail, on down the era of Bessemer steel to the present universal open-hearth, the steel rail has kept pace with the growth of the locomotive and the train.

Within the past few years a method of avoiding certain internal deficiencies has been developed. This process is known as "controlled cooling," or the "thermal treatment." The effect of this treatment has been the elimination of the inducing cause of one of the most troublesome type of rail defects, known as the "transverse fissure." Controlled cooling has eliminated the internal "shatter" of the steel structure, thus largely removing the cause of the broken rail.

On the 2,500 miles of New York Central track equipped with this rail there has been no such failure since it has been in use. But this treatment is not a cure-all for other rail troubles, including web or base failures and surface difficulties created by slipping drivers and the resultant burned spots. And there is the "shelling" or "flaking" of the steel on the "gauge corners," particularly on the high side of curves; also corrugations or washboard surface on the top of the head.

Ties are perhaps the next in importance in the make-up of the track. While many substitutes for wooden crossties have been considered and experimented with down the years, nothing as yet has been developed that is as practical and as economical as the good old wooden railroad tie. On account of the heavy equipment and increased loading of the present day, the larger-sized ties are generally standard. Nearly all ties are treated with preservatives. Careful attention has also been given to the drainage of storage yards, proper stacking for seasoning, and prompt treating after seasoning.

Changes in frogs and switches which provide for greater rigidity have resulted in smoother riding. So it goes all up and down the track, with every emphasis placed on speeding up traffic.

The Maintenance of Way Department, because of the many problems constantly arising, keeps in close contact with the Motive Power and Rolling Stock department at all times. There are, for instance, those matters relating to the effect of power on track, such as counterbalancing, wheel weights, and spacing. Again, on matters pertaining to clearance of power and cars in tight places, such as overhead bridges, tunnels, track centers, etc. Likewise with such destructive forces as brine dripping on the steel components, and stack cinders fouling the ballast.

These examples merely serve to indicate a few of the many and varied difficulties forever cropping up; yet all of which demand immediate countermeasures in this ceaseless tailoring of the tracks.

The Maintenance of Way Department works in close harmony with the Legal Department on matters relating to the right-of-way lines, highway crossings, power and transmission lines, and other matters. Contact is maintained with government and state agencies and various municipal authorities, and with the Transportation Department, in the furnishing and arranging for tracks, peak loads, and outsize shipments.

There is constant contact with the Operating Department on matters such as placing slow orders where work is in progress, the handling of work trains, track motorcars, and clearance of tracks at derailments, washouts, or for other causes.

The Clearance Car

In August of 1942 a strange-looking car rolled out of the Central's West Albany shops. It was a spiny creature, and it had not been on the road long before it was known as the "Porcupine Car." The New York Central called it a Clearance Car. Its number was X800.

When the war came along the railroads were confronted with the problem of hauling all manner of outsized shipments, from big guns to overseas locomotives. One of the first rules of How to Railroad is never try to enlarge an undersized tunnel by running oversized lading through it. A lot of oversize wartime equipment was loaded onto flatcars and gondolas, that was not included in the clearance calculations when the line was built. This meant that the railroads had to do a lot of measuring and a lot of detouring.

Before the X800 was built, clearance measurements on the Central were taken from a flatcar. This left much to be desired in the way of efficiency. The result was that the boys in the Maintenance of Way Department went into a huddle with a view to simplifying the process. Very shortly, H. Buckley, Clearance Engineer, came up with the construction details of the X800.

When it made its appearance on the New York Central's Boston & Albany lines, being pushed by a light engine, several heavy drinkers took the pledge. With its bristling array of spines and feelers, the X800 presented a startling and formidable aspect to the uninitiated.

The Clearance Car was remodeled from an old baggagesmoker. When in operation it is pushed by a locomotive, moving very slowly while taking measurements. It is manned by a crew of 5, including an engineer in charge, a draftsman, and 3 men from the Engineering Corps.

The peculiar appearance of the X800, viewed head on, results from the 112 projecting "feelers," or fingers, surrounding the round white face of a pantograph. These feelers, which are made of oak, are spaced 4 inches apart and extend in an arc around the car to a distance of 3 feet from the roadbed on each side.

Upon meeting an obstruction, the feelers swivel backward, holding their corrected position for measurement. They extend outward 7 feet 6 inches on the sides from the center line of the track, and to a minimum of 17 feet, 7 inches high.

Measurements of top clearance are ingeniously and accurately performed by a pantograph of stainless steel, more than 6 feet in diameter. This pantograph is connected to a small pantograph inside of the car which makes a reduction of $\frac{1}{12}$ and records the readings on drawing paper, thus making a chart of the clearance. The draftsman then plots out the finished drawing.

X800 is constructed with a large steel platform on its front end, with a steel ladder leading to the raised platform across the front of the pantograph. From this elevated platform the pantograph is operated. Inside, the car contains a platform for the operation of the small pantograph, storage space for tools, a drafting table, washrooms, and a shower. There are no sleeping quarters or kitchen, as stops are made at convenient sidings and yards.

The Ballast Cleaner

One of the railway housekeeping jobs that falls to the lot of the Maintenance of Way Department is keeping the ballast clean, and it is as important as attending to the drain under the kitchen sink. A clean stone ballast has a direct bearing on the safety, comfort, and speed of the trains.

Your housekeeper has various modern appliances for her convenience in cleaning house. So the railroads of late years have been provided with up-to-the-minute machines which make for speedy and thorough accomplishment of their many tasks. Not the least of these is the ballast cleaner.

The primary purpose of the ballast cleaner is to improve the drainage of the track. It removes the hard-packed accumulation of cinders, dirt, and decayed matter as efficiently as a vacuum cleaner sweeps your carpet.

Not long ago a huge machine weighing approximately 100 tons made its appearance east of Buffalo on the main line of the Mohawk Division. It was mounted upon a specially built railroad car and was incorporated as the principal unit in a work train. It began work in midsummer and started renovating ballast east from Schuyler Junction to Hoffmans on Track 4 of the New York Central System. From Hoffmans it doubled back on Track 3, continuing its labors until the ground became frozen.

On Track 4 it cleaned the ballast on both sides of the track, on the shoulder, and in the "6-foot," which is the area between tracks. On Track 3 it cleaned the ballast only in the "6-foot" between Tracks 3 and 1.

This machine is known as the Fairmont Ballast Cleaner. It is leased by the railroad and is operated by its own permanent crew of 18 men, divided into two 10-hour shifts per day. The remaining 4 hours, usually determined by the period when traffic on adjacent tracks is heaviest, are employed for refilling the fuel tanks of the motors and doing any necessary repair work.

The make-up of the work train consists of a Diesel switch engine, 3 loaded ballast cars, a caboose, a supply boxcar, the ballast cleaner, 2 dirt cars joined together in an articulated unit, and a tool car or machine shop.

In operation the Diesel locomotive and cars forward of the ballast cleaner move ahead approximately 40 yards, where they are anchored by setting the brakes. Cables stretching between the ballast cleaner and the supply boxcar are then wound up by a motor-driven windlass in the ballast cleaner so that the rear half of the train is pulled toward the anchored front half.

The ballast cleaner has two boxes, one on each side. It is the machinery in these boxes that does the digging, screening, and dumping of the clean ballast back into position beside the track. When not in operation or when a train is approaching on an adjacent track, one or both of these boxes are withdrawn into the side of the car.

When in operation the digger box plows into the ballast to a depth of 10 inches in the 6-foot or 14 inches in the shoulder. As the car moves forward, the digger at the front of the box scoops up the dirty ballast under the watchful eye of the operator in a cab in the car. Here a lever controls the lateral openings of the jaws of the plow, as the operator directs its movements and prevents it from damaging the tie ends.

The dirty ballast then travels upward over a conveyor chain and is thrown onto a heavy shaking screen. The cinders, dirt, and refuse are shifted onto a conveyor belt, which moves the matter thus separated to the dirt cars. Meanwhile the cleaned ballast is returned to the trough dug by the plow.

The dirt cars are provided only for loading when the ballast cleaner is working in cuts, adjacent to stations, or in locations where there is no room or place to dispose of this refuse. Otherwise the disposal is accomplished by means of another conveyor belt attached to a long boom which reaches beyond the ditch along the right of way. There Nature soon dresses it with vegetation.

Two gasoline motors operate the windlass, conveyor belts, and hydraulic lifting mechanism; also the digger. Two other motors generate electricity for the lighting system which illuminates the ballast car and track during night work.

Working two 10-hour shifts per day, the ballast cleaning machine has cleaned from 1.5 to 4 miles of track, depending upon local and traffic conditions.

Woman's work, it is said, is never done. This also applies to the house-cleaning activities of a railroad like the New York Central, as men and machines attack the demon dirt, forever accumulating down those endless miles carpeted by steel and stone.

Subsurface Grouting

The high-speed main tracks of the New York Central are maintained for passenger-train speeds of 80 miles per hour. These tracks, as well as the freight mains, carry an enormous tonnage freight—fast-traveling manifests and mile-long drags burdened with almost every commodity under the sun. To carry these loads the tracks must be maintained at peak efficiency.

As though ordinary wear and tear were not enough to keep the Maintenance of Way Department in a fret, Mother Nature takes a hand. At times she attacks openly and ferociously; again she smiles disarmingly; yet even then the invisible dagger in her hand is probing at the very heart of the roadbed structure, there in the subsoil beneath the ballast.

Spongy soft spots develop. These result in dangerous conditions of track and slow orders have to be issued, causing delays to train movements. For a time unstable subgrade conditions were accepted as part of the ills a railroad is heir to; then the railroad began to fight them.

These soft spots exist at intermittent intervals and are of various depths, ranging from 3 to 12 feet below the bottom of the ties. They occur at low points and obviously are affected by drainage conditions. Deep cuts and high fills are also susceptible to this water rot; in fact, wherever there are clays and silt or other soils which retain a high moisture content, soft spots are bound to develop.

The railroad problem was how to get rid of them—not a fly-by-night cure-all, but a permanent remedy. Maintenance of Way engineers scratched their heads and rolled up their sleeves and went to work, certain that there must be some way of ridding the track of this deep-rooted ulcer.

In 1936 the Pennsylvania Railroad attacked an 85-foot soft spot with a shot in the arm. They called it *pressure subsurface grouting*. The Maintenance of Way Department fashioned a railroad-size hypodermic needle which it jabbed into that portion of the roadbed afflicted with this soft spot and shot in a solution called "grout"; then awaited the patient's reaction.

The sick man responded to the treatment, and in 1940 the Michigan Central began experimenting with this method of grouting near Monroe, Michigan.

All previously accepted remedies for the soft spot disease were promptly abandoned on the New York Central, and tests were begun with this pressure subsurface grouting method. Careful study was made of a number of test sections, and much was learned from these observations. In most cases the soft spots consisted of very plastic soil without free water. This indicated that draining free water from the subgrade was not a cure for the condition. It was further discovered that the lowest point to which the pounding of the trains had driven the ballast was directly below or outside of the rail. Later it was revealed that this low point might be as much as 3 feet outside of the end of the tie, extending almost invariably to a point beneath the rail itself.

The original test sections were made after 6 weeks of drought, when periodic maintenance was still required. The line between the ballast and the soil was wet, and the soil was so plastic that it oozed from between the fingers when compressed in the hand. This liquefied condition had been caused by the successive poundings of the trains after sufficient moisture had reached the subsoil. The result was the formation of a series of soft spots which had been enlarged by the interception of additional water.

"Push-outs" along embankments, "squeezes" in cuts, and mud-caked ballast in the cribs and at the ends of ties provided evidence of the malignance of this hidden roadbed tumor. In some of the spots chosen for the original research it was necessary to surface the track only a few times a year, while at other points surfacing was required as often as three times a week to maintain the track in first-class condition.

It was agreed that the only way to cure the soft spots was to keep the moisture from reaching the subsoil, which, once deprived of this moisture, was bound eventually to dry out and stabilize itself.

Because the ballast directly above the subsoil was porous, cement grouting seemed to be the answer, as has been pointed out. This grouting, the engineers reasoned, would seal off the moisture seepage from the subsoil and at the same time distribute the impact of the wheels of the train. The tests surpassed even the fondest hopes of the Maintenance of Way Department.

The original grouting equipment included about the same paraphernalia as that in use at the present time. This consists principally of an air compressor, a combined grout mixer and pressure tank, 50 feet of 1½-inch rubber hose, and fittings and injection pipes of various lengths. The original air pressure of 70 pounds per square inch was reduced to 40 pounds, for the reason that the higher pressure caused a large number of line plugs and did not force additional grout under the track.

Of course, there is more equipment required, such as the driving caps which fit over the injection pipes, jackhammers for driving home the injection pipes, and pipe-pullers for withdrawing them.

Engine sand is used in the grout, for coarser sand, it was discovered, would not enter the subballast, and it had a tendency to create line plugs.

Roughly, the grouting procedure is as follows: The soft spots are located, and the equipment and grout material are moved to the site. The crew usually consists of a foreman and a crew of from 4 to 6 men. After the equipment has been set up, the injection pipes are driven with the jackhammer. They are started into the ballast about 1 foot outside of the end of the ties, slanting toward the track at an angle of about 30 degrees, which will place the tip of the pipe slightly outside of the rail for normal depths of soft spots. The depth of the soft spot is determined by the required length of the first or second injection pipe. Adequate clearance of the protruding injection pipe must be allowed for passing trains.

Approximately a day's supply of injection pipes is driven ahead of the grouting operations. They are spaced about 5 feet apart. This does not mean that grout can be injected into every pipe; in some cases the grout will be refused, but this is the exception rather than the rule. The depth to which these pipes are driven is determined by driving resistance. When the point enters a soft spot, there is an apparent decrease in resistance. Driving is stopped at this point.

A plug then is driven into the soft subsoil with a ramrod, and water is forced into the subballast under 40 pounds' pressure. This is to flush the fine clay and silt particles from the voids of the ballast and to produce a lubricating effect for the grout. If the water is refused at the first attempt, the pipe is pulled up about 6 inches and pressure again applied. These trials are repeated at successively shallower depths up to 2½ feet below the bottom of the ties. If the water is still refused, the grout mixture would of course not be accepted, and the operation moves to the next injection pipe.

Some concern has been expressed over the fact that in pressure grouting considerable water is injected into the subgrade before and with the grout. However, all of this is not free water, as a large portion of it is absorbed by the ballast and grout.

The amount of grout accepted by the injection pipes varies widely, as does the distance the grout travels underground. At times it will gush from pipes several yards away. When this happens the pipe is capped and the pressure is again applied. The watchful eye of the foreman is always on the lookout for grout breaking through the shoulder of the roadbed; also for a possible chimney under or between the ties. The pressure is then immediately reduced. If the break-through occurs in the shoulder there is no harm done, but if it is in the track it must be removed after it has hardened.

When the grouting has been completed, the track must be brought to line. Grouting does not require the issuing of slow orders.

The result of grouting is immediately apparent in the improved riding qualities of the track, as compared to soft subgrade conditions which require constant maintenance, and even then have a tendency to become rough between periods of surfacing.

It is interesting to note that certain sections grout-treated as long ago as 1941 have not required maintenance since grout was injected. The savings for 13 spots grouted the first year amounted to $2,343. The cost of grouting was $1,029.27.

As of February 1, 1945, cross sections were dug across the track to make detailed observations of the concrete formations produced by injecting grout into the subballast at 16 locations. The resulting concrete, we are informed, has a compression strength of at least 2,500 pounds per square inch.

Little or no moisture was found below any of these cement formations, and the subsoil underneath was so hardened that it was necessary to use picks to remove it.

Subballast grouting has been found to be adaptable to stabilizing the approaches to bridges, which usually require periodic maintenance in the maintaining of an even run-off from the end of the bridge structure. There have been cases where the ballast has become so stabilized by grouting that no further maintenance has been required.

Up to January 1, 1944, 113 spots were treated on the New York Central System west of Buffalo. These had a total length of 18,436 feet, and the cost average was $1.21 per track foot.

Sixteen grouting outfits were in operation on the Central in 1945. Many approaches to main- and branch-line bridges have been grouted, and soft spots are constantly being investigated in connection with continuing the grouting operations.

At this writing, 23 railroads in 21 states and 1 Canadian Province are employing this grouting treatment on their main lines. The bumps are being taken out of the steel rail, which spells smoother, safer, and faster train service.

Laying Steel

One of the first problems of railroad engineers was laying steel, and it is still a problem. It seems simple enough, and yet when you stand close beside a locomotive like the Central's Niagara and have to look up at the top of the drivers, when you look at the great boiler and remember that it will soon be traveling down the rail a lot faster than you ordinarily drive your car, you will begin to wonder how the rail can safely carry it.

New York Central engineers are still working on the original problem of rail laying, utilizing modern methods and materials. The result has been a swifter and safer movement of heavier equipment and loads over tracks of greater stability and longer life.

In May of 1941 there was a rail-laying demonstration on the Michigan Central west of Dearborn, Michigan. Engineers and trackmen gathered from all districts of the New York Central System to have a look at the latest methods of replacing rail. The roadbed at this point was standard on the Central. It consisted of straight and double-tracked section 8 feet above the surrounding depressed land and on an embankment of cinders and gravel. The ballast was broken stone about 12 inches in depth. The cinder shoulders were 1 foot wider than the required 2-foot, 1-inch minimum.

The rail-laying force consisted of 121 laborers, 5 foremen, 4 assistant foremen, a mechanic, 2 assistant mechanics, and a Burro Crane operator. The work was under the direction of General Foreman Philip Margraf. The job was the replacing of the 105-pound open-hearth rail with the 127-pound "control-cooled" rail which we mentioned earlier in this chapter. The track was westbound main line.

The total force was divided into 8 gangs, each with a specific job to do in the removal of the old rails, the preparation for the laying of the new rails, and the actual laying. Thus, with the operations spaced at intervals over approximately ¼ mile, they constituted an assembly line somewhat similar to that in mass-production factories.

When the force went to work, the heavier materials had already been distributed by work trains on previous days. The new rail had been laid out on the roadbed shoulder, with splice bars placed near the rail ends. Kegs of spikes had been set out at intervals. The tie plates had been placed between the ties on the outside of the track.

The lead-off man in the rail-laying force cut the bond wires.

He was followed by crews operating power spike-pullers and power wrenches for removing nuts from bolts. Some spikes and frozen nuts were dealt with by hand, yielding to claw bars and sledges and chisels.

Other men removed the rail anchors, splice bars, and bolts, renutting the bolts and placing them in a pile. Rails were then rolled to the shoulder with safety forks and the old tie plates removed with hooks. Next came the preparation of the ties for the new rail.

First, high ballast was raked to the center of the track, and tie plugs were inserted and driven into the old spike holes. Then 6 men, protected with goggles and armored guards for their legs and feet, planed the ties by use of power adzing machines so that the new tie plates would be placed in proper level. The ties not to be replaced in the near future were creosoted, and finally the new tie plates were set against the outside shoulder of adzed dapping.

A Burro Crane then picked up the new rail and set it down on the tie plates, guided by men with short bars. As each rail was laid, a proper expansion shim was inserted, according to the temperature of the rail. A push car carrying sharpening tools for the adzers was attached to the crane, which rolled forward over each new pair of rails laid.

Next in the assembly line were 2 push cars loaded with new spikes, bolts, and lubricants. Two spikes were dropped beside each tie. New bolts were distributed at the rail ends and the piles of old bolts picked up.

The web of the rails and splice bars were scrubbed with wire brushes to remove the mill scale, and lubricant applied where the bars would be set against the web of the rails. The bars were then adjusted, bolts inserted, and rail shims removed. Men with power wrenches then tightened the bolts, trailed by an adjuster with a speed wrench operated by hand.

The following gang drove the first spikes holding the newly placed rail as men with lining bars trued it off from the opposite fixed rails. Holes were bored in the ties, spikes set in position with hand hammers, and close behind came the spike drivers, working with air-operated tools. Anchors were then set on the rail base to prevent creepage, and a power unit drilled holes into the rail for the bond wires which complete the signal circuit.

The last gang in the fast-moving assembly line tamped the ballast around the loose ties, especially at the rail joints, and further did such miscellaneous work as driving odd spikes by hand and removing odd scrap from the track.

During the 3-day demonstration the track force laid rails at the rate of approximately 50 rails per hour. The rail laying ended at 1 o'clock to be ready for the Mercury, which passed over the track on its early-afternoon run from Detroit to Chicago.

Quality of workmanship, exactness, and elimination of delays were the primary goals of the methods and organization demonstrated. Thus the sequence of operations was laid out to prevent gangs, or the men individually, from interfering with or slowing down each other's work or duties.

Stress was also placed on the necessity of removing miscellaneous materials from the center of the track to avoid confusion between the old and the new, and distributing the new material in such a manner that it would be readily available at the proper time as the work moved forward.

Old materials—rails, tie plates, anchors, and spikes—were picked up by a work train the following day.

A permanent record of the demonstration was made with a moving-picture camera. Pictures were taken to detail each operation, thus establishing a complete illustrated memorandum of the laying of the steel. The films also will be of educational value for men of the Maintenance of Way Department.

In this age of rapid progress on the railroad, the trackman and the maintenance engineer march shoulder to shoulder in the big parade down the shining path of the steel rail.

CHAPTER XVIII

THE "GFX"

Santa Fe Green Fruit

The Green Fruit Trains—GFX—rank high in importance on the Santa Fe. Long trains of yellow reefers crawl out of "San Berdo"—San Bernardino—and start the climb over El Cajon, the pass that divides the ranges of the San Bernardinos and the San Gabriels. Up through the broad canyon's throat and into the narrowing hills; up from 1,000 feet above sea level to nearly 4,000 in 25 miles—up past Devore, Cajon Station, and Summit, to look down on the filmy haze of the great Mojave.

We are starting east toward Barstow and Needles, toward Arizona and New Mexico and Texas. Gleaming rails reaching on into Oklahoma and Kansas toward the big Argentine Yard, and still on into Missouri and Illinois toward Chicago and the Great Lakes. The Green Fruit Trains are rolling. Beyond the sprawling terminal tracks of the transfer lines, where the yellow reefers will be shuttled through busy classification yards, these cars of the fruit trains will be caught up by impatient engines of the B.&O., the Central, and the Erie, famed as the "route of the perishables," and rushed on east at close to express-train speed.

From the cupola of the way car we look across the roofs of the yellow reefers, past the spouting exhaust of the steam helper, across more cartops to the far-away blue-and-yellow Diesel and its 5,400 work horses, straining in the din of their tight steel corral as they spin the treadmill of the geared driving wheels in this beginning of the march of the Fruit Express. This is the beginning of the vital distribution of California's more than 100 varieties of fresh fruit and vegetables.

We look back now toward lusty San Bernardino, with its bustling business district, its comfortable homes, and the shops and yards of the Santa Fe. Crowding close to San Bernardino, in a vast checkerboard of greenery, are orange groves and vineyards, spread all of the way from the distant Santa Anas to the base of the San Gabriels mountain ramparts, which are crowned by snowy San Antonio Peak—"Old Baldy"—thrust 10,000 feet into the sky.

From the rich and fertile valleys dimming behind our markers come the citrus fruits and other perishables that ride eastward over the rails of the Santa Fe. To move these ripening fruits and vegetables, the Santa Fe maintains a fleet of over 14,355 refrigerator cars. To sustain and service this fleet the Santa Fe has established at San Bernardino—often called "Santa Fe Town" —a classification yard, precooling plant, reefer sheds, car and locomotive shops, and various other units.

To facilitate the handling of these crops the Santa Fe has developed a special Refrigerator Department, organized for the purpose of providing a complete protective service in the transportation of perishable freight, including icing plants and special departments peculiar to the fruit move.

The railroad leaves no stone unturned in an effort to deliver this fresh fruit at its destination as deliciously fresh as when it left the California fields and groves, and this is no simple matter, for much of this movement involves a 3,000-mile haul before it comes under the critical eye of the housewife.

The speedy handling of the fruit trains creates a problem which involves a hair-drawn timing, plus elaborate and intricate detail necessary to prevent spoilage. And once more fast freight plays its part in our daily lives, particularly in starting the day off with a breakfast-table smile.

Over the years fruit handling has been built into an enormous industry necessitating the construction of feeder lines into the principal producing areas, the building of ice plants and facilities at convenient points along the main line, the close co-operation of the railroad, the shipper, and the producer—all interwoven into a precise machine that has but one purpose, which is the delivery of fruits and vegetables to the table of the distant consumer as fresh and delicious as when harvested.

Better to understand the part that rail transportation plays, one must remember that the bulk of the perishable movement originates on the west coast, with most of the markets 2,000 and 3,000 miles distant. The products are of a highly perishable nature, and their movement is a year-round job. Many complications arise because of the fact that the fruit train, from the time that it leaves the packing districts, often experiences wide variations of temperature, from summer heat to winter cold.

Consider, then, that the Santa Fe alone handles an average of 100,000 carloads of California and Arizona perishables a year. Another 25,000 carloads move over the Santa Fe from the states of Colorado, New Mexico, and Texas, with 12,000 carloads of cantaloupes, onions, and assorted vegetables from Colorado; 4,000 carloads of carrots, cantaloupes, and lettuce from New Mexico; and 9,000 carloads of potatoes, peaches, cantaloupes, and watermelons from Texas.

Cross-country movement requires 5-10 days. The more important markets, such as Kansas City, Chicago, New York, and Boston have a sixth-, seventh-, and tenth-morning delivery respectively, as compared to from 2 to 3 weeks 40 years ago.

At this writing, about 2,000 of the Santa Fe's reefers have been equipped with Preco circulating fans, a refrigeration improvement device that is being installed in all new and rebuilt cars coming out of the Wichita shops. The Santa Fe is also experimenting with a new type of streamlined, stainless-steel refrigerator car which has a number of special features, including a sliding door to permit better clearance at loading docks, as well as a convertible light-weight bulkhead and a continuous duct system that can be cut in or out by means of adjustable louvers operated by a hand wheel over the door. This car is 5,000 pounds lighter than the older type of refrigerator car.

Ice is a big item in the fruit movement, and its use is being increased because of a growing movement of frozen fruits and vegetables. The manufacture and application of ice at strategic points en route, as well as at the originating points, is a big industry in itself, as indicated by the fact that in 1945 the Santa Fe used more than 1,000,000 tons of ice in refrigeration; 750,000 tons being used on the coast lines alone.

These icing plants are located at Los Angeles, San Bernardino, Bakersfield, Fresno, Stockton, Oceanside, Blythe, and Needles, California; Glendale and Winslow, Arizona; and La Junta, Colorado. In addition, icing service is provided at Albuquerque, Belen, and Clovis, New Mexico; Pueblo and Denver, Colorado; Waynoka, Oklahoma; Sweetwater, Temple, Cleburne, Fort Worth, and Galveston, Texas; Newton, Argentine, Dodge City, and Arkansas City, Kansas; Fort Madison, Iowa; and Corwith, Illinois.

The Santa Fe manufactures a large part of the ice used, and the daily capacity of its own 8 plants is as follows: Los Angeles, 150 tons; San Bernardino, 300 tons; Bakersfield, 400 tons; Fresno (Calwa), 200 tons; Stockton, 100 tons; Needles, 225 tons; Winslow, 200 tons, and La Junta, 100 tons. The current expansion program will increase the capacity of the San Bernardino plant to 450 tons; Bakersfield, to 650 tons, and the Stockton plant to 300 tons. Also, the Santa Fe has one of the largest precooling plants in America at San Bernardino.

Icing requirements are constant, regardless of the fact that thousands of cars move under ventilation only. In addition to icing requirements, there is the matter of temperature changes, which make necessary the use of heaters, and stations along the line are provided for this purpose.

For practical purposes, perishables are divided into five divisions, viz: citrus, deciduous fruits, vegetables, melons, and the new classification, fresh frozen fruits and vegetables. The latter promises to increase rapidly with the establishment of additional facilities.

The citrus fruits consist of oranges, grapefruit, and lemons, and these have maintained first place, making up approximately 40 per cent of the total movement. Grapes are second and potatoes third.

The perishable trains are on the move every day in the year, but the peak movement usually occurs in May and June, with citrus fruits and potatoes predominating. A second heavy movement takes place in September and October. At this time the citrus movement remains at the forefront, while the potatoes give way to grapes. The latter go to wine makers. During prohibition the Santa Fe hauled from 25,000 to 30,000 cars of grapes a year. These shipments, however, are now reduced, for the reason that more refineries have been established in California.

Although grapes still hold second place, the potato move is gaining, largely on account of an increased production in the San Joaquin Valley, particularly in Kern County, for which the Santa Fe is in a way responsible. The road aided in colonizing the Shafter-Wasco district, as it brought to the attention of farmers the opportunities for spud raising in this area. Reflecting these activities, California's early potato production increased from 3,456,000 bushels in 1934 to 23,350,000 in 1945. The Santa Fe also had a part in the development of the Palo Verde Valley. Here vegetable and melon shipments are on the increase.

While each group of perishables has certain standards of handling and refrigeration, certain commodities or individual shipments require special consideration, because of their inherent nature, weather conditions, and the distance to market. Also involved is the manner of packing. For this reason it is interesting to bear in mind that citrus fruits move in boxes and sacks, grapes in lugs, cantaloupes in crates, potatoes in sacks, green peas in hampers, and avocados in flats packed one high to prevent bruising.

As the fruit and vegetable crops begin to ripen, they are harvested and trucked to the packing plants scattered over each producing area. Virtually all deciduous fruits and cantaloupes are precooled, as most of them are picked during hot weather, and it is necessary to reduce the field heat quickly, thereby arresting the ripening process. This precooling is accomplished by placing the fruit in cooling houses where the temperature is brought down to transportation temperature, which ranges from 32 to 50 degrees.

Precooling, of course, depends on the season and other conditions. Citrus fruits are usually precooled for a period of 8 hours. On the road the average car is re-iced about every 24 hours; less, of course, during cool weather.

Refrigerator cars have already been precooled when they are spotted on the packing-house siding. This is accomplished at a central shipping point—San Bernardino in the case of the reefers rolling over El Cajon—where the cars are thoroughly chilled by cold air blown in through air-conditioning ducts, after which the bunkers of each car are filled with about 5 tons of ice.

When the fruit has been loaded, local freights pick up the cars on the packing-house siding and move them to the concentration point. Here the trains are made up and spotted at the icing plant. Workmen open the hatch covers, remove the hatch plugs, and chop down the ice in the bunkers; then new ice is added. The average icing operation requires about 1 minute per car, and is often less. As many as 80 cars have been re-iced in 20-25 minutes.

The standard refrigerator car weighs about 52,000 pounds and has a carrying capacity of approximately 32 tons. The walls, floors, roofs, and doors are heavily insulated. Refrigeration is accomplished by means of naturally circulated air, cooled by contact with ice or a mixture of ice and salt in the bunkers at each end of the car. Air circulation is aided by bulkheads, so placed in front of the ice bunkers that relatively warm air passes over the top to reach the ice; then, becoming chilled, it sinks to the floor, where it reaches the body of the car by passing through a space beneath the bulkheads.

A fruit train may leave California under summer conditions, but long before it reaches Chicago, temperatures may be encountered that require the placing of heaters in the bunkers. Again, due to weather conditions or a desire to lower the temperature of the car quickly to prevent premature ripening and subsequent deterioration, it may become necessary to "top" or "snow-ice" the perishables. In this case the car will be cut out of the train at one of the icing stations en route and spotted at a top-icing platform, where machines blow shaved iced over the fruit, covering it with a snow blanket some 6-8 inches in depth.

Vegetables and to a limited extent cantaloupes, in addition to regular refrigeration obtained from ice in the bunkers, require top-icing averaging 15,000-25,000 pounds, which, in the case of vegetables, is replaced at specified stations in transit, according to the desires of the shipper. Under present tariff requirements, cantaloupes may be top-iced by the shipper at the point of origin but cannot be re-top-iced in transit.

Top-icing is sometimes supplemented with pigeonhole or recess-icing. This means placing ice between the crates to secure and maintain even temperatures throughout the car. This practice has aided materially in putting vegetables and melons on the eastern market in field-crisp condition.

All fresh fruits are now placed in containers and move in refrigerator cars. Watermelons are the exception, and these go in bulk for short hauls, occasionally being handled in stock cars. Peaches are sometimes moved to near-by canneries in bulk in a similar manner. During the car shortage of 1926, stock cars were also used for hauling grapes, but without satisfactory results, and the practice of shipping potatoes in paper-lined stock cars was discontinued when the spud began moving long distances.

The heating of refrigerator cars is accomplished by placing small charcoal heaters in the bunkers. This sometimes becomes necessary in the mountain areas soon after leaving California. Again, the fruit trains may be well on their way to the East before heating becomes necessary. It is necessary to maintain regular heating stations, and at these points the icing process is reversed.

A fruit train on the road comes under the ever-alert eye of trained men whose business it is carefully to guard the contents of these reefers against the ills to which perishables are subject. This comes under the heading of specialized or protective service.

When conditions warrant, ventilating devices are manipulated to provide air circulation, or to exclude outside air of a temperature that might cause chilling. The circulation of air through a carload of perishables was a difficult problem until Preco circulating fans came into use somewhere around 1934 or 1935.

The advent of frozen fruits provided another avenue for the sale and marketing of fresh fruits and vegetables as this new method of preserving perishables was made available. The business has grown by leaps and bounds as the processors and shippers adjusted themselves to proper refrigeration requirements.

The quick-freezing of fruit began in a small way in about 1925, and it was adapted to vegetables some 10 years later. By 1942 the combined output had reached a large volume. The growth of the business is indicated by over-all statistics which reveal that 310,000,000 pounds of fruit and 260,000,000 pounds of vegetables were frozen in 1945. California's frozen fruit and vegetable pack in that year was 166,531,761 pounds of fruit and 48,074,479 pounds of vegetables, or a total of 214,606,240 pounds, the largest in the history of the business. Apricots, peaches, and apples made up 87 per cent of the California fruit pack; and asparagus, beans, broccoli, sprouts, and spinach made up 81 per cent of the vegetable pack.

The object of this quick-freeze of fruits and vegetables is to preserve their freshness and retain their vitamin content. The freezing operations begin within a certain time after picking. The fruit must be fully matured and the vegetables strictly fresh. The processing is accomplished by means of temperatures applied around 15 degrees below zero. This condition is maintained for 3-4 hours, after which the product is stored at temperatures ranging from zero to 10 below. There can be little or no fluctuation in this temperature.

To accomplish the transportation of frozen fruits and vegetables, the Santa Fe employs superinsulated cars. The composite felt insulation in these cars is 5 inches thick, as compared to 2½-3 inches in standard refrigerator cars. A salt application of 30 per cent is also used; salt serves to melt the ice and thereby absorbs the heat units more quickly. As the result of studies made by the Santa Fe and the shippers, the new type of refrigerator car will represent the last word in equipment for the handling of these quick-freeze products.

Once the fruit train is ready to start for eastern markets it travels on fast schedules and with a precision equaling that of the passenger service. However, there is involved a vast amount of detail as wheels within wheels are set in motion to the end that the shipper may receive the finest possible service at all times.

To begin with, the Santa Fe shops and perishable plant at San

Bernardino rank among the finest anywhere. A refrigerator car must be maintained in top condition, and the San Berdo shops render prompt and efficient service to this fleet that every day sends its yellow trains streaming eastward across the great Mojave. The locomotive plant prepares the big steam and Diesel engines for that grueling climb over El Cajon and the long miles beyond. The classification yard sorts out the cars and builds them into solid trains, for the busy San Bernardino Yard is the marshaling point. The way car is coupled on, and the air lines and all running gear, understructures, running boards, grab irons, drains, and hatch covers are inspected.

The conductor gathers up his stack of waybills and wheel report in the yard office, and with his clearance and train orders checked, he at last gives the signal that starts our Santa Fe Green Fruit—GFX—on its way.

Because of its heavy production and the distance to market, the west coast has taken the leadership in developing and meeting consumer demands for these fruits and vegetables. Products have been improved in quality, with particular attention to strains adapted to shipping, as well as sizes and flavors. Through better packing methods, modern refrigeration, advertising, diversions in transit, and other shipping privileges, the merchandising end of the business has arrived at high peaks of efficiency.

With such a vast volume to be disposed of, the keynote of the marketing policy involving perishables is uniform distribution, based on a constant knowledge of supply and demand. This has been worked out through close co-operation on the part of the railroads. Next to high-grade equipment, expert refrigeration, and fast, dependable train schedules, nothing is of more importance to distribution than the elaborate system of diversion and reconsignment effected by the carriers, thereby providing the shippers and jobbers with a choice of markets consistent with the demand. This service begins to function long after the cars have started to roll.

Diversions are made to meet changing weather conditions and all of the other elements affecting marketing needs, including varying requirements on the marketing end and the overlapping of crops. Under this diversion plan thousands of cars of perishables start eastward without a home, which is to say they have not yet been sold and will eventually wind up at those destinations which, in the opinion of the shipper, offer the better market. These cars are called "rollers," since they get under way to save time and may subsequently be diverted to any of a number of eastern cities before they find a buyer.

Shippers, with an accurate knowledge of market conditions, flash this information to their various sales offices throughout the country.

The quality of this diversion and reconsignment work is maintained at a high standard, necessitating as it does the prompt location of cars streaking down the rails on all parts of the system. It requires the utilization of the telegraph, the telephone, the teletype, and special messenger service, and no road is better prepared to provide this fast communication service than the Santa Fe. In an earlier Santa Fe chapter on railway communications I reviewed the complex but highly efficient manner in which a modern system of this kind works.

By means of this far-flung and magic "voice of the Santa Fe," the shipper or the consignee can remain in close contact with the fruit train, speeding across the mountains and plains, through every hour of the day and night. Never is it farther from him than the telephone on his desk.

Should it develop that certain markets are glutted, cars consigned to these points are diverted to other destinations. All the shipper or his representative has to do is furnish the railroad with the name of the new destination, and the change in routing will be made almost in a twinkling, and while the cars continue to move without interruption, as they are simply switched from one train to another.

The exact location of every car in transit is known at all times through the reporting system maintained by the Santa Fe. When a car is shipped it is given a symbol, and the car number and this symbol are conveyed to a central office. This office keeps a record of each movement, which is reported from time to time by various stations along the line. This service enables the shipper to determine when and where the fast-traveling fruit cars may be diverted to accomplish the distribution desired.

While diversions, reconsignments, and change of service have always been a part of the railroad's job, the practice is largely applicable to these fresh fruits and vegetables. Change in service includes icing and refrigeration, ventilation and heating, in accordance with shipper instructions, the weather, and other conditions affecting the safe delivery of the green fruit. On the Santa Fe these combined activities are handled by a department known as the Diversion Bureau, which has offices at the several grand division headquarters.

Diversion and reconsignment involves the following: a change in the name of the consignee; a change in the name of the consignor; a change in destination; a change in route at the request of the consignor, consignee, or owner; any other instructions given by these parties and necessary to effecting the delivery and requiring an addition to, or a change in, billing, or an additional movement of the car, or both.

The Santa Fe diversions in 1945 totaled between 90,000 and 100,000, representing constant day and night trigger performance.

Regular Diversion Bureaus are maintained at:

> Los Angeles, California
> San Francisco, California
> Phoenix, Arizona
> Shafter, California
> Bakersfield, California
> Lode, California
> Chicago, Illinois
> Kansas City, Missouri

The system of diversions was created by necessity and increased with the growth of the fruit and vegetable industry; also because of the growing competition, which developed not only between producers, but between different areas, as well as in the industry itself, as new products appeared on the market. In connection with the latter, I might mention avocados, which offered a new kind of salad. Too, there were different varieties of lettuce, while considerable rivalry developed between the many varieties of melons. Another reason was overlapping seasons, demanding speedy service.

For many years diversions were free and unlimited. That is, the shipper could reconsign a car as many times as he desired without extra charge. Leaving California billed to a broker or the owner, cars could be dropped out of a train at any time to be sent scurrying off in another direction. Shippers took advantage of this service, saving both time and demurrage. In these cases refrigerator cars served as traveling warehouses until their cargoes could be sold to advantage.

What is believed to have been the diversion record on the Santa Fe involved a car of potatoes originating in the Stockton, California, area. This car was diverted 29 times before it finally found a home at Fort Worth, Texas. On another occasion a carload of San Joaquin Valley peaches, originally consigned to Denver, Colorado, reached this point, only to be shunted around 24 times before finally being disposed of at an eastern city. Finally the Interstate Commerce Commission stepped in with regulations governing diversions, for in those days 10 or 20 diversions were common.

We have an example of the way in which shippers took advantage of this diversion privilege in an effort to obtain a top market in a carload of potatoes, shipped from Denver to Walsenburg, Colorado, on February 18, 1929. Walsenburg is only 160 miles from Denver. However, the spuds never reached Walsenburg. Instead, they were diverted 14 times, as follows:

Denver to La Junta—February 22
La Junta, Colorado, to Syracuse, Kansas—February 25
Syracuse to Garden City—February 26
Garden City to Dodge City—February 27
Dodge City to Kinsley—February 28
Kinsley to Stafford—March 1
Stafford to Hutchinson—March 3
Hutchinson to Newton—March 4
Newton to Wichita—March 5
Wichita to Florence—March 7
Florence to Strong City—March 8

Strong City to Ellinor—March 10
Ellinor to Saffordville—March 10
Saffordville to Emporia—March 11

Although shippers were well within their rights in this shuffling and holding of cars without paying extra charges, they abused the privilege, with the result that equipment was tied up and the service slowed down.

The new rules laid down in no way injured the shipper, while they relieved the railroads of a growing headache.

The first restricted tariff issued by the Interstate Commerce Commission went into effect August 1, 1932. This provided for 3 free diversions, with a charge of $2.70 for the fourth diversion; $6.30 for the fifth, and $9.00 for each subsequent diversion. This schedule included potatoes and certain fruits, vegetables, and melons. On June 1, 1935, the order was extended to cover all fruits and vegetables, with a charge of $6.30 applied to all diversions after the fourth. The present ruling allows 3 free diversions, with $2.97 for the fourth, and $6.93 for each diversion after that.

In order to establish a limit on diversions, the local freight rate applies, and this is usually high enough to be prohibitive. However, in most cases 3 free diversions are sufficient to give the shipper a choice of the big city markets, where auctions are held regularly, and the small additional charge for a greater number of diversions is considered reasonable and fair to all concerned. In fact, the restrictions placed in effect by the Interstate Commerce Commission, which put an end to the elements of speculation, have proved to be in the best interests of the shipper, the public, and the carrier.

It is estimated that at least 25 per cent of all cars of perishables leaving California and Arizona are subject to diversion. The first natural diverting point on the Santa Fe is at Belen, New Mexico, where the company's lines fan out in 4 directions. The next point is Kansas City, largest rail center in the Middle West. Then comes Chicago, which is not only one of the world's greatest markets, but also vies with Kansas City as an eastern gateway. Other important diversion points are at Clovis, New Mexico; Denver and La Junta, Colorado; Amarillo, Texas; Wichita and

Newton, Kansas; Oklahoma City and Tulsa, Oklahoma; and Sweetwater, Houston, Dallas, and Forth Worth, Texas.

To make its service as complete as possible, the Santa Fe maintains a special corps of experts who have been trained especially in the handling of perishables. These men have a full knowledge of the different classes of protective service essential to the transportation of such goods. They know train schedules, the location of icing and heater stations, transit privileges, together with a full understanding of other technical matters relating to transportation in general.

These experts are located in the principal producing areas, at icing and heater stations, and other important points along the line. They are on duty at all times, supervising and aiding in providing the protective measures necessary to the flight of GFX.

The reefers are inspected frequently to make sure that the service requested by the shipper is being maintained, and to determine whether or not the cars are moving in good shape. Contacts are maintained with district supervisors, who in turn report each movement to a central office.

Two men who have contributed greatly to the development of the fruit movement are the late J. S. Leeds and George H. Nelson. They are typical of the high class of railroaders on the Santa Fe.

Leeds was appointed manager of the newly organized Santa Fe Refrigerator Dispatch on April 1, 1903, and he served in that capacity until his death on March 12, 1918. During this period the department expanded rapidly, keeping pace with the increase of perishable shipments from California and Arizona.

George Nelson started as an office boy in the Chicago office on March 28, 1898, and he held various positions in the Chicago office until 1903. At that time he was appointed traveling agent at La Junta, Colorado. He was transferred to Topeka, Kansas, in the same capacity in 1907. In 1909 he was promoted to chief clerk and assistant to J. S. Leeds, serving here until his appointment as manager in 1908. The Santa Fe Refrigerator Dispatch was dissolved in 1918 and the Santa Fe Refrigerator Department was immediately organized.

Mr. Nelson was a member of the National Perishable Freight

Committee that wrote the first Perishable Protective Tariff, which became effective on February 28, 1920. At the present time he is senior member of this committee, having served continuously for 27 years. He is generally considered one of the leading authorities on protective-service matters and the handling of perishable freight by rail in the United States.

As we break over El Cajon and roar down on Victorville, hidden under a bench of this sloping land of sagebrush and Joshua trees, we mentally review the vast and complex machinery involved in the building of this fast-traveling fruit train—from the Mexican fruit pickers in the fields and groves; to the trucks and their loads of shooks racing along a dusty road to the packing house; to the cooling house, the busy fruit sorters and packers, the conveyor belt and its bulging boxes, delivering fruit at the door of the refrigerator car; to the local, puffing away to San Bernardino; to the yards and icing plant, where tanned college men wrestle with heavy blocks of ice; to busy billing clerks; to the call boy, rounding up the train crew. And then, at last, the conductor's highball.

And now we're riding the rear end, bound for Corwith Yard, Chicago.

This California fruit is delivered to thousands of American cities and towns, with some going to Canada and some abroad. Navel oranges start to move in November and continue to flow east on into the spring. The Valencia harvest keeps the refrigerator cars busy through the early spring and summer and on into the fall. In fact, oranges, lemons, and grapefruit move out of the Los Angeles area at the rate of about 200 cars a day throughout the entire year.

Our fruit train comes booming down on Victorville and speeds along the banks of the Mojave River—a river which later disappears from the face of the earth in the great Mojave Sink. We pass Oro Grande and its white-dusted cement plant, and Helendale, named for the daughter of a Santa Fe vice-president, and soon the Diesel horn is shouting at Barstow.

Here, following a crew change, GFX—the Green Fruit—picks up the slack, and the yellow reefers string out across the flats with the colorful Calico Mountains off on the left. Newberry Springs, Troy Dry Lake, Ludlow. This is a land of vast distances —the desert of the Mojave, with its tumbled mountains outlined against the sky. We pass Amboy and the famous Amboy Crater, out there on the right, and the 16-mile-long Bristol Dry Lake. Cadiz and the Ship Mountains, and we swing toward Danby, with the Old Woman Mountains to the south.

We have passed the little desert communities of Klondike and Siberia, back between Amboy and Ludlow. These names in a desert where summer temperatures often reach 110 degrees in the shade—and no shade!

Now we are dropping down into the basin of the Rio Colorado. We pass Ibis and, out there hardly a handshake away, the Dead Mountains. Below them, tucked away in a crook of the Colorado River, is the Mojave Indian Reservation. Approaching Needles, we look away to the east into Arizona and its mountain bulwark. No mountains anywhere have such rampant, primitive beauty.

The muddy, sullen river below us is mapped by a fringe of green, contrasting sharply with the ash-gray desert. Needles rests on the far eastern rim of San Bernardino County—the biggest county in the world. Starting from its western boundary, about 20 miles west of the city of San Bernardino, the rail distance across this sprawling county is some 270 miles, an expanse made up of volcanic mountains, desert valleys, and great flats. The floor of this desert, between Barstow and Needles, except for here and there a few cottonwoods and widely separated wells and springs, is without timber or water.

The county was named for St. Bernardinus, the famed founder of the charitable institution called in Spanish *Monte de Piedad* —the Hill of Pity.

At Needles we take on a new crew, and the refrigerator cars are checked and iced. And we roll on to the yellow river and the Santa Fe's great new bridge, which carries us across to Topock. We climb steadily from half a hundred feet above sea level to Seligman, at an altitude of 5,234 feet. This is the longest sustained grade in the United States—close to 150 miles.

We are on the tough Third District of the Albuquerque Division now, with the Supai grade and the Arizona Divide ahead of the blunt snout of our big Diesel. Our fruit train leaves Seligman at 2:30 p.m., mountain time, and we slide past Crookton at 3 o'clock, reaching Ash Fork at 3:35.

The PGX fruit train from the Fourth District is on the track beside us. This train, made up at Glendale and Phoenix, Arizona, will run through solid to Argentine Yard at Kansas City. The PGX trains have the same rights as our GFX, and they handle perishables from the fertile fruit and produce lands of the Salt River Valley.

A pusher is now on our rear end, and we highball out ahead of the PGX, starting up the 1.8 per cent Supai hill grade. From high above, we look back at the PGX with its Diesel road engine and steam helper, moving almost on our yellow block.

Our helper is cut off at Supai at 5:05 p.m., and our train moves on to Williams behind the 4-unit Diesel. There is a running inspection at Williams, and we leave at 5:18. Off on our left the white cones of the San Francisco peaks are visible now and then. We are storming past Bellemont at 6:06; Riordan at 6:15.

This is timber country, a beautiful land laid out close under the Arizona stars, so close that they seem like snowflakes just outside of the cupola windows. We are past Angell at 7:10, and at 7:24 we head in at Sunshine for First 24, the Grand Canyon Limited. The Limited, due at Winslow at 7:55, comes roaring through, and we head out at 7:40.

The lights of Winslow glimmer off there ahead of us, and soon we feel the surge of cars against the way car as the brakes are applied. Sparks spit from the wheels; then we are drifting on, finally weaving slowly into Winslow Yard. At 8:10 our precious perishables are standing on the icehouse track.

W. F. Taylor, our conductor out of Seligman, has told us that our train consists of 63 cars—57 loads and 6 empties—for a total of 3,350 tons. Diesel No. 162 has done a fine job over these 143 tough mountain miles. Our time from Seligman, 5 hours and 40 minutes, with 28 minutes dead time.

We leave Winslow with a new crew and full ice bunkers. Another crew takes over at Gallup, New Mexico, and silver ribbons spin out beneath the wheels of the way car. We have the feeling of riding an irresistible force and that nothing has the power to stay our flight—nothing but a pin point of red.

The perishables are checked for ice requirements at Belen, and we move onto the Pecos Division with a new way car and new faces here on the rear end. This is a Centralized Traffic Control district, and GFX becomes a little light winking across the C.T.C. board at Mountainair. A helper has been cut in at Belen to assist on the Abo Canyon grades. It is dropped at Mountainair, and C.T.C. shuttles it back to Belen.

On this district of push-buttons the man at the C.T.C. machine slides us in and out of sidings, several of which have a capacity of 200 cars or more. Scholle holds 270 cars, and that is a lot of siding.

The train is iced at Clovis, New Mexico, and there is a new crew at Amarillo, in the Texas Panhandle. We drop 102 fast miles behind our markers. Then 99 miles, Amarillo to Canadian; 106 to Waynoka, Oklahoma, with crew changes at 3 division points, and a check of ice bunkers at Waynoka.

GFX is in Kansas now—Wellington. Then Emporia. Argentine is ahead—the great Argentine Yard of the Santa Fe. The train is broken down at Argentine, classified and iced, and we pull out for Marceline, Missouri, 108 miles away. Shopton, Iowa. And we are reminded that it was here at Shopton one night in February, 1941, that the first Santa Fe Diesel—the famous 100 —began its test run to Los Angeles, 1,782 miles away, with 60 loaded freight cars—3,150 tons.

Chillicothe, Illinois. And the last crew takes over the job of rolling this Santa Fe fruit train in.

That's Corwith Yard out ahead where those lights are shining. Corwith Yard, Chicago. This is the journey's end for GFX. This is where they take the markers down. It is kind of like saying farewell to traveling companions at the station gates—friends who soon will be scattering to every nook and corner of the east, the north, the south. There are many tracks, many lines waiting to carry the cars of the Green Fruit Train to many destinations. Cars will roll to Chicago warehouses, to team tracks, to belt lines

Great Northern #5, the Cascadian, just after leaving the west portal of the Cascade Tunnel coming into Scenic Washington with streamlined electric Engine #5011, class Y-1. The grade is 2.2% descending. Photo by Wm. J. Pontin. Rail Photo Service.

Some of the 16,740-ton 180-car Great Northern ore trains after being broken up at the Superior, Wis., classification yard for grading special types of ore before being moved to the company's docks for loading into boats. Courtesy Great Northern Railroad.

New York Central #26, the eastbound Twentieth Century Limited, passing Fleishmans, N. Y., with a new 4,000-h.p. 2-unit locomotive. Courtesy New York Central Railroad.

Rotary snowplow on the Milwaukee's Second Subdivision of the Coast Division, clearing a siding 1 mile east of Hyak, Wash., at the east end of the Snoqualmie Tunnel. The heaviest snowfall in 20 years fell there in February, 1946. Courtesy Milwaukee Road.

Engine #5022 of the Santa Fe's great 5011-class, 2-10-4 type, running over C.T.C. territory on the Second District of the Pecos Division west of Willard, N. M., with a solid train of green fruit. Note the head brakeman looking the train over from the top of 25,000-gallon tank. Courtesy Santa Fe Railroad.

Rear end of Santa Fe way freight #75 descending the 3% grade in historic Apache Canyon at Canyoncito, N. M., on the Third District of the New Mexico Division. Courtesy Santa Fe Railroad.

The Santa Fe's call board in the Crew Dispatcher's office at San Berdo, Calif., Los Angeles Division. Note the GFX's engine crews that have been called. Photo by Delano. Courtesy Office of War Information.

Great Northern Extra 406 west hauled by a 5,400-h.p. 4-unit Diesel descending the 1.8% grade at Blacktail, Mont., on the Second Subdivision of the Kalispell Division. The mountains in the background are in Glacier Park. Photo by Wm. J. Pontin. Courtesy Rail Photo Service.

Looking toward the rear end of the world-famous New York Central Twentieth Century Limited from the second unit of the Diesel. The third car is the through New York-Los Angeles sleeper. Courtesy New York Central Railroad.

Measuring bridge #3021 clearances from a New York Central car especially equipped and used only for this purpose. Photo by G. Grabill, Jr. Courtesy Rail Photo Service.

Milwaukee's rotary snowplow approaching high-speed train order stand at Hyak, Wash., on the electrified Coast Division. Note the hole that has been dug in the snow to allow the operator to hoop up orders. Courtesy Milwaukee Road.

—to Hammond, Indiana, and the Erie, the road that will rush many of these cars to seaboard terminals on the Atlantic.

As fresh and delicious as when they left San Bernardino, California, and began the climb over El Cajon to start their flight to the markets and breakfast tables of America are these perishables that have traveled across deserts and rivers and mountains and plains aboard the refrigerator cars of the Santa Fe's Green Fruit Express.

CHAPTER XIX

SNOW-FIGHTING ON THE MILWAUKEE

The White Outlaw

The White Outlaw loots the tills of American railroads to the tune of millions of dollars every year. Swiftly he rides in from the Arctic, from Greenland, from the Siberian wastes, to lash and snarl at man and all his works. He rides behind a weather front, marshaling his legions through the trumpet call of the wind.

The White Outlaw is a bully and a fiend. Oceans and continents are his playgrounds. He is known by many aliases—the Storm King, Jack Frost, Old Man Winter—and, though smart young meteorologists may warn of his coming, there is nothing that anyone can do about it but prepare for the worst.

This Outlaw of the North may sulk in the frozen wastes through several winters, allowing folks to predict that the "seasons are changing," and then suddenly come roaring down with teeth bared to tangle communications, stall highway traffic, ground planes, and blockade the railroads.

It was the winter of 1935–36 that the White Outlaw hurled his forces at the Milwaukee Division and Superintendent Valentine in a series of assaults that almost—but not quite—tied up the railroad.

A storm was riding in from the Great Lakes, and whirling anemometer cups registered a wind velocity of 35 miles an hour. The thermometer at 8 o'clock in the morning was down to a shade below zero. Superintendent J. H. Valentine, of the Milwaukee Division, took a second squint at the thermometer, cocked an experienced weather eye at the sky—and wired Mitchell and Aberdeen, South Dakota, to start their rotary plows for Portage, Wisconsin—just in case.

Of course, there was a chance that the weather might moderate; still, the Superintendent decided, there was nothing like being prepared. The weather did not moderate; instead the mercury started to crawl farther into its hole.

Snow came slanting in from Lake Michigan, and before long there were reports of drifts—and trouble. Almost before you could say button-up-your-overcoat, the battle was on, and the Superintendent was in the middle of it. He spent long hours out on the line, and more wearying hours in his office in the Milwaukee depot.

The eastern end of the Chicago, Milwaukee, St. Paul & Pacific was toughened long ago to withstand the assault of the White Outlaw. In normal years the road takes winter in its stride without great difficulty, but this was not a normal winter, for which reason it has been chosen as an example of how a railroad battles blizzards when the chips are down. You can't judge a champion by watching him shadowbox or slap an inferior fighter around in the gymnasium. You judge him by his performance when he is in there with the challenger, slugging it out toe to toe.

This winter of 1935–36 was a real one. It snowed and the wind blew and the thermometer stayed in the cellar. On the fourteenth of February there were 38 inches of snow on the level and more in the making. Over a period of 34 days the mercury climbed above zero only four times. These "mild spells" proved but a snare and a delusion, for no sooner did the weather moderate a bit than Old Man Winter harnessed up another blizzard and rode it in from the Lakes.

From January 18 to February 20 the Milwaukee spent more than a million dollars for snow removal. Hard money right out of the till. But a railroad sells transportation, service. The trains must run, come hell, high water, or snow. On the other hand, the trucker and the bus operator, both of whom are also in the transportation business, stop rendering service when the highways are blocked and wait for the county or the state to open the road. You might call it a subsidy; certainly the trucker and the bus operator are handed a neat package on a silver platter, while the railroad, which provides faithful service always, has to go deep into its pocket when the blizzard strikes.

Ordinarily, Superintendent Valentine's division employs about 140 maintenance men, but during the periods of winter storm this number is increased by several hundred, and operating costs jump as much as 112 per cent.

During the entire period of the battle with the Storm King, the longest time any passenger was delayed on the line was slightly over 3 hours.

Considerable snow fell over the area composing the Milwaukee Division in the early part of January, but the fall was not above the average for other years. Wedge plows were employed in clearing the snow, and all schedules were maintained with little difficulty. And then, on January 17, trouble came in the form of that Old Outlaw of the North—the blizzard. In 9 hours 13½ inches of snow fell, which was 1.2 inches more than the normal fall for the entire month. But that was not too bad; it was the 35-mile-an-hour wind that cuffed the Milwaukee Division around. No sooner had the wedge plows opened the line than the tracks were buried in drifts again.

A wedge plow is what the name implies—a wedge-shaped affair that pushes the snow aside. But it is utterly useless for fighting heavy drifts. However, the January 17 storm abated the next day, and all concerned took a deep breath. Men had been rushed to critical areas, and by noon of the eighteenth all lines were open.

A little over a week later came a period of intense cold and high winds, and the Milwaukee Division began to take the kind of punishment that can even chill a champion. Round 1 had been just a warm-up, but in Round 2 the challenger came out throwing punches with both hands.

The first rotary arrived in Portage on January 26, but meanwhile things had been happening. Equipment capable of keeping the upper hand during an entire winter had been in constant use, and it had taken a fearful battering. Men were showing the strain of battling the ever-mounting drifts; the equipment began to fall apart. When you load a gondola with stone and place it behind a wedge plow, which is then rammed into a drift by a snorting engine at 20 miles an hour, and keep it up incessantly, something eventually has to give.

Side flanges buckled, support stays snapped, and wedge plows crumpled as though they were made of cardboard. The drifts packed and froze, and shovel gangs, working like beavers, tore into the great drifts which by now had reached depths in places of 9 to 17 feet. Men muffled to their eyes continued the battle. Repairmen, their hands numbed, struggled to repair the wedge plows. Workers stamped their feet, thrashed their arms, scrubbed frostbitten ears with snow. They uttered white-breathed oaths; they grumbled and growled—and kept right on digging.

The track had to be kept open. The trains must roll. There was No. 4, the Pioneer Limited, and the Fast Mail—the Milwaukee Postman—Nos. 56 and 57—and No. 58, and there were those long freight drags piling up in sidings and yards, with Old Man Winter screaming taunts at them.

The Milwaukee Division seemed to be dying on its feet when Superintendent Valentine got word that the first rotary had arrived at Portage. A division super may be an official, but when there is trouble on the line he puts on brass knuckles. He does not sit in a warm office and issue orders by wire—far from it. His job is in the front line. In this case, Superintendent Valentine climbed into his switchman's coat and headed for the yards.

Already a crew had been called, and a K-1 Prairie-type locomotive coupled onto a caboose in the Milwaukee Yards and headed for Portage. Here they hooked onto the rotary, brought in from Mitchell, South Dakota, listened carefully to instructions concerning clearances and other matters pertaining to its operation, and started out. Four miles an hour was the absolute maximum at which the plow could be run.

It was at Fox Lake, Wisconsin, that the rotary, which had been performing nicely up to this point, ran into trouble. The whirling blades continued to chew at the newly formed drifts, but the fluming, or discharge of the snow from the plow, stopped. Superintendent Valentine was out on the drift now, watching the proceedings. He observed that when the blades bit into the deep snow, the lower part of the frame enclosing the blades nosed upward instead of getting their teeth into the bottom of the drift. He waved at the operator in the cab of the rotary. "No good!"

Having decided that more power was needed, another K-1 was called out from Horicon. The second engine proved all that was needed to lick the drift, and the rotary completed the trip to Milwaukee.

A word here concerning the rotary snowplow. The one which we have seen in operation was an older type, in which the operator sat in a front cab of wood, built over an old locomotive from which the drive wheels and cylinders had been removed. A fireman in what had been the original cab kept up steam, which supplied the power to drive the rotary blades, and he also operated controls in answer to communication signals from the man in the front cab. The entire machine was, of course, pushed by a locomotive, with the engineer receiving signals for starting, stopping, and reversing.

The second rotary, arriving from Aberdeen, North Dakota, a short time later, was a new type, and its operator had a complete set of controls in the cab which governed the blades. He also had control of the air on the locomotive pushing the plow, but he still sent signals to the engineer as to direction and speed.

On January 28 the mercury climbed out of the basement, with a mere 6 below as a minimum on January 30. However, this "warm spell" ushered in a new series of storms. The rotary plows began attacks on the drifts, spouting snow like angry Arctic monsters. Superintendent Valentine dispersed his forces—50 men here, 75 there—and the battle was on again.

The wires were hot with word of trains stalled in giant drifts. Freight locomotives pulling work trains loaded with shovelers were rushed into the fray, with a plow breaking a path. Wedge plows bucked drifts, and snow was shot 25 feet into the air. Then it was back up and hit it again, with the crews braced against the impact as they listened anxiously for the sound of rending wood and metal.

Long freight trains were dragged from drifts that almost hid them from view. Flagging was done from the tops of 15-foot snowbanks. Cars were cut off and dragged to the nearest siding or crossover, while gangs moved in and shoveled snow away from the clogged wheels of that portion of the train held in the grip of the drift. At times as many as 4 cuts were necessary to dislodge the entire train. When this had been done the plow would move in to the attack.

It was buck and dig and push, until it seemed that neither man nor equipment could continue the battle. But these railroad men on the Milwaukee have hair in their ears, and they are never whipped so long as there are trains to be moved.

The Milwaukee staggered out of the January 30 fracas slightly slap-happy but triumphant. And then, on February 8, Old Man Winter came snarling from his lair again and set the road back on its heels.

About 4 p.m. the sky darkened, and a low scud moved in off Lake Michigan behind a strong east wind. Darkness closed down, and the world reeled under the impact of a blizzard of such ferocity that the oldest inhabitant was hard put to it to remember the likes of it.

Superintendent Valentine downed a couple mugs of hot coffee, took a hitch at his belt, pulled his cap over his ears, and rallied his snow-fighting forces. This was Saturday night. Six hundred men were out on the Milwaukee Division that night, together with every piece of snow-fighting equipment that could turn a wheel. Sunday morning found snow still falling, but everything was under control.

On this morning of February 9, No. 2 started from Milwaukee for Chicago with a locomotive and a wedge plow running ahead of her. Following No. 2 by about 5 minutes was No. 56. At Sturtevant, 23 miles out of Milwaukee, the plow unit stopped for water, which put a red block against No. 56 a mile north. The plow, followed by No. 2, went on, but by this time No. 56 was stuck fast in a drift. The dispatcher at Milwaukee, when there was no OS, or train report, coming in from Sturtevant reporting the passing of No. 56, sensed what had happened and promptly issued orders to Tower 68, 17 miles out of Milwaukee, to hold No. 16, the Olympian, which had pulled out for Chicago.

Upon receiving this information, Superintendent Valentine ordered out a rotary and a crew, quickly joining the rescuers.

No. 4, the Pioneer Limited, was about to pull out of the Milwaukee station; and the super, climbing into the cab, ordered the engineer to follow the rotary.

At Lake, 6½ miles from Milwaukee, the rotary and the Pioneer Limited crossed over to the left-hand main. Upon arriving at Tower 68, the rotary pulled ahead to the point where No. 56 was stalled, and the Pioneer stopped opposite No. 56. The tops of both trains were about level with the top of the snowbank beside the right of way, while between the trains was a wall of snow 6 feet high. Passages were shoveled through this, and the passengers on No. 56 were transferred to the Pioneer Limited.

There remained now the transfer of one more passenger—a passenger in a coffin in an express car of No. 56. When this was accomplished, the Pioneer proceeded down the left-hand main behind the rotary. Arriving at the signal where No. 2 now was stalled, passengers from this train were also transferred to the Pioneer Limited. The Pioneer then moved on to a crossover near Sturtevant, where it was switched over to the right-hand main and rolled on to Chicago, carrying a total of 350 passengers.

Until No. 56 and No. 2 were freed of the drifts, traffic was run around them. The delay for their passengers was a little over 3 hours, the longest delay suffered by any passengers on the Milwaukee Division during the entire period of the 1936 battle with Old Man Winter.

The Milwaukee Division consists of 5 subdivisions, totaling 637 miles of line, with a roadmaster in charge of each subdivision. The subdivision in charge of Roadmaster J. H. Johns is comprised of 130 miles of line, and the report which he sent to the office of the division superintendent on February 10 was something to cause even a hardened old railroader like J. H. Valentine to wince. It read, in part:

. . . 23 drifts between Atwater and Berlin; 18 between Ripon and Oshkosh; 10 between Horicon and Portage; 7 between Brandon and Markesan; 10 between Rush Lake and Winneconne. Total—68 drifts, 9 to 17 feet high and 100 to 3,000 feet long. . . . Pickett, Berlin, and Oshkosh report 5-foot drifts in cuts today, and—it is still snowing.

On February 12 the thermometer reached 14 degrees above

zero, virtually a thaw compared with the earlier cold snap. Superintendent Valentine was so encouraged by this break in the weather that he was on the point of sending the rotary plows back home. However, upon taking another peek at the sky, he decided to wait a little.

That night another storm slammed out of the northeast and hit the Milwaukee Division a resounding wallop. It almost seemed that Old Man Winter was peeved at not having been able to tie up the road completely; so now he unlimbered his heavy guns. By midnight the thermometer registered 6 below, and the wind was howling like a soul in torment.

The rotaries were shagged out and double-headed. More than 900 men donned mittens and Mackinaws and breasted the storm. On February 14 there were 38 inches of snow on the level and more piling up. The storm continued through February 16, with the mercury going lower and lower. It hit 17 below and never stopped. It was still going down at 20. It rang up a shivering 26 below and called it a day. The whirling anemometer cups wrote up a wind velocity of 53 miles an hour.

The driving snow hit the workers like bird shot, but they never quit. Don't say the man with a shovel is not a hero on the Milwaukee, but a man can't quit under fire when the Old Man is out on the line.

On the morning of February 18 the official snowfall for the month was more than twice the normal fall. At midnight of the eighteenth Superintendent Valentine left his office exhausted. He staggered home and fell into bed. At 3:30 a.m. the shrill call of the telephone jerked him out of a troubled dream of a fight to the death with a hoary outlaw who was trying to smother him in a snowdrift.

The agonized voice at the other end of the wire informed the super that hell was in its infancy. Seventeen freights were stalled —3 between Roundout and Janesville; 3 between Chicago and Milwaukee; 6 between Kittredge and Sturtevant; and 5 buried around Oshkosh and Portage.

Superintendent Valentine shivered into his clothes, all thought of sleep and weariness forgotten. This was his fight—the fight to keep trains on the Milwaukee Division moving. For 14 hours straight the super dogged, cajoled, and bullied every man on the division. He worked with them shoulder to shoulder; he fought frostbite and utter exhaustion. He rode the rotaries down the line between snowbanks higher than the roaring locomotives. From telegraph offices along the line he maintained a close contact with the dispatcher, giving orders that would relieve critical situations.

By 5 o'clock on the afternoon of February 20 all trains were free, all lines were open; and once more the Milwaukee had won its fight with the outlaw that rides its white charger in from the Great Lakes and the Arctic.

CHAPTER XX

THE ATLANTIC COAST LINE

Track Renovation

The Atlantic Coast Line, in preparing for a postwar era of super trains, is completing what is probably the greatest railroad rehabilitation program in the country. It is overhauling its right of way from the ground up, and from Richmond, Virginia, to Jacksonville, Florida.

There are no sacred cows in the railroad game any more. The day when the roads felt that what was good enough for dad was good enough for his son has passed. The folks who want to go for a hay ride will be down on the farm and not spending their hard-earned money for a railroad ticket. Back in the depression years, the forward-looking railroads in this country were starting to overhaul the old family bus. World War II delayed its rejuvenation somewhat, but look out now, for it is just starting to roll.

The railroads, hauling 90 per cent of the men and materials of war, had no time for more than the bare maintenance of their plant and equipment, but it is a different picture now. Not only do they have the time, but they have the inclination. Spurred by the realization that they are faced with some of the hottest competition they have ever experienced, the railroads are feverishly bending every effort toward providing the passenger and the shipper with the kind of rail transportation which will win both his approval and his patronage.

Amidst the airplane, the truck, the bus, and the family car, the railroad is going to have to dig deep into its bag of tricks; but if it doesn't come through with flying colors it will be the first time your railroad man has failed in his assignment when the pressure was on.

Just as an example of how completely the railroads are preparing to get into this fight, we will consider the case of the Atlantic Coast Line. In various chapters of this book I have placed emphasis on track work. Maintenance engineers all over the country are laying the groundwork for the coming of ultra-modern, high-speed trains, and the trackman is being paced by signalmen and the bright young men in the train-communication field.

The track rehabilitation work on the Atlantic Coast Line, we find, is a natural sequence to a mechanical improvement program carried out by the road during 1939–44, inclusive, in which it spent a far larger proportion of its net operating income for equipment—mostly Diesel motive power—than any other Class I road in the country. In 1945 operating expenditures for maintenance of way and structures along the line reached the millions, with some four and three quarter millions going into the track.

As early as 1943 work was in progress on the line, and by the end of 1947 this work is expected to be largely completed. The rehabilitation program includes heavier rail on all principal main and secondary lines, together with reballasting the track with crushed rock or washed and screened gravel, crosstie replacements, ditching and grading along the right of way, and roadbed stabilization through a general bank-widening program.

Eventually the Atlantic Coast Line will bring all branch lines up to the new high standards of track.

Because of a shortage of men and materials, little actual work was completed in 1943–44, but in 1945 things started to hum, and 326 track-miles were laid with 131-pound rail along the main line, with 213 miles of 100-pound relay rail being spiked down on secondary main lines; 1,822,509 crossties were renewed; 652,-986 cubic yards of crushed rock and 60,633 yards of gravel ballast were applied. Approximately 700 miles of main and secondary tracks were raised 4 to 6 inches and ballasted. This, however, represented only about 50 per cent of the main-line program and about 30 per cent of the work on the secondary main lines.

The new Western Division—the Atlanta, Birmingham & Coast, merged with the Coast Line in January, 1946—will eventually receive a similar renovation of track.

It is estimated that the end of 1946 will find 838 track-miles of new 131-pound rail spiked to close to 6,000,000 new crossties and ballasted with something like 1,700,000 cubic yards of crushed stone. A large amount of bridge work is included in the right-of-way program of the Atlantic Coast Line. This involves the strengthening of important steel bridge spans. The elimination of timber trestles has been under way for more than 20 years, and eventually all such structures will be replaced with concrete or ballasted deck trestles.

Carpenter gangs and paint gangs in 1945 began the task of renewing and refreshing station, office, and roadway buildings. And right here I should like to point out that this is something railroads all over the country should include in their plans for the future. It is a sizable project, I admit, but one that would pay dividends. Many local railroad stations are an eyesore and a blot on the landscape. They are grimy and dismal and ill-kept, malodorous within and frowzy without, huddled beside the track like beggars at the city gates.

The Atlantic Coast Line's renovation of its station at Orlando, Florida, is an example of what can be done to make a railroad station attractive. The road has completed extensive improvements at its wharves and docks in Savannah, Georgia, and Norfolk, Virginia. It has built new electrically operated concrete coaling stations at Harrisburg, Florida, Savannah, and Wilmington, North Carolina, replacing obsolete timbered coaling trestles.

The replacement of the semaphore-type block signals on the Atlantic Coast Line represents another part of its modernizing program, as it substitutes the latest searchlight-type signals. Studies are being made relative to the installation of Centralized Traffic Control, with "reverse running," to facilitate the operation of trains over certain bottleneck sections of double track.

Few main lines in the eastern United States offer such possibilities for high-speed operations as we find on the Atlantic Coast Line. The double-track road traverses the rolling coastal plains along the Atlantic seaboard. There are few curves, and the grades are light. Excluding movements through terminals, the route traveled by fast Coast Line passenger trains is 93.4 per cent tangent. The remainder has an average curvature of between

1 and 2 degrees. The ruling grades exist around north Petersburg, Virginia, and Fayetteville, North Carolina. These are of 0.6, but can be operated as "momentum" grades.

Both main-line tracks between Richmond and Jacksonville will be laid with 131-pound rail, as well as all single track between Jacksonville and Tampa. Further, much of this new heavy rail is end-hardened at the mills. However, when this is not done it is so hardened in the track soon after being laid. The rail is joined by head-free joint bars, and the joints are bonded with railhead-type bonds. Double-shoulder tie plate is being used. On tangent track the rails and tie plates are fastened by two gauge spokes and two or more hold-down spikes per tie plate. Full-spiking is generally used on curved track and bridges. Ten anti-creepers are applied per 39-foot rail, 8 against the current traffic and 2 to prevent movement in the opposite direction.

In connection with the main-line relay work, No 10 turnouts with spring-rail frogs and 16½-foot switch points are standard, except at the ends of double track, where No. 20 switches are laid. These have 30-foot switch points and rigid manganese-insert frogs. All main-line switches have six adjustable rail braces and heavy insulated gauge plates, the same as are standard for interlocking switches. This permits accurate control of gauge and switch adjustments and will simplify future installations of interlocked power switches.

As the new rail is laid, the 100-pound relay rail thus released is applied to passing tracks and important sidings. This rail before being laid is cropped, and a large rail yard and cropping plant was set up at south Rocky Mount, North Carolina. This plant has a friction saw, an electrically operated gang drill, and a straightening press.

This cropping process involves cutting 18 inches from each end of all rail to be used for relaying secondary main lines. It is at the end of the rail that batter occurs, and the removal of this eliminates secondary batter and also exposes hidden defects in the vicinity of the old joint bars, which might have escaped detection by the Detector Cars. These Detector Cars have long been a part of Atlantic Coast Line equipment, and they are an invaluable sleuth of the rail, as they record possible fractures within the rail structure.

Most track work is done under traffic, except rail-laying, for which the track involved is usually killed.

Relaying rail on track that does not require tie renewal proceeds at a rapid pace. The steel gang is preceded by a cribbing gang; cribbing machines expedite the work. In connection with the rail-laying, one work train works ahead and one behind this crew. The work train ahead unloads and distributes all materials as needed; the second work train picks up the released rail and discarded materials, working ½-1 mile behind the track layers. The rail-laying is accomplished by completely mechanized steel gangs, with an assistant roadmaster in charge.

The acquiring of the enormous number of crossties needed in this vast program was a big job in itself. The Coast Line purchases ties direct from producers. During the war most of the labor formerly engaged in cutting ties was either cutting pulpwood or working on defense projects. Railroad representatives went into every tie-producing area in the territory served by the road. They finally got their ties, which began to move to the company-owned tie-treating plant at Gainesville, Florida, and thence to the waiting track gangs.

The Coast Line, like many other railroads during the war, took all crossties they could get, including many slightly less than the standard 9-foot tie. About 80 per cent were pine, the remainder being oak and gum. All of these ties were given a 100-per-cent creosote preservative treatment by the Rueping process.

Tie renewals, tie spacing, and the initial surface on new ballast are accomplished together under traffic. Ties are spaced 19½ inches apart, center to center, to provide 24 ties under each 39-foot rail and a 3-tie support for each joint.

The ballast used on all main tracks is a crushed granite secured from commercial quarries, screened and washed to meet A.R.E.A. specifications. In main-line surfacing, an average of 40 cars, or about 1,750 cubic yards, of crushed rock is used per track-mile.

The Coast Line enjoys an advantage in traversing the coastal plain where the soil is a sandy loam, which packs well and drains readily. Consequently the roadbed is very stable, and there are no water pockets (described in Chapter XVII) of any material consequence on the entire line between Richmond and Jacksonville.

Train Communication

Early in 1944 the Atlantic Coast Line began an extensive study of electronics as developed during the war years, with a view to employing these technological advances in the communications field. Two distinct communication systems at that time were undergoing tests and experiments. The one employed "space" radio, in which transmission is accomplished by means of electromagnetic waves of very high frequency radiated directly between transmitting and receiving points. The other used the inductive-carrier principle, wherein transmission is accomplished by means of electromagnetic waves of low frequency impressed by induction upon adjacent wayside line wires and the rails.

These tests indicated that space radio is quite satisfactory for distances of 15 to 20 miles, and has wide appeal for end-to-end service, and yard and terminal service. On the other hand, the inductive-carrier type provides a range between trains and wayside stations of from 40 to 60 miles, indicating greater possibilities for line-of-road operation—where line wires are available— than does space radio.

During 1945 the Atlantic Coast Line completed plans for an experimental installation of the inductive-carrier type of train communication (explained in Chapter II).

With a view to expediting both freight and passenger traffic on its lines between Rocky Mount, North Carolina, and Wilmington, and between Wilmington and Florence, the Coast Lines began the installation of Union Inductive Train Communication. Approximately 18 to 20 road locomotives used in freight and passenger service, 14 caboose cars, and 4 terminal wayside stations were involved in this road-line experimental installation. To provide adequate wayside communication directly with terminal dispatchers, 2 intermediate automatic unattended repeater stations were provided, 1 between Rocky

Mount and Wilmington and 1 between Wilmington and Florence.

The inductive-carrier equipment supplied by the Union Switch and Signal Company consisted of a frequency-modulated transmitter using the reactance-tube method of varying carrier frequency with voice modulation. This can be switched to operate on 2 carrier frequencies of 88 and 152 kilocycles. Carrier frequency deviation ratio is 1-to-1 for voice frequency modulation from approximately 200 to 3,000 cycles. Two receivers of the superheterodyne type are provided, 1 tuned for 88 kc. and 1 for 152 kc. in order that both frequencies might be continuously protected.

Primary power in the locomotive installation is obtained from a 32-volt turbogenerator which supplies energy directly for tube filaments and to a dynamotor to obtain d.c. high-voltage for tube plate supply. Caboose installations employed a 32-volt storage battery, provision being made for terminal recharging.

For transmitting, a large loop—which includes vehicle frame and rails between trucks—is energized on locomotive tender and on caboose to create sufficient electromagnetic field to induce energy into wayside line wires. For receiving, smaller receiver coils are provided, one for the 88 kc. receiver and one for the 152 kc. receiver. These receive energy by induction from the electromagnetic field surrounding the wayside line wires.

Wayside station equipment is directly connected to the line wires through appropriate coupling units. Operation of the inductive system in connection with wayside line wires in no way interferes with simultaneous transmission of usual telegraph and telephone messages over such wires.

The operation of the equipment from locomotive cab and caboose involves a small control box with volume-control knobs for loud-speaker and handset receiver, an on-off power switch and pilot light, noise-suppressor controls for receivers, switch levers for changing the frequency of the transmitter and for transmitting tone signal. A handset with push-to-talk button, as described in Chapter II, is provided on a switch hanger on one side of the control box.

In operation, one frequency is used for end-to-end and intertrain communication, while the second frequency is for train-to-wayside communication, although either frequency may be used for any station break-in or emergency purposes. With the handset in place on its hanger, the loud-speaker will respond to calls received on either frequency.

Upon receiving a call, the engineman, conductor, or dispatcher removes the handset and moves the frequency change-over switch to proper frequency, which automatically transfers output of receiver on that frequency to handset, leaving the loud-speaker to respond to calls on the other frequency. The transmitter is also switched to operate on the desired frequency. Upon identifying himself, the called party may proceed with the conversation—pressing handset button to talk and releasing it to listen.

When the conversation is finished, the handset is restored to the hanger, which automatically restores frequency switch to neutral position, and the channel is cleared for further use.

That the economic benefits to be derived from the use of a more rapid form of communication might be fully investigated, as applied to freight-yard operation between the yardmaster and switching crews, the Coast Line has planned to experiment with the inductive system in its south Rocky Mount freight yards. The apparatus employed will be similar to that described, and will employ 2-frequency operation of 103 and 174 kc.

The south Rocky Mount Yards are divided into two general areas of supervision, and one frequency will be assigned to each area. Thus, any equipped switcher may work in either yard area and at the same time be able to receive and respond to calls made on either frequency.

The experimental line equipped with I.T.C. includes the double-track portion of track from Rocky Mount to Contentnea, North Carolina; the single-track line from Contentnea to Pee Dee, by way of Wilmington, and that portion of the double-track line from Pee Dee to Florence.

In addition to the immediate advantages derived from this system of train communication, the Atlantic Coast Line expects to gain experience in methods of utilizing these advantages in other main-line operations under consideration.

So we find the Coast Line, the "Speedway of the South," keeping well abreast of the times, from roadbed to electronics, in this bright modern era of railway transportation. The road's progressive activities have been planned and prosecuted under the able leadership of its president, C. McD. Davis, and its new Chairman of the Board of Directors, F. B. Adams, a wide-awake railroader and all-round businessman.

CHAPTER XXI

THE ERIE

History in the Making

Before we take up fruit handling on the Erie, let us talk for a little about the Erie Railroad itself. The Erie is an old American institution, and it boasts many firsts in American railroad history. The first iron rails made in the United States were rolled in Scranton, Pennsylvania, for the Erie Railroad over 100 years ago. In September of 1851 the first train order ever issued flashed over a telegraph wire on the Erie. In November, 1875, the Erie inaugurated a through train service over its own and connecting lines between New York and Chicago. The Erie, its roots put solidly down in American soil, survived some tough business depressions and persisted in developing into one of the nations great railroads.

More remarkable still is the fact that the Erie literally crawled out of a swamp to blazon a page in history. Its first rails were spiked to piles as the Erie thrust out trembling steel fingers that ultimately squirmed across York state to Dunkirk on Lake Erie. Erie presidents came and went. Ten miles from Piermont, on the Hudson, the builders took time out for a rootin', tootin' celebration, and we mean *tootin'!* The Erie was on the way to the Great Lakes. The track reached Goshen, 46 miles from tide-water, after a struggle. In December, 1848, trains were whistling for Binghamton—a small matter of 7 years later. The railhead stood at Corning in December, 1849. On April 19, 1851, the last spike was hammered home, and news of the momentous event went by wire to President Millard Fillmore.

The President of the United States himself, accompanied by old Dan Webster and other notables, was invited to come and see what the Erie had done, and the first through passenger train from the Hudson River highballed over the rails of the Erie for the Great Lakes. Those rails, by the way, were laid to a 6-foot gauge. Gad Lyman was at the throttle of the bustling locomotive, Rogers 100. Sad to relate, the Rogers finally stalled on a grade, and it was necessary to substitute a grimy engine borrowed from a convenient work train. This engine had been built by a man named Swinburne, a rival of the Rogers outfit, and it was thought she would never make it, but the new engineer, Josh Martin, opened up the throttle and almost scared the notables to death. The Swinburne 71 huffed and puffed and groaned, but it rolled into a town called Deposit on time.

That night the special laid over at Elmira, some 280 miles from the starting point. The remainder of the trip to Dunkirk was completed the next day, amid much horn-blowing and rejoicing. The fatted calf was killed and toasts were drunk—and Erie officials stuck out their chests and took a bow.

The Erie, as a result, found itself included in the *American Railway Guide* of 1851. From this old guide we glean numerous interesting names along the line, including Shultz Turnt, Shin Hollow, Lackawaxen, Mast Hope, Basket Turnt, Nobody's Turnt, Painted Post, Friendship, Tunungwant, Bucktooth, Carraragus, Turnout, and—Dunkirk, on Lake Erie.

The Erie's firsts include the ticket punch, iron bridges, water tanks, the bell-cord communication signal between the train and the engineer, and many more. The battle-scarred Erie, through its will to survive, extended its rails and its service, and in 1888 the *Official Guide* registered the first famous Erie trade-mark. Also, it coined the slogan, "Ship and Travel by the Fast Erie Service."

Fruit Trains

The first shipment of transcontinental deciduous fruit was loaded into Central Pacific car 1974 at Vaccaville, California, in the spring of 1887, and was consigned to the Erie Railroad's Jersey City Terminal, where it arrived on June 28. From that small beginning, the movement of perishables on the Erie has grown to enormous proportions.

A pioneer carrier of fruit, the Erie today is known as the "Route of the Perishables." Long trains of yellow reefers are constantly booming down the rails of the Erie to eastern markets, and the road takes particular pride in the speed and efficiency with which this fruit movement is handled. The fruit trains roll at close to a mile a minute on many stretches along the line.

Citrus and deciduous fruits converge on Chicago from California, Arizona, Oregon, and Washington. Transfer engines move those cars consigned to the eastern seaboard and intermediate points to the tracks of the Chicago & Western Indiana Railroad and on down to Hammond, Indiana, 16 miles away. Here they are classified and trains for various destinations made up.

NY-98 (New York-98) is a crack Erie perishable train, and we find it made up and ready tonight—close to 100 cars of citrus fruits which the Santa Fe has rushed through from the Southwest. A big Berkshire locomotive of the S-3 class is on the head end. The conductor has checked the train, and his lantern swings the highball. Soon the markers are glimmering pin points of red moving east on the Erie.

Back at Hammond, complete reports of the make-up of the train are on the teletype. Thus the consignee is informed of the movement as he keeps a watchful eye on the eastern markets. In this way it is possible to reroute certain cars and take advantage of prices at cities other than the original destination while the fruit is in transit. In 1940 the Erie installed the teletype as a special service in expediting the movement of perishables.

The conductor writes up his wheel report, while the swing brakeman and flagman keep a close eye on the fast-moving train in the caboose cupola. Arriving at Huntington, Indiana, NY-98 picks up cars of garden produce from Louisiana that have come in over the Wabash from St. Louis. Huntington is a division point, and there is a new crew on the rear end when the fruit pulls out of the yard.

More cars of perishables converge on the route of NY-98 at Lima and Marion, Ohio. At Marion there are cars from the

Erie's Dayton and Cincinnati line; also cars from the Big Four. Marion Yard is crowded with jostling cars and busy switch engines, as trains are broken down and reshuffled for movement to various destinations. Cars requiring re-icing are switched to the icehouse track. Icing has been reduced to a highly specialized art. The time required to ice and salt the bunkers of a refrigerator car consumes from 60 to 90 seconds. One to 1½ tons of ice is used per car.

The icing plant has a track on either side with a capacity of 21 cars on each track, and here our eastbound perishable is speedily iced in the gray dawn. We now have 99 loads—4,680 tons—which include 3 cars of livestock, with a 5,400-horsepower Diesel coupled on ahead in place of the steam locomotive.

The conductor waves us out of town, and the motors of the Diesel roar up. NY-98 thunders over the rolling Kent and Mahoning Divisions. Arriving at Kent, Ohio, 114 miles to the east, the 3 livestock cars are dropped. The drover, who has been riding in the caboose, goes with his charges. The conductor turns in the 3 waybills, and a new crew takes over.

A check of his waybills reveals to the conductor that there are cars for Buffalo and Rochester, New York. These are set out at Meadville, Pennsylvania. The cars billed to points in northern New England are set out at Binghamton, New York, for the D.&H. Others move to Maybrook, New York, en route to points in southern New England.

NY-98 continues then to Croxton, which is the official designation for the big New Jersey receiving yard at the west end of the Bergen Tunnel. This is the end of the flight of the fruit trains. We think of fast freight as involving a train of 40 or 50 cars or so speeding between two metropolitan centers, but one of the biggest movements in the country is the march of the fruit trains, and "march" is hardly the word, for they move fast. These trains, often made up of 100 cars, beat out the miles at increasingly high speeds as the roads make way for the reefers. Fruit that once was a luxury has become a necessary part of the menu.

During 1945, freight conductors on the Erie entered 30,000 cars of fruits, vegetables, and melons in their wheel reports; 30,000 waybills were turned over to the yard clerks at Croxton.

As soon as the reefers are checked and carded, they are switched to the Croxton fruit-holding yard. Here the icing platform is 850 feet long. Icing inspections are made daily.

Notice of arrival is delivered to the consignee, which information shows all cars moving in since the last previous report. When the fruit rush is on, as many as 500 cars have been in the Croxton Yard awaiting orders, with approximately the same number booming through from Hammond. Erie traffic representatives have their fingers on these cars always.

The fruit consignee places orders with the agent at Duane Street Station in Manhattan on or before 2 p.m. for the following day's delivery. The various cars ordered are then grouped by the agent, who uses a letter designation, such as "Group A," citrus fruits; "Group B," deciduous fruits; "Group G," vegetables, melons; "Group Y," pears for heater barge. Switching then begins, and the cars are classified according to this grouping.

Perishables move from Croxton Yard to the float bridge in Jersey City in trains of 40 to 50 cars and are loaded 10 to 16 to a float. The floats are towed across the Hudson to the Duane Street Station. The Duane Street Piers, each about 1,000 feet long, are leased from the Harbor Department of the City of New York. The warehouses on the piers are, of course, heated in winter.

A maximum of 16 car floats can be docked here at one time, which means a minimum of 160 cars. The fruit, sorted and displayed on the piers, has been unloaded during the night, and the buyers arrive early to make their inspections and selections; then go to the auction room on the second floor. As many as 367 cars a day are handled at the Duane Street Piers.

In addition to the movement of the fruit trains, the Erie, because of a freedom from tight clearances, handles many "high and wide" loads.

A side light on the infinite detail involved in handling perishables is the fact that the Erie employs a large force of men who do nothing but repair the broken boxes and crates. The material is purchased from western mills in order that it may match as closely as possible the wood used in the original container.

CHAPTER XXII

THE BOSTON & MAINE'S YANKEE EMPIRE

Industrial New England

"Fish or cut bait" is an old New England axiom, and it pretty well typifies your New Englander. Thrift, industry, and stead-fastness of purpose are essentials that make for butter in the pan-try—and bread to put it on. A lot of long hard winters have made this Down Easter a pretty rugged individual. And that includes the Boston & Maine Railroad.

New England is known as an unsurpassed vacation land, and the Boston & Maine has done much to make vacationing attrac-tive, but there has to be something else to support a community or a railroad. If a New England farmer depended on summer boarders for his livelihood, he would starve to death. Taking sum-mer boarders provides a means for making a few extra dollars, but summer boarders are merely a by-product. No region or sec-tion of any country can hope to remain prosperous if its chief re-sources are not turning out and selling goods 12 months in the year.

Northern New England and the Boston & Maine have had their postwar problems, along with everybody else. These prob-lems began respectively at the close of the Revolutionary War and the War between the States. Postwar and economic prob-lems in general, it seems, are a kind of chronic ailment—like Aunt Mathilda's "spells." But Aunt Mathilda discovered long ago that what goose grease won't cure, elbow grease will.

"Some folks," says Aunt Mathilda, "enjoy poor health, and they work harder at it than they would at a fair-to-middlin' job."

The products of northern New England are travelers, and they reach into every corner of the earth. They begin their journey on the Boston & Maine and its feeder lines—the Central Vermont, the Rutland Railroad, the Bangor & Aroostook, the Maine Central—and flow ceaselessly to tidewater and many Boston & Maine gateways.

Shall we start with the potato? The Aroostook Aristocrat. This State of Mainer begins its long trek from the northern tip of Maine. Four million bushels came out of Aroostook County in 1943, which means that the Boston & Maine moved 50,000 carloads, delivered on its doorstep by the Bangor & Aroostook.

From the lumber camps deep in the great spruce forests of Maine, New Hampshire, and Vermont comes pulpwood. Down wood roads and streams, down the mighty rivers of northern New England to the mills in log drives, prodded on by the lumberjack. From the mills its moves by rail in the form of wood pulp or paper.

Nowhere in the world is man's ingenuity and resourcefulness and skill so completely built into the products of his labor as in New England. Turret lathes from the hills of Vermont, blankets from the looms on the banks of the Merrimack, stitching machines and shoes and gloves. The stencils on the packing cases read, Akron and Alexandria and Angora; Melbourne and Montreal and Mangitogorsk. The first wheel reports of the freight cars that carry them are written by conductors on the Boston & Maine.

When trainloads of steel for the shipyards on the Maine coast are rushing through, it is the Boston & Maine that delivers them on schedule. An automatic thread grinder starts out from Springfield, Vermont. The little spinning pump known as the Mechanical Silkworm, performing for the nylon industry what the heart does for the human body, was designed, developed, and produced in Waltham, Massachusetts, there beside the B.&M. tracks.

Freight cars loaded with paper roll into Concord, New Hampshire, and from the Rumford Press at Concord other hurrying cars carry every month 15,000,000 pieces of finished printing in the form of the *Reader's Digest*, the *Atlantic Monthly*, *Harper's*, *Yachting*, and other magazines.

Coal mining is not a northern New England industry, but the manufacture of coal-mining machines is. These machines speed the production of coal, sulphur, and salt all over the world. Built at Claremont, New Hampshire, we find a 15-ton machine that can block out a 300-ton chunk of coal in 2 hours flat as it gnaws a 5-inch groove, or "kerf," at the rate of 9 feet every 2 minutes.

From a textile research laboratory in Everett, Massachusetts, comes a chemical which reduces wool shrinkage. From Keene, New Hampshire, comes a delicate cable-marking machine. Nylon stockings of the finest texture come from a famous mill in Franklin, New Hampshire. From Windsor, Vermont, come insect-killing chemicals.

There are toys from Winchendon, fine tools from Athol, chairs and the latest type of passenger-coach seats from Gardner, Massachusetts. The list is endless. Industry and the steel rail march hand in hand in northern New England.

The Boston & Maine is both an institution and a tradition.

Let's go back a little. This is September 20, 1848. The place is Causeway Street, Boston. A Whig Congressman, on his way to speak in Cambridge, enters an imposing granite-walled building with 4 massive castle-like towers. The structure has been completed but little more than a month, and it is the pride of the Fitchburg Railroad, later a part of the Boston & Maine.

This Congressman is from Illinois, and he towers head and shoulders above his companions as he strides toward his waiting train. His name is Abraham Lincoln.

Above the depot in this building of Fitchburg granite, we enter a great hall, the largest in New England, which is packed with a concert audience. A woman on the stage is singing, a famed operatic soprano—Madame Otto Goldschmidt. Jenny Lind!

The old Fitchburg is gone now, but there is another and greater depot, and another and greater hall—the Boston Garden.

The Fitchburg depot lived out its span, to bow to the hand of the wrecker at the ripe old age of 80 years. The station served as a passenger terminal until 1894, at which time trains on the Fitchburg Railroad began rolling into the first North Union Station, eventually replaced by the present modern terminal. Between 1894 and the time it was razed, the Fitchburg depot served as an office building.

The Boston & Maine is part of the tradition of rock-ribbed New England, the bone and sinew of which went into the building of the old Fitchburg depot. Like Christianity, New England was founded on a Rock. It has preserved and treasured these traditions, as the Locomotive Historical Society has preserved the replica of the Alvah Crocker, the first engine on the Fitchburg Railroad, which once occupied a place on the front of the old Fitchburg depot.

In the year ending December 31, 1944, the Boston & Maine Railroad issued its 112th annual report. It has been a long span between the days of the old Haymarket Railroad Station in Boston and the present North Station, a short distance from the present Haymarket Square.

The Boston & Maine has made long strides, keeping pace always with the growth and development of this northern New England which it serves. How great has been the road's advancement we find embodied in the properties of the North Station, a monument there on Causeway Street to the railroad of which it is a part.

Of the hurrying thousands who daily pour through the portals of this terminal, few realize that on the face of all this earth there is no other railroad station like it. When I make this statement, I am not dealing in fantasy, but cold fact. Preposterous? Not a bit of it. One sentence sums up the all-embracing facilities of the Boston & Maine's North Station: A baby born in North Station could grow to maturity there and enjoy the fruits of a full life, including every comfort and luxury. There is only one thing lacking, and that is educational advantages. The North Station does not include a school system, but we feel that this is but a temporary oversight.

Let's assume that a baby *has* been born in North Station. This is a mythical baby, and we are going to grow up with her. We have chosen a girl baby for the reason that as she grows older she will require a greater variety of certain luxuries than a boy. We will call her Sally—Sally North.

Sally is born in a comfortable suite at the Hotel Manger,

which the Boston & Maine owns and rents to the operating hotel company. She entered this world with the house physician in attendance.

Sally's babyhood is spent with her parents in the Manger. The roof-walk on top of the hotel provides the necessary air and sunshine. Sally's childhood toys are purchased in the North Station concourse; her children's books come from the newsstands. Her kindergarten is the various exhibits on display in the station, including Mother Goose and all the rest. Here we meet the difficulty of Sally's progressing education by providing a tutor.

Baby food and all infant needs have been provided by the station drugstore. Clothing for herself and her mother comes from the women's shops. There are flowers from the station florist.

Entertainment? Well, what youngster doesn't have fun at the circus—the circus in the Garden, the greatest sports arena in a railroad station. And there is the rodeo, the Ice Follies, hockey, basketball, and track meets.

As Sally grows older, there is beauty treatment in the beauty shop. There is a wrist watch and other trinkets from a shop on the mezzanine; up-to-the-minute frocks from the dress shop, which also provides cleaning service. If Sally had happened to be a boy, he could have been completely outfitted at the ready-to-wear shop, from hat to shoes.

There are, of course, cocktail lounges in the hotel, and dancing in the ballroom. At Christmas there are carols in the concourse. There are all manner of Christmas and greeting cards. If Sally, grown up, wants a job, she will find it in the railroad offices or with any of the score of industrial firms who maintain offices in the North Station Industrial Building.

There are radio news broadcasts in the waiting room, and radio programs are always available in the hotel rooms. Sally can attend religious meetings in the Garden, political rallies, the poultry show, professional hockey games, and many other events.

The Boston Garden is comparable in size to Madison Square Garden in New York. It was opened in 1928.

It is a little difficult to imagine where you would find a better example of Yankee thrift and inherent shrewdness than right here in North Station, for every time a cash register rings up a sale there is more money in the bank for the Boston & Maine. The railroad receives a percentage of all sales.

From where we stand, it looks as though the Boston & Maine has plenty of bait and plenty of fish.

As for Sally North, we can well imagine that she eventually marries a railroad man, and that they will ride out of North Station on a "Honeymoon Special" behind a locomotive bearing the name "Sally North."

Fish Move

Possibly nothing is more symbolic of industrial New England than the codfish above Faneuil Hall in Boston's market district, for Boston has trafficked in fish from the beginning.

The Boston & Maine plays an important part in the movement of the codfish and all the other varieties almost from the moment that the trawler and the commercial fisherman dock. This fish traffic out of Boston is an important and highly developed business, for it originates the movement of an enormous amount of sea food which eventually arrives on the dinner table over a large part of America.

Once landed at the Boston Fish Pier, or other points, your codfish and halibut and haddock and all of their cousins and their aunts are soon on their way to distant markets. Soon after the fish has been hoisted from the pens of the trawler or the dragger, it is packed by dealers and rushed by a fleet of Railway Express Agency trucks to either the North or the South Station. (At the latter point it is handled by the Boston & Albany and the New York, New Haven & Hartford roads.) It is then loaded into waiting refrigerator cars, which are switched into fast passenger trains or made into solid express trains for large cities in New York state, Pennsylvania, Ohio, Michigan, Illinois, and Missouri.

Through the medium of this fast express service, fish leaving Boston on the late afternoon or early evening trains is being delivered to dealers, hotels, and restaurants the next day at points as far west as Chicago, and early the second morning in St. Louis, Missouri.

During 1945, 570,926 packages of fish, with an approximate weight of 63,801,260 pounds, were handled by this express service. In addition to this, fish shipments originated at other New England coast points, such as Gloucester and Lynn, Massachusetts; Portsmouth, New Hampshire; Portland, Boothbay Harbor, Rockland, Machias, Calais, and Eastport, Maine. The shipments from these communities include millions of pounds of live lobsters.

The lobster is a cherished member of the fish family—the aristocrat of sea food. He is fragile and perishable and requires specialized handling if he is to arrive at his destination in top condition. Special containers are necessary.

This thorny crustacean of the Atlantic, who retains his green coloring until cooked, is kept in large lobster pounds, or cars, secured to the wharf. Thus the lobster remains alive in his native element until prepared for shipment, at which time he is packed in a barrel. The barrel has a built-in container. The lobster is placed in the container with some seaweed, which acts as a sort of wet excelsior and prevents bruising. Ice is packed around the container. Lobsters can live out of water about two weeks if the gills are kept moist.

Lobsters shipped from points in Maine, such as Rockland, Boothbay Harbor, and Portland, on early morning trains, arrive over the lines of the Boston & Maine in Boston in the afternoon. Here they are quickly transferred to refrigerator cars on the Boston & Maine's crack Minute Man and start west over the Fitchburg Division for Chicago and intermediate points, being transported by the B.&M. as far as its western gateway on the Hudson River. These lobsters arrive in Chicago the next day in time to be served for dinner that evening.

In his normal element the lobster travels backward, through the medium of a flip of his powerful tail, but on the railroad he travels forward—and fast.

New England ships lobsters to all large cities on the Atlantic coast all the way to Florida and west to Missouri and Kansas. The tonnage runs into the millions of pounds. In one year, the lobster crop from Maine alone reached a total of 14,056,795 pounds, or more than 50 per cent of the total fishing industry of the state.

Through the use of refrigerator cars moving on fast trains, the lobsters are protected from extreme cold during the winter months, and in the hot weather they are cooled by the use of ice in the bunkers of the cars. A temperature very near to that of the natural habitat of the lobster is maintained during the movement.

A novel shipment originating in New England is that of live fish. These fish are transported to dealers in what are called "fish tank cars."

This car is of a special type, with built-in tanks on both sides and an aisle running full length between the tanks. These tanks are partially filled with water, and in one end of the car is an electricity-driven pump which forces air into the tanks to insure sufficient oxygen to keep the fish alive. Eels and an occasional car of river shad are the variety of fish mostly shipped in this manner.

Gloucester, steeped in fishing tradition, is one of the principal fishing ports along the New England coast. Rare indeed is the inlander who at one time or another has not enjoyed fish in some form from those famous Gloucester fish-packing plants. (Gloucester is pronounced Glosster, and not Glouchester, as some radio announcers mangle it.)

Fish products move out of Gloucester over the Boston & Maine in the form of frozen fish, salt fish, pickled fish, canned fish, and fish meal—products that reach into almost every far-flung corner of these United States.

About half of the rail distribution consists of frozen fish. This is shipped in refrigerator cars, precooled at Boston and sent to Gloucester for loading. When they are loaded and ready to move, complete instructions are given for icing, thus insuring the ultimate delivery of the fish in proper condition. This frozen fish is shipped largely to points in the Middle West, the South, and the Southwest, including the Pacific coast. During July and August there is also quite a swordfish movement, this fish commanding the highest price of all that swim the seas.

Pickled and salt fish move in smaller volume only as far as the Mississippi. Fish meal provides a fertilizer ingredient because of its high protein content, and the movement runs up to 20 cars a month.

The sardine, small but vastly important, makes up one of the big movements of fish out of northern New England, with some 19 canning factories scattered along the Maine coast from Portland to Eastport and located in such towns and cities as Robbinson, Lubec, Pembroke, Machiasport, Jonesport, Prospect Harbor, McKinley, Southwest Harbor, Belfast, Rockland, and Yarmouth. Sardines are caught in weirs, though seining is the usual method employed.

During 1945 there were approximately 2,600,000 cases of sardines, or the equivalent of 2,150 carloads, packed in the state of Maine. A record of 3,200,000 cases was established in 1944, with a money value of $12,000,000. Sardines are usually shipped in cases containing 100 cans each, with a weight of about 40 pounds per case. These sardines go to practically every state in the Union, and some are exported. During the last war year nearly 80 per cent of the entire pack was taken by the government.

Even the humble fish cake is a New England traveler, and 21 cars of this product were shipped in 1945. A company at Eastport puts them up, and they are highly recommended, particularly when served with fried eggs.

In seasons when the alewives (a species of herring) are running, 15 to 20 cars of this fish are shipped from Newcastle and Damariscotta Mills to New York City markets.

In connection with the sardine-canning industry there are also various by-products, such as fish scrap, fish oil, and fish meal, traveling by rail in this great New England fish move. And it is by no means a small item. In 1945 there were 103 cars of fish scrap, 23 cars of fish oil, and 16 cars of fish meal, which besides its fertilizer value supplies an ingredient used in poultry feed. It is produced by cooking, drying, and grinding fish waste.

Another by-product of fish waste is liquid soap, made by mixing the waste with a chemical solution. Seventy-one cars were shipped from Eastport, Maine, in 1945, being taken by the government.

Returning to the frozen-fish move, we find that several hundred cars are shipped from Rockland, Wiscasset, and Portland, Maine. These shipments move to Chicago, St. Louis, Omaha, Kansas City, Milwaukee, and other western cities. There is also a substantial market for this product in the South. Approximately 175 cars of pickled, smoked, and salt fish are shipped annually from Eastport and Lubec to these same markets. Down from the Boston & Maine's gateway at Portland, Maine, over the Portland Division, roll fish from the North Atlantic, moving to the ceaseless chant of singing wheels.

So we find in the fish move another page in the story of industrial New England.

Snow Trains

The Boston & Maine was the first railroad in the country to operate a Snow Train. The idea originated with Frederick T. Grant, General Passenger Agent, in 1930. Mr. Grant felt there was an opportunity in the railway field for the transportation of winter-sports enthusiasts to resorts in the mountain areas of northern New England. Why, he reasoned, only provide excursion trains in the summer? During the winter the White Mountains have a surplus of snow, and Boston a surplus of young folks full of vim and vitality.

It remained only to get them together. With this end in view, the Boston & Maine got busy. It was not entirely a benevolent undertaking, leaning slightly to the "fish or cut bait" rule. The hauling of passengers produces revenue, which any railroad is not above considering, particularly a Yankee railroad.

Other railroads around the country quickly seized upon the idea, but it took a Down Easter to start the ball rolling. It was the same kind of Yankee ingenuity employed by a small New Hampshire manufacturer who, when metal replaced one of his principal products, turned to making sticks for lollipops, which were even more profitable than the former article.

We can imagine that when the Boston & Maine's first advertisement announcing its Snow Trains appeared, there was a great rustling of Boston papers as Junior and Sister sprouted into action. Until this time the major snow activities of the young folks around Boston had been confined largely to Franklin Park, but now new horizons were opening, it seemed. The run on department stores and sporting goods establishments had all of the earmarks of an early-day gold rush.

The first Boston & Maine Snow Train went into operation in the winter of 1930–31. It carried 197 slightly giddy winter-sports enthusiasts. The business grew by leaps and bounds, and by 1934 this Yankee railroad was hauling as many as 3,000 lovers of the open spaces on a single week end. Snow Trains were running in 6 sections, and you could hardly see the coaches for skis, snowshoes, sleds, and ski caps.

Business fell off somewhat in 1933, but this was occasioned by the bank holiday when folks did not have the money to spend.

Let's just run down the list of passengers which one-day and week-end trains carried out of North Station during the 12 seasons of 1931 to 1942 inclusive.

1931	8,371
1932	10,314
1933	7,703
1934	14,974
1935	17,943
1936	24,240
1937	10,039
1938	13,383
1939	14,529
1940	12,431
1941	10,039
1942	15,753
	159,719

There are fluctuations, you have observed, largely caused by economic conditions. The spirit was willing but the purse was weak. However, the Snow Train is here to stay; no doubt about that. Junior and Sister have become snow enthusiasts, and you might include Father, Mother, and many others, who will like it if it kills them.

The patronage of the Snow Trains is made up of about 80 to 90 per cent skiers—budding amateurs and seasoned experts. The remainder consists of the snowshoe element and the young fry, who go in for sliding and skating. There are also the usual camera addicts who find the winter scenes a dish greatly to their liking. A few just go for the ride, wanting to enjoy the out-of-doors, cold feet, red noses, and wear the becoming ski clothes.

Most of the Boston & Maine's winter-sports announcements appear on the sports pages of the Boston papers. There are also moving pictures in natural colors of all the fun, which are shown at clubs, schools, and other places. Each year a booklet covering the activities for the coming season is issued. This contains a list of hotels and boardinghouses in the various localities. Also, half-sheet display posters are distributed.

Practically all the Snow Trains have been operating into central New Hampshire because this territory is ideally situated geographically. The snow lasts, and the locality is far enough from the seacoast to be free from fogs, which melt the snow. Of late years Vermont, Massachusetts, and Maine have developed their own winter-sports facilities, and these areas are attracting increasing attention.

The Sunday Snow Trains operate to North Conway, New Hampshire, and they offer a full day of good clean fun at a price so reasonable that you feel that you will lose money if you do not take advantage of it.

If you feel that you cannot sufficiently expose yourself to chilblains in one day, there is the week-end Snow Train. This was originated back around 1935. The week-end Snow Trains leave Boston on Saturday, returning late Sunday night.

The Snow Train provides an excuse for many northern New England communities to dust off the old pung and oil up the sleigh bells. A pung, in case your knowledge of such things is a bit hazy, is a boxlike sleigh. A long one filled with straw and drawn by a spanking team offers a means for the young folks to become better acquainted. The local folks also organize hockey games, skating parties, and other entertainment such as you will only find in New England.

Snow Train followers find a Snow Train at their disposal each week end during the season. Also, the schedules of regular trains during the week, as well as on Sundays, are so arranged that the snow enthusiasts can reach their favorite spots whenever they desire.

A sports-equipment and luncheon car is carried on one section of the Sunday Snow Train. This car offers for sale and for rent a limited supply of ski clothes and other equipment, including ski wax, ski straps, and books on skiing. Other sections of the Snow Train offer for your convenience a limited supply of these incidentals. The Sports Car is available to other patrons before departure and upon arrival at the destination.

If you are planning to spend the week end in the snow-sports country you may make reservations through the Passenger Traffic Department, or by direct communication with the hotels, at your pleasure.

We gather that the Boston department stores and sporting-goods establishments warmed to the Snow Train idea with no reluctance whatsoever. The original Snow Train, of course, was new and unique, and newspapers in Boston, New York, Chicago, and other cities seized upon this meaty morsel at once, for it provided many a feature story. National magazines ran articles about it, and the movie weeklies played it up.

Your Yankee railroad stood up admirably under this barrage of unsolicited publicity. In view of all the commotion stirred up, the Boston & Maine contrived to continue doing business at the same old stand.

I have obtained no definite figures on the increased sales of sports wear since the Snow Train was originated, but soon after it was established, stores all over Boston began featuring "Snow Train Departments" and "Snow Train Lodges" and such. This did the B.&M. no harm.

The stores before long were increasing their orders for snow equipment, which meant a corresponding increase in shipments moving over the lines of railroads entering Boston, with the Boston & Maine hauling its share.

Store owners in other parts of the country, upon reading the advertisements in the Boston papers, promptly investigated this winter sportswear boom as they scanned the local countryside hopefully for anything resembling a snowbank. So contagious was the idea that California was starting to organize a snow-sports movement almost before the early returns were in from the New England territory.

We will write of California snow sports in another chapter, for obviously you cannot ignore a winter playground that has seen a snowfall of 67 feet in one winter.

During the late war and immediately afterward, the needs of war transport outranked the Snow Train, but it is back now, bigger and better than ever.

The Snow Train was a bright thought, and it has grown into big business in railroad transportation, in store sales, and in manufactured goods. It has been a pay-roll producer. It has been a body-builder, and many a G.I. Joe among the Ski Troopers of our armed forces during World War II first learned the high art of skiing through the medium of the Snow Train.

A brief summary of the Snow Trains moving for the most part out of Boston during the winter of 1941–42 shows that there were 11,574 one-day passengers and 4,179 week-end passengers, for a total of 15,753 riding the Boston & Maine's special and regular trains.

Many a snowball has started an avalanche, but never one with the far-reaching, soul-satisfying results of that snow tide set in motion by that first Yankee Snow Train. Skiing and salt-water fishing are the two greatest outdoor crazes of the present time, and were for 8 years before the war.

Two other great railroads join with the Boston & Maine in providing Boston and New England with the best in railroad transportation. They are the Boston & Albany, a division of the New York Central, and the New York, New Haven & Hartford.

In a month-long exhibit at the Boston Museum of Fine Arts, in January, 1945, these 3 roads united in sponsoring 2 huge mural paintings. The canvases, 7 feet high and 30 feet long, portrayed the future port of Boston, with the railroads playing an important part in providing a link between tidewater and New England's farms and factories in this great Yankee Empire whose hospitality and welcome are always tops.

CHAPTER XXIII

FLAGMAN OF THE CHICAGO & NORTH WESTERN

Mars Headlight

A man from Mars is flagging on the Chicago & North Western. He is a thousand times faster than the human flagman, starting out to protect the standing train; his lantern is a thousand times more powerful. The beams of his light flash across the sky like the brilliant sweep of the aurora borealis.

The man from Mars leaps into action the instant there is an emergency application of the train brakes. It makes no difference whether the engineer has swung the lever of the brake valve to the last "big hole" notch—full emergency—or whether the brake application was caused by the rupturing of the train line because of a break-in-two; the mechanical flagman automatically begins to swing his powerful electric lantern. Above the trees and across the hills the crimson banners fan out, crying that a train has stopped and all enginemen beware.

On clear nights these oscillating red lights are visible for several miles, and they have considerable penetrative power in rain or fog. Also, they can be seen over a long range in daylight.

In the field of astronomy, we find that Mars is a planet conspicuous for its red light. In the railroad field the powerful Mars oscillating figure-eight red light at both the front and rear end of the train is a prominent safety feature, and a recent contribution of the Chicago & North Western Railway System.

The purpose of this new development, created by the Chicago & North Western, working in conjunction with the Mars Signal Light Company of Chicago, is further to protect trains making emergency stops from rear-end collisions or, in event of a derailment, from being sideswiped by trains moving on adjoining tracks.

The automatic operation of the Mars lights involves a new principle which utilizes the sudden release of air-brake pressure. The Mars lights are also hooked up so that the engineman or fireman may operate them by means of a switch in the cab of the locomotive.

This new Martian equipment has been installed and tested on the streamliner Twin Cities 400 with highly satisfactory results. According to L. L. White, Vice-President in charge of Operations of the North Western, who personally supervised this new development, the Mars light is one of the most important features of railroad safety research in recent years, for it represents another step forward in the high art of railroading.

The story of the research that went into these lights is not only interesting, but further illustrates the manner in which one new achievement may lead to greater events. The experiments with the Mars light resulted in 4 distinct accomplishments, each so successful as to attract the attention of other railroads, many of which soon began installing similar lights on their trains.

In 1936 the Chicago & North Western and the Mars Signal Light Company developed the first oscillating headlight. This was installed on the original streamliner 400 as a supplement to the conventional headlight. Its purpose was to attract the attention of motorists and pedestrians at crossings, warning of the approach of a fast-moving train. This flashing white light, whipping across the sky long before the train itself was in sight, could not help but catch the eye of the motorist or pedestrian. Further, there was no chance of the train's headlight so merging with automobile headlights or the lights of town or city that it might fail to be immediately identified as an oncoming train.

The Mars light was of such proven value that it was quickly adopted by many railroads for their high-speed trains. Still the North Western was not satisfied, feeling that there was an opportunity here for greater improvement. Thus, in July of 1944, it announced a second development—an oscillating headlight that would flash either a red or a white light, whichever the engineer desired.

This dual-purpose light was not simply a single reflector with a red and a white bulb; it went further than that. Before the final drawings were O.K.'d, there were various problems to be solved and bugs to be worked out. At last the North Western and the Mars people came up with a headlight that was all they felt it should be.

Instead of the headlight containing a single reflector, there were two. At the touch of a switch these reflectors could be reversed, with the light also changing from red to white. The mechanism was comparatively simple; it was sure and foolproof. And another hurdle had been cleared. Feeling now that the head end of the train had been taken care of, the engineers turned their attention to the rear.

In January of 1945 a portable oscillating red light had been developed for the rear end. This light had for its purpose the prevention of rear-end collisions, and it was designed so that it could be attached to any car.

The result of the development of this light, which came close on the heels of earlier developments, was that the North Western was the first road to provide mechanical flagmen for its trains. But there was still work to be done.

The first of the portable rear-end lights was constructed of steel, and it weighed 123 pounds. While it could be set in position, it was too heavy for one man to handle easily.

Vice-President White insisted that the weight of the light be reduced. There followed a series of tests and experiments with various materials. A light was built of aluminum. This resulted in a reduction of 58 pounds, but Mr. White was not satisfied, for he thought 65 pounds was still too much weight. A new housing was built; this time of magnesium, and now the weight dropped to a comfortable 41 pounds, thereby reducing to a minimum the grunting and profanity attendant on its movement.

At this writing the automatic rear- and head-end lights are in service on the fast Twin Cities 400, and the portable light is performing its duties as a silent flagman on a host of North Western trains, including the San Francisco Overland Limited, the Challengers, the Pacific, the Portland Rose, locals No. 15

and 16, and mail trains Nos. 8 and 9. These trains operate between Chicago and Omaha.

And there is the North Western Limited between Chicago and the Twin Cities, the Duluth-Superior Limited between Chicago and Duluth, the Mondamin from Minneapolis and St. Paul to Omaha, the Rochester-Minnesota Special from southern Minnesota to Chicago, the Ashland Limited between Chicago and Ashland, Wisconsin, the Iron and Copper Country Express between Chicago and the upper Michigan peninsula, and the North American between Omaha and Minneapolis and St. Paul.

Twenty-eight passenger and mail trains on the North Western now employ the portable rear oscillating lights—the new flagman.

Rules Governing the Flagman from Mars

Upon the installation of the red oscillating rear-end light, the following rules become operative:

On passenger trains equipped with red oscillating rear-end lights, trainmen and enginemen will be governed by the following instructions:

When a train comes to a stop or is moving under circumstances in which it may be overtaken by another train, the trainman acting as flagman will immediately turn on the red light.

The operation and use of this device will not in any way relieve trainmen from compliance with Rule 99.

Enginemen on approaching trains will take notice and immediately reduce speed and be prepared to stop.

The rules governing the use of the red headlight read as follows:

In every case where the air-brakes are applied from any cause other than in normal operation by the engineman, or when the engineman finds it necessary to stop his train due to some defect or under circumstances which might cause derailment, thereby fouling the adjacent main track, enginemen will immediately turn on the red emergency light, and when this is done, enginemen on approaching trains on adjacent tracks will take notice and immediately bring their train to a stop, and proceed only after finding track clear. These instructions are applicable at all times, both day and night. This emergency headlight must not be used for any other purpose.

The operation and use of this device will not in any way relieve enginemen or trainmen from complying with the last paragraph of Rule 102.

Rules 99 and 102 are flagging rules. These instructions, incidentally, will be modified to make allowance for the new automatic feature.

On the Twin Cities 400, both red-white oscillating headlight and the rear-end red oscillating light are connected to operate simultaneously and automatically. The automatic feature of these lights is controlled through air-connected switches cut into the brake pipe. One is located on the Diesel locomotive to control the red-white headlight, and one is located on the rear end of the observation car to control the red light there.

On the 400 the red light is built into the curvature of the roof at the rear as a permanent feature.

The automatic control of these lights assures that whenever the brake-pipe pressure drops below approximately 30 pounds for any cause while the Mars headlight is operating, the light will revolve from white-oscillating to red-oscillating and immediately shut off the regular fixed headlight.

When the pressure of the brake pipe is pumped up above approximately 43 pounds, the red light will turn out and automatically revolve back to white-oscillating, the regular fixed headlight again lighting.

In daytime operation the Mars headlight is off, and all switches, except the automatic switch, remain in off position. However, again, if for any reason the brake-pipe pressure should drop below approximately 30 pounds, the light will turn to red-oscillating and, as before, remain in this position until the brake-pipe pressure has again been pumped to at least 43 pounds.

The oscillating light on the rear of the 400 shows red position only, but its operation is the same as the Mars headlight on the locomotive.

The air switches governing these headlights are of the dia-phragm type. Whenever the brake-pipe pressure is above the predetermined upper setting, the contacts on this switch are held open, and the white light is in operation. When pressure drops to the low limit, the contacts on the air switch close, energizing the polarity-change relay, and the rotating motor will turn the barrel of the Mars light from white to red, at the same time energizing the power-cutoff relay to the standard stationary headlight, turning this light out.

At all times when the red-oscillating light is in operation there is no other light displayed to an approaching train.

The combination red-white headlight on the locomotive re-ceives its power from a 64-volt battery through a 12-volt motor-generator set. The lamps used on the red and white positions are 480 watt, 12-volt, bipost type. The red light on the rear end is a 250-watt, 32-volt standard headlight lamp, taking its power from the car battery.

In the case of the portable rear light, there is no automatic operation. These lights are switched on by the flagman just be-fore he gets off to post his train in the event of an emergency stop.

The value of the lights in preventing sideswiping has been demonstrated. There was, for instance, a train on the North Western that was stopped by an application of brakes from some cause unknown to the man at the throttle. He immediately switched on his oscillating red light, which at that time was not of the automatic type.

The flagman from Mars instantly went to work, waving his light across the sky—bold, bright crimson flashes reaching far down the rail.

Close to the moment when emergency air set the brakes on this train, a speeding train was approaching from the other di-rection on the adjacent track. Far around the curve, the engineer caught the red beams flashing and instantly slowed his train, brought it to a stop. There had not been time for a flagman to gather up his lanterns and fuses and go out, no time for the crew to recover from the slamming shock of locked wheels.

Investigation revealed that several cars of the train stopped by the emergency brake application had been derailed and were fouling the opposing track. No human brakeman could possibly have flagged down the swiftly approaching train in time to avert disaster. It was the first actual and indisputable evidence of the efficiency of this new flagman of the Chicago & North Western.

Lives and property had been saved, and the reward for long and painstaking experiment was contained in this one incident. The flagman from Mars had earned a place on the railroad honor roll.

CHAPTER XXIV

BUSINESS CAR ON THE SANTA FE

Field Headquarters

The Business Car is probably the least known and understood piece of railroad equipment, from the layman's viewpoint, and yet it is enormously important to the successful operation of the railway system. In the same sense that the caboose is the command car of the freight train, the Business Car is the field headquarters of the railroad.

A great many people hold to the opinion that a high railway official never takes his feet off his desk. In this chapter we offer evidence quite to the contrary, and in contradiction to the assertion of a boomer friend that "you could lop off the head of every official above a superintendent, and the railroad would still run." It is possible, but it would be running downhill. The top-drawer officials of the railroad, as in any other business, are the masterminds who spell the difference between a going concern and "two streaks of rust."

In the first place, the Business Car on the rear end of a train is exactly what the name implies, and is not in any way associated with a joy ride. When he is out on the road, your operating official is not only confronted with many duties and problems along the right of way, but he carries the additional burden of transacting the business connected with his home office. Stacks of mail, papers, and telegrams are delivered to him in the Business Car while he is traveling. I have seen George Minchin, Operating Vice-President of the Santa Fe, send 14 messages and dictate 17 letters in an hour and a half in attempting to keep abreast of routine company business while he was on an inspection trip. His usual office work is simply transferred to him when he is on the road, often as much as 2,000 miles from his Chicago head-quarters.

The Business Car provides the railroad official with the only effective means of keeping in close touch with the railroad. Here at first hand he has an opportunity to observe the condition of the track, the right of way, sidings, bridges, towers, interlockings, signals, highway crossings, house tracks, and the tracks which serve industries along the line.

Almost any other business executive can view most of his plant from the window of his office. Not so the railroad official, whose plant and facilities cover thousands of miles in perhaps more than half a dozen sprawling states. Hence this car at the rear end of the train, which many folks mistakenly believe to be a private car. It is, of course, private so far as the public is concerned; but it is not a place of luxury and frolic. On some railroads, it is called Office Car.

If you were to hear a railroad man say, "The Old Man's car is on," you may be assured that the train is hauling a Business Car. It may be carrying the president of the road, an operating vice-president, vice-president in charge of traffic, general manager, assistant general manager, general superintendent of motive power, chief mechanical officer, assistant to the operating vice-president, or the division superintendent.

The smaller roads, of course, operate only 3 or 4 Business Cars, and these are usually assigned to the president, operating vice-president, and chief engineer.

A superintendent spends much of his time out on the division, but if you do not see his Business Car on the rear end it is no sign that he is not around. In fact, most superintendents cover more miles in the locomotive cab or in the caboose than they do in the Business Car. When things are happening, the super is always on the firing line. In time of storms, traffic jams, or just all-round hell and high water, you will find him in the thick of it. You remember in a preceding chapter when Old Man Winter started shutting down the railroad, Superintendent J. H. Valentine, of the Milwaukee, was out there on the line with the snow fighters.

All business cars are equipped with speed indicators, and most of them have air gauges which allow the official in the Business Car to check on the braking of the train. Nearly all Business Cars are equipped with floodlights located behind the rear trucks. These are for the purpose of inspecting the track during night runs, and they are constantly in use.

The Business Car provides a meeting place for superintendents, division engineers, signal supervisors, roadmasters, and other officials of the Operating and Maintenance departments. When the car is laying over at various points on the line, railroad men of varying rank are constantly coming and going. Problems of the district are threshed out on the ground; also the headquarters official obtains a firsthand picture of conditions and train operations on the line.

The Business Car also serves as a place where department heads may invite city and town officers and others in to discuss community problems in countless localities, which, aside from the service rendered by the railroad, are after all contributing factors to the livelihood and well-being of the railroad itself.

Few other than railroad men ever ride in the Business Car. Except in the case of the Military, if a house guest does squeeze in, he pays full transportation and Pullman fare. Besides its dining facilities, the average Business Car provides sleeping accommodations for from 4 to 8 people. Aside from the fact that the car is often set off at points where there are no hotel accommodations, the busy rail executive prefers to remain in his car. His duties often keep him at his desk until a late hour; also he may find it expedient to order the car coupled onto a train during the night for a move to the next stop, where, following a few hours sleep and breakfast, he will pick up his work where he left off.

The railroad official puts in many days each month on the road, and I have seen top-ranking railroaders watching the track from the rear of the Business Car while eating their meals from their laps.

Obviously you will never see a Business Car attached to the rear end of a train with an observation car. Most officials, unless they are going through, pick the slower trains. This allows for a closer inspection of the right of way, and also they come in contact with more of the personnel at the various stops.

Two ditching machines removing eroded materials from a cut, thereby improving track drainage on the A.C.L. The earth removed is relaid so as to strengthen the roadbed. Courtesy A.C.L. Railroad.

Freight conductor in caboose using new I.T.C. telephone. Courtesy Union Switch & Signal Co.

Flagman on the rear end of the B.&M. #5, the Alouette, gets a highball from section foreman, who had inspected his train from the ground. Motor car in foreground. Courtesy Boston & Maine Railroad.

Perishable train on the Erie pulling out of Marion, Ohio, with Engine #3329, 2-8-4 type, class S-3, with fruit for the eastern market. Courtesy Erie Railroad.

Santa Fe #17, the Super Chief, descending the west slope of Glorieta Pass, N. M., on the 3% grade, Third District of the New Mexico Division. Courtesy Santa Fe Railroad.

B.&M. freight conductor demonstrates use of conductor's valve for applying train brakes from caboose in freight service. Courtesy Boston & Maine Railroad.

B.&M. freight trainman displaying lighted 5-minute red fusee in holder provided for that purpose on each end of both sides of B.&M. cabooses. Courtesy Boston & Maine Railroad.

B.&M. flagman in freight service holding day-time clear-weather flagging signals used on that road. Red flag, torpedoes, and fusees. Courtesy Boston & Maine Railroad.

How the torpedo, sometimes called gun, looks when fastened to the railhead. The use of 1 or 2 torpedoes means the same thing: reduce speed. Courtesy Boston & Maine Railroad.

Westbound Santa Fe Fast Mail #7 running around #75 Southern Kansas Division way freight at Olathe, Kan., with Engine #3451, 4-6-4 type, on the Eastern Division. The operation is left hand. Courtesy Santa Fe Railroad.

Santa Fe #1703, 2-10-2 type, helping at the rear of a 26-car coal drag as it climbs the 3.3% grade on the west slope of Raton Pass, 1 mile below Lynn, N. M. Photo by Preston George.

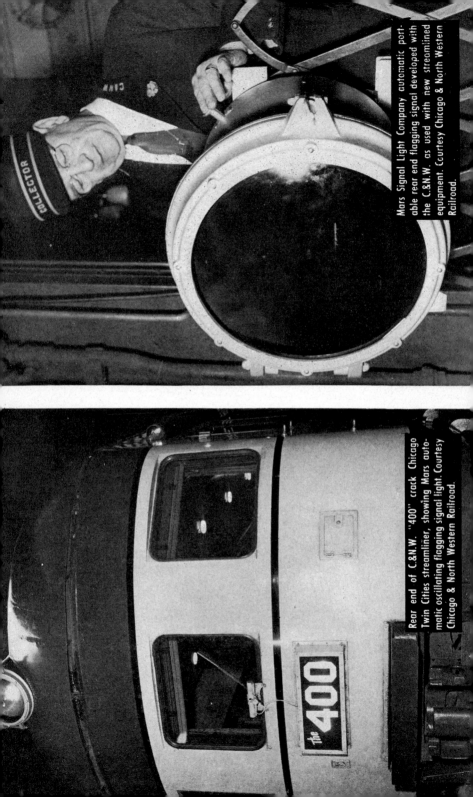

Mars Signal Light Company automatic portable rear end flagging signal developed with the C.&N.W. as used with new streamlined equipment. Courtesy Chicago & North Western Railroad.

Rear end of C.&N.W. "400" crack Chicago Twin Cities streamliner, showing Mars automatic oscillating flagging signal light. Courtesy Chicago & North Western Railroad.

14,000 tons of coal, 165 loads, en route to Lambert Point and Tidewater, east of Crewe, Va., on the Norfolk Division, hauled by Engine #2101, 2-8-8-2 type, class Y-5. Courtesy Norfolk & Western Railroad.

N.&W.'s modern steel coal loading piers at Lambert Point (Norfolk, Va.) with cars ready to be dumped into the waiting collier. Courtesy Norfolk & Western Railroad.

Balancing way cars on the First District of the Sante Fe Plains Division. Note the highballers that perform excellent work in passing signals to the head end and are in service on several flat divisions on that road. The train is Fwd. 43, snapped on Curtis Hill, Okla., just east of Quinlan, where the new line has just been finished. Note the fresh grading. The track still has a slow order on it. Photo by Preston George.

Sante Fe #27 the Antelope with the 4-6-2 type Engine #3415 running along the Washita River near Arbuckle, Okla., on the First District of the Northern Division. Note the business car on the rear end. Photo by Preston George.

Now let us take a typical trip on a Business Car. We are riding with F. A. Baker, Assistant General Manager of the coast line of the Santa Fe. At the time of this trip Mr. Baker had jurisdiction over the First, Second, and Third Districts of the Arizona Division, extending from Mojave and Barstow, California, through Needles to Seligman, Arizona; and the First, Second, and Third Districts of the Albuquerque Division, from Seligman through Winslow, Arizona, Gallup, New Mexico, to Belen, New Mexico, including all branch lines such as the line from Cadiz, California, to Phoenix, Arizona; and the Fourth District, Phoenix to Ash Fork, Arizona.

The Assistant General Manager's car, No. 18, has been coupled onto the rear end of Second No. 8, the Fast Mail, at Los Angeles. This train handles overflow express and is the slow section. Mr. Baker did not want to burden the first section with an extra car, for First No. 8 is a fast, heavy train.

District Engineer R. E. Chambers, of the coast lines, another crack railroader, is making the trip with us. We go to bed at midnight. At Barstow, at 5:30 a.m., the car is cut off. Mr. Baker is up at 6 o'clock and takes a turn around the yards and looks over the new Diesel shops. At 7 o'clock he has the trainmasters stationed at Barstow and two mechanical men in for breakfast with him.

In the meantime, a switching crew has turned the Business Car on the wye and coupled it onto the rear end of a westbound "main" train of 12 cars. This main train is carrying hospital battalions en route to Pittsburg, California. Here on San Francisco Bay these hospital battalions will board transports for theaters of war in the Pacific.

Before we pull out of Barstow, Mr. Baker invites the army "train commander" and his second in command to make the trip in the Business Car. This is a practice religiously pursued by all railroads and officials when Business Cars are attached to main trains.

Our train heads into a passing track at Muroc to meet an eastbound troop train. None of the soldiers aboard the train are allowed to detrain.

At Mojave we are joined by the Santa Fe trainmaster in

charge of the jointly operated territory between there and Bakersfield. We pick up a 1600-class 2-10-2 locomotive to help our regular engine, the 3726, a fine performing 4-8-2. Our helper is cut off at Tehachapi, the top of the Hill, and we continue single to Bena over C.T.C. territory.

Traffic is heavy in the Tehachapis. We meet 6 trains, but are only stopped once, and then because of a sticking brake west of Caliente. This run of 33 miles is reeled off in 66 minutes, with all speed limits on the many curves strictly observed. Some of these curves, including the famous Tehachapi Loop, range up to 10 degrees.

We pull into Bakersfield at 2:30 p.m. and say good-by to our friends of the main train. Mr. Baker has business at a local packing house, which provides me with an opportunity to visit my old friend E. F. Wasem, the chief dispatcher of the Southern Pacific's San Joaquin Division and look over the S.P. C.T.C. machine.

Another crack railroader of the Santa Fe is E. E. McCarty, General Manager of the Santa Fe Coast Lines. He served with distinction as rail transportation head of the O.D.T. through 1945 and the early part of 1946. C. R. Tucker, present Assistant Vice-President of Operations, served under him as assistant and acting general manager, while Mr. McCarty was in Washington.

Our Business Car is lined up to leave Bakersfield on the rear end of Second No. 2, the Scout, and we pull out 5 minutes late behind the first section with 11 cars and a 3800-class 2-10-2 helper, which is cut off 2.2 miles east of Tehachapi at Summit Switch.

This is April, and the San Joaquin Valley is carpeted with miles and miles of lupines as blue as the Pacific, and here and there fields of bright yellow poppies. Too, the great Mojave Desert is putting on its annual spring flower show, with the gnarled Joshua trees flowered out with solid clusters of white blossoms. Strange as it may seem, no flowers anywhere can begin to compare in variety and in beauty and delicacy with those of Mojave. (Mojave is pronounced, and often spelled, Mohave—Mo-hahv-ay)

We arrived at Mojave at 8 p.m., right on the money, and are

on First No. 2's block all the way to Barstow, pulling in at 10:20. Here Mr. Baker receives his mail and railroad paper work for the first day. It consists of a stack which requires the attention of himself and secretary until late into the night.

At 6:10 a.m. we leave Barstow on the rear end of the second section of No. 24, the Grand Canyon Limited, 10 minutes late. Our train is made up of 11 cars. This 10 minutes, however, is easily made up on the Second District in the 165.7 miles, Barstow to Needles, with one stop at Cadiz.

A. J. Smith, then Superintendent of the Arizona Division, is waiting for Mr. Baker in Needles. We have in the car now trainmasters, the road foreman of engines, and some track supervisors. The more you ride with railroad men on these Business Cars, the more you become impressed with their interest in the maintenance of the track and their insistence that it be 100-per-cent perfect at all times. This is understandable, because the rails and roadbed are, after all, the most important part of a railroad.

At Needles Mr. Baker receives another stack of official papers; these in addition to papers handed to him before we pulled out of Barstow.

The first place a railroad official heads for when his Business Car arrives at a division point is the dispatcher's office, for here the DS has his finger always on the hot pulse of throbbing trains. The first question usually is, "How's the railroad and what have you got coming?"

On the coast lines of the Santa Fe there are always three things of major importance that never for an instant are out of an official's mind. Let's examine them in the order of Mr. Baker's rapid-fire interrogations.

"What shape was No. 19 in when we received her at Albuquerque?" No. 19 is, as you possibly know, the westbound Chief. He follows this up with, "What time did she get into Barstow?"

Then he switches to the eastbound Chief. "In what shape was No. 20 when we turned her over to the New Mexico Division?" And now he turns his inquiry to the Fast Mail, Nos. 7 and 8. A Santa Fe man never lets Uncle Sam's mail out of his mind.

The third big question, though it is always saved for the last, is, "How many loads did we put into Belen [New Mexico]?"

This refers to the last 8 hours. Then, "What's coming east out of San Bdno [San Bernardino] and Bakersfield? How many loads out of Barstow?"

This information is all-important, for it concerns freight movements, and in wartime or peace freight is constantly under the watchful eye of the railroad official.

Mr. Baker has a word or two with just about everybody around the Needles station. We go then to inspect the new icehouse track; then there were other yard tracks. These have recently been raised, for every year Old Man River, in the form of the Rio Colorado, seems to grow bigger and hungrier. In the past the Colorado has often flooded the Santa Fe yards at Needles, interrupting service and chasing the inhabitants, the majority of whom work for the Santa Fe, to higher ground. However, of late years some of this danger has been lessened through raising yard and main-line tracks and the construction of additional culverts, bridges, and dikes. But you never can tell in this country, for terrific heat, cloudbursts, flash floods, and other conditions that no man may safely predict provide a constant threat. Never does anyone ever feel that he is free from the clutching hand of this sudden and unpredictable river. But the railroad men have to think and plan ahead.

Needles is, indeed, an amazing town. Needles and the red Colorado. It is unlike any other American river, and could be the Ganges or the Yangtze, for its uncivilized behavior. Fray Francisco Garces passed that way in 1775–76, and it was called Colorado, which is the Spanish word for red.

After lunch we rode a rail motorcar to Topock to inspect the Santa Fe's magnificent high-speed double-track railroad bridge across the Colorado. Here the tracks of the Santa Fe enter Arizona. A big 5,400-horsepower freight Diesel is trumpeting in the distance, and waiting beside the operator under the "clear" order board over the Topock station, we notice big flocks of Canada geese and many canvasbacks and redheads resting on the river, preparatory to continuing their flight north.

The new Santa Fe bridge is good for any speed, and is one of the finest examples of bridge engineering ever built. It has replaced the old single-track bridge, erected over 40 years ago, with curves of 10 degrees at both approaches. The old bridge was presented to the state of Arizona and California for a highway bridge.

We follow a main train back to Needles. In the next 2½ hours Mr. Baker is in conference with various railroaders. We have supper at 6 o'clock and then go to the station to see No. 20, the eastbound Chief, pull out at 6:45.

For an hour our Assistant General Manager is with the Chief Dispatcher, checking on train movements. This is followed by a meeting at 8 o'clock, attended by gang foremen, section foremen, supervisors, and roadmasters, which lasts until midnight. That winds up the day's work.

And now we are moving again, leaving Needles at 10 a.m. on the rear end of Second No. 24. From Franconia to Yucca, Arizona, on the First District, they are laying new 131-pound steel, and the main line is single-tracked between these points. Mr. Baker and our District Engineer, Mr. Chambers, are all attention as they inspect both the finished and unfinished sections, paying close attention to the position of supplies, equipment, and tools pertaining to the job, relative to their location and convenience.

We are out of Kingman, Arizona, 37 minutes late due to slow orders and having left Needles half an hour off the schedule. However, our 3700-class engine and its 1300 helper pick up 22 minutes between Kingman and Yampai, where the helper is cut off. The distance from Needles to Yampai is 126 miles.

We leave Seligman, Arizona, at 3:40 p.m., mountain time, 15 minutes late, and now are on the Third District of the Albuquerque Division. Between Needles and Seligman we have met 8 westbound freight trains, all pulled by 5400-horsepower Diesels. Four more show up between Seligman and Ash Fork.

At Ash Fork, Arizona, Superintendent A. B. Enderle boards the Business Car and rides with us as far as Winslow, Arizona. We are still 15 minutes late when we pull out of Ash Fork at 4:35. We have no helper and the 3721 has her job cut out for her. This type engine is small beside the 4-8-4's, but that 4-8-2 of ours really buckles down and does a job. The sound of her exhaust coming back to us, there on the rear end, is something to remember.

This 3721, with 20 miles of 1.8-per-cent grade trying to awe her, settles down to work, and, believe it or not, at Supai, 50 bruising minutes later, she has picked up 5 minutes on 24's time. Our cars are all heavyweight, but the 4-8-2 handles them beautifully. There are 50 of these locomotives on the Santa Fe, and they are turning in exceptional service. I have never seen an engine with a sweeter valve motion.

We are looking back at Bill William's Mountain and ahead are snow-capped San Francisco peaks over 30 miles away now. At Canyon Diablo we are right on First No. 24's block, and we roll into Winslow, Arizona, on time.

Mr. Baker hurries off to the dispatcher's office for the usual check. Later there is another meeting; this time with the master mechanic, the road foreman of engines, and other members of the mechanical department. The next morning there is an inspection of the Diesel repair shop, the yard, and icing facilities, and more conversations with various railroad men. And again there is a pile of paper work and the writing of more letters in the Business Car.

At 1:50 in the afternoon the car is attached to the rear of No. 2, the Santa Fe's great economy train, the Scout, and, accompanied by the trainmaster of the Second District, we roll into Gallup at 4:30. We leave Gallup at 4:37, meeting the westbound Chief on the double track at Bluewater, as we roll on east to Belen, New Mexico, through a land of color without compare.

Looking into the west from the rear windows of the Business Car, we watch the sun going down, watch those kaleidoscopic hues changing constantly. The sky flames up in yellow splendor, while the purples of the peaks and high mesas deepen to meet the night stalking from the canyons.

Something about that country gets you, whether you are riding the front or the rear end, and futile is the pen or the paint brush that attempts to record its glory.

At Belen Mr. Baker puts in a busy evening. This is the eastern terminus of the coast lines, and he will start back again tomorrow on No. 1, the westbound Scout. He always tries to arrange his crowded schedule in such a manner that he will cover most of his territory in daylight. A week or 10 days hence our Assistant General Manager will be riding this way again, going through much the same routine.

The General Manager also rides the Business Car on the rear end, frequently in the company of the railroad president or the operating vice-president. These men not only maintain close contacts with the various grand divisions, but with the entire railway system as a whole.

Leaving Mr. Baker at Belen that day, I climbed into the cab of a 5011-class Santa Fe freight hauler, went up to Mountainair, New Mexico, to spend some time looking over the Pecos Division C.T.C. Later I rode a way car back to Belen to catch No. 14, coming through from El Paso for Albuquerque, where I later boarded the Chief for Chicago.

Now let's move out onto the line again; this time with a mechanical official, J. M. Nicholson, Mechanical Assistant to the Vice-President of Operations, of the Santa Fe, on No. 5, the Ranger. The Ranger is the road's crack Chicago-Texas train, and we are going to take a swing that will include some of the Santa Fe shops.

The first stop is Topeka, where one of the Santa Fe's 4 largest shops is located. Mr. Nicholson remains in Topeka 2 days, holding many meetings in the Business Car.

On the third morning he leaves on the Fast Mail for La Junta, Colorado, his car having been taken over to Emporia, Kansas, by No. 5. Arriving at La Junta at 5:20 on No. 7, he remains until the following day, when again his car is coupled onto No. 7, which hauls him to Albuquerque, New Mexico. Here are located the largest shops on the system.

Two days later Mr. Nicholson moves on to Winslow, Arizona; then to San Bernardino, California, with shops second in size to those of Albuquerque. From San Bernardino he moves east again over the Southern District to Clovis, New Mexico; thence over the Texas lines to Brownwood and the system's fourth largest shops at Cleburne. He returns to Chicago by way of Oklahoma City, pausing for another stop at Topeka.

Yes; this railroading from the rear end, as I discovered a long time ago, is a vital part of a railway system.

Milwaukee Business Car

J. E. Bjorkholm, General Superintendent of Motive Power of the Milwaukee, covers a vast territory in his Business Car, as do all officials of these far-flung roads of the West. Mr. Bjorkholm is a great mechanical genius and student of motive power, and he never misses a trick. He has been with the road since 1905, and, like J. T. Gillick, the then Operating Head of the Milwaukee, is one of the most charming and likable railroad men I have ever known.

J. E. Bjorkholm has his headquarters at Milwaukee and operates from that point, traveling south to Chicago and Kansas City, and west to Seattle and Tacoma, Washington. He is possessed of a vast store of energy and is constantly on the go, riding the road's steam, electric, and Diesel motive power.

Going west, his Business Car is usually attached to the rear of the second section of the Olympian, with Miles City, Montana, the first layover.

At Miles City, Mr. Bjorkholm will look over the shops, hold numerous meetings with motive-power men, then move on to Deer Lodge for another 24 hours of inspections and meetings. At Deer Lodge are located the main shops of the Milwaukee's electrified territory.

And again the Business Car is lined up for Second No. 15— the Olympian—and Mr. Bjorkholm heads for Avery, Idaho; then to St. Maries for an inspection, and back to Avery. Once more the Business Car moves west to Othello, Washington.

The Milwaukee, as you know, is electrified from Harlowton, Montana, to Avery, Idaho—440 miles—and from Othello to Seattle and Tacoma, Washington—216 miles. In this electrified territory the Superintendent of Motive Power gives close attention to all powerhouses and substations.

The Business Car makes its final lap to Seattle and Tacoma; then begins its eastward swing back to Milwaukee. The distance from Milwaukee to Tacoma is 2,206 miles, or pretty close to 4,500 miles for the round trip.

So the Business Car plays its part, close to the battle front that is the roaring main line.

The Business Car in Chile

I have ridden many Business Cars on many roads, but the tiniest Business Car and one of the most unusual railroads I have ever seen was the Ferrocarril de Tocopilla Al Toco in Chile. The Business Car is maintained and operated for W. E. S. Tuker, Superintendent of the Port of Tocopilla, and Superintendent and Chief Engineer of the railroad.

The road operates from Tocopilla, the largest nitrate shipping port in the world, up over the Coast Range to the nitrate cities of Maria Elena and Pedro Valdiva, where the mines are located. The railroad hauls only nitrate and occasionally that little Business Car and is owned by the Cia. Salitrera Anglo-Chilena.

The rail lifts from sea level to a little over 5,000 feet in about 19 kilometers, climbing much of the way over 4 per cent grades and around one switchback. The road is electrified for about 22 kilometers; the remainder of the distance the motive power is 0-6-6-0 oil-burning Mallets, which were originally built for the Russian government during World War I, but never got any farther than Seattle, Washington, where they were purchased for use on this Chilean nitrate road. Some of the yard engines were built at Leeds, England, as long ago as 1880.

Most of the nitrate is brought down in bulk, and a train usually consists of 18 loads. The air-brake system is the Westinghouse Automatic ET. They also have another system, similar to the old SA straight air, which was used in the United States before the ET equipment came along.

The Chilean railroaders never touch the automatic brake, but drop their trains down the mountain with straight air and regenerative braking. The trains are operated with train orders and clearance cards. They handle 18 empties up the mountain, and often an added car or two of supplies and a couple of water and oil cars.

The electric engines were built by American Locomotive and the General Electric Company in 1928, and they are maintained in perfect condition. The speed limit is 30 miles an hour, and the track is meter gauge, or about 39 inches.

The Chileans are very able railroaders. As there are no cabooses, the trainmen ride the cars. They always carry tea, and when the train stops you will see them running to the block stations for hot water. All Chilean working people wear neckpieces, and it is a colorful sight to see these trainmen sitting on the snow-white nitrate, their tasseled scarf-ends fluttering in the wind as you look down on a train beneath you on the mountain.

W. E. S. Tuker, in addition to being a very fine railroad man, is a fine fisherman, and he holds the record for the largest swordfish ever caught on rod and reel—860 pounds, which, by the way, tops my best efforts by 7 pounds. He also pioneered the saltwater angling of that grand country, the world's finest for outdoor sports.

Whenever I ride a Business Car, I always think of Mr. Tuker and that little Business Car coupled onto the rear end of 18 cars of nitrate, with the Chilean porter serving an excellent meal while we rode over excellent track in well-shopped equipment, high up above the waters of the blue Pacific.

CHAPTER XXV

BLACK DIAMONDS OF THE NORFOLK & WESTERN

"Fuel Satisfaction"

The coal that moves over the rails of the Norfolk & Western comes from seams in which this black wealth of the Appalachians has been in the slow process of formation longer than ordinary bituminous coals, with the result that nature has had time to complete its refining process, thus creating the purest of fuels.

Because coal is the life blood of the Norfolk & Western, the road has taken an active part in its distribution and marketing. Its empire is the great coal fields it serves. As we have pointed out in Chapter XI, the term "Fuel Satisfaction" in 1928 was adopted as the name most accurately describing the coal mined along its lines. Fuel Satisfaction is more than a name for a variety of excellent coals—it is a mark of distinction, for these coals are famous not only in America, but in all of the far corners of the earth where fires are kindled by this black monarch of the hills.

Strategically located and readily accessible in relation to the industrial centers of the Midwest and the East and with a great steel jugular to tidewater, the mine gates of the coal fields pour forth their treasure as a contribution to the well-being and security of a greater America.

The main line of the Norfolk & Western extends from Norfolk, on the port of Hampton Roads, through rich agricultural, livestock, and mineral sections of Virginia, through the coal fields of West Virginia, and on to Columbus and Cincinnati, the western terminals. The road is double track over the 673 miles between Columbus and Lambert Point, at Norfolk, and over this line moves the greater part of the coal tonnage.

The converting of coal, the raw material, to the needs of industries and individuals is a process which involves expert knowledge and infinite care. Let us start with the miner, working deep in the bowels of these rugged hills. Present-day mining operations, for the most part, employ modern and highly efficient methods. The miner himself is a skilled artisan of underground, engaged in a hard and dangerous work as he wrings from the earth this richest of economic minerals.

In the mines the coal seams lie flat, or nearly so, and they are pierced by main and cross haulageways driven into the seams. Actual mining is done on the "room and pillar" system, with pillars supporting the roof while the coal is removed from adjacent rooms. When the coal has been removed from a room, the overhanging strata are allowed to cave in. A maximum recovery with a high degree of safety is thus obtained.

The actual mining operation in a room begins with the undercutting or the overcutting of a portion of the seam. This work is performed by electrically operated machines which cut out a thin layer of coal about 4 inches thick and penetrate the coal face to a depth of about 6 feet.

The second operation is drilling. This is usually done by an electric drill. This block of coal is then ready to be "shot down," and explosives are tamped into the drill holes. The shot is made electrically. The coal thus released from the seam is scooped up by power loading machines and loaded into mine cars. These cars are assembled by electric motors and hauled to the mouth of the mine, and thence to the head house, or the point where the coal is dumped for processing and sorting into the various sizes. Having been sized and treated, it is ready to be loaded into Norfolk & Western coal cars.

When the seam of coal being mined is on the same level as the tipple, the mine cars are unloaded into hoppers at the top of the tipple itself. After being unloaded into these hoppers the coal is moved by means of conveyors as it continues by production-line methods from raw to finished state. Coal as it comes from the mine is known as "run of the mine" coal.

The Norfolk & Western, the carrier of Fuel Satisfaction, has developed its facilities and services to keep pace with the progress in the mining and preparations of these coals for the consumer. Coal, nature's bountiful gift to mankind, regardless of the care and preparation given it at the mines, would still be of no commercial value without adequate transportation from tipple to market, and this is the service provided by a great coal road like the Norfolk & Western.

Well-built and efficiently maintained track, sturdy and capable cars, expert railroaders, and powerful motive-power equipment provide the basic formula necessary to the movement of the millions of tons of Fuel Satisfaction every year starting its journey down the steel rail.

Nothing could more clearly demonstrate the Norfolk & Western's efficiency than the road's remarkable engine terminal at Roanoke. Here production-line methods in the servicing of locomotives make possible the handling of 135 giants of the rails every 24 hours.

Maintaining Fuel Satisfaction means precision railroading 24 hours a day and 365 days a year. There can be no car shortages; no locomotive shortages—no breakdown of facilities, ever.

Heavy rails are used on all main and important branch lines. All trains are amply protected by adequate automatic block signals. Coal cars range from 50- to 90-ton capacity. Yard capacities range from 10,300 at Portsmouth, Ohio, to 5,400 at Williamson, West Virginia. The great storage yard at Lambert Point has a capacity of 6,200 cars. The total yard capacity of the Norfolk & Western stands at 34,910 cars.

Coal is usually sold and all freight charges assessed on railway scale weights, and the Norfolk & Western employs the best car scales obtainable at both its Roanoke and Portsmouth yards. These scales are balanced daily and frequently tested, and the weighing is done by men especially trained for this work. The weights are typed on the original mine tags by an automatic recorder, thus insuring accuracy. Tidewater coal is weighed at Lambert Point, where similar precautions are taken to insure absolutely correct weight.

A. D. 231-E
(Revised 11-41)

NORFOLK AND WESTERN RAILWAY CO.

(1)
Car Initial_____ (2)
Car No._____

(3)
Marked Capacity of Car_____Pounds

(4)
Name of Mine_____
(As Shown in N. & W. Ry. List of Coal and Coke Operations)

(5)
Mine No._____ (6)
Billing Station_____
(As Shown in N. & W. Ry. List of Coal and Coke Operations)

(7)
Date Tagged_____ (8)
Contents_____
(IF COAL STATE GRADE)

(9)
Tagged to
Shipper or
Sales Agent

{ _____
_____

Roanoke, Va., Scales

(10)
Consignee_____

_____

(11)
Destination_____

(12)
Delivering Railroad_____

_____

(13) PREPAID OR COLLECT (See Back of Tag)	(14) The carrier shall not make delivery of this shipment without payment of freight and all other lawful charges.
	_____
	Signature of Consignor

(15)
Rate_____ (16)
W. B. No._____

(17)
Freight_____ (18)
Prepaid_____

(19)
SCALE WEIGHTS

Gross_____

Tare_____

Net_____

(20)
Name of }
Shipper } _____
(SEE INSTRUCTIONS Nos. 1 AND 3 ON BACK OF TAG)

Behind these important weighing activities is the railway's progressive scale department, with its own shops and repair facilities and its own master scale, one of but 19 existing in the United States (16 are owned by railroads, 2 by state governments, and 1 by the national Bureau of Standards). The Norfolk & Western's master scale is located at the Roanoke Scale Shop. It was installed and is maintained in accordance with the specifications of the Association of American Railroads and the U.S. Bureau of Standards.

The mines along the lines of the Norfolk & Western vary in capacity. The larger mines are capable of an output of from 100 to 175 cars per day—measured in terms of 50-ton cars.

Practically all of the high (and medium) volatile bituminous coals along the Norfolk & Western are mined in the Williamson Field, lying in Mingo and Wayne counties, West Virginia; Buchanan County, Virginia; Pike and Martin counties, Kentucky; and in the Clinch Valley Field, which lies in Tazewell, Russell, and Wise counties, Virginia.

Named in order of their importance, as measured by production, the seams mined are: No. 2 Gas (Pond Creek, Freeburn, Warfield), Cedar Grove (Thacker, Red Jacket), Bull Creek, Clintwood, Winifrede, Upper and Lower Banner, Raven Red Ash, Eagle, Alma, and others.

Coal from No. 2 Gas (Pond Creek, Freeburn, Warfield), Clintwood, Bull Creek, and Alma seams is used principally for making manufactured gas and for metallurgical and by-product purposes. These coals are also superior for steam and domestic use.

The Cedar Grove (Thacker, Red Jacket) and Winifrede seams produce a coal that is blocky, hard, and stands transportation and storage without deterioration. It ranks high as domestic fuel, steam coal, and for gas-producer use. The Cedar Grove coal, because of its long flame-burning characteristic, is especially adapted for brick burning and both ceramic and cement manufacture.,

The Upper and Lower Banner and Red Ash seams produce a coal of high quality for steam, domestic, and railroad purposes. Many other seams produce coals of uniform high quality, and all have had a part in the creed of Fuel Satisfaction, so prominently a part of the Norfolk & Western and the great coal fields it serves.

The tidewater terminals at Lambert Point are equipped with two modern steel coal piers for the transferring of coal from railroad cars into the holds of vessels. Pier 5 has been described as the most modern and efficient coal pier in the world. It is equipped and operated with a view to eliminating breakage in the handling of coal, and yet it performs its operations with magic speed.

Under normal working conditions this great coal pier can handle 2,000 tons an hour. A bunkering barge enables vessels to take bunker coal and cargo at the same time and without either operation interfering with the other.

Pier 4 is 1,200 feet long and provides berthing space for 6 large vessels. It is equipped with 3 loading machines which have telescopic chutes. These operate in such manner that breakage is negligible, and at the same time the coal is almost perfectly trimmed in the hold. As much as 61,500 tons of coal have been dumped at these piers in a day.

Further to facilitate efficient service at the Lambert Point terminals, ample storage yards have been provided—yards that can not only accommodate today's enormous tonnage, but are of sufficient capacity to fulfill the requirements of tomorrow. Experience has demonstrated the fact that these tidewater terminals are capable of handling 1,200,000 tons of coal per month.

Coal moving over the Norfolk & Western to the Columbus, Ohio, gateway is speedily dispatched by connecting lines to the Great Lake coal docks at Sandusky and Toledo, Ohio. Through its rail connections at Columbus and Cincinnati and other Ohio junctions, fuel consumers in the Chicago district, in Cleveland, and in the Youngstown and Pittsburgh districts, in Michigan and Canada and throughout the Middle West, are reached with ease. Coal moving via Winston-Salem, Durham, and other gateways in the Carolinas finds its way swiftly into the Southeast. From the Hagerstown gateway coal rolls down the rails to the Middle Atlantic and New England states. So Fuel Satisfaction spreads out across the world from the tracks of the Norfolk & Western.

In a preceding Boston & Maine chapter we spoke of salesmanship, co-operation, and courtesy as attributes of successful railroad operation. These 3 factors play a big part in any undertaking, whether it is running a neighborhood store or a nation. Achievement in any field is largely a matter of go-getting and "hoss" sense, and the Norfolk & Western demonstrated this when they opened up a little side line in the form of a number of bureaus of public relations. They called it a Coal Bureau.

We outlined it briefly in Chapter XI, but it is worth enlarging on a little. The idea was to render every possible aid to coal consumers, and also to supply pertinent information to any prospective users lurking in the offing. The success of the first bureau, opened in Chicago in 1929, led to the establishment of similar bureaus at Detroit, Cleveland, Winston-Salem, Boston, Cincinnati, and St. Louis.

These bureaus were manned by fuel experts—the gentlemen who knew all of the answers to Fuel Satisfaction. They were the handy men who were there to iron out the rough spots for producers, distributors, and consumers—anything from helping to correct boiler-room firing methods to advising the proper adjustments for the kitchen stove.

The Norfolk & Western also reorganized its official personnel, creating a Coal Traffic Department charged primarily with seeing that the railway's helpful-hint activities were successful. Here again was evidence that this thing called Fuel Satisfaction was being backed by all the resources of a great railroad.

At one time it became apparent that there was an urgent need for accurate and dependable information regarding the performance of various sizes and types of coal in domestic automatic stokers. The Norfolk & Western immediately volunteered to conduct a series of impartial and exhaustive experiments. It bought special equipment for this purpose and delved into the matter with enthusiasm. When these railway fuel experts were convinced that they had the correct solution, the Norfolk &

Western published and distributed two booklets packed with informative facts.

Similarly, through a series of experiments and tests that included oil and gas, the railway experts on fuel demonstrated by means of a practical installation in their own shops at Roanoke that pulverized coal is the most economical and efficient for use in heavy forging and metallurgical furnaces.

Another factor in this industrial partnership is the large volume of coal advertising, both national and local, placed by the Norfolk & Western—advertisements explaining the superiority, consistency, and availability of coal. This campaign is further supplemented by a wide distribution of literature, photographs, and motion pictures produced by the railway.

In a less spectacular but equally essential manner, the Norfolk & Western maintains a consistent program of scientific research into ways and means of getting the most out of coal, both for industrial and home use.

A pertinent fact worth remembering in connection with this black monarch of the hills, so carefully nurtured by the Norfolk & Western, is this: The bituminous coal tonnage mined on 1 average day contains potential energy equal to the total power generated by the Bonneville and Grand Coulee Dams combined, operating at capacity continuously for 3 years.

CHAPTER XXVI

MANIFEST TRAIN ON THE C.&O.

Motive Power

The Chesapeake & Ohio class K-4, 2-8-4 Berkshire-type locomotive was designed for fast freight service between Cincinnati, Ohio, and Hinton, West Virginia. It was named for a river—the Kanawha. The first 2-8-4 locomotive, the Berkshire, was designed to whip the heavy grades in the Berkshire Hills in western Massachusetts and made its bow on the Boston & Albany in 1925.

This class K-4 of the Chesapeake & Ohio is rugged and powerful. The Kanawha is good to look at and sweet to listen to, cracking through at the head of the Manifest Train No. 92. A great engine. Ask C. O. Boyer or W. W. Fouts, or any of the other enginemen who have run this class K-4 locomotive. They know what the Kanawha can do with a train of fast freight.

The American Locomotive Company built most of these Kanawhas, and when you see the Alco name plate on an engine you know that here is another example of fine American craftsmanship. The Kanawha incorporates the latest in feature and design as it takes its place in the high ranks of motive power.

For those who like to study the specifications and make-up of an engine like the Kanawha, I include in this chapter tables that reveal its innermost secrets. But, after all, it is performance and availability that make the dollars ring in the railroad's cash register. The pay-off is not made on paper, but out on the main line.

We are dealing for the moment with the head end, but don't forget that for every working locomotive up ahead it takes a pair of markers to make it a train.

The railroad strives constantly to improve its service. The road benefits, it is true; so also do the shipper and the passenger. The customer is always right. Little old John Q. Public. When he lays his dollar on the line, he expects full value. If the article he buys—whether it is transportation or a Sunday suit—is not "all wool and a yard wide," you are going to hear about it.

The railroads of the country and the locomotive builders are today dealing in honest cloth, not shoddy.

Prior to 1943 the Chesapeake & Ohio's manifest service between Cincinnati and Hinton was handled by a class K-3, 2-8-2 type engine designated the Mikado. This locomotive had a tractive effort of 67,700 pounds, and while it gave a good account of itself, it was not considered entirely satisfactory.

There was a growing demand for higher speeds and higher availability in manifest service. That was when the C.&O. and the American Locomotive folks went into a huddle. They sharpened their wits and their pencils, with the result that a better engine for the job was developed. It was the K-4, the Kanawha.

The characteristics of the K-3 were studied and certain improvements incorporated in a machine of ultra-modern design. In the first place, it was evident that a higher wheel was required. Further, the boiler pressure was too low for maximum efficiency. The boiler, while having a relatively high potential horsepower, did not have sufficient heating surface to produce the maximum amount of steam required by the cylinders at a low firing rate, which is conducive to fuel economy.

After a study of roundhouse maintenance records, it was found that the availability of the locomotive could be materially increased by the application of roller bearings to all wheels. Too, it was apparent that the use of cast-steel locomotive beds and cylinders, multiple-bearing crossheads, and other modern specialties would reduce running repair time and cost.

Studies of operation indicated that the K-3 engines, with 67,700 pounds tractive effort and 2,824 cylinder horsepower, were not powerful enough to make desired schedules with full-tonnage trains. Therefore it was decided to increase the tractive effort to 69,350 pounds and to design for 2,978 cylinder horsepower. With this as a basis, and with the understanding that the boiler should produce a horsepower equal to 100 per cent, or better, of that produced by the cylinder, when figured by Coles Ratios, the highest wheel permissible to stay within clearance limitations was found to be 69 inches in diameter.

The general dimensions, weights, and proportions of these locomotives, as well as those of the class K-3 engines previously used between Cincinnati and Hinton, are shown in Table I.

TABLE I

Railroad Classification	Class K-4	Class K-3
Wheel arrangement	2-8-4	2-8-2
Cylinders, diameter & stroke	26″ x 34″	28″ x 32″
Boiler pressure, working	245 PSI	200 PSI
Driving wheel diameter (over tires)	69″	63″
Tractive effort (engine)	69,350 lb.	67,700 lb.
Tractive effort (booster)	14,400 lb.	. . . . .
Tractive effort (total)	83,750 lb.	67,700 lb.
Factor of adhesion—main engine—minimum	4.21	4.05
Factor of adhesion—booster—minimum	4.48	. . . . .
Weight on drivers, working order	292,000 lb.	273,500 lb.
Weight on engine truck, working order	44,500 lb.	31,000 lb.
Weight on trailer truck, front, working order	59,000 lb.	. . . . .
Weight on trailer truck, back, working order	64,500 lb.	53,500 lb.
Weight of engine, total	460,000 lb.	358,000 lb.
Wheel base, rigid	12′ – 2″	11′ – 2″
Wheel base, driving	18′ – 3″	16′ – 9″
Wheel base, total engine	42′ – 0″	37′ – 5″
Wheel base, engine and tender	93′ – 2″	86′ – 2¼″
Highest point of locomotive above top of rail	15′ – 7⅞″	15′ – 2″
Maximum width of locomotive over windshield	10′ – 10¾″	11′ – 1″

All machine parts, such as axles, crank pins, crossheads, wrist pins, frames, guides, piston rods, main rods, side rods, etc., are designed for a maximum thrust of 132,750 pounds.

The Locomotive Boiler: To insure against intercrystalline cracking and other boiler troubles, it was decided to make all longitudinal boiler seams of the low-efficiency type and to use plain carbon steel. This, of course, increased the sheet thickness, which resulted in some increase in the total weight of the locomotive. To keep from additional sheet thickness and boiler-weight increases, a nominal boiler pressure of 245 PSI was selected.

In calculating the boiler horsepower, Coles Ratios were used

311

throughout, and no allowance was made for the Type "E" super-heater or the feed-water heater as is done by some designers. This policy was followed because experience on the Chesapeake & Ohio indicates that if the boiler is overcapacity, steam can always be produced at comparatively low firing rates, with the result that maximum fuel economy is accomplished.

In fact, this is no doubt one of the contributing factors to the Chesapeake & Ohio's excellent fuel record, and the road is fortunate in having the very high permissible axle loads which permit such design.

TABLE II

Railroad Classification	Class K-4	Class K-3
Inside diameter boiler, first course	86″	87″
Outside diameter boiler, largest course	98″	98″
Firebox length at mud ring, inside	135$\frac{1}{16}$″	120$\frac{15}{16}$″
Firebox width at mud ring, inside	96$\frac{1}{4}$″	96$\frac{1}{4}$″
Grate area	90.0 sq. ft.	80.8 sq. ft.
Length over tube sheets	19′ – 0″	19′ – 0″
Tubes, number	73	248
Tubes, outside diameter	2 – $\frac{1}{4}$″	2$\frac{1}{4}$″
Tubes, thickness	12 BWG	11 BWG
Flues, number	202	50
Flues, outside diameter	3$\frac{1}{2}$″	5$\frac{1}{2}$″
Flues, thickness	11 BWG	9 BWG
Arch tubes, number	2	5
Arch tubes, outside diameter	3$\frac{1}{2}$″	3″
Siphons, number	2	. . . . .
Superheater units, outside diameter	1$\frac{3}{16}$″	1$\frac{1}{2}$
Heating surface, tubes	812 sq. ft.	2,760 sq. ft.
Heating surface, flues	3,496 sq. ft.	1,360 sq. ft.
Heating surface, firebox & comb. chamber	343 sq. ft.	302 sq. ft.
Heating surface, arch tubes	19 sq. ft.	36 sq. ft.
Heating surface, siphons	103 sq. ft.	. . . . .
Heating surface, total evaporation	4,773 sq. ft.	4,458 sq. ft.
Heating surface, superheater	1,932 sq. ft.	1,173 sq. ft.
Evaporation from tubes	7,154 lb. per hr.	5,175 lb. per hr.
Evaporation from flues	33,247 lb. per hr.	13, 998 lb. per hr.
Evaporation from firebox & comb. chamber	18,865 lb. per hr.	16,610 lb. per hr.
Evaporation from arch tubes	1,045 lb. per hr.	1,980 lb. per hr.
Evaporation from siphons	5,665 lb. per hr.	. . . . .
Evaporation from total boiler	65,976 lb. per. hr.	57,763 lb. per hr.
Boiler horsepower	3,172	2,776
Cylindrical horsepower	2,979	2,824
Boiler hp percent of cylinder hp	106.5%	98.3%

The general dimensions and proportions of the boiler are shown, as in comparison with those of the K-3 class locomotive, in Table II.

Running Gear: The foundation of the locomotive is a cast-steel engine bed with cylinders cast integral. The boiler is supported by sliding shoes at the second course and at the front and rear ends of the firebox. Roller bearings are applied to all driving and truck wheels. These are the Timken dual roll design with split housings over the driver bearings. Alco Lateral Cushioning Devices are applied to the front wheels, which materially shortens the rigid wheelbase and assists in negotiating maximum curves of 20 degrees, for which the engines are designed.

The engine and trailer trucks are General Steel Castings Company's design and are equipped with outside Timken roller bearings. General wheel and axle dimensions are shown in Table III.

TABLE III

| | | AXLES | | | WHEELS OR TIRES | |
Location	Material	Solid or Hollow	Bearings	Journal Size in Inches	Type of Material	Diameter in Inches
Front truck	Carbon steel	Solid	Timken	8¼	Rolled steel	33
Main driver	Carbon steel	Hollow	Timken	13	Cast steel	69
Other drivers	Carbon steel	Hollow	Timken	12⅛	Cast steel	69
Trailer, front	Carbon steel	Solid	Timken	8¼	Rolled steel	36
Trailer, rear	Carbon steel	Solid	Timken	10	Cast steel	43
Tender	Carbon steel	Solid	Friction	7	Rolled steel	36

Cylinder and Steam Distribution System: With a 69-inch diameter wheel and 245 pounds boiler pressure, it was found that cylinders having 26-inch diameter would produce the required tractive effort and that the stroke could be 34 inches without producing excessive piston speeds.

The 14-inch piston valves are driven by Baker Valve Gears equipped with needle bearings. This gear provides a maximum valve travel of 8 inches with $1^{11}/_{16}$-inch lap, $^3/_{16}$-inch lead, and $^1/_{16}$-inch exhaust clearance.

Considerable care was exercised in the cylinder and steam-pipe design in order to provide large steam passages from the boiler through the cylinders and into the stack. Table IV shows principal areas maintained in passages from boiler to exhaust nozzle.

TABLE IV

	Sq. In.
Internal area of dry pipe	72.7
Minimum area through superheater units	72.6
Area through throttle valves (full open)	73.1
Internal area of one steam pipe	56.7
Area through ports one valve bushing (full opening)	77.3
Exhaust area number one of exhaust stand	59.7
Area of exhaust nozzle ($8\frac{1}{2}''$ bore)	56.7
Area of one cylinder	530.9

Lubrication: The lubrication is provided for by one Nathan Type DV-7 and one Detroit Type B Lubricator. The Detroit Lubricator distributes valve oil, and the Nathan distributes engine oil. The distribution of each is shown in Table V.

TABLE V

Kind of Oil	No. of Outlets	Destination of Outlets
Valve oil	4	Steam pipes
Valve oil	4	Cylinders
Valve oil	4	Guides
Valve oil	1	Feed-water pump
Valve oil	1	Stoker
Valve oil	1	Air pumps
Engine oil	4	Engine truck pedestals
Engine oil	4	Valve crosshead guides
Engine oil	1	Engine truck main equalizer pin
Engine oil	4	Engine truck bottom rocker bearing
Engine oil	2	Boiler bearing under second boiler course

Engine oil	1	Engine truck center casting
Engine oil	1	Trailer truck radius bar seat
Engine oil	16	Driving box pedestal faces
Engine oil	4	Spring equalizer pins
Engine oil	2	Radial buffer
Engine oil	2	Trailer truck bottom rocker bearings
Engine oil	16	Driving wheel lateral wear plates
Engine oil	8	Trailer truck pedestal faces
Engine oil	4	Furnace bearers under firebox
Engine oil	4	Trailer truck main equalizer pins

In addition to the foregoing, three 1/4-pint Kirchoffer Lubricators are connected in the air pump, the stoker, and the feedwater-pump steam line to provide lubrication when engine is at rest. The lubrication to the booster is taken care of by 1 pint-size Kirchoffer Lubricator connected in the steam line between the idling valve and the booster engine. The lubrication of all rods, valve motion, spring rigging, etc., is taken care of by Alemite fittings. International Lubrication is used on the main pins.

Cab Arrangement: Considerable care was exercised in the cab design and back-head arrangement. In fact, when the first locomotive was completed and before leaving the American Locomotive Company's plant, representatives of the Brotherhood of Railway Engineers and Firemen were invited to inspect the engine and make suggestions as to the accessibility of the various operating valves, levers, etc., in the cab.

The cab length is such as to provide 4 comfortable seats. There is ample knee room in front of the 3 seats regularly used by the engineer, fireman, and head brakeman.

As a further step to comfort, the cab is equipped with 4 steam radiators, 1 opposite each seat. There is a large ventilator in the center of the roof, as well as 1 small foot ventilator in each side near the neck and ahead of the radiators.

One of the special features of the cab is that it is mounted independent of the boiler. In other words, it is bolted rigidly to brackets from the rear of the frame, and all fastenings to the boiler are flexible to allow for expansion and contraction of the boiler during the fire-up and blowdown periods. A seal is also provided around the front cab wall to protect the engine crews in cold weather.

Front-End Arrangement: The improved master mechanic's front-end arrangement was used and the AAR recommended practice was generally followed as to principal gas areas. These are shown in Table VI.

TABLE VI

Areas in Percentage of Tube and Flue Areas

	Area Over Arch	Through Tubes & Flues	Max. Under Table Plate	Min. Under Table Plate	Under Draft Sheet	Through Netting	Stack
C.&O. K-4	128	100	111	80	66	106	24
AAR	110 to 120	100	95 to 110	80 to 95	65 to 80	110 to 140	25

Spring Rigging: The spring rigging is more or less unique in its design in that, first, a nest of coil springs is applied over the main wheels in place of the conventional semielliptic springs; second, the hanger pins are large enough in diameter to hold bearing pressures down to 2,300 pounds per square inch in equalizer fulcrums, and 1,500 pounds per square inch in equalizer ends and hangers; third, where clearance will permit, lateral flexibility is provided by the use of knuckled hangers.

Specialties and Miscellaneous Equipment: The terrain over which the K-4 locomotives operate and the speed maintained on the road do not generally favor booster operation on ascending grades. However, previous experience indicated that time schedules could be improved by faster acceleration from starts if boosters were applied. Also, it was found that in making starts with the booster, much rough handling could be eliminated, which would result in a decrease of damage to equipment and at the same time lessen freight-damage claims against the road.

A partial list of specialties and equipment applied to these locomotives is shown in Table VII.

TABLE VII

Device	Type	Make
Bell ringer	V	Trans. Devices Corp.
Low water alarm	B	Nathan Mfg. Co.
Driving box bearing	Roller	Timken Roller Bearing Co.
Lateral device	Cushioning	American Loco. Co.
Water column	WOA-Long	Nathan Mfg. Co.
Blowoff muffler	20-C	Wilson Eng'r. Corp.
Radial buffer	E-2	Franklin Ry. Supply Co.
Fire doors	But. #8	Franklin Ry Supply Co.
Grate bars	Firebar	Waugh Equip. Co.
Headlight	20-F-145	Pyle-National Co.
Injector	4000 – "G"	Nathan Mfg. Co.
Feed-water heater	5½ SSA	Worthington P. & M. Co.
Mechanical lubricator	16 pt. "B"	Detroit Lub. Co.
Mechanical lubricator	14 pt. DV4	Nathan Mfg. Co.
Valve gear	Baker (needle)	Pilloid Co.
Air-pump lubricator	Fig. 219	Edna Mfg. Co.
Booster lubricator	Fig. 220	Edna Mfg. Co.
Washout plugs	S-34	Huron Mfg. Co.
Arch tube plugs	Housley A-2	American Loco. Co.
Reverse gear	Precision F-2	Franklin Ry. Supply Co.
Sanders	AX	Morris Brewster Co.
Smoke-box hinges	Okadee	Okadee Co.
Stoker	MB	Standard Stoker Co. (Note A)
Superheater	E	Superheater Co.
Crossheads	Multiple bearing	
Cylinders	Steel, cast integral with frame	
Tender frame	Water bottom	
Throttle	Multiple	American Throttle Co.
Booster	C-2-L	Franklin Ry. Supply Co. (Note B)
Frame cradle	C.S. engine bed	
Air-brake equipment	8-ET	

Note A: Engines 2700-2739 have MB Stokers. Engines 2740-2749 have HT Stokers.
Note B: Engines 2700-2739 have C-2-L Boosters. Engines 2740-2749 have E Boosters.

Tenders: The tenders behind these locomotives carry 30 tons of coal and 21,000 gallons of water, which permits them to operate with minimum stops for coal and water. They are equipped with 6-wheel Buckeye trucks, with 36-inch wheels, and 7-inch x 14-inch journals. The foundation of these tenders is a General Steel Castings Company's water-bottom frame. The stoker engine is carried on the tender.

The general dimensions and weights of the tenders are shown in Table VIII.

Type of tank	Rectangular
Type of frame	Water bottom
Type of truck	Buckeye 6-wheel
Tank capacity, water	21,000 gallons
Tank capacity, coal	30 tons
Weight, loaded	390,000 lb.
Weight, empty	155,070 lb.
Over-all length front buffer to rear coupler	48'—9⅜"
Wheel base, tender	37'—1"
Wheel base, truck	10'—0"
Height of filling hole from rail	12'—8⅜"
Height of top of slope sheet from rail	15'—1"
Width of tank, inside	10'—3"
Height of tank, inside	95"

In general, these locomotives have been so successful that in 1945 a duplicate order was placed for 10 additional units. These new engines are identical with the 40 delivered to the Chesapeake & Ohio in 1943 and 1944, except they have Standard Type HT Stokers instead of Type MB. They have Franklin Type E Boosters, instead of Type C-2-L, and they have the air reservoirs cast in the locomotive bed. These modifications will result in a slight increase in weight. However, this will not be sufficient to limit their operation in any territory where the first Kanawhas are in service.

We have moved through the American Locomotive Company's shops with this K-4, and now we will go out onto the open road with her. We will not ride the cab this trip, but watch the engine's performance from the rear end. Today our point of vantage is 95 cars back of engine No. 2741.

Manifest Train No. 92

Fast freight is today writing history on the railroads of America. It is moving perishable and l.c.l. freight at a pace never dreamed possible a few years ago. It is crowding right on the heels of fast passenger service, and day in and day out is delivering the goods.

The fast freight may be hauling livestock, requiring the rest and feeding and watering of animals; it may be moving those perishables which demand icing or heating of the refrigerator cars; its shipments may include foods and silk and machine tolls. It may move from coast to coast; it may cover but a few hundred miles between metropolitan areas. But wherever it moves and when, it moves fast. Today thousands of head of horses, sheep, and cattle are being shipped to Europe through Newport News over the C.&O.

Let us take, for example, Train No. 92 on the Chesapeake & Ohio. This train operates over all divisions between Chicago and Newport News. It handles freight not only from western points but from points along the C.&O., delivering to destinations all along the line.

Train No. 92 on August 31, 1945, on that part of its run between Stevens, Kentucky, and Hinton, West Virginia, handled a total of 156 cars. These cars carried a vast assortment of shipments, including butter, beverages, milk, cotton, vegetables, flour, feeds, cereals, potatoes, grapes, soap, building materials, sheet iron, machinery, automobiles, fruit, horses, and many cars of miscellaneous merchandise.

This consist originated in Minnesota, Texas, Indiana, California, Georgia, Illinois, Ohio, Wisconsin, Iowa, Virginia, Kansas, Missouri, Colorado, New York, Michigan; it came from Oregon, North Dakota, Kentucky, Tennessee, Maryland, and West Virginia. In all, 21 states were represented.

These goods were consigned to various localities in Virginia, West Virginia, Ohio, Kentucky, South Carolina, North Carolina, and Tennessee. Much of the consist consigned to Virginia was eventually shipped to foreign ports.

The rush of fast freight continues interminably. It is handled by specially designed locomotives like the K-4 in many cases. Again, it rushes through behind big dual-purpose locomotives, built to haul famous limiteds, mail trains, or manifest. Down the years fast-freight movements have grown from a few regularly scheduled trains to great fleets. They have become the life-blood of the nation.

This is the early morning of August 31, 1945. We are at Stevens, Kentucky, on the Cincinnati Division of the Chesapeake & Ohio. Conductor Frank Brackin and Engineer Boyer have received a 3:30 a.m. call, together with their crew.

At 3:45 class K-4 engine No. 2741 backs onto the train, and the air hose is coupled up. Ninety-five cars away stands the caboose, its marker lights gleaming in the darkness. Conductor Brackin has his waybills, and the brakes have been tested. At 3:52 there is the highball from the rear end. The whistle of the 2741 barks twice, and Engineer Boyer drops the reverse lever into the corner and eases the throttle open. The slack runs out, and the caboose starts with a little lurch. No. 92 is getting out of town with 4,845 tons.

The speed increases. Conductor Brackin settles down at his desk, the yellow glow from his shaded lamp shining on his wheel reports. The watcher in the cupola is looking away toward the place where the 2741 is crying its sharp-voiced chant.

No. 92 has passed CS Cabin at 4 o'clock. Rails are slipping away behind the caboose. Towns slip past, towns nestling in the beautiful Ohio Valley along the south bank of the river. Augusta, Maysville, Vanceburg, Greenup, Kentucky. No. 92 reduces speed to comply with local ordinances; then the exhaust shouts again, brusque, impatient.

There is a slow order at Trinity, Kentucky, because of excavation work south of the eastbound main. Again there is a forward surge of cars ahead of the caboose, and 92 resumes her maximum speed. The conductor has completed his office work. He glances at his watch, and his face reflects approval of the job the 2741 has done. The 2741 and Engineer Boyer. The manifest is approaching the great Russell Yard in Kentucky now. Russell, one of the largest yards in the country, is a division in itself and consists of 149.8 miles of track. It is a teeming world of shining rails and cars and engines.

The wheels of the caboose clatter over frogs and switches as the pace of the train slows, drifts on past the car shops to come finally to a stop at MS Cabin at 7:06 a.m. Signals then beckon the manifest into the Eastbound Yard, and it stands in the clear at 7:13. That is all for Conductor Brackin and Engineer Boyer.

The manifest train soon is being classified, and those loads for Ashland, Kentucky; Huntington and Charleston, West Virginia; Columbus, Ohio, and other Big Sandy and Ashland Division points are switched out, leaving 41 through loads. There are added 16 through loads from the Northern Subdivision, the Big Sandy and the Ashland divisions, making 57 loads for No. 92 out of Russell.

Meanwhile the 2741 has been serviced. It has taken on coal and water and returned to the head of its string of fast freight.

Conductor W. E. Fleck and Engineer W. W. Fouts take charge of No. 92 at this time, having been called to go on duty at Russell Yard at 9 a.m. Conductor Fleck receives his waybills, his orders, and the clearance and climbs aboard the caboose. The highball is given at 9:41, and the flight of the manifest is resumed; this time with 3,170 tons.

The train pauses at Ashland to pick up one through load, and again its eastward rush is checked at the Elk Yard in Charleston, West Virginia, to gather 3 more loads into the fold. The waybills on Conductor Fleck's desk now represent a total of 3,315 tons moving behind the tireless 2741. This, by the way, is the beautiful country of the Kanawha. Here our big K-4 got her name, and she seems to shout her greeting over every hill and into every valley.

There is a stop at Handley for water, and the shop forces clean the fire and service the locomotive for the dash to Hinton. Soon our fast freight is again battering the miles behind her.

Included in the consist of No. 92 are 14 cars of horses for Belgium, and the caretaker is riding in the caboose, going ahead to inspect them when the train stops. At Sewell, West Virginia, the operator "hoops up" a message, requesting that the manifest be stopped at CS Cabin to allow a check to be made, as it was reported that some of the horses were down.

The stop was made at CS Cabin at 2:55 p.m., and the caretaker and conductor went forward to inspect the stock cars. The horses, however, were all on their feet and in good shape. Writing up a 10-minute delay, No. 92 gets under way again, driving through to Hinton, West Virginia.

Here the manifest pulls into the upper yard, and the arriving time is 4:01 p.m. The engine is cut off and rolls down the lead. A hostler relieves Engineer Fouts, who writes up his work report and calls it a day.

Conductor Fleck turns in his waybills and reports at the yard office, and his part in the eastward movement of Train 92 is finished.

The run from Milepost 651 at Stevens, Kentucky, to Milepost 357 at Hinton, West Virginia, was covered in 13 hours and 2 minutes, including all stops. The distance was 294 miles, with an average running time of 22.6 miles per hour and a maximum speed of 50 miles per hour. An examination of the log of No. 92 reveals a delay en route of 4 hours and 26 minutes. Of this time, 2 hours and 28 minutes was charged to servicing the locomotive and classifying the train at Russell Yard.

As shown in the following log of Train No. 92, the running time for the 294 miles was 8 hours and 36 minutes, which indicates that, except for the delays, the manifest was doing some fast wheeling. And, remember, there were 95 cars in the train when it left Stevens, Kentucky. But that's the way they railroad on the C.&O. every day of the year, from President R. J. Bowman and ex-Vice-President A. T. Lowmaster, two great railroaders, right on down the list.

LOG OF TRAIN NO. 92—STEVENS, KY., TO HINTON, W. VA., AUGUST 31, 1945.

Crew—Stevens to Russell

C. O. Boyer, Engineer
Employed Fireman 8-17-1907
Promoted Engineer 8-14-1911

Frank Brackin, Conductor
Employed Brakeman 11-6-1908
Promoted Conductor 5-9-1917

Great Northern first #1, the Empire Builder with Engine #2506, 4-8-2 type, class P-2, picking up orders at Blackfoot, Mont., on the Kalispell Division. Photo by Wm. J. Pontin. Courtesy Rail Photo Service.

Type of superintendent's business car used on many western roads. Superintendent W. R. Minton, of the Great Northern's Kalispell Division, makes this one his office while inspecting the road. Photo by Wm. J. Pontin. Courtesy Rail Photo Service.

Swing brakeman H. C. Zweifel turns over to his conductor, R. H. Allen, who has 26 years' seniority, a check he has made of the train as it leaves Bakersfield, Calif., for Mojave. San Joaquin Division. Courtesy Southern Pacific Railroad.

S.P. swing brakeman keeps an eye on the cars of his train from the cupola of the caboose. Note the conductor's valve close at hand and order hoop hanging up. San Joaquin Division. Courtesy Southern Pacific Railroad.

Eastbound coal drag running over the electrified portion of the N.&W.'s Pocahontas Division between Eckman and Bluefield, W. Va. The train is climbing the famous 2% Elkhorn grade, and the electric engine is class LC-2, 1-D-1+1-D-1 type. Courtesy Norfolk & Western Railroad.

Modern coal tipple located on the N.&W. in McDowell County, W. Va. Courtesy Norfolk & Western Railroad.

Santa Fe first #4 eastbound California Limited crossing the picturesque Canyon Diablo bridge, Ariz., on the Third District of the Albuquerque Division. The road engine #3772, 4-8-4 type, is one of the 3765 class, the second series of this type put in service; and the helper is a 1300-class 4-6-2 type. Courtesy Santa Fe

C. & O. Engine 2720 2-8-4 type Class K4 with =94 Eastbound Manifest train near Charleston, West Va. Photo by G. Grabill, Jr. Rail Photo Service.

C.&O. steel gang with rail-laying plant near Thayer, W. Va., on the New River Subdivision of the Hinton Division. Courtesy Chesapeake & Ohio Railroad.

Business car on the rear end of the supply train on the Ferrocarril De Tocopilla Al Toco. The tank cars contain oil for the steam locomotives. Wire train in background. Courtesy W. E. S. Tuker.

Motor car running ahead of rail auto inspection car on the meter gauge electrified nitrate railroad above the port of Tocopilla, Chile. The grade is 4% descending. Courtesy W. E. S. Tuker.

Rear end of an S.P. freight train with AC-class helper near Truckee, Calif. Courtesy Southern Pacific Railroad.

Southern Pacific's snow-spreader pushes snow aside at Eder, Calif., on the Mountain Subdivision of the Sacramento Division. Courtesy Southern Pacific Railroad.

Burlington Engine's #906 west, 2-10-2 type, and #6308 coupled, both class M-3, leaving Keensburg, Col., on the C.T.C.-equipped Denver Division. Photo by R. H. Kindig.

Interior view of a drovers' car on the rear end of the C.B.&Q. crack stock train #62 en route to Chicago from Denver. Courtesy Chicago, Burlington & Quincy Railroad.

. W. Fouts, Engineer
mployed Fireman 11-5-1903
omoted Engineer 10-20-1906

W. E. Fleck, Conductor
Employed Brakeman 12-1-1903
Promoted Conductor 4-13-1907

tevens to Russell—Engine 2741—95 loads—4,845 tons.
ussell to Hinton—Engine 2741—61 loads—3,170 tons.

ATION	ARRIVED	DEPARTED	DELAY	REMARKS
tevens (Called)	3:30 a.m.	4:00 a.m.	30 min.	Put engine on train, test brakes, clear yard.
S Cabin	7:06 a.m. Clear	7:13 a.m.		
ussell	7:13 a.m.	9:41 a.m.	2 hr. 28 min.	Service locomotive, re-classify train, cutting out short manifest and adding through manifest from Northern and Big Sandy Divisions and clear yard.
Russell (Called)	9:00 a.m.	9:41 a.m.		
NC Cabin	9:46 a.m.	9:55 a.m.	9 min.	Waiting for Extra 1249 west, troop train, before crossing to freight main.
Ashland	10:03 a.m.	10:12 a.m.	9 min.	Pick up one load.
Elk Yard (Charleston)	12:19 p.m.	12:34 p.m.	15 min.	Pick up three loads.
Handley	1:16 p.m.	1:30 p.m.	14 min.	Water and clean fire.
CS Cabin	2:55 p.m.	3:05 p.m.	10 min.	Stopped for caretaker to inspect 14 cars of horses on which it was reported some of the horses were down.
Hinton	4:01 p.m.	4:32 p.m.	31 min.	Pulled train in upper yard. Bring engine back to passenger station.

Total time:	13 Hours 2 Min.		Consumed 49,500 gallons water, 25 tons of coal.
Delays:	4 Hours 26 Min.		
Running time:	8 Hours 36 Min.		

CHAPTER XXVII

THE S.P.'S BIGGEST RUSH

Mountain Railroad

They do a lot of railroading out there on the Sacramento Division's Mountain Subdivision. They handle a lot of freight on the Hill. And tonight, superimposed on the movement of long freight drags out of Roseville, California, and the regular passenger trains, we find other trains—the troop trains that are bringing the men home.

Up from the Sacramento Valley come big cab-ahead Articulateds, their exhausts roaring—9 sections of No. 88; 2 sections of No. 14; 4 sections of No. 28! Seventy inches of snow at Norden Summit, and still snowing. Up from the Nevada desert —3 sections of the westbound Overland, No. 27; 8 sections of No. 87! The Big Parade is on.

A headlight shows around a curve. A whistle shouts, and a green dot glimmers ahead. Clear board! Cars roll past, marker lights slip away; the blast of the panting helper fades. Then another burly 4-8-8-2 comes stamping up the Hill with its long train of darkened coaches. And another. And another. Nine sections of 88! This is a 2.6-per-cent grade they're climbing. Colfax to Emigrant Gap.

The silver blade of a headlight slashes the mountain blackness, lights briefly a snow plow in a siding, moves on toward Norden. Cars stream past. Still they come. Two sections of 14 out of Roseville, far below. Through Rocklin, Newcastle, Auburn. Through Clipper Gap, Colfax, Gold Run. The thunder from the squat stacks tears the night apart. Dutch Flat, Emigrant Gap, Yuba Pass, Soda Springs, Norden! Soldiers from the

South Pacific war theater are riding the rail—heading home, but damn glad to see snow again.

Deadhead (empty) coaches are rolling west to help move the biggest rush the S.P. has ever seen. Trains are thundering out of Sparks, Nevada. Eight sections of 87. Through Reno, Truckee. This is the way of the Forty-Niners. On past the ghosts of the ill-fated Donner Party, echoes awakening in the rock-walled canyons. It is a battle of iron giants, iron men, against a mountain range. Every exhaust of these charging locomotives is the heartbeat of a railroad.

And out in the thick of it all we find Superintendent M. L. Jennings of the Sacramento Division. Not an S.P. man but knows that the Boss is on the Hill tonight; he always is when the going is rugged.

Yes; that was his Business Car on the rear of No. 22, the eastbound Pacific Limited out of Roseville. After 3 days and 3 nights on the Hill with the plows, the super is going back. Likely they'll be needing him.

I wanted a look at the Hill under fire, so I went along. I wanted to see how they railroaded from the rear end when the pressure was on. I found out.

Everything was moving like clockwork when we reached Norden, so the Business Car continued on to Sparks. Superintendent Jennings thought he might grab a little sleep, but on arrival at Sparks, they handed him a message. He smiled thinly, shook his head. "It's snowing on the Hill again. Want to ride back to Norden with me?" I said I did, and Mr. Jennings ordered his car attached to the rear of No. 9, the westbound Fast Mail, first out on the line-up west.

They cut the car off at Norden, and we went out with the plows. When it snows at Norden, look for about 6 inches an hour. We took a siding for the two 14's about 3 o'clock in the morning. They were coming east now—4 sections of 28, 9 sections of 88. The last section showed at Norden at about 7:30 in the morning. They did a lot of railroading on the Hill that night, a lot of it.

Superintendent Jennings ordered his car put on Eighth 87, and we dropped down the grade to Roseville. I was feeling mighty proud of the S.P. about that time, proud of these S.P. railroaders.

Once more I had seen the importance of the Business Car. There were the makings of a lot of trouble on the Hill that December 10, but the Superintendent had set his Business Car right down in the middle of it as he marshaled the snow-fighting equipment and kept his finger on the pulse of one of the biggest movements of important trains that the S.P., or any other railroad, has ever been called on to handle in a like period.

Homebound Troops

Now we'll explain why all these trains were on the Hill. The Sacramento Division of the Southern Pacific bore the brunt of moving the tidal wave of returning troops landing in California late in 1945, with the Santa Fe, Union Pacific, and Western Pacific also doing their utmost to relieve the congestion at the debarkation points. The same condition existed, of course, in the North with the Milwaukee, Northern Pacific, and Great Northern working desperately to keep pace with the inrush of home-hungry veterans from the Pacific war area.

All of these railroads were faced with the task of transporting thousands upon thousands of soldiers across the United States in a few short months—fighting men it had taken two or three years to send overseas. There wasn't a railroad official in the country but understood and sympathized with the returning soldier, but there was not the equipment.

Given the cars, the Southern Pacific and other railroads could have handled the thousands pouring ashore from transports, but during the war the building of passenger equipment—except for some troop sleepers and kitchen cars—had been prohibited by the government. The railroads, in keeping with ODT orders, had discontinued sleeping-car runs of 450 miles or less; they had reduced the amount of space available to civilians until by October, 1945, 100 per cent of the coach space and 80 per cent of the Pullman space of regular eastbound trains out of San Francisco was assigned to military personnel.

The public was demanding speedier discharge for the veterans, and the Military aimed to oblige, with the result that in November of 1945 the west coast saw 450,000 being disembarked. In December 590,209 men arrived in Pacific ports. The railroads had fought a war; locomotives and cars were war-weary, and the job of moving 22,000 men a day from Pacific coast ports seemed impossible. And yet in the two weeks preceding Christmas, over 25,000 soldiers were transported every day.

On December 1 there were 48 special military trains rolling over Southern Pacific tracks alone. Strikes had held up the building of berths and mattress equipment for 1,200 new troop sleepers, and the S.P. and the other lines had to go along with what they had, or could beg and borrow. Cars were rushed from eastern roads—anything that looked like a passenger car and could turn a wheel.

Four-fifths of the soldiers landing at Pacific ports were destined for points east of the Mississippi, which meant a 2,000-mile haul. These cars returned empty in special trains. But there were not enough of them; there was not enough of anything, including Pullmans. A railroad cannot handle the same number of men on a long haul that it can on a short haul because of the necessity of providing sleeping accommodations. However, if the 1,200 troop sleepers had been delivered to them on time, there would have been no delays or congestion.

During the holidays men piled up on the west coast, but the jam was broken at the turn of the year, despite storms which hampered other means of transport. The trains went through. The Southern Pacific had the track room and the locomotives to move the servicemen, but they did not have the cars. And yet the railroads moved 95 per cent of all organized troop traffic. The remaining 5 per cent traveled by air and motorbus.

Veterans continued to pour into west coast ports at the rate of half a million a month. From Guam and Saipan they came; from New Guinea and the Philippines and bloody Okinawa; from the Marshalls and Hawaii and Japan—homesick kids and war-scarred veterans, wanting nothing so much as to get home to Mother and Dad, to their wives and their youngsters. The railroads bent every effort toward providing them with safe and speedy transportation. Passenger and operating departments worked in close co-operation; railroads everywhere gave everything they had, interchanging equipment and stepping up joint schedules; but there was always that old bogy of car shortage, created by shortsightedness in high circles and strikes. But the men were a lot better off being held up in Pacific ports than they were on Pacific islands for their Christmas holidays.

But that is all water over the dam now. However, the lesson remains. The steel rail and the trains that ride it are the first—and last—line of supply for the armed forces in time of war.

The Southern Pacific and all railroads of the country, geared for peacetime movements, suddenly found themselves looking at the bared teeth of the god of war. Overnight, the American Railroad cleared the decks for action, and through the bitter years of conflict and the reconversion they maintained the American tradition of entering the fight as the underdog and returning—the champion!

Snowball Special

"Nevada" is a Spanish word meaning "snow." "Sierra" likewise is a Spanish word, and it means "mountains." Hence, Sierra Nevada means "Snowy Mountains." And those explorer priests of long ago could not have selected a more appropriate name for this majestic range, the sawtooth peaks of which are thrust up against the sky between Tehachapi Pass, to the south, and Lassen Peak, to the north, a distance of some 400 miles as the crow flies.

In an earlier chapter we spoke of a California snowfall of 67 feet, a statement which some might challenge, for 67 feet is a lot of snow. However, the fact remains; for it is a matter of record.

Let's consider, for instance, just one snowstorm. It began on February 1, 1938, and continued with only one day's break through the night of February 14. We will disregard the snow already on the ground and consider merely the fall of this storm, which reached a recorded depth of 341 inches. Another 15 inches fell during the remainder of February, for a total of 356 inches for the month.

This old thumper of a blizzard struck at Norden Summit, and Norden and vicinity are a snow-sports fan's idea of heaven, as, conversely, it is a Sacramento Division railroader's idea of a winter hell, if there can be such a thing.

Trainmen, sectionmen, signalmen, and linemen fight the Snow King, while the ski and snowshoe enthusiast worships at the old fiend's shrine.

The Sierra Summit area around Norden has become one of the leading snow-sports centers of the world. Promotional work and special train service on the part of the Southern Pacific were responsible for the development of snow sports in this area. It all began in the winter of 1931–32. At this time the Southern Pacific inaugurated their Snowball Specials, which included recreation cars, Ski Hut cars, and coaches or sleepers.

Round-trip fares with a 10-day limit were reduced to a low figure to encourage week-end snow trips. Ski equipment was rented or sold on the trains, and hot meals were served, making for a most attractive outing for those who wanted to get away from low-country sunshine.

Since their inception, these Snowball Specials, except during wartime and immediately thereafter, have proved immensely popular. Of course they did not operate during the war emergency, but before and since they have been hauling folks to the high rims of the Sierra Nevadas for their fling at winter play.

Various lodges have been established, with investments running into hundreds of thousands of dollars. Snow here, as elsewhere in the country, has become big business.

So popular have the Southern Pacific Snowball Specials become that often 3 or more of them are required to handle the crowds over a single week end. On the pine-clad snowy slopes many sports facilities have been installed as at the Sugar Bowl, including ski lifts, rope tows, and toboggan slides and jumps. There are schools for skiers and excellent hotel accommodations.

Many of the skiers detrain at the Southern Pacific's Ski Hut at Norden. The Ski Hut is a "house within a house," for it is built under the protection of a railroad snowshed. Here there are sleeping and eating accommodations, a store, checkroom, warming and drying rooms, ski racks, and other facilities. The interior of the Norden Ski Hut is paneled in knotty pine, which gives it an informal, cheery atmosphere. Here the snow-sports fans rest and eat.

The habit of organizing week-end snow-sports parties and the reservation of space on the Snowball Specials has been acquired by many clubs, employee groups, and other organizations in the San Francisco Bay area. Catholic groups, confronted by the alternative of missing the fun or missing Mass, organized a "Skier's Mass" in the snow-sports area, with blessing of the skiers and their skis included in the impressive ceremony.

Most popular of the Snowball Specials leave San Francisco late on Saturday night, arriving at Norden about 7 o'clock Sunday morning. Returning trains leave Norden at 3 or 4:30 p.m. Sunday, arriving in San Francisco at 9:30 or 11:10 p.m.

Internationally known skiers who have ridden the ski trails of the outstanding winter-sports resorts of the globe have pronounced the Norden region the finest in the world. Long gentle slopes make this area ideal for skiing. And there is, of course, this enormous snow blanket.

Where you find Old Man Winter piling up pretty close to 30 feet of snow in one storm, you have the groundwork for just about as fancy a skier's dream as there is in the book. And, whether or not you are one of those rugged souls who revel in snow sports, going along just for the ride is not a bad idea. The scenery alone will leave you as breathless as a fast run on skis.

The beauty of it is that when you have had your fill of snow you can again in a few hours plant your dizzy feet on bare ground.

The Southern Pacific is doing all right in this snow business, to the mutual satisfaction of all concerned, and it is the first time since the Central Pacific, the daddy of the S.P., started rolling trains across the summit of the mighty Sierra Nevadas that anyone has gotten any fun out of that frowning old graybeard, the Storm King.

CHAPTER XXVIII

THE BURLINGTON

Streamlined Station

The streamlined train opened a new era in railroad transportation when the Burlington's first Zephyr flashed down the rails in 1934. In keeping with the modern trend, a streamlined railway station arose from the ashes of the old depot at Burlington, Iowa, 10 years later.

With its numerous gables and towers and decorative trim, the old Burlington "deepo" reflected the day of gingerbread mansions, bustles, and Pintsch-burner lamps in open-end passenger coaches. It belonged to the past. The new structure may well be the pattern of the railroad station of tomorrow.

The railroad depot has become an institution and a symbol in the community, but today it is as outmoded as the meeting-house shed that once sheltered the churchgoer's horse and buggy. Dingy, unattractive, its waiting room often smelling faintly of disinfectant, the average railroad station is entirely out of keeping with the fashionable trains it serves.

It is small wonder that station signs are so hard to find, a complaint frequently registered by travelers. Apparently the railroad feels that the passenger has no particular interest in the localities along the line, and the towns are not bragging.

The streamlined railroad station at Burlington, Iowa, is entirely in keeping with the forward-looking Burlington system. The traveler passing through receives a favorable impression of the city because of the striking appearance of the attractive structure clearly labeled Burlington.

You do not in any way associate this station with the word "deepo." The Burlington station stands as a tribute to the railroad, the city, and its builders. H. R. Clarke, Chief Engineer of the Burlington, and H. G. Dalton, Structural Engineer, have made a fine contribution to railroad architecture.

You are strongly impressed by the station's pleasing exterior design, and still more favorably impressed by the interior, with its sparkling club-lounge atmosphere, the lighting arrangement and color schemes.

The station, which overlooks the Mississippi River, is a two-story structure, with the exception of the restaurant section, which is rounded and all glass. Adding to the streamlined appearance of the station is a flat overhanging roof extending beyond the walls of the main building and restaurant. The exterior is faced with random ashlar masonry; the interior walls, of hollow tile, are faced with polished Montana Travertine and black marble.

The waiting room is spacious and decorated with drapes, potted plants, and other modernistic appointments. The furniture is much the same as you will find in any well-ordered hotel. In fact, you lose all sense of being in a railroad station. There is concealed indirect lighting, together with floor and table lamps. The decorative motif and color scheme of the restaurant are similar to those of the waiting room. Settees and stools are of green leather. The window sash and mullions are white, and the windows have yellow draperies, matching the color of the pillars.

The terrazzo floor of the waiting room is bordered by a black asphalt baseboard. The ceiling is of acoustic tile. All lockers and telephone booths have walnut trim and are recessed in the wall. Glass-faced electric signs indicate ticket offices, telephones, toilets, and other facilities.

All offices and office corridors have black and green asphalt tile floors. In all offices and office corridors, which would normally be dark, we find large panels of block glass to transmit light from adjacent rooms. All radiation is concealed.

Offices on the second floor are occupied by various railway employees.

On the outside the station is illuminated by lights along the side of the building and under the entrance canopies. A large

"Burlington" sign of Tymestone covered with gold leaf fairly shouts this proud old name.

There is only one fault I have to find with the Burlington station—you hate to leave it. The upholstered oak chairs in the waiting room, the upholstered double settee, the end tables, small tables, cozy lamps, all tastefully arranged for the convenience and privacy of small groups—well, you just can't bring yourself to the realization that this is a railroad station. Certainly it is a far cry from the old railroad "deepo."

The Burlington station was designed to provide efficient operation and to avoid congestion. The ground floor is divided roughly into 3 parts—restaurant and waiting room, office section, and baggage room. The waiting room is spacious and occupies the full two-story height of the building. Included in this room are the railway and bus ticket offices, located in the southeast and southwest corners of the room.

The entrance to the restaurant is in the northeast corner. The main entrances to the waiting room proper are on the town and track sides of the building, opposite each other near the south end and convenient to the ticket counters. A large area of the waiting room between these entrances and along the east side to the restaurant is unobstructed, which makes for the convenience of traffic to and from trains and to and from the restaurant.

From the south end of the waiting room a wide corridor extends through the center of the station to the baggage room. The corridor is wide enough to allow free movement. Along it are located the telephones and the parcel-checking lockers; also the entrance to the rest rooms. There are also offices off this corridor, a meeting room, and a record room.

Between the doorway to the tracks and the entrance to the restaurant there is a pleasant alcove with windows overlooking the tracks. The wall in this area and the large square pillars are faced with black marble to the top of the windows.

The station entrances have large glass-enclosed vestibules. The one on the track side extends into the waiting room; the one on the town side extends outward toward the driveway. These entrances and the alcove windows provide exterior light in the daytime in addition to that supplied by the large two-story window at the northwest corner of the waiting room. This window occupies half of the wall space on the west side and nearly a third of the wall at the north end of the waiting room.

The northwest corner of the waiting room, furnished with the kind of chairs and lounges you find in a hotel lobby, looks out through the two-story window upon a landscaped park north and west of the station. It is separated from the remainder of the room by banks of radiators which are concealed with metal covers capped with black marble.

Just to the right of the town entrance, engraved in the Travertine wall, we find the following inscription:

Here in 1852 the Burlington and Missouri River Railroad was incorporated.

In 1855, Chicago, Burlington and Quincy rails from Chicago reached East Burlington.

In 1868, the Burlington Bridge across the Mississippi River replaced the car ferry. From 1881 to 1901 Charles E. Perkins, of Burlington, was president of Burlington System Lines.

In 1887, George Westinghouse perfected the air brake on West Burlington Hill.

In 1934, the Burlington Zephyr, first Diesel streamlined train in America, was exhibited here, and in 1935 service to St. Louis by the Mark Twain Zephyr was established.

The restaurant is strikingly attractive. You enter it from the waiting room through two doors with large solid glass panels, while the remainder of the partition between the restaurant and waiting room is also of glass, affording a full view of the interior from the waiting room. You may also enter the restaurant from the outside from the sidewalk on the west side.

The restaurant has a terrazzo floor and is composed entirely of large windows overlooking the landscaped area outside. In addition to the lunch counter, an upholstered circular settee is built into the circular window area. Tables with black composition tops are placed in front of the settee. The walls are black marble, and the ceiling is acoustic tile. The restaurant also contains a magazine and newspaper stand, a cigar and candy counter, and a baggage-checking counter.

The woman's rest room has a floor of black and green asphalt tile. The walls are buff, and there are yellow curtains, green settees, and a large mirror. All trim is walnut. The men's room has a terrazzo floor and Cararra glass and plaster walls.

The station has 5 station tracks and 4 concrete platforms about 1,000 feet long. Two of these platforms are protected with butterfly-type canopies with center draining. Platforms and station track are lighted by floodlights on the ends of each canopy; also the platform area under the canopies is lighted by 100-watt bulbs at 19-foot intervals.

A large depressed driveway at the south end of the station provides room for trucks to turn and back to a concrete platform level with the baggage-room floor. The baggage room has large overhead doors on all 3 sides, 2 facing the tracks, 1 facing the south platform, and 1 facing west into a driveway on the city side.

West of the station, between the station and the street, is a sidewalk or platform; a wide, one-way drive; and a parkway. Traffic in this drive is routed past a saw-tooth platform between the baggage room and the station entrance. Parking space is provided for busses. The one-way drive extends on past the entrance into a wide parking area for private cars.

The remainder of the grounds north and west of the station are landscaped with large elm trees along the street, a lawn, shrubbery, and flowers.

As I have said, you lose all sense of having arrived at a railroad station at Burlington. It is almost as though your train or your car had drawn up at some fashionable and modernistic hostelry, an impression further emphasized upon entering the waiting room. If this is an example of what we may expect from the railroads in this new era of rail transportation, we can prepare to bid farewell to the unsightly and slightly smelly old railroad "deepo."

Improvements at the Burlington station, including track work, cost a cool half-million dollars, but no railroad ever made a better investment. Just as the Burlington road offered a new kind of rail transportation when it introduced those first silver Zephyrs, so now this famous rail line offers the traveling public the last word in a streamlined and luxurious railroad station.

Rear End of No. 62

"This little pig went to market." One of these fine days they will have to amend this old nursery rhyme to, "This little pig went to market at 90 miles an hour!" Fast freight has just about quit playing tank towns and is heading for big time. We've had red-ball trains for quite some time, but it has only been a warm-up. American railroads are getting down to business and in a very short time when you hear a freight whistle you had better hold your hat.

Look for lightweight cars with high-speed trucks—and roller bearings—before you can say Chicago, Burlington & Quincy. Look for a 4-8-4 or a freight Diesel on the head end, and count 10, and you will be looking at the marker lights going out of sight around the bend.

Back in 1941, the Burlington was shooting livestock from Denver to Chicago in a little over 31 hours, and they were calling it their No. 62, the fastest livestock train in America. No. 62 made no job at all of wheeling from Denver to Akron, Colorado, 112 miles, in 2 hours and 19 minutes. It seemed that a livestock train hardly got under way before it was time to change crews.

Livestock moves from Denver to the eastern seaboard in 80 hours, with 2 stops for feeding and rest of stock en route. If it wasn't for the fact that they are stepping up the passenger schedules, we might have the picture of the limiteds being side-tracked to let the fast freights go by.

The rear end of a livestock train plays an important part in its make-up, for here ride the men who are in charge of the live-stock. In the old days they rode in the saddle when the cattle drive was on, but since the railroads took over the job of moving beef to market, they travel in the drover's car. The drover's car goes through, while the caboose and its crew are changed at division points.

The drover's car is usually an old passenger coach that has

336

seen better days. It is fitted up with bunks, a stove for heat and cooking, and a couple of oil lamps. The stockmen, as they did in the days of the old Chisholm Trail, bring along their own chuck, skillet, coffeepot, and a meager handful of eating "impliments." They "spit and argue," and keep an ever-watchful eye on the stock. Except for the built-in bunks, the car retains its old red plush seats and a thousand memories of an earlier railroad era.

The purpose of the livestock train is to get the stock to market with a shrinkage in weight of 10 per cent or less if possible. The hauling cost is about $1\frac{1}{5}$ cents per pound. The men in the drover's car are always on the lookout for cripples or "downers." A downer is a steer or other animal that is down and in danger of being trampled.

A stock train is frequently made up of stock owned by different outfits, each represented by its own drover, who remains with the animals of his brand until they reach their destination. A man, say, with 4 or 5 cars of feeders—cattle going to Midwest areas for fattening—will be dropped with his charges at Galesburg, Illinois. Other cars may move direct to the stockyards at Chicago or the eastern seaboard. The average shrinkage of a steer will be replaced in a week's feeding at the stockyard.

Some ranchmen have facilities for fattening their beef before it is shipped. Many range cattle have the frame but not the tallow after the roundup; these will go to feed lots in the Middle West.

Stock movements occur in seasonal surges—spring and fall. Then cattle come out of the Southwest, lambs from Colorado and western Kansas, hogs from the Corn Belt. When the range starts to dry up, the steer moves to the feed lot for finishing off—putting on beef and that little layer of fat that makes your beefsteak tender and tasty.

The law requires that animals in transit must be unloaded, fed, and watered after they have been in transit 28 hours. This is a costly operation, and the stockman is continually seeking routings and service that will eliminate these stops so far as possible. The answer is fast freight, and the railroads are answering the problem with fast-moving livestock trains like this No. 62 of the Burlington. The carrier and the drover have but one purpose, and that is to see that the animals move quickly and safely. Poundage lost en route can mean the difference between profit and loss. The margin is close, both for the railroad and the cattleman. A hog or a steer can cause more gray hairs to the transportation department than a whole trainload of extra-fare passengers zipping through on the road's crack flier. That is why the railroads are giving close attention to fast-freight movement, particularly livestock.

The conductors of all trains handling livestock must consult the wishes of the men in the drover's car in matters pertaining to the care of the stock. They are further required to allow the stockmen an opportunity to examine and care for the stock when stops are made, and also render all possible assistance at any time.

Livestock cannot legally be confined to cars in excess of 28 hours, unless at the written request of stockmen, which must be attached to the waybill. At such time the confinement may be extended to 36 hours. In warm weather arrangements must be made to water hogs as often as necessary. If it becomes necessary to set out a car of livestock, the conductor promptly wires the trainmaster in order that repairs can be made immediately.

The conductor must report to the superintendent of transportation by wire all red-ball cars set out short of destination.

A freight conductor is expected to ride in the cupola of the caboose when his duties will permit. This, of course, applies to all freight as well as livestock. The Burlington has a fine fleet of freight Diesels, and 35 modern 4-8-4 type class O-5 engines to meet their fast freight requirements. And with the forward-thinking Ralph Budd running the railroad, you can bet they will always do it.

CHAPTER XXIX

"SPUD SPECIALS" OF THE SANTA FE

The Story of the Potato

The humble spud has produced one of the greatest mysteries known to man. Where did it originally come from? All efforts of botanists and plant experts to discover the parentage and the native habitat of the potato have met with failure, and there is little likelihood that this botanical mystery will ever be solved. Search as they will, the professors have been unable to determine where the potato is indigenous or where it was first introduced.

There are those who cling to the belief that the potato is a native of Chile, and others are as firmly convinced that it was first cultivated in Peru. Many good things and people come from these neighbor countries of western South America, and it is entirely possible that the potato was one of them. We do know that there are burial grounds in the arid regions on the Pacific slopes of Peru and northern Chile in which not only mummies have been discovered, but also withered products of the soil. Dried potatoes in these graves lead to the belief that they were grown prior to the conquest of England by William the Conqueror in 1066.

The Spaniards first discovered potatoes in the region that is now Quito, Ecuador. An examination of the records left by these explorers provides evidence that the natives raised several varieties of potatoes, which the Indians dried and carried over from one harvest to the next. When dried, this tuba was called Chunus, and it was highly prized as a food. The surplus crop, records reveal, was stored against years of crop failure and famine. The tubers also were used by these aborigines to make bread, first being cooked and then ground into flour.

There is not much data on the development of the potato as a field crop in North America, but it is said that the potato as a dish was first served in this country during a Harvard College dinner in 1707. In the early part of the eighteenth century potato culture was introduced at New Londonderry, New Hampshire, by a colony of Irish immigrants. And we know that early Americans, a particularly healthy lot, raised potatoes.

However, prior to 1850 little progress was made in potato breeding either in America or Europe. In 1851 the Reverend Chauncey Goodrich, of Utica, New York, received a small quantity of South American potatoes for breeding purposes. These potatoes included a vigorous variety which Goodrich named the "Rough Purple Chili."

Luther Burbank was another pioneer in the development of the potato, and the variety that bears his name was originated in 1883 from a seed-ball produced from an Early Rose plant. The true Burbank potato is grown almost exclusively in the Stockton districts of California.

Potato Growing in California

The majority of potato varieties grown in the United States today may be traced to the "Garnet Chili," a seedling of the Rough Purple Chili grown by Goodrich. The United States Department of Agriculture, through constant experimentation, has furnished potato growers with many new varieties, and also organized a national breeding program having as its aim a standard set by the American housewife, who choses potatoes of convenient size, regular exterior, and freedom from dirt. And in particular she wants a potato that will be tender and mealy when cooked.

We find this kind of potatoes in the rich agricultural districts of California, Arizona, New Mexico, Texas, Oklahoma, Missouri, and Kansas—districts served by the Santa Fe Railway System.

All potatoes raised in these areas are of an early and intermediate-crop variety, with the exception of California, which produces potatoes throughout the year. Irrigation is employed in potato growing in California, Arizona, and New Mexico, and because of the skill of the growers in supplying the exact amount of moisture necessary to the growing plant, these potatoes are in great demand.

Almost every sort of irrigation is practiced by the California potato grower, from culture under winter rainfall to irrigation on alternate days, a near subirrigation and, in San Diego County, overhead irrigation.

Since around the turn of the century potato breeders have improved and developed many varieties, with a goal centering around an early type, yield, quality, and disease resistance. While the White Rose is the principal variety grown in California, there are also many others, including the Burbank, the Netted Gem— also known as Russet Burbank and Idaho Russet—Garnet Chili, British Queen, and Bliss Triumph.

A potato called the Irish Cobbler is produced in limited quantities as an intermediate crop in New Mexico. The Irish Cobbler was originated by an Irish shoemaker who discovered the variety in his garden among plants of the Early Rose. This was back in the seventies.

Grown under favorable soil and climatic conditions, the White Rose of California is smooth, well-shaped, and makes an attractive appearance in the market. The sandy soils and warm spring weather are favorable to the production of this variety in the Shafter-Wasco and Edison-Arvin districts in the southern part of the San Joaquin Valley during May, June, and July.

Although the potato has long been considered a cool-weather plant, high yields are secured in the districts named, as well as in the Sacramento–San Joaquin Delta district in central California, where summer temperatures frequently top 100 degrees. Under these conditions, the soil temperature is kept relatively low, either by frequent irrigation in the sandy soil or by constant irrigation in the Delta districts where the water level is 18-24 inches from the soil surface until the crop approaches maturity.

Burbank and White Rose potatoes are grown in the peat lands of the Sacramento–San Joaquin Delta. The digging season begins in July and continues through February the following year. High

341

soil fertility and close planting have made high acre yields possible.

The Burbank, a late variety, has long been a standard variety in the coastal and interior districts of northern California. The Netted Gem is grown extensively in the coastal and interior districts of California, particularly in the Delta region.

The Garnet Chili, probably the oldest variety grown in America, is raised in California for the early market. Its growing season is long, but when planted in the fall it is considered an early crop.

The British Queen is a standard variety for California's winter crop. It is more strictly limited by climatic requirements than other varieties, and the plant and tuber will develop normally only in a constant cool humid climate.

The Irish Cobbler is raised in the Kaw Valley in Kansas and the Orrick section of Missouri, reaching maturity in July.

The Bliss Triumph leads all varieties grown in the dry-farmed areas of Oklahoma, Texas, Missouri, and Kansas. In southern Arizona this potato is harvested twice a year—in May and November. Seed potatoes of this variety are grown around Flagstaff in the high altitude of northern Arizona. Throughout the Southwest the Triumph is harvested in May and June.

The Bliss Triumph was introduced in Connecticut in 1878, and is one of the earliest commercial varieties in this country. It is claimed to be a seedling of the Peerless crossed with the Early Rose; hence is a direct descendant of the Garnet Chili, first produced by Chauncey Goodrich in New York in the early fifties. The Triumph has rapidly increased in popularity in California because it matures early and is of a high culinary quality.

A long reefer train moves south out of Bakersfield, California, and slowly climbs the grades of the Tehachapis. It snakes around the famous Tehachapi Loop and points away into the purple haze of the great desert of the Mojave—eastward bound. And another "Spud Special" is rolling on the rails of the Santa Fe.

The lowly potato, once scorned as an article of food by the Englishman, the German, and the Frenchman, is riding high

342

steel aboard a thundering special as it rushes to the markets of America.

No gleaming passenger train in the fleet of magnificent limiteds is more carefully guarded than this train of spuds. The last word in motive power is assigned to it; block signals guard it; Centralized Traffic Control, the push-button dispatcher, magically slips it in and out of passing tracks. G. R. Buchanan, Assistant General Manager of the coast lines of the Santa Fe, keeps his eye on it from the vantage point of his Business Car—for on the Santa Fe the potato move out of Bakersfield is important.

The demand for the many varieties of potatoes grown in territories served by the Santa Fe is demonstrated by the fact that the growers do not store their products in potato warehouses, but immediately start their potatoes to market. As a rule, potatoes are on their way 12 hours after coming out of the ground.

An unusual and outstanding advantage of the Sacramento–San Joaquin Delta is the fact that the raiser can use the ground as a natural warehouse throughout the season, digging potatoes to meet current market conditions.

Potatoes produced in California travel in refrigerator cars of the Santa Fe Refrigerator Department, and they travel on fast schedules. Diesel locomotives accelerate the speed of San Joaquin Valley shipments.

The average load of one of these Santa Fe reefers is 360 sacks of potatoes, each sack weighing 100 pounds. The early crop from Kern, Madera, and Fresno counties is moved in iced cars, while other California shipments may be either ventilated or iced as the shipper desires.

The same equipment is used in ventilated service as in the refrigerator service. These cars are provided with 2 hatches at each end, and these open into the ice bunkers. In the transportation of potatoes in the un-iced cars, the hatch covers are raised for ventilation; thus the outside air has free access to the car, and the circulation is accelerated when the car is in motion.

The planning of crop rotation, the preparation of the soil, the digging, grading, and shipping are only part of the problem of the potato grower. The shift in location of supplies, changes in transportation methods, increasing competition from other districts, a longer shipping season—all these factors have combined to create a constant marketing problem in the industry.

These problems are worked out daily by the grower and the railroader, for the success of the grower depends upon the co-operation he receives from the railroad that serves him; while the railroad, in turn, feels that it is in partnership with the farmer and the industrialist along its lines. It is the old story of "united we stand, divided we fall."

We have seen the benefits of this co-operation between the carrier and the shipper in industrial New England, in the coal regions, in the land of the Empire Builder of the Northwest. And when war came along there was the same kind of partnership between the government and the railroads. It was so in the movement of ore, of food, of guns, of men and—Material X, which made the atom bomb.

We find this same kind of co-operation existing between the Santa Fe and the potato growers. The Santa Fe maintains a Perishable Diversion Department, a part of the Santa Fe Refrigerator Department. The Diversion Department handles the re-consignments of shipments in such a manner that the grower is able to take advantage of a favorable market whenever and wherever it exists. Through this department the potato shipper may bill his cars to a temporary destination, then reconsign his potatoes to markets in accordance with the demands.

Better to provide a picture of the potato industry of California, I present the following figures through authority of the Federal-State Market News Service, U.S. Department of Agriculture, of San Francisco, California.

CALIFORNIA POTATO CROP, 1945

Total acreage	121,000 acres
Total yield	37,280,000 bushels
Total shipments	35,998 cars
Estimated value of crop	$57,784,000
Average value per bushel	$1.55
Average yield per acre	308 bushels
Early crop acreage	73,000 acres
Late crop acreage	48,000 acres

The figures in the following table represent shipments made over all railroads serving the territory.

CALIFORNIA POTATO CROP, 1945

Annual Carlot Shipments of Potatoes, 1945

COUNTY	NUMBER OF CARS
Contra Costa	250
Fresno	284
Humboldt	13
Inyo	10
Kern	22,368
Lassen	1
Los Angeles	270
Madera	816
Modoc	172
Monterey	1
Napa	7
Orange	37
Riverside	1,436
Sacramento	10
San Bernardino	572
San Joaquin	4,281
San Luis Obispo	14
Santa Barbara	241
Santa Clara	1
Siskiyou	3,463
Tulare	1,747
Yuba	4
Total	35,998

Though the origin of the lowly potato probably will remain a mystery to the end of time, its value as an article of food has long since been established, even though it took famines to bring a realization that this strange tuber contained vital elements of nutritional value.

If, when hunger threatened nations long ago, a wise man had arisen to proclaim that the potato contained vitamins A, B, C,

345

and G, and that it was rich in phosphorus and iron and an ideal food for children and grownups, the people would still have been very much in the dark, and no doubt would have chopped off his head. And yet when war again came to Europe it was the potato that fed the hungry.

After an 18-months' study in industrial centers of this war-ravaged Europe, the Health Committee of the League of Nations recommended that workers and their families eat more potatoes because of the life-giving minerals and vitamins they contained.

Cooking the potato with its jacket on, the experts tell us, conserves the maximum mineral value, of which about 10 per cent is lost in peeling.

The chemical composition of the potato varies with the variety and the conditions under which it is grown, but the potato that rode into the port of Santa Fe aboard the slave ship *Jesus of Lubeck* remains in any form the King of the Dinner Table, as today it rides the Spud Specials of the Atchison, Topeka & Santa Fe.

CHAPTER XXX

ROLLER BEARINGS FOR FREIGHT CARS

Wings on the Wheels

The long-suffering freight car, from all present indications, is just about ready to take off. They are going to put wings on the wheels—wings in the form of roller bearings. Already many boxcars equipped with roller bearings are being regularly operated as head-end cars in fast passenger trains.

In this book I have placed considerable emphasis on fast freight. The Santa Fe, as stated in an earlier chapter, has built a lightweight streamlined steel refrigerator car. Many roads are seriously considering roller bearings. Old Bill, the Great Northern's Rocky Mountain goat, is traveling farther and faster on a G.N. freight car than ever before, thanks to roller-bearing trucks.

That little pig going to market on the Burlington's No. 62 livestock train will without doubt one day glide over the rail on roller bearings. The freight car is lining its sights for high speed. There is no counting the hours freight in transit has been delayed by hot journals. And trains have been piled up because of bearing failure. But the day is coming when there will be no more replacing brasses and souping-up hotboxes.

The merit of roller bearings on freight cars is coming in for a lot of discussion in railroad circles, and the increasing number of all types of freight cars now being equipped with roller bearings speaks for itself. Roller bearings remove all speed restrictions, so far as bearings are concerned. Look, too, for the little red caboose on the rear end to follow suit.

Of course, when roller bearings go in, there must also be high-speed brakes, wheels, and draft gear. But the trend right now is toward the development of "one-speed—high-speed" rail-roading. All we have to do is look at the foundation being laid, starting with the track. Every up-and-coming road is tailoring the track for the safe movement of fast trains, as I have indicated in preceding chapters.

Again I point out that in tomorrow's railroading many a fast freight is going to be right on the block of the limited. In this development of high-speed freight, the use of roller bearings will play a key role. Roller-bearing-equipped locomotives and passenger cars demonstrated during World War II the fact that they could accomplish much in reducing maintenance costs, at the same time increasing the availability and the dependability of rolling stock.

The use of roller bearings on freight cars, as well as on locomotives and passenger cars, will offer the railroads the largest return of any single equipment investment that they can make. The roller-bearing rods are tops and should increase the life of this country's steam locomotives by 50 years.

Certainly I do not foresee the immediate installation of roller bearings on all existing freight cars, for many cars are too old and travel-weary to warrant such an investment. But many officials with whom I have talked feel confident that an increasingly large percentage of the new freight cars and cabooses placed in service each year will be ready to roll up many more revenue miles because of roller-bearing equipment.

The fact is recognized that some railroads may be reluctant to make an additional investment for roller bearings if cars thus equipped are to be used largely on lines other than those of the car owner. A certain road purchased 500 spanking new box-cars of modern design, and that was practically the last the owner saw of them, as they went to work hauling freight on almost every road in the country except the home road. Take, for example, a certain boxcar of a big eastern line. In slightly over a year it rolled up 15,000 miles, almost all of which were on the rails of other lines.

Roller-bearing-equipped freight cars will cost approximately 10 to 15 per cent more than a car with friction bearings, and naturally an assured return on the additional investment must be provided.

Such an assurance may be brought about by two developments. One, a steady increase in the number of high-speed freight trains which will operate as units, shuttling back and forth between large cities where such trains will not be broken up when arriving at a terminal, but will remain permanently in the service of the road owning them, and thus allow the home road the benefits derived from the use of such roller bearing equipment.

Two, to remunerate the owner of roller-bearing-equipped freight cars for their use. An arrangement might eventually be worked out, whereby the car owner would receive a higher per-diem rental for such modern equipment than for friction-bearing cars when it was in service on foreign lines. For instance, as against the present per-diem rate of $1.15 for standard cars serving on other lines, owners of roller-bearing cars might receive $1.25 to $1.50 a day.

Because of the low starting resistance of roller bearings, the necessity for taking slack is either eliminated or greatly reduced, permitting closer coupling of cars. The slamming shock caused by the large amount of slack in the present-day freight train often causes considerable damage to both lading and equipment. Again, roller bearings will reduce stresses and maintenance costs of draft gears, couplers, and other parts; not forgetting those claims for damage to lading.

The roller bearing is affected little, if any, by variable railroad operating conditions, but the friction bearing is directly and adversely affected by these conditions, particularly in those sections of the country which experiences extreme cold.

Many a freight car has rolled into a big classification yard with its friction bearings in good shape, and a few hours later it has gone out, a potential troublemaker, the result of hump-yard operation. As cars bang together, the shock, it has been discovered, momentarily disengages the brass from the axle, and the moving axle stirs up the waste packing so that strands may get between the brass and the axle, causing what is calling a "waste grab," which may in turn result in a hotbox—and trouble.

The brass friction bearing contacts less than a third of the circumference of the axle journal (28.9 per cent for 5½ inches x 10 inches; 30.8 per cent for 6-inch x 11-inch size) at the top. A roller bearing, on the other hand, completely surrounds the axle journal 100 per cent and is in contact 360 degrees of the circumference, which eliminates any possibility of displacing the bearing from the axle. It also offers more stable conditions in regard to braking and shocks. With roller bearings, waste packing is entirely eliminated, the bearing being lubricated by operating in a bath of oil. In all my railroading I have only seen one hotbox with a roller-bearing-equipped journal, and that was on an electric locomotive.

All vertical, radial, and end-thrust loads and combinations of each are taken in a tapered roller bearing itself, and no wear can occur on the surface and shoulders of the axle journal.

The friction in a roller bearing itself is represented by less than .05 per cent of the load imposed upon the bearing at starting and at all operating speeds. Expressed in another way, the friction within the bearing itself is "less than 1/2,000 of the load imposed upon it."

All of these statements are brought down to the cold fact that if a piece of freight car equipment can be so constructed that its rolling characteristics will be the same at all temperatures—which has been accomplished with roller bearings—then we have eliminated one of the most troublesome variables in the hump yard.

Roller-bearing-equipped freight cars will improve hump-yard operations for the reason that the bearing friction is practically the same at all speeds and at all temperatures; therefore "a more uniform braking or retarding pressure can be established for such cars."

More and more American railroads are using roller bearings on modern locomotive and passenger equipment, and without exception the roller-bearing locomotive is far outperforming a similiar locomotive with friction bearings.

From figures submitted by railroads having roller-bearing-equipped steam locomotives, the increased amount of work done, expressed in mileage by locomotives after being converted to roller bearings, ranges from 33 per cent to 133 per cent. A fair and conservative average would be 75 per cent increased work performed. This increased locomotive performance means a lot to the railroads in the handling of traffic, in particular when the motive power is being used to the utmost capacity.

I know of one instance where the chief executive of a railroad stated that his road would have been unable to handle the increase in traffic if a large number of their locomotives had not been converted to roller-bearing equipment before World War II. During the emergency it was hard to get men to maintain motive power, a situation at times acutely critical, and further aggravated by costly delays directly traceable to bearing trouble. The miracle of it was that war transport delivered the goods when the chips were down, not so much because of friction bearings—but in spite of them. The comparison of wartime engine failures between two of our largest eastern roads, one with roller bearings and one without, is unbelievable.

An indication of the increased availability for service made possible by the use of roller bearings was recently revealed by a large transcontinental road which reported that mileage figures over a period of 6 months showed that steam passenger locomotives equipped with roller bearings, which comprised 32.9 per cent of the ownership, made 51.9 per cent of total passenger locomotive miles. Roller-bearing steam freight locomotives, which comprised 6.5 per cent of the ownership, accounted for 15.8 per cent of total locomotive freight miles.

There are a number of important advantages to be considered in connection with roller bearings, including high speeds made possible, reduced starting resistance, improved fuel economy, greater hauling capacity, less "in shop for repair," to name a few. A further point to be considered is no change in tonnage rating between summer and winter service. Roller bearings show a reduction of 88 per cent in starting resistance on freight cars. Milwaukee passenger tests revealed a reduction of 90 per cent in starting resistance.

These are things you can't laugh off.

The railroads were skeptical at first, and roller bearings cost more. That was in the days of Old Man Depression. The Timken Company, with faith in its product and the future of the railroads and the nation, built a locomotive for demonstration purposes. They completely equipped it with roller bearings and started it down the railroad.

The Timken people were convinced that what the roller bearing had done for the automobile, the truck, and the bus, it could do equally well for the railroad, and they were willing to lay a few dollars on the line to that effect. Roller bearings then were viewed with dark skepticism in many railroad circles. The old problem of the wheels and the axle was just about where it was in the days of the Roman chariot races when a wheel turned around a thingumbob. All the railroads had ever done was to create a device whereby both the wheel and the axle turned; then they brassed the axle, packed it with waste, squirted in some oil now and then, and hoped for the best. And that ancient contraption has been "running hot" ever since.

We took our eternally shameful track gauge from the Roman chariot and adopted the friction bearing, with some small refinement, from the Romans, and have been sweating it out under those two handicaps ever since. It has been argued that once a freight train is under way it doesn't make much difference whether it is equipped with friction or roller bearings, so far as the tonnage rating is concerned. Be that as it may, from a sound engineering and economical standpoint, the advantages of a roller bearing far outweigh its disadvantages.

To get back to the locomotive that Timken built. This engine ran up over a million miles on 14 roads, and certain rail systems began applying roller bearings to motive power. About that time World War II came along, and roller bearings for the most part took the siding to let the war trains roll.

And now, during a slightly hectic reconversion period, they're clearing the rail for a bright new era in railroading. There are improved designs in trucks, antislide wheel devices, new cars, new car seats, vista-dome coaches; they have taken the jerk out of passenger-train starting with something called Waugh twin-cushion draft gears, and they have improved car wheels and brakeshoes.

Yes, and they are putting wings on the wheels in the form of roller bearings. The Burlington alone has rolled up an amazing

25,000,000 miles with roller bearings on its famous fleet of Zephyrs.

We are entering a period of "precision" railroading, and roller bearings will continue to play an increasingly important role.

True, there are still problems to be worked out before we will find roller bearings on all freight cars, cabooses, and passenger equipment, but they will be whipped eventually. The day is coming when roller bearings will have a bigger part in giving America even better rail transportation than she has today, and that's the world's best.

CHAPTER XXXI

THE ROAD OF POCAHONTAS

The Norfolk & Western's Balance Sheet

When Captain John Smith sailed up the Chickahominy River in Virginia he did not discover the Pacific Ocean, for which he was searching, but he did find high adventure—adventure that left its bright imprint not only on the pages of American history, but on railroad history as well. Probably the most famous coal in America today bears the name of the Indian maiden who befriended the explorer of the Chickahominy, there in old Virginia —Pocahontas.

It was only natural that in the course of time the Norfolk & Western's crack limited should be named Pocahontas, after the great coal mining district of that name.

And when a modern postwar train, all shiny and new, went flashing down the rails of the Norfolk & Western, the spirit of a great Indian chieftain returned from the Happy Hunting Grounds to ride it. This all-coach luxury flier which began operation between Norfolk, Virginia, and Cincinnati, Ohio, on April 28, 1946, bore the name "Powhatan Arrow."

Powhatan, the Indian chief, and his daughter Pocahontas are symbolic of America, exactly as they are symbolic of an American railroad, the Norfolk & Western.

Primarily a coal road, the Norfolk & Western Railway operates approximately 100 passenger trains per day over its system. The road owns 380 passenger car units, including 81 locomotives, 159 passenger cars, 13 diners, together with baggage, postal, combination, and express cars.

The principal motive power in passenger service is the sleek and beautiful streamlined J steam locomotive of the 4-8-4 type.

Westward caboose hop from Minot to Williston, crossing Gassman Coulee on the Third Subdivision of the Minot Division. Photo by H. W. Pontin. Courtesy Rail Photo Service.

New Great Northern aluminum box car built at the St. Cloud shops for high-speed freight and passenger service, equipped with Timken roller bearings as well as steam heat and signal lines. Courtesy Great Northern Railroad.

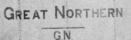

GREAT NORTHERN RY.

SEE AMERICA FIRST
GLACIER NATIONAL PARK

GREAT NORTHERN
G.N.
2500
CAPY 100000
LD.LMT. 123400
LT.WT. 45600 FB·45
BX

Santa Fe #12, the streamlined Chicagoan, crossing the Missouri River on the Sibley Bridge, Mo., hauled by Diesel #50, built by Alco. Second District of the Missouri Division. Courtesy Santa Fe Railroad.

The climb is over. Rear end of Santa Fe westbound Chief entering Raton Tunnel at the top of the 3.5% grade on the historic pass of that name. Courtesy Santa Fe Railroad.

Loading ewes for the Colorado feeding ground from the Burlington stock pens at Armito, Wyo. Courtesy Chicago, Burlington & Quincy Railroad.

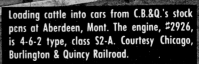

Loading cattle into cars from C.B.&Q.'s stock pens at Aberdeen, Mont. The engine, #2926, is 4-6-2 type, class S2-A. Courtesy Chicago, Burlington & Quincy Railroad.

Colonel Frank Russell, U.S.A., and S. Kip Farrington, Jr., pose with army engine crew running a U.S.A. oil-burning 2-8-2 type locomotive at Calcocan Shops outside of Manila, P.I. Courtesy U.S. Army.

Luzon Military Railway special hauled by 350-h.p. Diesel switcher built by the American Locomotive Company. With Colonel Frank Russell, U.S.A., and the author standing alongside. Courtesy U.S. Army.

N.&W. Engine #2055, 2-8-8-2 type, class Y-3A, assisting a mixed-tonnage train eastbound at Blue Ridge, Va., on the Norfolk Division. The grade is 1.2%. Courtesy Norfolk & Western Railroad.

The Timken roller-bearing application can be used in all kinds of freight-car trucks. Courtesy Timken Roller Bearing Co.

Santa Fe #22, eastbound El Capitan, de luxe all-coach streamliner, climbing the 3.3% grade above Keota, N. M. Engines #1695, 2-10-2 type, #5000, 2-10-4 type, and Diesel #15 (2 units) are on the head end. Photo by Preston George.

The forerunner of a great class. Santa Fe's experimental Engine #5000, built in 1930, helping #39 Colorado-California-Texas fast freight up Raton Pass where she is now in service. Photo by Preston George.

Caboose and rear end of a New York Central NB-2, providing fast Pacemaker freight service from Buffalo to New York with high-speed specially built equipment. Courtesy New York Central Railroad.

Rear end of the New York Central #25, the westbound Twentieth Century Limited, at Peekskill, N. Y., on the Hudson Division. Courtesy New York Central Railroad.

Mr. and Mrs. S. Kip Farrington, Jr., leaving Chicago en route to the Southwest Pacific with the U.S. Army Special Service Division and the U.S.O. They covered over 20,000 miles by air after leaving Hamilton Field, Calif.

This engine might easily be termed one of the most striking engines in the country, with its torpedo streamlining, bright Tuscan red stripe extending the full length of locomotive and tender, and those sharply contrasting silver side rods.

This engine has 70-inch drivers and a tractive effort of 73,300 pounds. It is equipped with Timken roller bearings on the engine truck, drivers, trailing-truck and tender-truck journals, and on wrists and crank pins and valve gear. These locomotives have an assignment of 15,000 miles per month and accumulate an average of 238,000 miles per engine before going to the shop for classified repairs. They have proved themselves capable of mileage greatly in excess of 15,000 miles a month on a railroad where the locomotive could be assigned to longer runs.

These engines pull the Pocahontas Nos. 3 and 4, running between Norfolk, Virginia, and Cincinnati, Ohio; the new Powhatan Arrow; and other fast trains of the Norfolk & Western.

Beside the Pocahontas and Powhatan Arrow, other crack trains of the Norfolk & Western are the Cavalier, running between Norfolk and Cincinnati; the Tennessean (trains 45 and 46) operating between Washington, D. C., and Memphis, Tennessee; the Birmingham Special (trains 17 and 18) between New York and New Orleans, Louisiana; and the New York, Chattanooga, and New Orleans Limited (trains 41 and 42), between New York and New Orleans, which are operated jointly by the Southern Railway and the Norfolk & Western, over the Norfolk & Western line from Lynchburg, Virginia, through Roanoke and down through southwest Virginia to Bristol on the Tennessee-Virginia border. Complete dining-car and Pullman service are provided on each of these trains.

A particularly scenic route of this great coal road is that from Roanoke, Virginia, to Hagerstown, Maryland, up the famous and beautiful Shenandoah Valley. The distance is 238 miles, and connections are made at Hagerstown for points to the north and east. The Shenandoah Valley, rich in scenery and historic lore, is a veritable fairyland, and it was named by the Indians the "Daughter of the Stars."

Two lines from Virginia into North Carolina make connections at Winston-Salem and Durham for the South. A line running from the main line at Walton to Bristol, 131 miles, passes through the heart of southwest Virginia, making connections at the latter point for Tennessee, Mississippi, and Southwest destinations. The line from Bluefield, West Virginia, to Norton, Virginia, traverses the beautiful Clinch Valley sections.

Traveling on the Norfolk & Western, you not only are given an opportunity to see something of its enormous coal operations as they pertain to transport, but view scenery beyond compare —the mountains and valleys and rivers of the Virginias, North Carolina, Ohio, and the edge of Kentucky, touched by the road's gleaming rails.

The Norfolk & Western is a modern, progressive railroad. Because it is a coal road, you perhaps rather gain the impression that it is a burly, muscular, and grimy giant lacking in polish and style. True, it is a hard-working railroad, with its endless caravans of coal cars; but it is also a well-dressed and precise railroad, its track and rock-ballasted right of way having a clean, scrubbed look.

Prior to our entry into World War II, the Norfolk & Western had embarked on an extensive replacement and improvement program, purchasing modern de luxe coaches and rebuilding and modernizing coaches already in operation. Some of this work was completed; some was necessarily deferred through the war and demobilization period. Motive power and other equipment on the road had always been maintained to the highest degree, but, as in other industries, war shortages seriously curtailed extensive equipment replacements and other improvements.

Passenger-traffic men were faced with acute problems in servicing the teeming military areas on the system, particularly around the great port and naval base at Norfolk and the army camps such as Camp Lee at Petersburg, and Camp Pickett at Blackstone, Virginia.

Prior to 1871 Congress granted large acreages of land to a number of railroads to aid in the construction of their lines. The grants required those railroads to carry government troops, property, and mail at reduced rates. The Norfolk & Western did not receive such land grants, but, like other roads which did, was compelled by competition to join in through rates at the lowest

356

level available to the government via land-grant routes. Such reductions, by act of Congress in 1940, were limited to the transportation of troops and military or naval property of the United States.

These reductions saved the government many times the value of the lands granted. The savings to the government have been substantial in the war years. The railroads, the Interstate Commerce Commission, and others interested in the subject have urged for a long time that such reduced rates should be abolished.

By act of Congress, approved December 12, 1945, the provisions for the land-grant reduced rates were repealed, effective October 1, 1946. Thereafter the government will pay full commercial rates for the transportation of troops and property. This enactment is of value to the land-grant railroads as well as the Norfolk & Western and other roads.

During and following the war, the Norfolk & Western has carried forward a program of additions and betterments to its plant and equipment. At Lambert Point, Virginia, a new pier and supporting yard of 280-car capacity and new warehouses, costing nearly $6,000,000, will accommodate simultaneously 4 of the largest seagoing freight vessels afloat. Sprinkler and firebreak curtains have been installed at the warehouse piers. At Norfolk, at this writing, a new bascule-type drawspan of 190 feet in length over the eastern branch of the Elizabeth River is under construction.

A modernization of automatic signals between Williamson and Fort Gay, West Virginia, has been completed. High-tension signal transmission lines have been rebuilt between Roanoke and Walton, Virginia, and between Vera and Columbus, Ohio. Between Pulaski and Bristol, Virginia, a distance of 98 miles, Centralized Traffic Control has been installed.

Passing sidings, team and storage tracks have been constructed at numerous strategic points to accommodate increased traffic movements. Industrial sidings and extensions have been completed at 43 locations. Three tunnels in the vicinity of Pounding Mill, Virginia, were enlarged to accommodate oversize ship-

357

ments. New 131-pound rail has been laid, making a total of 3,205 miles of track now laid with 130- or 131-pound rail.

The Pocahontas Land Corporation, all of whose capital stock is owned by the Norfolk & Western, is a coal landowning company which does not itself mine or sell coal. Of the road's holdings of approximately 307,000 acres, largely underlaid with bituminous coal, in Virginia, West Virginia, and Kentucky, about 180,000 acres are under lease to operating companies.

Men like William J. Jenks, Chairman of the Norfolk & Western Board and R. H. Smith, President, crack railroaders, who have come up from the bottom, know and appreciate the value of dollars earned the hard way. And the same thrifty habits acquired in their climb to the top they now apply to the management of the railroad they represent. The Norfolk & Western Railway System has not only achieved success through hardheaded business principles and "hoss" sense, but also because of the loyalty of its close to 22,000 employees—the men and women on the line.

During recent years the Norfolk & Western has designed and built 116 modern steam locomotives. By the term "modern" I mean a locomotive with a high-capacity boiler, equipped with roller bearings on all engine and tender wheels, one-piece cast-steel bed frame, improved counterbalancing, and complete mechanical and pressure lubrication. And if a locomotive is intended for high-speed passenger service, rod and valve gear connections should be equipped with roller bearings, as on the Norfolk & Western streamlined locomotives which I have mentioned. This engine, primarily designed to handle heavy passenger trains over the mountains, has, where grades and curvature permitted, recorded speeds in excess of 100 miles an hour.

The modern steam locomotive, as compared with engines built back around 1930, has far greater utilization and costs over 50 per cent less to maintain. Of the Norfolk & Western's fleet of freight locomotives, one-third are of modern design. This 33 per cent hauls 68 per cent of the road's total steam freight mileage.

A feature of no little importance on the Norfolk & Western's locomotives is an automatic telltale valve located under the engine truck. If at any time the engine truck should be derailed, the brakes will be instantly applied. This telltale valve is of particular value on a road where so many Mallets are in operation, for there have been cases on this type of locomotive where the engine crew were unaware that the engine truck had become derailed until the locomotive went on the ground.

The Norfolk & Western freight motive power is exceptionally rugged, with a high record of availability. The 2-6-6-4 Articulateds, in working order, have a total weight of engine and tender of just under a million pounds—951,600 pounds, to be exact. They have a boiler pressure of 300 pounds; 24-inch x 30-inch cylinders, and a tractive effort of 114,000 pounds. This is a very fine engine, easy on coal and one of the nicest engines for the fireman I have ever fired. It is my favorite of the Norfolk & Western fleet.

The 2-8-8-2 locomotives, in working order, weigh 961,500 pounds. The driving wheels are 57-inch, and the boiler pressure is 300 pounds. These engines are compound Mallets, with the 2 high-pressure cylinders measuring 25 inches x 32 inches, and the 2 low-pressure cylinders measuring 39 inches in diameter, with a 32-inch stroke. Their tractive effort is: simple, 152,206 pounds; compound, 126,838 pounds. They do an amazing job.

War Record

Strategically located, splendidly equipped through the expenditure of millions of dollars, and experienced in providing precision transportation, the Norfolk & Western Railway and its employees played a vital part in the nation's war effort.

From the outbreak of the war in Europe in the fall of 1939, through 1945, the Norfolk & Western spent or authorized the expenditure of $92,000,000 in a sweeping program of additions, betterments, and expansion in order to meet the demands of war and further to expedite the movement of the staggering volume of war traffic.

During these war years, the Norfolk & Western moved the greatest volume of freight traffic in its history. In 3 of the 5 war years it carried the heaviest freight traffic, measured by ton-miles per mile of line per day, of any railroad in the United States more than 350 miles in length.

The job of handling the troop and civilian passenger traffic alone was a gigantic task. This traffic in 1942 was 5 times greater than in 1939. In 1943 it was 9½ times greater. The peak was reached in 1944, when the passenger-train movement was 11 times greater than in 1939. It dropped in 1945 to 9 times greater.

This traffic included hundreds of special troop trains, and the movement of additional hundreds of thousands of other servicemen and civilians.

In another chapter I have said that the movement of bituminous coal reached a peak of 54,400,000 tons, with an average in each year of the war of 52,000,000 tons, an increase of 33⅓ per cent over 1939.

One thing that stands out in the American railroads' contribution to the war effort is the fact that, so far as I know, no accident occurred in connection with the transportation of explosives.

The Norfolk & Western, in addition to rebuilding thousands of its own coal cars, constructed many new locomotives and at the same time maintained its rolling stock as a whole in top-notch condition. The great Roanoke shops filled 88 orders for war equipment for other industries and for the Army and Navy, including the manufacture or processing of more than 349,806 separate equipment parts.

The Norfolk & Western helped maintain the rolling stock on neighboring railroads by overhauling 241 locomotives and more than 2,000 freight cars.

This brawny giant of the coal fields not only moved the war load thrust upon it with the motive power on hand, but it sold 62 locomotives to other lines. On top of that, it leased 2,700 of its coal cars.

When all over America the cry was being raised that the railroads were on their last legs, the Norfolk & Western and other of the nation's roads were doubling up their fists preparatory not only to doing the impossible, but also to swatting the carpers hip and thigh.

When William Mahone, hero of the Battle of the Crater,

plunged into Virginia's Dismal Swamp with his silk-lined shoes, the cry was raised that the proposed rail line was a crazy man's idea. But William Mahone showed them. William Mahone was President of one of the Norfolk & Western's parent roads.

When A. C. Needles, late Chairman of the Norfolk & Western, was one day showing a party of friends through the railway shops, he casually mentioned a machine that bored square holes. A few eyebrows went up, while one of the party suggested that Mr. Needles must be joking.

A. C. Needles was not joking, and he showed the doubters the machine that was boring square holes—not only square holes, but triangular holes, holes in the shapes of hexagons and pentagons; any old kind of a hole, in fact.

The Norfolk & Western at the start of the war was in a position to lease many of its port facilities at Norfolk to the government. This included piers, warehouses, and land. The road moved an unprecedented volume of troops and materials to the port of Norfolk, contributing in no small way to the outstanding record of Hampton Roads as the nation's third most important port.

In spite of manpower and material shortages superimposed on the war burden it was carrying, this coal road proved itself a typically hornyhanded railroader by installing 118 miles of Centralized Traffic Control, by double-tracking heavy grades, by extending passing tracks, and by performing other chores on the Shenandoah Valley Line. By so doing the railway was able to handle 17,000,000 more tons of bituminous coal over this route —coal that was being diverted from Norfolk because of the submarine menace. An important but little realized contribution.

The Norfolk & Western, further, constructed a storage yard at Windsor, Virginia, for the accommodation of the carloads of explosives awaiting the arrival of convoys at Norfolk.

The Norfolk & Western is not a big railroad, as railroad giants go, but it contributed in no small way to victory through the payment of $180,000,000 in taxes. And just by way of doing its bit in a less spectacular manner, the road collected and disposed of 456,000,000 pounds of scrap metal, 122,700 pounds of rubber, and 1,224,000 pounds of paper.

Norfolk & Western employees, through the pay-roll savings plan, bought nearly half a million War Bonds having a par value of $12,596,850. Of the Norfolk & Western railroaders, 4,815 entered the armed forces, and to the 107 who died in their country's service, William J. Jenks, then President of the road, paid a special tribute in the company's annual report for the year ending December 31, 1945.

Form A. D. 58-H
Revised 2-15-35

1

550-NORFOLK AND WESTERN RAILWAY COMPANY- 550
Coal and Coke Freight Waybill
ORIGINAL

STOP THIS CAR AT	FOR			

Gross Weight of Car and Contents for Engine Rating	Car Initial and Number	Mine No.	Mine Tag Date	If "X" appears in this space the carrier shall not make delivery of this shipment without payment of freight and all other lawful charges.
TONS	N.&.W. 96207	100	1/9/46	X

TRANSFERRED		WAYBILL DATE	WAYBILL NUMBER
TO	AT	1/11/46	52008

Route (Show each Junction and Carrier in Route Order to Destination of Waybill)

VXing-C&O,Fost-NKP,M.City-CSS&SB,Chgo-CRI&P

FROM STATION	STATE
4262	Berwind,W.Va.

No. ( )

TO STATION	STATE
Iowa City, Iowa	

All correspondence pertaining to this Waybill should be addressed to Weighmaster at

(Portsmouth, Ohio.)

Consignee, Address (Final Destination and Additional Routing)	Full name of shipper and previous waybill reference when rebilled
Lampert Yards Inc.	Berwind Fuel Co.

Commodity	WEIGHT	RATE	FREIGHT	ADVANCES	PREPAID
Briquets	WEIGHED AT Portsmouth, Ohio. GROSS 137.8 TARE 43.6 NET 94,200 LF	500	235.50		

Destination Agent's Freight Bill No

All Yard Stamps to be Placed on Back of the Waybill in Spaces Provided

JUNCTION FORWARDING AGENTS WILL SHOW JUNCTION STAMPS IN THE SPACE AND ORDER PROVIDED BELOW

FIRST JUNCTION	SECOND JUNCTION	THIRD JUNCTION	FOURTH JUNCTION	DESTINATION AGENT WILL STAMP HEREIN STATION NAME AND DATE REPORTED

Additional Junction Agents' Stamps Must be Shown on Back of Waybill in Spaces Provided
550—NORFOLK AND WESTERN RAILWAY COMPANY—550

CHAPTER XXXII

LUZON MILITARY RAILROAD

Railroading in the Philippines

This is the story of military railway operations in the Philippines and the man who virtually performed a railroad miracle—Colonel Frank E. Russell.

My own remarks are more in the way of a preface and to set the stage. This chapter really belongs to Colonel Russell. Like his father before him, Frank E. Russell, Sr., he is a Southern Pacific railroad man and a good one. He started on the S.P. as a special apprentice at Sacramento and worked his way up to Master Mechanic at El Paso, Texas. In August, 1942, he was advanced to Assistant Superintendent of Motive Power at Los Angeles, California.

He entered the armed forces in September, 1942, and was commanding officer of the 754th Railway Shop Battalion (sponsored by the Southern Pacific). He went to Iran in February, 1943, where he distinguished himself in the supervision of heavy repairs to engines and freight cars on the Trans-Iranian Railway. He was awarded the Legion of Merit.

When the Persian Gulf Command became inactive, Russell went to the Philippines to aid in re-establishing rail transportation. And it was here that I saw at firsthand the kind of a job our American railroad men performed in World War II. I wish that I could name all of the officers and enlisted men of those Railway Battalions, as well as the railroads they represented, in all of the far-flung war theaters throughout the world. The job they did and the conditions under which they had to work and the difficulties they surmounted are beyond description. I only

363

wish it could be understood, and half appreciated, by the American public.

The men of the U. S. Army's Railway Operating Battalions made history, and they showed the world how to railroad. They picked up where enemy demolition squads left off, and, often working under fire, opened the line and started the trains rolling again. Books could be written concerning their activities, and probably will. Major General Carl Gray, their commanding officer in several theaters, who has returned to the Chicago & North Western as vice-president, hopes to see at least a little of the story of the Railway Battalions recorded, as does Major General Frank E. Ross, U.S.A., commanding general of the Transportation Corps in Europe, himself the son of an S.P. man.

I will never ride a locomotive again without regretting that I could not have played a part in the work of these American railroaders abroad, but Army and Navy doctors here and in Canada looked me over and shook their heads just on account of a lung condition. But when the Special Service Division of the Army asked Mrs. Farrington and me to visit the European theater with the U.S.O. to show our fishing and *Field & Stream* shooting moving pictures to the troops, I jumped at the chance. Then the war in Europe ended and our itinerary switched to the Pacific.

We arrived in Manila October 20, 1945, after flying from Hamilton Field, California, under the auspices of the A.T.C., too late to see any of the actual hostilities. We had shown our pictures every evening for about 3 weeks at various camps and depots around Manila, Lieutenant General W. D. Styer, U.S.A., commanding general of the Armed Forces of the Western Pacific, introduced me to Brigadier General G. C. Stewart, who headed the Transportation Corps in that theater. General Stewart in turn arranged with Colonel Frank E. Russell, who was in charge of the Luzon Military Railroad, to take me out on the line.

The Luzon Railroad would have been the road nearest Japan if our Army and Navy had been confronted with a fighting invasion, and its importance would have been great, on account of the fact that all supplies moving up from the Manila area would have been transported to San Fernando, U., its northern terminus on Lingayen Gulf, which is 265 kilometers north of Manila. The railroad also extended to Batangas, 112 kilometers to the south, and to Mondagua, 237 kilometers to the southeast. The volume of troop movements to all of the various encampments situated near the line was tremendous.

When Colonel Russell arrived on Luzon he found that the Army Air Force, which had preceded him after the landings along the Lingayen Gulf, had a 90-mile pipe line carrying high octane gas laid on the ties. This, of course, had to be moved off the track, but so little a thing as a pipe line on the track was the least of the Battalion's troubles. The Japs had had a field day staging head-on collisions between the road's locomotives. They had destroyed bridges, communications, and rolling stock, made a mess of the shops, and removed all the brass from the journals.

Nothing can so much resemble a junk yard as a smashed-up railroad. You can't even start from scratch, but have to wade through the debris, hoping you can find something with the wheels intact. Colonel Russell at last located one locomotive, a 4-8-2, built by the American Locomotive Company in 1922. This these Yank railroaders soon had in shape to run, and that was the beginning.

When at last the standard 2-8-2's began to arrive, they required 2-3 weeks' work to put them in shape. This was a sad condition, it seems, in many war theaters. Railroad men and locomotive builders in the States protested, but to no avail, and locomotives continued to be shipped with no lights of any kind on them, not even a headlight, and with many other ridiculous things on them, such as oil lubrication for the rods, steam sanders, and hand reverse gears.

By the time the mechanical forces had the motive power in shape, the track gangs had the railroad ready for them. The gauge in the Philippines is 42 inches; the rail is from 60- to 80-pound. Because there were practically no air brakes, the speed of all trains was limited to 20 miles per hour. The track gangs did a heroic job, often working in water and jungle and rice fields that were infested with every variety of insect and two or three reptiles, including one charming little leaf-green snake with yellow stripes called a "pit viper." The pit viper is a cousin of the water moccasin and the fer-de-lance. This viper, rarely over 2 feet in length, often is found in branches or vines, and its bite is painful and sometimes fatal. Many a railroader was bitten. And there were also many species of the deadly cobra.

Until the late fall of 1945 there was always the threat of roving bands of Japs moving stealthily down from their mountain hide-outs to destroy the track or attack the trains. Everybody wore side arms.

When the regular Philippine railroad crews were put back on the trains, a pilot engineer always rode the engine, with a pilot conductor on the train. On freight trains the caboose was a box car, and the last car of passenger trains was reserved for military use.

Two passenger trains a day operated between Manila and San Fernando, U. The morning train left Manila at 10:00 and arrived at the northern terminus at 20:30. The evening train left at 20:00 and arrived at San Fernando, U., the next morning. Returning trains left at 10:00 and 20:00, arriving in Manila at 20:15 and 07:00 hours respectively. I quickly named these two jobs the "Daylight" and the "Lark," in honor of the Southern Pacific colonel who was running the railroad.

The Filipinos would wait all day and all night to board the trains at both terminals, and if the seats had been reserved they would have been taken days ahead. However, there were no such things as seats—just wooden benches—and no lights. But such minor inconveniences bothered the Filipinos no more than the holdups and thieving that went on nightly. The Military Police found it difficult to cope with this banditry, for it was executed with stealth and cunning in the darkness. Twelve cars were usually the limit of passenger trains, with about double this number in freight service.

The cars were equipped with every kind of coupling, from the old link-and-pin on up. Some of the locomotives of the Luzon Railway were built in England in the eighties and nineties, and were practically museum pieces, but if there was ever a locomotive the boys in the Railway Battalions couldn't put in shape I never heard of it.

The shops were located at Caloocan, just outside of Manila.

The division point was at Tarlac, 119 kilometers from Manila, and the train crews changed there.

Mrs. Farrington and I felt highly honored when General Stewart and Colonel Russell ran a special for us. The make-up of the train consisted of the late President Quezon's private car, a cook car which was used for a diner, and a tiny boxcar on the head end for the train and engine crew. The locomotive was a 350-horsepower Alco-General Electric Diesel switcher, one of the 10 received from the States.

The private car, which we used as a Business Car, was constructed of wood, and when the President used it, had had an airconditioning system, but it was no longer in operation. It gave me rather a queer sensation to sit in a straight-backed chair looking out of its tiny windows in its small rear end. The dust was as bad as the old dust-bowl days, and we were white with it in a short time. There were air brakes on 2 cars, and at times we could run 35 miles an hour.

Trains were operated with line-clear tickets, a form of clearance card. Few train orders were issued, and there were, of course, no automatic block signals. As in many foreign countries, there was a switch tender on duty at all passing tracks, and you never knew whether he would head you in, allow you to hold the main track, or throw the switch under your train.

Form TRANS. 230
500 Pads. 200-sht. (D)

LUZON MILITARY RAILWAY
DUPLICATE

Explotacion
Operation

Movimiento
Transportation

CERTIFICADO DE VIA EXPEDITA, NO EXISTIENDO BATUTA
LINE CLEAR CERTIFICATE, STAFF NOT BEING AT ISSUING STATION

No·
No

AL NORTE
NORTHBOUND

Estacion de .... a .... de .... *Nov. 16* .... de 1945
Station   Date

Al Maquinista del Tren No.
To the Driver of Train No.

Puede V. seguir hasta .... sin batuta; la linea esta expedita.
You may proceed to   without the staff; the line is clear.

La batuta esta detenida en .... por............
The staff is retained at   on account of

y el Jefe de dicha estacion avisa que detendra
and the Agent at said Station advises that

la batuta hasta la llegada de este tren.
he will retain the staff until the arrival of this train.

....
Jefe de Estacion

367

At most of the highway crossings, no matter how isolated, we found the inevitable guard or watchman. Often the traffic consisted only of a plodding water buffalo, or caribou, as they call them, and a native driver. Some of these crossings were equipped with pole gates.

When a train order was issued it was usually called "across" instead of a "meet." Such an order would not only include the train and engine number, but also the number of cars. The order hoops were bamboo reeds about a third the size of those used in the States. When they were thrown from a train, every Filipino kid around raced up the tracks after them.

As in many countries, the Philippine railroaders will never run an extra train, and every movement must be scheduled well in advance, including the wrecker or anything else. Our extra was known as TS-8 and TS-9.

In these Railway Battalions you meet railroaders from everywhere, and what a kick you get out of talking to them. A grand bunch, and there are no railroaders on earth to compare with them. Here you find them, 8,000 to 11,000 miles from their home terminals. Transportation men from the Central's DeWitt Yard at Syracuse, a road foreman of engines from the Florida east coast, a master mechanic from the Grand Trunk, a trainmaster from the New Haven, an engineer from the Coast Line, a yardmaster from the Norfolk & Western. They all came from roads and division points where I had been many times, and we had a lot of fun talking of the men and the railroads we all knew so well.

The crew on this special of ours was made up of a Union Pacific engineer from the Los Angeles Division. The fireman was from the Columbia Division of the Southern, the conductor was off the Southern's Birmingham Division, the brakeman was off the Katy, out of Parsons, Kansas, and the flagman was "made on" the Louisville & Nashville, "Old Reliable."

There is no such thing as a 16-hour law for these American railroaders in the Railway Battalions, and often they are on duty endless hours.

Colonel "Red" Barrett, who was a member of the engineering staff of the Rio Grande, came to call on us at San Fernando, U.

He was in command of the transportation facilities at the port. He nearly fell off his chair when I pulled the Rio Grand profile book out of my brief case. "Gee!" he exclaimed, "I never expected to see one of those things out here."

But I think one of my biggest thrills was when I got off the engine of our special to talk to the flagman of a freight train. He was stripped to the waist, like all the rest of them, looking lean and hard and brown. The boys preferred comfort to clothes, even if it meant exposing themselves to mosquitoes and the often-resulting malaria. That heat was worse than anything I have ever encountered anywhere, and I have spent a lot of time fishing in the tropics of many hot countries.

I asked this freight flagman what road he had worked on in the States, and he said the Santa Fe—Vaughn, New Mexico, Second District of the Pecos Division. I told him I had been there 6 months before, riding 43, the California Fast Freight. The tears came into his eyes.

"Boy, put her there!" He told me then that the last trip he had made on the Santa Fe he had been flagging on 43. When his train started to pull out, he gripped my hand again. "This is a hell of a way car," he said, jerking his head at the lousy little boxcar on the rear end, which served as caboose.

"Not much like the Santa Fe," I called after him.

He shook his head disconsolately as he piled aboard. I can see him yet, hanging out of that side door and looking back. His train moved on into the jungle under one of those blood-red sunsets that every evening dip into the China Sea, and which always reminded me of fire, pestilence, and death.

The natives use the railroad as a main street and a highway, dodging off the track or climbing under bridges when a train comes along. They dried great quantities of rice on the ties, and once I saw about two dozen dogs being driven along the track. These dogs, I was told, are considered a great delicacy by some of the tribes, and this bunch was on the way to the pot.

Such is life in the Philippines.

Lieutenant Colonel Frank E. Russell was appointed Assistant General Manager of Stores of the 3rd Military Railway Service at Teheran, Iran, in April, 1945. In May of that year he made a tour of the European Theater to study landing setup of rolling stock in connection with invasion tactics. Later he was assigned to the Pacific as Assistant General Manager of Equipment to handle railroads in the Philippines in preparation for the invasion of Japan. In September, 1945, he was promoted to a full colonel and so became Director and General Manager of Military Railway Service.

A railroad writer searches out certain facts and then polishes them up, but no words of mine could so clearly illustrate the enormous task performed by the railroad troops as the factual record that follows.

This was jungle country. Bear that in mind. It was a land of heat and pestilence and death, but there was a job to do and American railroaders did it. And here I present the story of Colonel Russell and his men:

Military Railway Operations on Luzon

Reported by Frank E. Russell

The first railroad troops to land on the Islands of Luzon were the members of the 790th Railway Operating Company, who disembarked at Lingayen Gulf on January 14, 1945. They established camp on the Manila Railroad at San Fabian.

This organization, consisting of 4 officers and 139 enlisted men, was activated in New Caledonia and followed the invasion forces ashore, preparing the railroad for the hauling of supplies to support military operations.

Preliminary reconnaissance of the road was made and work on rehabilitation begun south of San Fabian on January 16. One steam locomotive and 22 cars were located near Dagupan. Emergency repairs were made, and the transportation of supplies began on January 22. These supplies consisted of gasoline, ammunitions, and rations, and they were moved from San Fabian and Dagupan to Bayambang, a distance of 27 miles.

The United States Army Engineers began work on reconstruction and repair of bridges, and the Maintenance Platoon of the 790th, together with civilian laborers, started restoration of the track. The Locomotive and Car Repair Platoon and civilian mechanics rehabilitated additional locomotives and cars. On the thirtieth of January supplies were being transported from San Fabian and Dagupan to Tarlac, a distance of 57 miles. The rolling stock at this time consisted of 83 cars, 4 road locomotives, and 5 switch engines. This equipment was picked up on the railroad or at sugar mills.

Two of the locomotives were oil-burners; the balance were fired with wood, coal being unavailable. Frequently it was necessary to tear down shacks along the road for fuel. Water was supplied by the bucket-brigade method.

The advanced echelon of the 775th Railway Grand Division arrived at Mangaldan on January 25. Immediately they began drawing plans for the rehabilitation and operation of the railroad. They rendered technical assistance to the 790th Railway Operating Company. The balance of the 775th Railway Grand Division landed at Lingayen Gulf the tenth of February.

The 775th Railway Grand Division assumed responsibility for the operation of the Luzon Military Railroad as of February 15, with the 790th Railway Operating Company attached as an operating unit. The Rail Highway Traffic Officers assigned to the Transportation Command handled all rail traffic problems.

Because of the shortage of railroad operating personnel, enlisted men and officers of the 775th Railway Grand Division and as many experienced railroad men as could be procured from other units in the vicinity were placed in service with the 790th Railway Operating Company. Former civilian employees were hired and placed on their old jobs as fast as they could be located. Rehabilitation of all railroad facilities continued at a rapid rate. An advance echelon of the 775th Division set up headquarters in Manila to organize the former railroad workers and to repair the rail facilities in the Manila-Caloocan area and on the line between Manila and San Fernando, Pampanga.

The 790th Railway Operating Company, working from the north end, soon had the railroad open for traffic as far south as San Fernando, Pampanga, and north to Alacan jetty.

371

The first U.S.A. rolling stock started to arrive late in February, and by the second of March one U.S.A. Diesel-electric switch engine and two U.S.A. steam locomotives of the 2-8-2 type were placed in service. During the month of March the work of restoring facilities and equipment continued. The San José Branch, consisting of 33.8 miles of track between Tarlac and San José, was opened to traffic. The main line from San Fernando to Manila was placed in operation, and General Mac-Arthur rode the first train into Manila Station on the fifteenth of March.

Reconnaissance south showed the right of way littered with damaged rolling stock. Numerous bridges had been demolished, and there had been many locomotives wrecked, together with demolition of various kinds. All stations north of Manila had been burned, and water and oil facilities destroyed. There were locomotives run into turntable pits, and the train yards were pock-marked with bomb craters.

The following railroad units arrived during March and were attached to the 775th Railway Grand Division:

> 737th Railway Operating Battalion
> 749th Railway Operating Battalion
> 131st TC Railway Workshop (Mobile)
> 132nd TC Railway Workshop (Mobile)
> 133rd TC Railway Workshop (Mobile)

Additional locomotives continued to arrive from the United States, and also freight cars. They were immediately assembled and placed in service.

On March 15, Headquarters of the 775th Railway Grand Division were established at Tutuban Station, Manila. The first troop train was operated on March 21. The 793rd Base Depot Company arrived during April and immediately took over the procurement of material and supplies for railroad operation.

During April work continued on railroad repair, and with the completion of the bridge over the Pasig River the line south of Manila to Santa Rosa was opened; also the Carmen Branch from San Fernando, Pampanga, to Del Carmen. The new tracks to the docks in the North Harbor at Manila were completed, and rolling stock from the United States was being unloaded at Manila.

During the month of May the main line was open north to San Fernando, La Union. Numerous improvements were being made; the main locomotive and car shops at Caloocan were being rehabilitated, and new air compressors, electric generators, and a steam engine to drive the overhead line shafting was installed. Army machine-tool equipment had arrived and was being installed in the various shops and enginehouses.

The assembly of U.S.A. locomotives and cars was completed during the month of June. The following U.S.A. equipment had at that time been placed in service:

43	2-8-2 steam locomotives
10	0-4-4-0 Diesel-electric locomotives (switchers)
100	30-ton box cars
100	5000-gallon tank cars
800	30-ton gondolas

Limited civilian passenger and freight traffic was inaugurated on the sixteenth of May.

The rehabilitation work continued through June and July, and many Manila Railroad employees were hired, and the various civilian road departments were set up. Plans were formulated to train civilian employees for the ultimate return of the railroad to civilian control.

On July 3 the 5250th Railway Shop Battalion (Prov) was organized and assigned to Caloocan Shop to assist in maintenance and repair of rolling stock.

With the cessation of hostilities in August and the possible necessity for railroad troops in Japan, the following railroad units were relieved from assignment with the Luzon Military Railroad and were staged for redeployment:

> 737th Railway Operating Battalion
> 790th Railway Operating Company
> 793rd Base Depot Company
> 131st TC Railway Workshop (Mobile)

Because of the loss of these units, it was necessary to start an immediate program to turn over the various parts of the operation to civilian employees under military supervision. During the latter part of August the operation and maintenance of the railroad, Tarlac and north, under military supervision, was turned over to the civilian employees.

Additional track was placed in service when the line was open south from Santa Rosa to College and from Calamba to Makiling. As of the end of August, there were 6,674 civilian employees on the road.

During September, the 753rd Railway Shop Battalion arrived from Europe and was assigned to Caloocan Shop.

Definite plans were made in September for the return of the railroad to its civilian owners. Steps were taken to complete the organization of the various railroad departments and train civilian employees.

The first of January, 1946, was set as the date for the return of the railroad to the civilian owners.

The way Colonel Russell has told it, you rather get the impression that it was just routine and as simple as performing a bit of railroading in the United States. I can assure you, after having been on the ground and observed conditions, that it was actually a far different story. Colonel Russell has not told you of the long heartbreaking hours, the enormous difficulties overcome, the unbelievably wretched conditions under which he and his men had to work. He has not once, in this terse military report, hinted at the toil and sweat and bodily torment involved in the reconstruction of the Luzon Railroad.

Men worked in the jungle's living hell—a green hell of insects and pit vipers and slime and muck, dust and dirt. The terrible humidity, the crushing heat, the interminable hours of backbreaking labor were enough to break the spirit of any man; but it couldn't whip these American railroad men. They cursed and growled at the Army, the Japs, the bugs, and all the rest—but they did the job.

They suffered from jungle fevers, skin diseases, and utter homesickness; but they rebuilt the Luzon Military Railroad, and they ran trains over it, hauling close to a million tons of military supplies, half a million military passengers, almost a million revenue passengers.

This is a list of net tons hauled:

NET TONS HAULED—PASSENGERS HAULED

February 15 to December 31, 1945

Month	Military Tonnage	Military Passengers	RR Emp. on Pass	Revenue Tonnage	Revenue Passengers
15 – 28					
February	12,047	—	—	—	—
March	43,645	6,060	—	—	—
April	64,041	13,001	111	—	939
May	94,945	20,538	24,136	680	9,620
June	115,049	48,543	28,853	2,222	32,267
July	147,454	77,502	34,359	2,956	54,458
August	115,058	65,660	35,370	2,360	70,936
September	119,185	165,124	30,255	2,371	78,113
October	90,005	78,697	34,486	3,602	134,349
November	62,279	51,910	30,844	5,387	225,950
December	34,688	19,816	30,909	5,353	307,525
TOTAL	898,396	546,851	249,323	24,931	914,157

And that, in a small way, is the story of the Luzon Military Railroad—from San Fernando, U., on the north to Mondagua to the southeast. It tells a little, but there is so much more that it does not tell. But whether he is railroading in Luzon or Texas, our hat is off to the American railroad man.

A final word concerning Frank E. Russell. He came up from the ranks to night roundhouse foreman, to machinist foreman, to supervisior of construction on the big cab-ahead Southern Pacific Articulateds at the Baldwin Locomotive Works, to master mechanic, to assistant superintendent of motive power. He served honorably and with distinction in the armed forces.

And as of March 1, 1946, following his release from the Military Railway Service, he became Superintendent of Motive Power at Sacramento on the Southern Pacific.

CHAPTER XXXIII

MILK FOR TEN MILLION

The New York Central Milk Service

Milk is the most vital of all commodities involved in rail transportation. It is the life-giving blood of the 10,000,000 people crowded into greater New York's metropolitan district.

The rattle of milk bottles and the clatter of cans has become so much a part of the city's awakening that the milkman making his rounds in the eerie dawn stirs only a sleepy protest from the householder, whose somnolent mutterings would quickly become a loud howl if the familiar milk bottle was not on the stoop beside the morning paper.

The city dweller, beyond a hazy notion that milk is in some way associated with a farmer and a cow, for the most part remains ignorant of the enormous effort and planning involved in the delivery of the milk bottle at his door. If told that the locomotive engineer on the New York Central was a milkman in reality, he no doubt would utter a hoot of derision. And yet it is the railroad and the man at the throttle upon whose shoulders rests the responsibility of delivering at New York Central terminals 4 solid trains, or about one-quarter of the milk delivered and consumed every 24 hours.

One million gallons of milk per day!

New York's milk shed covers a vast area, including the states of New York, Pennsylvania, New Jersey, Vermont, Connecticut, and Massachusetts. And the transportation of this milk has created a pretty sizable business in its own right. The Central's stake in this traffic, handled by its Milk Service Department, reaches a gross revenue of more than $2,000,000 annually.

Because of the enormous consumer market, milk must in

many cases be brought in from points more than 400 miles distant from New York City. The swift movement over these distances resolves itself into an important rail-haul problem for the carriers. Clanking cans start their journey from far-off rural communities, many of whose citizens have themselves never been to New York and yet who contribute a vital part to the life and health of this great metropolis and its swarming millions.

Hospitals, hotels, and restaurants create an enormous demand for the product of the humble cow, but it is the apartments, the tenements—the homes—that daily consume the greater part of the white flood flowing down the steel rail from the farming areas.

It is reported that the first known movement of milk by rail to New York occurred in 1842, when the New York & Erie brought 60 gallons from Orange County, New York, in a churn in the baggage car of a passenger train. Just why a churn was employed is not quite clear, but anyway the operation seems to have been a success, for subsequent shipments increased until the following year 1,000,000 gallons of milk rode into the New York market. The railroads soon were organized to handle the growing movement of milk.

Following the first churn delivery, milk was shipped in cans, varying in size from 5- to 15-gallon capacity. The railroads supplied insulated cars which were equipped for high-speed use in passenger trains. In the summer ice was placed around the cans to prevent souring.

As the city's population and the demand grew, solid milk trains were inaugurated for daily service. The first of these was operated by the New York, Ontario & Western on February 1, 1871.

The first tank car for milk was built in 1903. These early tank cars consisted of a glass-lined tank housed within an insulated car. Later tank cars had a stainless-steel inner tank, which was provided with insulation and a streamlined outer shell. A further development provided for the removal of the tank, as a matter of convenience, at the originating milk station and at the terminal in New York.

377

The tank car is a time- and labor-saver, eliminating the work of handling cans and the packing of the cars with ice. With the tank car precooled milk is pumped in at the milk stations at originating points and pumped direct to tank trucks at receiving terminals, from which point it is taken to pasteurizing plants. These tanks are owned by the National Fitch Corporation, subsidiary of the Fruit Growers Express. Their trucks pull alongside the car, and the tank is moved off the car onto a trailer by power from the truck's motor, which is kept idling. The milk is then taken wherever it is wanted.

This system has returned much milk business to the railroads, and will soon mean more. It is a great help both for the farmer in loading and the receiver in unloading. It is also a cleaner and cooler method. The National Fitch Corporation plans soon to have cars in service for hauling flour to bakeries.

About 73 per cent of the equipment used in the Central milk trains consists of tank cars, which number 150; the remainder are can cars. The tank cars, with a 6,000-gallon capacity, are privately owned. The can cars are owned by the railroad. All equipment is built for high-speed service.

Operated in solid trains, specially built and heavy "rider" cars carry the train crew.

Of the 4 solid milk trains moving into the metropolitan area daily, 3 carry milk from the counties along the Mohawk Valley and from counties north and west of the Adirondacks to the St. Lawrence and Lake Ontario; the fourth train, bringing milk from the Catskills, moves down the River Division (West Shore) from Kingston to Weehawken. The first 3 trains terminate in the 60th Street Milk Yard on the west side of Manhattan. The fourth train terminates in a special milk yard at Weehawken.

The milk traveling the greatest distance originates at stations along the Rutland Railroad, beginning at Lisbon, in upper New York, almost at the Canadian border. It rushes across the state, across the upper end of Lake Champlain, traveling south then through Burlington, Vermont, and back into New York, to be picked up by the Central at Chatham and sped on to Manhattan.

Other cars are picked up south of the Mohawk Valley by the Delaware & Hudson road and delivered to the Central at Albany.

Here they join ranks with others of the milk fleet and whirl down the Central's roaring main line to New York City.

The collection of milk from the most distant points begins at about 8 o'clock in the morning. Farmers make their deliveries to receiving stations on the railroad, where the milk is tested, weighed, and loaded into the cars, which have been spotted in the various sidings during the night.

The milk-car pickup moves from station to station by local trains, until a final assembly point has been reached. For the most part these milk cars travel in passenger trains.

The solid milk trains generally begin their runs to New York late in the afternoon, arriving during the night. They are promptly unloaded at the city terminals and soon begin their return trip to the distant collection point. Where possible, a 2-day cycle is established for each car.

The longest run of a milk car on the New York Central starts away up in St. Lawrence County at Massena, New York—410 miles from the 60th Street Milk Yard. Train No. 16 on the St. Lawrence Division originates here every morning at 7, running to Watertown, gathering in cars en route.

The start at Massena involves 1 car of milk cans. Another car is added at Norwood, a can car contributed to the milk move by the Norwood & St. Lawrence Railroad. A third can car is picked up at Potsdam. Then 1 or 2 tank cars are picked up at Canton, depending on the day's supply. At DeKalb there's a tank car off the DeKalb Branch from Heuvelton; at Gouverneur a can or a tank car; at Antwerp a cheese car; at Philadelphia a local tank car, plus another tank car from Douglas Crossing, and a can car from Lafargeville, off the Clayton Branch; at Evans Mills a can car. At Watertown a local tank car is picked up, in addition to another from Limerick and Cape Vincent, off the Cape Vincent Branch, and one from Black River.

These milk cars leave Watertown for Utica in Train No. 70, which carries 2 passenger coaches. It makes another milk collection at Richland. These cars at Richland were picked up by a Milk Extra out of Watertown at 8 a.m., some hours ahead of No. 70. This Milk Extra picks up a can car at Adams Center; 2 tank cars at Adams; 1 can car at Pierrepont Manor; 1 tank car at La-

379

cona. These cars are combined at Richland with 2 tank cars from the Oswego Branch at Pulaski.

It is like a snowball starting down a mountain, soon assuming the proportions of an avalanche—an avalanche of milk, building into 1,000,000 gallons.

Upon its arrival at Utica, train No. 70 is combined with Train No. 64. No 64 meanwhile has collected 10 milk cars from the Utica-Carthage Branch. It is on this Carthage Branch, at Boonville, that the demountable, or "slide-off," Fitch tank is used. Here a tractor and trailer unit moves the tanks from the car to West Leyden, 10 miles off the line, where they are loaded at a milk station conveniently placed for farmers' delivery. When filled, the tanks are returned to the rail siding at Boonville.

The combined train, Nos. 70 and 64, now becomes No. 184, which pulls out with still other cars added from St. Johnsville and Middleville. The leaving time is 5:05 p.m. No. 184 picks up the last car at Fort Plain and rushes on to Rensselaer with 34 cars of New York-bound milk. After changing crews at Rensselaer it goes booming through to New York City, pausing only at Harmon to change to electric power.

At Spuyten Duyvil 1 tank car is dropped for the Bronx Terminal Market. The next stop is at the 130th Street Milk Yard on the West Side to drop cars billed to this point. The Milk Run is done with the arrival of the train at the 60th Street Milk Yard, where approximately 50 per cent of the cars are delivered at 11:30 p.m.

A second milk train originates as train No. 188 at Syracuse at 8:41 in the morning. It runs over the West Shore, picking up 5 or 6 milk cars in addition to some freight work, between Syracuse and Albany.

These milk cars are combined in the Rensselaer Yard to make No. 182, which hauls milk cars collected by the Delaware & Hudson from as far west as Harpursville and as far north as West Chazy. With an average of 20 cars it makes its daily run down the Hudson Division to pull into the 60th Street Terminal at 12:20 a.m.

The Rutland train, which we have mentioned, originates at Ogdensburg, New York, and, starting with the first car at Lisbon, builds up to a train of 20 cars by the time it turns the milk over to the Central at Chatham. It then moves down the Harlem Division, crossing over the wye at the Mott Haven Yard to drop 1 car at the Bronx Terminal Market. It drops more cars at 130th Street and arrives at 60th Street at 3:20 a.m.

The fourth milk train originates as No. 528 on the Catskill Mountain Branch of the West Shore at Oneonta. No. 528 provides passenger service between Oneonta and Kingston as it picks up 7 to 8 milk cars on the way. Out of Kingston it operates as a Milk Extra to the Weehawken Milk Yard, arriving at 8 a.m. At this point the cars are unloaded to milk trucks, which cross the 42nd Street Ferry en route to the pasteurizing plants in New York City.

These 4 trains account for all but 5 cars, which are loaded at points off the regular runs. These move into the city in regular passenger trains. These cars are cut off at Harmon for West Side movement to the 60th Street Yard.

With the reverse movement, the first empty milk cars leave Weehawken at 1 a.m. Cars for Syracuse leave 60th Street as No. 793 at 2:45 a.m. The next train returning cars leaves as No. 183 for the Delaware & Hudson at 5:30. The empties for the St. Lawrence Division and points west of Utica depart as No. 185 at 8:30 a.m. The last empties are those for the Rutland connections, leaving 60th Street at 1 p.m.

During the summer months can cars are stocked with ice at Richland and Carthage before being spotted at milk station sidings. The Milk Service Department of the New York Central cuts and stores some 14,000 tons of ice each winter. Of this about half is required for the icing of milk cars during the summer.

No. 8, of the Erie, serving Newark and northern New Jersey, through the efficient Alderney Dairies, is another fine milk train. That dairy handles an average of 16 tank cars a day. It also has cars for Brooklyn and New York City.

Lehigh Valley No. 36 and Delaware, Lackawanna & Western's No. 44 are other crack milk trains running into Hoboken and Jersey City, serving Brooklyn as well as Manhattan. Trucks have made a severe dent in the milk haul of the Lackawanna, which at one time operated 3 milk trains. These cars are returned solid by these 2 roads the next morning as trains 37 and 47 respectively.

The truck, with no right of way to support and maintain, has the advantage of direct haul over state highways from the country milk station to the distributing point in the metropolitan area. However, on the long haul, and in the keenly competitive postwar era of modern transportation, the railway milk run will offer the shipper an increasingly fast and dependable service.

The railroads that so ably served America in wartime will as ably continue their peacetime partnership with the nation if given the opportunity.

New Pacemaker Fast Freight

The first completely standardized fast-freight boxcars in the United States made their bow on the New York Central in May, 1946. They paraded in all of their spanking newness and colorful splendor on the New York–Buffalo run, inaugurating the Central's Pacemaker Fast Freight Service and establishing the first step in a brilliant postwar program of superservice for shippers.

To say that the Pacemaker "sparkles" is an understatement, for this new kind of a fast freight is as pretty as a spring sunrise, as clean-looking as hills after a rain, and as bright-hued as a rainbow. Every car is identically the same, in shape, size, and color scheme.

The upper halves of the cars and doors are painted vermilion; the lower halves are dark gray. Roofs, underframes, and trucks are black, and all lettering is white.

The New York Central's Pacemaker—NB1 and BN2—is at once a challenger and crusader, and it marks the dawn of a new railroad era. We have repeatedly stressed the fact that fast freight service in America is on the way to setting the rails afire, and these statements are borne out by the unveiling of this speed merchant of the Central.

The Pacemaker Fast Freight Service operates dawn-to-dusk trains, daily except Sundays and holidays, in both directions between New York City and the Niagara frontier, where connections will be made to and from other cities on the system.

A pool of 425 cars was made available upon the inauguration of this fast freight service, and 575 are being added as the service expands. These cars are from the Despatch Shops, Inc., East Rochester, New York.

There was a time when a boxcar was a hobo, traveling on many roads in many places and never too particular about the company it kept. It grew increasingly disreputable in appearance, and it developed ailments, and its passing plaints were many. But the cars of the Pacemaker Freight Service are of a different breed to begin with, and they will be reserved for the high-speed service for which they are designed.

The standardization of boxcars has been a matter for considerable thought by railroad men for a long time, but it has never quite made the hurdle, for various reasons. However, the New York Central perhaps has started a trend, and we can look for other roads to come up with a car of like specifications for service on manifest runs between terminals along their lines.

Car designers and coupling manufacturers some time ago took the slack jerk out of the modern passenger coach, and now they are eliminating it from boxcars. Of course, without slack the mile-long freight train became an immovable body. The steam locomotive, in starting, bunched the slack and went about the matter of getting under way, you might say, by starting one car at a time, until at last the caboose joined the parade by making a prodigious leap which practically unjointed the vertebrae of the hapless occupants. These lunging starts did the lading no good, often wrenching pained shrieks from the consignee.

This bunch-and-jerk method has largely been eliminated in the cars of the Pacemaker through the application of Waughmat Twin-Cushion, double-acting, rubber draft gears.

All the boxcars of these new trains are equipped with Barber high-speed freight-service trucks, having built-in stabilizers and bolster lateral-motion device. Special brake equipment is used. This is known as the AB-1-B type, and was designed specially for high-speed freight service. All cars have one-wear, rolled

383

steel wheels. They are of modern steel-sheathed, wood-lined design and have a marked load limit capacity of 50,000 pounds.

The cabooses have Barber-Bettendoft swing-motion trucks, and also are equipped with the Waughmat Twin-Cushion draft gears for smooth and cushioned action. And this innovation is indeed a far cry from the not-so-good old days when it was no trick at all to catapult a brakeman through the rear window of a caboose.

The word hot-shot has variously been applied to fast trains of any sort, and particularly to fast freights. The New York Central's NB1 and BN2 is a hot-shot in every sense of the word. It has an authorized speed limit of 65 miles an hour with 75 cars or less. It will blaze over the 429 miles between New York City and Buffalo in 10 hours and 50 minutes. This elapsed time will include stops to pick up and drop cars at Albany, Utica, Syracuse, and Rochester. And that is fast freight service.

In the opening chapter we reviewed a typical fast freight run of 424 miles, for an average of 40 miles an hour. Our Seaboard Dispatch, however, was a lighter train for the reason that heavy grades were encountered over portions of the run.

The average speed of the Pacemaker freights will be 39.6 miles per hour, including all stops. Twenty-five tons per car is the limit.

The motive power of the Pacemaker will be the famous L-4 Mohawks, the Central's road name for the 4-8-2 Mountain type locomotive. The Mohawk, 5-400-horsepower, was developed by the New York Central Equipment Engineering Department for both fast passenger and fast freight service over its Water Level Route. The Mohawk paved the way for the development of the Central's new and mighty 6,000-horsepower Niagara, which we reviewed in Chapter VII.

Tracing the westward run of NB1, the train leaves St. Johns Park Freight Terminal in New York City at 7 p.m. It pulls out of the 33rd Street Yard at 8 p.m. The 33rd Street Yard is the final make-up and departure point of the Pacemaker.

NB1, its colorful cars rolling behind the roaring Mohawk locomotive, moves swiftly up the Hudson Valley on passenger express train schedule. It arrives at Rensselaer (Albany) at

11:20 p.m., departing at 11:30. It reaches Utica at 1:35 a.m. and leaves at 2:10. Syracuse, in at 3:10 and out at 3:30. It pulls into Rochester at 5:05 and departs at 5:20. It arrives at Buffalo at 6:50 in the morning. NB1 then moves on from Buffalo to Black Rock, reaching there at 7:25, finally to take down its markers at Niagara Falls at 7:50 a.m.

Niagara Falls is the originating point of BN2, eastbound.

This Pacemaker Fast Freight Service will possibly have been extended to Chicago before this appears, with its vivid vermilion and gray fleets swiftly spanning the miles between the great metropolitan centers of New York and Chicago with Dunkirk, Erie, Cleveland, Toledo, South Bend, and other great cities of trade benefited.

Certainly the Pacemaker was rightly named, for it is a pioneer in an age when fast freight is rapidly forging to the front as the railroads' contribution to a greater America.

CHAPTER XXXIV

SANTA FE WHEAT BIN

The Battle of the Wheat Trains

Wheat, aside from being the staff of life, can be a tremendous headache, particularly to a railroad when the grain rush is on. The Santa Fe, which handles a large share of the nation's annual wheat crop in the form of grain, flour, or feed, has made an extensive study of new methods and techniques for expediting grain movements.

The bulk of the Santa Fe boxcars employed in the wheat movement are specially built, for to prevent damage to flour and feed cargoes, they must be moistureproof. Keeping these grain cars on line for its own use has been a problem with which the Santa Fe has had to cope for a good many years. Frequently when grain arrives at a terminal the cars are transferred to elevators on other lines. Then when they are unloaded they often are diverted to destinations off line.

To meet this situation, the Santa Fe erected its own elevator at Kansas City. The first section of this elevator was built as far back as 1904. It was enlarged in 1915 and again in 1925, and today it will house 10,500,000 bushels of grain—the largest elevator under one head house in the world.

However, when the war came along even this great elevator could not remedy the mounting troubles on the line and at the wheat-country elevators in the grain belt. When the wheat begins to move it comes in an enormous golden flood, and to care for and confine it railroaders have to strain and stretch and improvise. And if you see a man pacing up and down the track in the vicinity of a grain elevator in Kansas and counting on his fingers, it is safe to assume that he is confronted with the job of promptly moving many more carloads of grain than there are cars for.

Just any old wandering boxcar will not do, though it may be seized upon in a pinch. Most boxcars not built to handle wheat require a lot of work to get them in shape. Rough-merchandise cars from other lines, when and if they are available, need a lot of coopering and patching, and some have to be paper lined— all requiring materials, manpower, and time. In the meantime the grain continues to pour in.

The cry was raised that people were starving, and the railroads with a lot of cars worn out from hauling war cargoes, and denied the chance to buy new cars, were left holding the bag. It is fashionable, when things reach an impasse, to blame the railroads. Then the buck-passers and the GAIC boys—the "Gosh am I confused" crowd—rear back and give it to the poor old Iron Horse with both barrels. And what does the railroad do? If the railroad stops, everything stops; so the railroad simply takes another hitch at its pants and continues to do the impossible.

During the war considerable public and political pressure was directed against the railroads in an effort to place the blame for failure to move the staggering wheat tonnage of 1944–45. Wheat bins were bulging, elevators were overflowing, and all through the wheat-growing country grain was piled on the ground—and there were just not enough boxcars. Given the cars, the Santa Fe and all the other roads could have handled the wheat, and more.

The Santa Fe, at a time when it needed all of its cars which had been designed for the grain move, could not get them. They were scattered from Maine to California, hauling everything but wheat, and if they had come home, many of them would have required a lot of work to get them in shape.

However, the Santa Fe did have a small surplus of hopper-bottom cars and some ballast cars on the Western Division at Dodge City. Some Santa Fe man cast an appraising eye that way. Hopper cars?

Santa Fe men put their heads together. "How about using those hoppers? They'll hold wheat."

"What if it rains?" someone said glumly.

Another said, "The wheat would blow out of those open cars like nobody's business."

It was suggested that the wheat might as well blow away as rot on the ground, and so the experiment was begun—an experiment that may revolutionize old methods as they concern the hauling of wheat to market.

The Santa Fe people approached the hopper idea with their fingers crossed. One of the first obstacles that presented itself was the fact that receiving elevators were not equipped to unload hopper cars. Boxcars, yes—but not gondolas. However, an elevator operator was found who was willing to co-operate. He took a chance and installed a grain dump for handling wheat from hopper cars. And that obstacle was conquered.

Other elevator operators were skeptical, and they stood back and watched the experiment, apparently of the opinion that the whole thing would flop with a dull thud.

The hopper cars were cleaned up, loaded with yellow wheat and started on their way, for better or for worse. The funny part of it was that the scheme worked. It didn't rain, and the wheat did not blow away. Not only was the loss and damage slight, but the new method of unloading proved to be a great time- and labor-saver.

Other elevator operators climbed off the fence, expressing a willingness to receive grain in hopper cars. The result was that a fleet of this type of equipment was assembled for the 1945 harvest, and the railroads had licked another major problem in the transportation field.

The bulk of America's hard winter wheat is produced on that vast expanse of semiarid plains that gradually slope upward from the Missouri River and roll westward to the Rockies. This is the breadbasket that not only feeds the people of the United States, but also contributes a large loaf to the population of Europe in times of want.

The wheat harvest in this area has grown from a thin golden trickle, spread from June to November, to a deluge that is ready for market in a tight span of 3-4 weeks. Better to present the case of the railroads, I will briefly review the history of wheat. In the meantime, let's keep in mind that just one of the roads that serve this titanic wheat bin hauls annually as much as 100,000,000 bushels, or more than 70,000 carloads, and this does not include wheat products. The railroad we have chosen as a gauge for this wheat move is the Santa Fe.

The growing of wheat began with the westward expansion—the movement of settlers from the East. This gradual flow of population by 1825 had reached the Mississippi. By 1850 it stood at the banks of the Missouri. The movement from this point was in a large measure due to the opening of the prairies, which were easily brought under cultivation.

From the day the sodbuster first broke the land with the furrow that plowed under the cattle trails, to and through World War II, including the postwar era, the movement of wheat has grown from a weak infant to a lusty giant in the economic scheme of things.

The yellow fields of wheat, scattered here and there over the prairies, were first cradled, or cut, by hand. The wheat was tied into sheaves, placed in shocks, and allowed to cure; then it was threshed, sacked, and hauled to market. Some of this wheat was ready for market in July. The cradling and threshing continued on through July and into August and September and October, even into November. There were years of bumper crops, years of crop failures, but the planting of wheat continued to increase.

Came the development of farm machinery and the introduction of the McCormick Reaper, which came into use about 1860. Drawn by 2 horses, it could do the work of 20 men using the cradle. The reaper was followed by the self-binder, which both cut the grain and bound it into sheaves. More horses were required to operate it; more wheat was harvested in less time. This self-binder gave way to the steam-driven thresher. A steam-driven gang plow made possible the breaking of 35-45 acres of ground a day, as it turned 12 furrows at a time.

Wheat raising advanced in strong stride, and the professor took a hand. Agriculture went to college, and scientific principles were applied to wheat growing. Through a greater knowledge of soil conditions, climatic hazards were reduced. There were fewer crop failures as hardier wheat was developed at the agricultural experimental stations. More acreage went into wheat.

The harvest period was shortened through the use of the combine harvester, which cut, threshed, cleaned, and measured the wheat and put it into sacks. With a crew of 4 men the combine could harvest and sack 3,000 bushels in a day.

Already grain elevators had sprung up at stations along the railroads. Here the wheat was stored as it awaited shipment. Before the wheat harvest got under way, the Santa Fe and other railroads in America's great wheat bin began assembling empty boxcars from all parts of the country. These cars shuttled back and forth between shipping points and the great wheat terminals at a speed limited only by the inspection and unloading facilities at the terminals.

The railroads and the shippers, working in close co-operation, were just about able to keep pace with the ever-increasing tempo of the harvest, but they did keep pace through an efficiency born of long experience. And then suddenly a cloud appeared on the horizon of the wheat belt. Like a prairie thunderstorm, it boomed up out of a clear sky. For a time it looked as though it might be just a passing squall, but black war clouds merged with these economic thunderheads—clouds crisscrossed by gun flashes and the boom of cannon—and chaos threatened.

When the Commodity Credit Corporation came into being, the wheat surplus was carried over from one harvest to the next. This surplus wheat went into storage at terminals and sub-terminals, but when the next harvest season came along the railroads were faced with the job of moving thousands of cars of stored wheat to tidewater terminals and at the same time transporting the crop then in the process of being harvested. It proved a superhuman task, but the shippers and the railroads, working hand in hand, performed an all-time miracle. Cars were rushed into this vast wheat bin from north, south, east, and west, and the big rush was on.

But when the wartime industrial production hit its stride, the railroads and the shippers found themselves in real trouble—trouble that made the previous mad scramble seem like a picnic. Suddenly a car shortage loomed. In addition, there was a shortage of wheat storage space and outdoor wheat piles sprang up, pending the day the wheat could be absorbed by the country's markets. Canada, too, was crying for cars to move its own wheat crop, and the hard-pressed American railroads supplied our neighbor to the north with 250 cars a day, at the same time keeping a worried eye on those growing wheat piles and the weather. Happily, there was little deterioration because of a normally dry climate throughout western Kansas, Oklahoma, and Texas, where most of this wheat was awaiting cars.

Most present-day wheat growers own their own combines and do not, as they once did, have to wait for the arrival of a threshing machine in their neighborhood. Dozens of combines will be at work in the same area at the same time, while fleets of trucks rush the grain from the fields to the nearest elevator. The wheat rolls in in a growing flood—moving to elevators built to handle grain at the threshing-machine tempo instead of the present-day combine speed.

In addition to its limited storage capacity, the average elevator is located on a side track in proximity to that of a competitor or competitors. Frequently but 2 or 3 cars can be spotted for loading at one time, and when the rush gets under way there is a delay caused by the necessity of waiting for a local freight to switch out the loads and spot empty cars. The railroads have met this situation by operating extra trains to service these local elevators. However, under war and postwar conditions, it was next to impossible to get the crews and equipment to operate enough of these extra trains to keep pace with the demand during the short harvest season.

Few wheat growers have facilities for the storing of grain in an amount that will permit a gradual marketing of the crop. In fact, many wheat growers in the West and Southwest have no facilities whatsoever, as the operator lives in town and his acreage is without buildings of any kind. The result has been the railroads have been called upon to forward freight cars from all over the country in a frantic effort to keep pace with the deluge and haul the wheat to elevators at wheat terminals.

The markets and the mills naturally are not equipped to receive and unload wheat in such volume, with the result that serious congestion has developed. Often side tracks as much as 100 miles from terminals have been jammed with loaded wheat cars awaiting their turn at unloading elevators.

Of late years the flour milling industry has extended its facilities into the wheat belt, and milling centers have sprung up at Wichita, Hutchinson, Salina, Dodge City, Kansas; and at Enid, Oklahoma; Amarillo, Texas; and other points. These centers are constantly enlarging their storage capacity in an effort to relieve the annual harvest overflow.

At the same time another factor has entered the picture which lessens the advantages gained. Farmers, seeking to increase their production, are growing types of wheat of poor milling quality; and western millers, specializing in bread flour, are forced to import the high-grade type of grain they require from distant points, while the locally produced wheat is hauled elsewhere to be used in making macaroni and pastry flour. This involves a double haul and a triple handling, further complicating the wheat movement from farm to market.

Now let's go back to those Santa Fe hopper cars.

The Santa Fe, during the war emergency, moved wheat in those open-top cars all the way from Kansas elevators to the Gulf of Mexico, where it was dumped into the holds of ships for export. Taking the bull by the horns at a time when rail transport was engaged in the greatest battle of all time, the Santa Fe met and whipped a situation that seemed close to getting out of hand.

A long time ago the Santa Fe proved that where there is a will there is a (rail) way, and there could be no better example than that of a veteran wheat-hauling road moving grain in hopper cars. As we pointed out in connection with the potato industry, the railroad and farmer are united in a business partnership, each dependent on the other, and none are more aware of their responsibilities and obligations than the men of the Santa Fe.

Santa Fe men pressed idle stock cars into service along with the hopper cars. They grabbed empty refrigerator cars and old boxcars, made them usable, loaded them with wheat, and started them down the rails with grain for Europe's starving millions.

Workmen slatted and lined the stock cars with paper, and the wheat tonnage mounted. In 1944, 147,138 wheat cars rolled on the Santa Fe. In 1945 there were 164,946 carloads of wheat rushing to wheat terminals. To accomplish this enormous grain move, the Santa Fe used, in addition to box and refrigerator cars, 1,175 open-top hopper cars, 275 covered hoppers, and 796 stock cars—all reconditioned under the urge of necessity for the job that was to be done.

The Santa Fe, planning for the future, applied old steel box-car tops to the hoppers and sent them hurrying south to Gulf ports—a grimy, clanking caravan of hopper cars, joining rank with all of the others in the greatest wheat rush in Santa Fe history.

This record wheat move was under the supervision and personal direction of 3 crack railroad men, George H. Minchin, Operating Vice-President, G. C. Jefferis, General Manager of the western lines, and H. B. Lautz, of the eastern lines, who proved their mettle in the Battle of the Wheat Trains.

The Crucible of Men and Locomotives

Santa Fe men of iron will carved a railroad empire out of the raw frontier, and a great system spread its network across the West. Tried in the crucible of the wilderness and hardened under fire, these men built a trail carved in burnished silver across the mountains and the plains.

The railroad builders perhaps did not know it then, but they were molding tradition—the tradition of Santa Fe men. And down the years other Santa Fe railroaders have manned the trains—the Chief and the Scout and the El Capitan; the oil trains and the wheat trains and the Green Fruit Express—the trumpeting calls of their big steam and Diesel engines echoing triumphantly through the passes of Raton and the Arizona Divide and El Cajon.

From the trackman on the high mesas to men in the Business Car, the railroaders of the Santa Fe have served the farmer and the industrialist and the nation. The Santa Fe and all the other American railroads, a few of which it has been my privilege to review in a small way in this book, have contributed always to the greater glory of our country. And they stand today on the threshold of a bright new transportation era.

I can think of no better way to pay tribute to the railroad and the railroad man than to lift the curtain on a test run of a railroad locomotive, which to me seems to symbolize the baptism of fire through which a man, a machine, or a railway system must pass before the words "well done" signal its acceptance by those to whom it will render service.

I give you the story of engine No. 5011. The 5011 and Cardy Hill.

In general appearance and outline, the 5011 is very much like the Santa Fe's famous 3785-class and their later 2900's, both 4-8-4's. It is not until your eye, after running down the great barrel of the boiler, notes the wheel arrangement that you become aware that this brawny giant is a 2-10-4 freight hauler. A 5011 class.

This Santa Fe 2-10-4, or Texas type, was built primarily for service on the tough Pecos Division, but this last batch won their spurs on the First District of the Missouri Division, when, after test runs over various districts and divisions, they threw it at Cardy Hill. The 5011 and 89 loaded tank cars—5,004 tons—on the train they call CUX.

The CUX hauls oil from Cushing, Oklahoma, in solid tank trains, and the going is tough. When the 5011 thundered at Cardy Hill that fourteenth of June, 1944, she was working steam at full throttle, and her exhaust was blasting hard. The weather was clear, the rail dry, making for almost perfect conditions; and yet there was a kind of grim tenseness in the cab, a tension reflected in the faces in the way car, 89 cars behind the roaring locomotive, for this was Test Run No. 10, and they were sending the 5011 against Cardy Hill.

Cardy Hill is near Marceline, Missouri. The realignment work recently completed there is another reason why they're rolling 'em faster on the Santa Fe. With the straightening of the curves on Cardy Hill, freights were able to get a 6-mile running start for the climb out of the valley of the Chariton River. Freight drags now easily handle 200 to 300 more tons per train over the hump, and with a saving in time. In the old days heavily loaded freights often stalled on Cardy, making it necessary to "double" the hill, which means cut the trains in two. This slowed down schedules of both freight and passenger trains.

Coupled in behind the 5011 was the Dynamometer Car No. 29, staffed with coldly scientific test engineers. They were taking her temperature, her pulse, her blood pressure. Their stethoscopes were on her heart, her lungs. They were checking her reflexes, measuring the strength of her in tractive effort and drawbar pull. The locomotive dietician was measuring her fuel consumption; the chart operator was watching those automatic pens that record speed, distance, steam pressure, and all the rest of it. Santa Fe scientists had the 5011 in a test tube and were measuring her ability to stand up under fire, to take it.

When she hit the bottom of the hill, the 5011 was giving everything she had. She came out of the sag, a roaring avalanche of iron and steel, her 74-inch drivers biting savagely at the rail. She threw herself at Cardy Hill, feeling the first stubborn thrust of the lifting grade, the heavy hand of those 5,004 tons like a giant's clutching fist at her drawbar. Power was exploding in the 30-inch x 34-inch cylinders, the power that strained to overcome the 19,000,000 foot-pounds of drag. The side rods fought to keep the drivers turning, to beat back those swiftly building forces called inertia.

Every inch of the 5011 is a battleground. The boiler, carrying a working pressure of 310 pounds, shackles a seething volcano —310 pounds of pent-up force to the square inch, seeking to escape at every seam. Tubes and stay bolts and mud ring fighting back.

Flame at white heat roars against the flash wall. The 249 3½-inch tubes are livid barrels of fire. The smokebox is an inferno; the stack a hot cannon's mouth, hurling its blast at the sky. The 5011 rocks and sways, a panting, furious giant charging Cardy Hill.

The big freight hauler has come storming onto the grade at 56 miles an hour, with 5,004 tons. This is the battle line. The 5011 and Cardy Hill. Cardy Summit, taunting in the distance. Cardy Hill was there before the 5011, before the Santa Fe, before the covered wagons rolled west. But men had conquered it, and now a locomotive—a rookie—was fighting it out there, with Cardy Hill and 89 slogging tankers arrayed against the 5011.

Men in the cab and the distant way car watched the contest, tight-lipped, straining unconsciously in support of the 5011's mighty effort. The test crew hung over their instruments and their charts, reading the story in the making—stolid scientists concerned only with facts and figures.

Page after page of reports and diagrams were piling up for Test Report No. 87542—"Performance of Locomotive No. 5011" —59 pages of "road profile," closely written data, of "power performance curves" before the final signature of the Santa Fe Engineer of Tests.

The speed began to drop—50 miles an hour; 45 now; 40. The grade was .87 per cent. The momentum that had given the 5011 her start was swiftly being absorbed by the grade and the drag. Thirty miles an hour. The big freight hauler was slugging it out with the tonnage and the hill.

At 42 minutes and 55 seconds past 7 a.m. the 5011 had started moving back in the yards at Marceline, Missouri. At 7-46-50 she passed Marceline station. At 7-57-40, by the engineers' timing, there in the Dynamometer Car, the train had passed Bucklin. Elmer, 8-21-20. Cardy was ahead. The exhaust of the 5011 had settled to a steady thundering chant. The tension in the cab and the way car had eased; the 5011 was close to the summit—shouting her defiance at Cardy Hill.

At 8-29-55 the 5011 blasted past Cardy. The instruments in the Dynamometer Car registered 23 miles per hour, with 68,000 pounds drawbar pull. There was a stop of 5 minutes at Baring for water, and the 5011 started her train again.

Train CUX pulled into Shopton, Iowa, at 10-41-00. From the time the oil train had passed Marceline station to the end of the 112.2-mile run, the running time had been 2 hours and 53 minutes. With 5 minutes dead time, the time was 2 hours and

58 minutes. The engine had consumed 24,370 gallons of water, 2,150 gallons of fuel oil.

The 5011 had earned her right to a place on the roaring main line. Two hours and 58 minutes elapsed time for a fraction over 112 miles with 5,004 tons is something for the book.

But it was not all for the 5011. There were still Test Runs 11 and 12 and 13. The big 2-10-4, on Run 11, hauled 121 cars—38 loads and 83 empties—3,861 tons—from Shopton to Marceline—112 miles—with a running time of 3 hours and 16 minutes. She rolled on to Argentine Yard in Kansas—107.6 miles—with a running time of 4 hours and 11 minutes.

On Test Run 12, the 5011 pulled 94 cars—93 loads and 1 empty, 5,426 tons, Argentine to Marceline—in 4 hours and 46 minutes.

The time on Run 11 included taking water twice, servicing of the locomotive at Marceline, and the change of crew and way car, air pulled from the rear because of brakes sticking, a red block, and two "red pots."

On Run 12 there were several stops for a red block, dead time picking up and dropping a helper, and waits for Nos. 2 and 12, the Scout and the Chicagoan. The helper was used through the Kansas City terminal.

Test Run 13 was from Shopton, Iowa, to Argentine Yard, Kansas, and involved a crew change, servicing locomotive, taking water, a number of red blocks, and several waits. At 9:50 on the evening of June 16, 1944, the test runs ended. The 5011-class, when all of the Dynamometer Car reports were checked and tabulated, was ready for regular road assignment.

The tonnage rating of these 2-10-4's had been established, and the 5011-class found work cut out for them on the tough Pecos Division, over which passes the greater proportion of the Santa Fe's transcontinental freight tonnage.

At the time of her initial road test, the 5011 had approximately 500 miles of service to her credit. Test equipment was applied at the Topeka shops, and break-in trips were made between Topeka and Argentine.

Dynamometer Car 29 recorded drawbar pull, speed, air-brake pressure, Foam-Meter operation, time of starting, stopping, and passing stations, as well as locations at which Dynamometer Car and locomotive cab instruments were read. The amount of water and fuel oil used was measured, and the quantity of condensate delivered to boiler from feed-water heater was calculated.

Test equipment located in the locomotive cab, from which observations were recorded on charts in the Dynamometer Car through telephone communication, made recordings of boiler pressure, valve, chest, and back pressure, position of throttle and reverse lever, superheated and exhaust steam temperature, and height of water in boiler-gauge glass. The cab observer also kept a record of temperature of oil in tank and to burner, feed-water temperature, and duration of pops.

These new 5011's, like their famous Texas-type predecessors, have 74-inch driving wheels, the only 10-coupled engines having drivers over 70 inches, and they are equipped with the longest 1-piece engine beds ever built.

A great engine, the 5011, and doing a great job on the Santa Fe—"West of the Pecos." I have ridden a number of engine tests and followed many more, but that 23 miles an hour at the top of Cardy Hill was really something with that train.

I rather like to think this work-horse locomotive possesses the salient characteristics of railroad men in general and Santa Fe men in particular—men who do not know the meaning of the word "quit." The kind of men who fought and won the Battle of the Wheat Trains.

DRAG TONNAGE RATING FOR 5011 CLASS
PECOS DIVISION
Belen—Clovis

Eastbound		Westbound	
Tons	Cars	Tons	Cars
Without Helper			
3,070	60	4,840	80
3,020	70	4,750	90
2,970	80	4,660	100
2,920	90	4,570	110
		4,480	120
		4,390	130

With Helper [1]

6,250	100
6,200	110
6,150	120
6,100	130
6,050	140
6,000	150

[1] With 5001—5011 Class Helper, Belen to Mountainair.

REPORT OF TEST 87342

(Performance of Locomotive 5011)

Power Performance

	Drawbar Pull, Pounds			Drawbar Horsepower		
Speed	5011 Class	5001 Class	Diesel 100 Class	5011 Class	5001 Class	Diesel 100 Class
0	105,200	105,500	230,975	0	0	0
5	101,100	94,500	—	1,350	1,260	—
10	95,500	91,200	—	2,540	2,430	—
13	91,500	88,900	134,100	3,170	3,080	4,650
15	88,400	87,500	117,750	3,540	3,500	4,710
20	80,100	81,400	90,400	4,270	4,340	4,820
25	72,500	72,000	73,500	4,830	4,800	4,900
30	65,900	63,800	62,100	5,260	5,100	4,970
35	59,200	57,000	53,900	5,530	5,260	5,030
40	53,100	49,800	47,250	5,660	5,310	5,040
45	47,000	44,200	41,750	5,630	5,300	5,010
50	41,000	39,600	37,200	5,450	5,280	4,960
55	35,200	35,800	33,300	5,150	5,250	4,890
60	29,400	32,000	30,100	4,700	5,120	4,810
65	—	—	27,200	—	—	4,720

The drawbar pull for Locomotive 5011 at speeds above 50 m.p.h. is actual maximum values obtained in test, but not necessarily maximum performance because opportunities for running at speeds above 50 m.p.h. were limited.

CHAPTER XXXV

SEE AMERICA BY RAIL

Through Coast-to-Coast Service

On March 31, 1946, the American railroads drove another gold spike. The rails were joined, and for the first time the transcontinental traveler could go through without changing cars at Chicago Junction.

If anything else was needed to prove that the railroads were out to provide America with the last word in rail transportation, that did it. It supplied the finishing touch to the blazing of a postwar trail of modern rail travel that is as far ahead of anything that has gone before as the first passenger coach was superior to the stage coach.

The tracks have been tailored, the motive power groomed, the coaches and sleepers lavishly dressed, and all the brasswork polished—and the line forms on the right.

Now we find the new service in operation, and we are going to run down the list of trains and railroads that have made this service possible.

Sleeping cars are operated daily in both directions between New York and Los Angeles, via the New York Central Railroad between New York and Chicago and the Santa Fe between Chicago and Los Angeles; also via the Pennsylvania Railroad between New York and Chicago and the Santa Fe between Chicago and Los Angeles. The service east of Chicago is carried in the New York Central's Twentieth Century Limited and in the Pennsylvania's Broadway Limited; west of Chicago the cars are operated in the Santa Fe's Chief. Through Pullman service without change has also been established between Washington and Los Angeles in the Baltimore & Ohio's Capitol Limited between Washington and Chicago and the Santa Fe's Chief between Chicago and Los Angeles.

Sleeping-car service between New York and Los Angeles, in connection with the Chicago & North Western and Union Pacific Railroads west of Chicago, is also operated daily over the Pennsylvania Railroad and New York Central Lines. Westbound, this service is carried in the Pennsylvania's General, No. 49, and the Central's No. 67, the Commodore Vanderbilt, New York to Chicago; and the Chicago & North Western–Union Pacific's Transcontinental, Chicago to Los Angeles. Eastbound, the service is operated in the Union Pacific–North Western's Transcontinental, Los Angeles to Chicago; and in the New York Central's Commodore Vanderbilt, No. 68, and the Pennsylvania's General, No. 48, Chicago to New York.

New York and San Francisco daily through sleeping-car service in both directions is also operated without change, via the New York Central and Pennsylvania railroads, east of Chicago, in connection with Chicago & North Western, Union Pacific, and Southern Pacific railroads. Westbound sleeping cars are carried in New York Central's No. 19, the Lake Shore Limited, and the Pennsylvania's Manhattan Limited, No. 23, New York to Chicago, and from Chicago to San Francisco in the San Francisco Overland Limited, No. 27, of the Chicago & North Western, Union Pacific, and Southern Pacific roads. Eastbound, the service is operated in the San Francisco Overland Limited from San Francisco to Chicago and the Pennsylvania Railroad's Pennsylvanian, No. 78, and the New York Central's No. 64, the Water Level Limited, from Chicago to New York.

Through daily sleeping-car service is also provided in both directions between Washington and San Francisco in the Pennsylvania Railroad's No. 79, the Golden Arrow, and Chicago & North Western, Union Pacific, and Southern Pacific railroads' Pacific Limited, No. 21, westbound. Eastbound, the car is carried in the Pacific Limited, No. 22, over the Southern Pacific, Union Pacific, and Chicago & North Western and Pennsylvania railroads' No. 22, the Manhattan Limited. The B.&O. also operates a car on its Shenandoah between San Francisco and Washington, both ways, using these roads and Pacific Limited west of Chicago.

Additional coast-to-coast through sleeping-car service is provided, New York to San Francisco, via the New York Central's Commodore Vanderbilt and Pennsylvania's General, both eastward and westward, with daily connections to and from Chicago, Burlington & Quincy's Exposition Flyer to Denver, thence over the Denver & Rio Grande Western to Salt Lake, and the Western Pacific from Salt Lake to San Francisco.

The Pennsylvania and New York Central are also operating through cars from New York to Los Angeles via the Golden State Route, comprising the Rock Island and Southern Pacific railroads.

Through service has been installed also between New York and Washington via the B.&O. and Pennsylvania, and from New York to San Antonio, Galveston, El Paso, and other Texas cities as well as a through car to Mexico City via the New York Central. Through cars run through St. Louis via the Missouri Pacific, Katy, and Frisco roads, the last named also handling cars to Oklahoma cities. The C.&O. also put on through-car service from Washington to Texas cities on their George Washington and the M.P. Sunshine Special.

After their rendering valiant service in transporting something like 95 per cent of the war transport load in the United States, it was unfortunate that the railroads' reconversion program should have been severely hampered because of the epidemic of labor difficulties. The delivery of urgently needed equipment was almost stalemated for months, with the result that the new train-service schedule suffered dreary delays everywhere. The airlines were more fortunate in their ability to procure new planes, and consequently were in a position to begin new air service soon after the war's close.

The manufacture of both de luxe and low-cost coach equipment was slowed to a dribble, with every railroad caught in the paralyzing grip of car shortages at a time when all rolling stock was the worse for wear, following merciless war service. However, cars are being delivered as this is written, but far from the number required.

New Santa Fe bridge over the Colorado River at Topock, Ariz., on the First District of the Arizona Division, with westbound freight. Courtesy Sante Fe Railroad.

Luzon Military Railway business car with Colonel Frank Russell, U.S.A., standing on the rear end. This car was used by the late President Manuel Quézon of the Philippines. Courtesy U.S. Army.

This locomotive, a 4-8-2 built by Alco in 1922, was the only one found in running condition when the Railroad Battalion took over the Luzon Military Railway. Courtesy Signal Corps.

Westward Sante Fe freight train rounding the famous Tehachapi Loop, Calif., on the Southern Pacific San Joaquin Division over which the Santa Fe has trackage rights. Note the third of three 3900-class 2-10-2 type engines coming out of the tunnel. Photo by G. M. Best. Courtesy Rail Photo Service.

Interior of cab of Sante Fe Engine #2906, latest oil-burning 4-8-4 type. Courtesy Santa Fe Railroad.

Left side of the cab of a Santa Fe oil-burning 2-10-4 type, 5011-class locomotive. Courtesy Baldwin Locomotive Works.

Right side of the cab of a Santa Fe 2-10-4 type, 5011-class locomotive. Courtesy Baldwin Locomotive Works.

Eastbound Erie fast freight rounding the big curve at Pond Eddy, N. Y., on the Delaware division along the river of that name. Note the green fruit in train. Courtesy Erie Railroad.

Santa Fe 4-unit 5,400-hp freight Diesel with the PGX Phoenix Glendale Fruit running through solid from the Great Salt River Valley, Ariz., to Argentine, Kan., coming down the hill into Williams, Ariz. Third District of the Albuquerque Division. Courtesy Santa Fe Railroad.

Denver & Rio Grande Western #3407 with auxiliary water car, 2-8-8-2 type, class L-95, assisting Engine #3616, 2-8-8-2 type, class L-132, with 55 cars west of Tolland, Col., on the Pueblo Division. The grade is 2%. Note James Peak in the background. Photo by Otto C. Perry.

Denver & Rio Grande Western Engines #3501 and 3503, 2-8-8-2 types, class L-107, helping Extra #1404 west up Soldiers Summit, Utah, at Castle Gate, Utah, on the Salt Lake Division. The grade is 2.4%. Photo by Otto C. Perry.

New York Central Engine 2600U, new 4-8-4 type, class S-1A, with solid milk train. Note the Fitch tank cars. Courtesy New York Central Railroad.

The railroads, naturally, are anxious to unveil their sparkling new equipment, and also have an eye to getting in on the post-war traffic which is straining at the leash. Once the shipper and the passenger have an opportunity to try out the new service the railroads are offering, I feel free to predict they will be sold on this modern rail transportation.

The Chesapeake & Ohio, for instance, besides planning to operate some of the vista-dome coaches on their two new day-time trains between Washington and Cincinnati, have curved some of the aisles and corridors so there is not a single right-angle turn from one end to the other. These trains carry their own motion-picture theaters, lending libraries, news tickers, and train telephones. Also, a system is being worked out that it is believed will eliminate all waiting for meals.

The Norfolk & Western has come up with a splendid new daylight train from Norfolk to Cincinnati. The Louisville & Nashville, and Nashville, Chattanooga & St. Louis have a new daylight service from Cincinnati to New Orleans and St. Louis to Atlanta soon to go into operation.

The Great Northern's new Empire Builder, which I have mentioned in another chapter, running between Chicago and the Twin Cities to Seattle and Portland, is in service on its new 48-hour schedule. The Northern Pacific's new North Coast Limited, and the Milwaukee's new Super Olympian—although it may not be so named—will probably be running soon after this book appears. The old Olympian will handle local business.

And there is the Southern Pacific's new Shasta Daylight between Portland, Oregon, and San Francisco. It will in every respect be equal to the Southern Pacific's other Daylights, and there can be no higher praise. The Noon Daylight, via the Coast Route between San Francisco and Los Angeles, is also back in all of its vivid-hued glory. The S.P.'s overnight economy train, the Coaster, is operating on a new, faster schedule, as is the San Joaquin Daylight and the Owl. The latter is an over-night train, operating through the San Joaquin Valley, and the West Coast is another that has been speeded up from Los Angeles to Portland, Oregon.

The Southern Pacific's Cascade is on an 18½-hour schedule

between Portland and San Francisco, and is equipped with new lightweight sleeping cars. The Beaver operates over the Shasta Route, and is an economy train, with chair, tourist, and lounge cars.

Early in 1947 the Southern Pacific will put in operation their new triweekly 39¾-hour streamliner between Los Angeles and Chicago over the Rock Island Railroad from Tucumcari, New Mexico. The Golden State Limited is now completely equipped with lightweight streamlined cars and is offering a 48-hour eastbound and 49-hour westbound service between Chicago and the Coast.

The U.P. Cities of San Francisco, Portland, and Los Angeles, have been speeded up and the last named soon is to go on a daily schedule. They have put on a new City of St. Louis and Transcontinental with all of their schedules speeded up.

The new California Zephyr, operating between Chicago and San Francisco over the Burlington-Rio Grande-Western Pacific, will also be one of the country's finest trains, and takes the place of the Exposition Flyer on a 48-hour schedule.

The Katy and the Frisco, as well as the Missouri Pacific, have streamlined their new Texas and Sunshine Specials and are running them on fast schedules from St. Louis to Texas points.

The Santa Fe, while not having a great deal to improve in the matter of train service and equipment, has reduced the running time of the Super Chief and El Capitan to 39 hours and 45 minutes and will soon place them on a daily schedule. The time of the westbound Chief has been reduced 1 hour and 40 minutes, and the eastbound 24 minutes, with an over-all time westbound of 48 hours and eastbound 47 hours.

Both the Chief and Super Chief have new equipment and still carry their 3 lounge cars and other special service features, including Fred Harvey meal service which is standard all over the system. The Chief is now powered with Diesel locomotives right through.

Westbound, the Grand Canyon Limited has reduced its schedule 5 hours and 15 minutes; eastbound, 9 hours and 35 minutes. The California Limited has shaved its time 3 hours and 45 minutes westbound; and ½ hour eastbound. The Santa

Fe's economy train, the Scout, now makes the coast run to Chicago in 59 hours and 15 minutes, a reduction of 3¼ hours. Eastbound, the running time is reduced by 1 hour and 45 minutes.

The Santa Fe, in the spring of 1945, received the last of 164 modern high-speed, lightweight passenger cars, and Nos. 11 and 12, the Kansas Cityan, running from Chicago, have been extended to Fort Worth, Dallas, Houston, and Galveston, operating on a schedule of approximately 19 hours, Chicago to north Texas, and 25 hours, Chicago to south Texas. Between Kansas City and north Texas, Nos. 11 and 12 make the run in 10 hours and 45 minutes, and they provide south Texas with a running time of 16 hours and 55 minutes.

The crack Texas trains Nos. 5 and 6, the Ranger, are also fully equipped with lightweight stainless-steel cars and are powered with Diesel locomotives. The schedules are only about 1 hour slower than the streamlined Kansas Cityan. This new Santa Fe service provides both morning and evening departure from Chicago, with morning and evening arrivals in north Texas and mid-morning arrivals at Houston and Galveston.

When the Santa Fe has received all of its new equipment, the road will have a fleet of 424 lightweight streamlined passenger cars. Certainly the car builders and the railroads have gone all-out in their efforts to provide the traveling public with appointments befitting royalty, and you get it for the price of a railroad ticket. Any trip you take is going to be a big adventure, with new gadgets and conveniences every way you turn.

The slogan coined by the Great Northern, "See America First!" might easily be changed to, "See America by Rail!"

The person who has not ridden a modern train will find the new railroad equipment as exciting as it is gratifying. It is as different from the old-type train as the shabby country hotel is different from the brisk new city hotel. The trouble is going to be to get the folks off at the end of the line.

The improvements include nonfogging windows, improved lighting—some of the fluorescent type—improved heating, new air conditioning. The sleeping cars provide a new type bedroom, with late-design fold-away beds which allow the use of 2 comfortable chairs for daytime occupancy. They are equipped with enclosed toilet facilities.

The new chair cars have specially designed reclining and adjustable chairs with foam-rubber cushions of form-fitting contour. Other features include an adjustable leg rest which slides under the seat when not in use, easily accessible ash trays, and finger-tip control for seat regulation. Window spacing has been arranged to permit the greatest possible vision.

The new Santa Fe fleets have radios, wire reproducers, and public-address systems, as do most of the others. All equipment is decorated in the latest color combinations, with particularly attractive decorative schemes. Lunch-counter diners created by Henry Dreyfuss provide an added feature.

The Illinois Central's new day train from Chicago to New Orleans, the City of New Orleans, is a daylight counterpart of the famous Panama Limited. The Chicago & Eastern Illinois also have a new Diesel-hauled streamliner between Chicago and Evansville.

The Erie is streamlining all passenger trains, with new coaches and sleeping cars, which will be hauled by new Diesel passenger locomotives.

Scenery is high on the list of the passenger's desires, and the Baltimore & Ohio has it. The line between Washington and Cincinnati is also rich in historical background. This road's new daylight trains, the Cincinnatian, between these two cities, and between Chicago and Washington, will afford the traveler an opportunity to view a country unequaled anywhere for charm and beauty, particularly when the Old Master wields his autumn paint brush.

Again, on the B.&O. we find the new trains wheeling through behind sleek Diesel locomotives.

The New York Central has ordered over 700 new cars of all types for both its name trains and those in the less aristocratic bracket. The name trains will be handled by new Diesel passenger locomotives. The renowned Twentieth Century Limited is again running between Chicago and New York on its old 16-hour schedule. The Commodore Vanderbilt is again on its 17-hour running time. The Southwestern Limited and the

Knickerbocker, between St. Louis and New York, are operating on materially reduced schedules, as is the Ohio State Limited between New York and Cincinnati.

All during the war the New York Central maintained a surprisingly high degree of service in spite of its staggering war burden.

The Pere Marquette's two beautiful new streamliners are in service between Detroit and Grand Rapids.

The Richmond, Fredericksburg & Potomac, the justly famed "biggest little road in the country," is operating a new streamlined train between Washington, the nation's capital, and Richmond, the Virginia capital. This train has all modern equipment, which speeds down the rail behind the road's beautiful new 4-8-4 steam locomotives.

Service to Florida is in keeping with the pace of these other trains of the nation, with the Florida Special, soon to be restored to service, running via the Atlantic Coast Line and the Florida East Coast. This is the oldest winter train in the United States. Other trains are being provided with new equipment as it becomes available. Thousands of cars will be required to re-equip and modernize the speed-queen fleets, and the railroads are loosening their purse strings to engage in an improvement program that in the next 2 years will mean the spending of close to $2,000,000,000 over and above capital expenditures.

The Southern's streamliners, the Tennessean, the Southerner, and the Crescent, running between New York, Memphis, and New Orleans, are to be completely re-equipped, the schedules shortened, and new Diesel motive power assigned.

The Norfolk & Western, the great coal-hauling road, has reduced the running time of its famous Pocahontas, Nos. 3 and 4, between Norfolk and Cincinnati by 1 hour and 40 minutes. Other changes include additional passenger service and better connections for through passengers between Norfolk & Western points and Richmond.

A proud retired trackman of the Norfolk & Western, Leonard A. Scott, of Dry Branch, Virginia, has played a part in the road's postwar program, and when a brand-new streamliner began its scheduled flight between Norfolk, Virginia, and Cincinnati, Ohio, it bore the name suggested by this veteran of the road—the Powhatan Arrow!

The Powhatan Arrow is a reserved-seat, all-coach day train which will give the passenger an opportunity to view the glorious scenery of the Appalachians from this magic carpet. The train's interior decoration is in pastel blues, with chrome trim and full-color photo-murals. There are soft-cushioned adjustable seats, individual seat lights, over-all fluorescent lighting, rubber tile flooring, and the last word in smoking rooms and washrooms. Powhatan is a proud name—a chief's name—and the crowning touch to a proud new train, the Norfolk & Western's Powhatan Arrow.

It is impossible to begin to review all of the new trains which are offering America a new kind of service, but every section of the country is represented in the roster of fascinating speedliners, every one of which offers the traveler a new experience and a new thrill.

You can experience no greater luxury or freedom of movement in your favorite hotel than aboard these brilliant and restful postwar trains. You enjoy full relaxation en route, you get the "feel of the country," which you cannot get in an airplane, and you arrive at your destination clean and refreshed, for the railroad offers advantages entirely out of reach of competitors.

Air travel is faster, it is true, but there are associated discomforts and uncertainties. These discomforts present themselves particularly during the sleeping hours. Again, you arrive at the airport and find it "closed in"; planes grounded. You remain "alerted," but nothing happens, while somewhere you hear a locomotive whistle and you glimpse the sparkle of lights in the soggy night, and yawningly envy the traveler asleep in a comfortable Pullman berth, as you more fully appreciate the fact that the trains *always* run.

Busy executives and traveling men have discovered that the race is not always to the swift, and that the new train service provides a means of combining business with pleasure. To the vacationist, the tourist, the train is a magic carpet gliding smoothly and swiftly through an ever-changing world of enchantment—your America.

You ride trails blazed by the pathfinder and the pioneer, the wagon train, the stagecoach, and the Pony Express rider. You thread historic valleys and mountain passes and swing onto the river curve. You cross prairies and high mesas to the rhythm of singing wheels. You roam on silver rails through the land of the old cattle trails and the red men, the explorer priests, and the *Conquistadores*. Your magic carpet carries you down the beautiful Connecticut Valley, across the Hudson, the Ohio, the Mississippi, the Missouri, the Canadian, the Red, the Rio Colorado—rivers rich in story and legend.

There is an ancient Indian pueblo in New Mexico, a cowtown in Arizona, an Old Spanish town in California, a low green valley in New England; there are the Cumberland Mountains, the Great Smokies, the Blue Ridge, the Colorado Rockies gleaming with summer snow, Marias Pass and Glacier Park, the Sangre de Cristos and the Siskiyous and the Sierra Nevadas. The wonderland that is your heritage is outside the train window. The bright murals of your train are there in reality beside the rail.

The track that is the Main Street of northern New England is the Main Street of the Pacific Northwest, the West Coast, the Deep South. You dine and sleep and dream—dreams come true—aboard this American train. You turn slowly the pages of history and geography, filling a book of memories.

The marvel of it is that the railroads which so quickly adapted themselves to war have so swiftly adjusted themselves to peace. And whatever the future holds, the destiny of our nation depends upon our continued partnership with American railroads. But they cannot go ahead and continue to give improved service if they are not given adequate freight rates, and right now it is most vital that they receive the 19-per-cent increase for hauling freight.

Remember, the rails you ride are the rails that transport the red ore of the Iron Range—the ore that becomes a plowshare or a sword.

INDEX

414

4¹7

425